IB DIPLOMA PROGRA...

Engli... ...age ...ure

...NION

Rob Allison
Brian Chanen

OXFORD
UNIVERSITY PRESS

OXFORD
UNIVERSITY PRESS

Great Clarendon Street, Oxford OX2 6DP

Oxford University Press is a department of the University of Oxford.
It furthers the University's objective of excellence in research, scholarship, and education by publishing worldwide in

Oxford New York

Auckland Cape Town Dar es Salaam Hong Kong Karachi
Kuala Lumpur Madrid Melbourne Mexico City Nairobi
New Delhi Shanghai Taipei Toronto

With offices in

Argentina Austria Brazil Chile Czech Republic France Greece
Guatemala Hungary Italy Japan Poland Portugal Singapore
South Korea Switzerland Thailand Turkey Ukraine Vietnam

First published 2011

British Library Cataloguing in Publication Data

Data available

ISBN- 978-0-19-913542-4

10 9 8 7 6 5 4 3 2 1

Printed in Singapore by KHL Printing Co Pte Ltd

Paper used in the production of this book is a natural, recyclable product made from wood grown in sustainable forests. The manufacturing process conforms to the environmental regulations of the country of origin.

Author biographies

Brian Chanen has taught high school English for the past twenty years in Egypt, Thailand, Poland, and India. He holds a Ph.D. in English and has published on the influence of the digital environment on print narrative structure. Brian is currently Deputy Chief Examiner of Language A1 English and was a member of the team that developed the new curricula in Language A: Literature and Language A: Language and Literature.

Rob Allison has taught high school English for the past two decades in Egypt, Thailand, Australia, and India. He holds a Ph.D. In English and has published on the affective nature of experimental literature. Rob is currently Deputy Chief Examiner of Language A1 English, and was a member of the team that developed the new curricula in Language A: Literature and Language A: Language and Literature.

Acknowledgments

INTERNATIONAL BACCALAUREATE DIPLOMA PROGRAMME: ENGLISH A: LANGUAGE AND LITERATURE by Brian Chanen and Rob Allison
The authors and publisher are grateful for permission to reprint the following:
Chimamanda Ngozi Adichie: extract from *Purple Hibiscus* (Fourth Estate, 2004), copyright © Chimamanda Ngozi Adichie 2004, reprinted by permission of HarperCollins Publishers; extract from '"African Autheticity" and the Biafran Experience', copyright © Chimamanda Ngozi Adichie 2008, published in *Transition* 99, 2008, reprinted by permission of the author c/o The Wylie Agency UK. All rights reserved.
Edward Albee: opening extract of *Zoo Story* (Coward-McCann, New York, 1959), reprinted by permission of WME for the author.
Glora Anzaldua: extract from *Borderlands/La Frontera: The New Mestiza* (Aunt Lute Books, 1987), reprinted by permission of the publishers.
Margaret Atwood: 'You fit into me' from *Selected Poems* (OUP Canada, 1976), copyright © O W Toad 1976, reprinted by permission of the publishers, House of Anansi and Houghton Mifflin Harcourt Publishing Company, USA. All rights reserved.
James Barron: 'Storm Batters East, Closing Schools and Halting Flights', *New York Times*, 20.2.2010, copyright © 2010 New York Times. All rights reserved. Reprinted by permission of Pars International Corp and protected by the Copyright laws of the United States. The printing, copying, redistribution, or retransmission of this Content without express permission is prohibited.
Roland Barthes: extract from 'The Death of the Author' (1968) from *The Rustle of Language* translated by Richard Howard (University of California, 1989), reprinted by permission of Farrar, Straus & Giroux LLC.
Elizabeth Bishop: 'The Imaginary Iceberg' from *Complete Poems* (Chatto & Windus, 2004), reprinted by permission of Farrar, Straus & Giroux LLC.
Stephen Brunt: 'Historic Goal gives South Africa the moment of national exultation it had craved. It would not be enough for an outright win, but Bufana Bafana can still feel triumph', *The Globe & Mail*, Toronto, 12.6.2010, reprinted by permission of the author and The Toronto Globe and Mail.
Raymond Chandler: extract from *The Big Sleep* (A Knopf, 2002), copyright © Raymond Chandler 1939, reprinted by permission of Alfred A Knopf, a division of Random House, Inc.
Hélène Cixious: extract from 'The Laugh of the Medusa' translated by Keith & Paula Cohen, *Signs: Journal of Women in Culture and Society*, 1:4 (1976) 875, reprinted by permission of The University of Chicago Press via Copyright Clearance Center.
David Crystal: extract from '2b or not 2b?', *The Guardian Review*, 5.7.2008, from *Txting: The Gr8 Db8* (OUP, 2008), reprinted by permission of Oxford University Press
Tony Cozier: 'Ganga or Gayle: Who will lead the Windies?', *The Trinidad and Tobago Express*, 25.10.2009, reprinted by permission of the author.
E E Cummings: 'In Just-' from *Complete Poems 1904-1962* edited by George J Firmage (Norton, 1994). copyright © 1991 by the Trustees for the E E Cummings Trust and George J Firmage, reprinted by permission of W W Norton & Company.
Daily Mail Reporter: 'How using Facebook could raise your risk of cancer', *The Daily Mail online*, 19.2.2009, reprinted by permission of Solo Syndication.
William Dalrymple: extract from *City of Djinns* (HarperCollins, 1994), reprinted by permission of the publishers.
Emily Dickinson: poem 1129 'Tell all the Truth but tell it slant' from *The Poems of Emily Dickinson* edited by Thomas H Johnson (The Belknap Press of Harvard University , 1983), copyright © 1951, 1955, 1979, 1983 by the President and Fellows of Harvard College, reprinted by permission of Harvard University Press; facsimile of poem-letter 'Is this frostier?' from www.emilydickinson.org, reprinted by permission of The Emily Dickinson Archive.
Joan Didion: extract from 'Marrying Absurd' from *Slouching Towards Bethlehem* (Farrar, Straus & Giroux, 1968), reprinted by permission of the publishers.
Joan Morris DiMicco and David R Millen: extract from 'Identity Management: Multiple Presentations of Self on Facebook', from the *Proceedings of the 2007 International ACM Conference Supporting Group Work*, copyright © Association for Computer Machinery, Inc, 2007, reprinted by permission of ACM via Copyright Clearance Center.
Fyodor Dostoevsky: extract from *Crime and Punishment* translated by R Pevear and L Volokhonsky (Vintage, 1993, 2007), reprinted by permission of the publishers, The Random House Group Ltd and Random House, Inc.
Fyodor Dostoevsky: *Crime and Punishment* translated by Constance Garnett (Dover Publications, 2001), first published 1914 by Wm Heinemann, reprinted by permission of the pbulishers.
Carol Ann Duffy: 'Mrs Lazarus;' and 'Mrs Aesop' from *The World's Wife* (Picador, 1999), copyright © Carol Ann Duffy 1999, reprinted by permission of Pan Macmillan. London.
The Economist Editorial 'South Africa's World Cup: Who Profits Most?', *The Economist*, 13.5.2010, copyright © The Economist Newspaper Ltd, London 2010, reprinted by permission of The Economist Newspaper Ltd.
Larry Eigner: 'the knowledge of death, and now' from *Selected Poems* (1971) and *The Collected Poems of Larry Eigner* edited by Curtis Faville and Robert Grenier (Stanford, 2010), reprinted by permission of Stanford Univeristy Press.
Michael Evard: extract from *Um: Slips, Stumbles, and Verbal Blunders, and What They Mean* (Pantheon, 2007), reprinted by permission of Random House, Inc.
Louse Erdrich: opening of *The Last Report on the Miracles at Little No Horse* (HarperCollins, 2001), reprinted by permission of HarperCollins Publishers, USA.
William Faulkner: extract from 'A Rose for Emily' from *The Portable Faulkner* edited by Malcolm Cowley (Penguin NY, 1978), reprinted by permission of Curtis Brown Ltd.
Edward Gay: extract from 'I should have asked my wife to check email', *New Zealand Herald*, 10.11.2009, reprinted by permission of The NZ Herald/ APN Holdings Ltd.
Anand Giridharadas: 'Reflections on the start of the 2000s', *International Herald Tribune* 5-6.12.2009, copyright © 2009 IHT/iht.com, reprinted by permission of Pars International Corp and protected by the Copyright laws of the United States. All rights reserved.
Louise Gluck: lines from 'The Drowned Children' from *The First Four Books of Poems* (HarperCollins, 1980/Ecco Press 1995), reprinted by permission of the publishers.
Witold Gombrowicz: extract from *Ferdydurke* translated by Danuta Borchardt (Yale UP, 2000), reprinted by permission of Yale University Press.
Grahame Greene: opening of *The End of the Affair* (Penguin, 1999), reprinted by permission of David Higham Associates and Penguin Group (USA).
John Gugala: 'Desiree Davila targeting Chicago and a fast time this fall: Fast times on track indicate good potential on the roads', *Running Times*, Sept 2010, reprinted by permission of the author.
Claude Hagege: extract from *On the Death and Life of Languages* translated by Jody Gladding (Yale, 2009), reprinted by permission of Yale University Press.
Seamus Heaney: 'Mint' from *The Spirit Level* (Faber, 1996), reprinted by permission of Faber & Faber Ltd.
Madelaine Hron: extract from 'Ora na-asu nwa: The Figure of the Child in Third-Generation Nigerian Novels, *Research in African Literatures*, 39:2 (2008) 27, reprinted by permission of Indiana University Press.
Langston Hughes: 'Harlem (A Dream Deferred)'from *Collected Poems of Langston Hughes* (A. Knopf, 1994), reprinted by permission of David Higham Associates and Random House, Inc.
IHT Reporter: 'Successes fuel hope for green therapy resurgence' *International Herald Tribune*, 7-8.11.2009, copyright © 2009 IHT/iht.com, reprinted by permission of Pars International Corp and protected by the Copyright laws of the United States. All rights reserved.
Vivien Jones: extract from introduction to Jane Austen: *Pride and Prejudice* (Penguin Classics, 1996), introduction and notes copyright © Vivien Jones 1996, reprinted by permission of Penguin Books Ltd.
Deena Kamel: 'A language without limits', *Toronto Star*, 19.8.2008, reprinted by permission of Torstar Syndication Services.
Megan Kelso: extract from *The Squirrel Mother* (Fantagraphics Books 2003), reprinted by permission of the publishers.
Giuseppe Tomasi di Lampedusa: extract from *The Leopard* translated by Archibald Colquhoun (Collins & Harvill, 1960), reprinted by permission of The Random House Group Ltd and The Wylie Agency.
Philip Larkin: 'Church Going' from *Collected Poems* (Faber, 2003), reprinted by permission of Faber & Faber Ltd.
Tamar Lewis: 'Teenagers' Internet Socializing Not a Bad Thing' *New York Times*, 20.11.2008, copyright © 2008 New York Times. All rights reserved. Reprinted by permission of Pars International Corp and protected by the Copyright laws of the United States. The printing, copying, redistribution, or retransmission of this Content without express permission is prohibited.
Ian McEwan: extracts from *Atonement* (Jonathan Cape, 2001), reprinted by permission of The Random House Group Ltd and the author, c/o Rogers Coleridge & White Ltd, 20 Powis Mews, London W11 1JN.
Ben Macintyre: 'English grows into strange shapes when transplanted into foreign soil', *The Times*, 24.3.2007, copyright © The Times/NISyndication 2007, reprinted by permission of News International Syndication.
Ben Marcus: opening of *Notable American Women* (Vintage, 2002), reprinted by permission of Random House, Inc.
Arthur Miller: extract from *Death of a Salesman* (Penguin Classics, 1961), reprinted by permission of Rogers Coleridge & White Ltd, 20 Powis Mews, London W11 1JN.
T J Mitchell: 'An Interview with Barbara Kruger', *Critical Inquiry* 17 (Winter 1991), reprinted by permission of The University of Chicago Press via Copyright Clearance Center.
Toni Morrison: extract from *Beloved* (Chatto & Windus, 1987), reprinted by permission of The Random House Group Ltd and International Creative Management.
Bharanti Mukherjee: 'The Management of Grief' from *Middleman and Other Stories* (Grove Press, 1988), copyright © Bharati Mukherjee 1988, reprinted by permission of the publishers, Virago Press, an imprint of Little, Brown Book Group (UK), Grove Press (USA) and Penguin Group (Canada).
New Zealand Herald: extract from 'SPCA blocks contentious crayfish game', *New Zealand Herald*, 9.2.2010, reprinted by permission of The NZ Herald/ APN Holdings Ltd.
Michael Ondaatje: extract from *Running in the Family* (W W Norton, 1982), copyright © Michael Ondaatje 1982, reprinted by permission of the publishers, W W Norton & Company Inc, Bloomsbury and McLelland & Stewart, Canada.
Walter Ong: extract from *Orality and Literacy: The Technologizing of the Word* (Routledge, 2004), copyright © Routledge, 2004, reprinted by permission of Taylor & Francis Books UK.
Brian Ott and Robert Mack: extract from *Critical Media Studies: An Introduction* (Wiley-Blackwell, 2010), copyright © Brian Ott and Robert Mack 2010, reprinted by permission of Blackwell Publishing Ltd.
Steven Pinkner: extract from *The Language Instinct* (Penguin, 1994), copyright © Steven Pinkner 1994, reprinted by permission of Penguin Books Ltd and the Brockman Agency.
Richard Powers: 'How to speak a Book', *New York Times*, 7.1.2007, copyright © 2007 New York Times. All rights reserved. Reprinted by permission of Pars International Corp and protected by the Copyright laws of the United States. The printing, copying, redistribution, or retransmission of this Content without express permission is prohibited. Extract from *The Echo Maker* (Farrar, Straus & Giroux, 2006), reprinted by permission of ** the publishers.
Annie Proulx: extract from 'Brokeback Mountain' from *Close Range: Wyoming Stories* (Scribner, 2000), reprinted by permission of Simon & Schuster and Darhansoff & Verrill, Literaty Agents for the author.
Salman Rushdie: extract from *The Moors Last Sigh* (Jonathan Cape, 1995), reprinted by permission of The Random House Group Ltd and Random House, Inc.
Peter Schaffer: extract from *Equus* (Penguin, 1977), copyright © Peter Schaffer 1973, reprinted by permission of the publishers, Penguin Books Ltd and Penguin Group USA.
Benjamin Shores: extract from 'Squatters take on developers', *Miami Herald*, 1.10.2007, copyright © 2007 by McClatchy Company, reprinted by permission of McClatchy Company via Copyright Clearance Center.
Wallace Stevens: 'Disillusionment of Ten O'Clock' from *Collected Poems* (Faber, 2006), reprinted by permission of Faber & Faber Ltd.
Wislawa Szymborska: 'Soliloquy for Cassandra' and 'Lot's Wife' from *View with a Grain of Sand* translated by Stanislaw Baranczak and Clare Cavanagh (Harcourt, 1995), copyright © Wislawa Szymborska 1993, English translation copyright © Houghton Mifflin Harcourt Publishing Company 1995, reprinted by permission of the publishers, Houghton Mifflin Harcourt, and Faber & Faber Ltd.
Deborah Tannen: 'The Talk of the Sandbox; How Johnny and Suzy's playground chatter prepares them for life at the office', *The Washington Post*, 11.12.1994, adapted from the book *Talking From 9 to 5: Women and Men at Work* (Wm Morrow, 1994), copyright © Deborah Tannen 1994, reprinted by permission of the author.
Thornton Wilder: extract from *Our Town* (Harper Perenniel Classics, 1998), reprinted by permission of HarperCollins Publishers, USA.
William Carlos Williams: 'This is Just to Say' from *The Collected Poems Vol 1* (Carcanet/New Directions), reprinted by permission of Pollinger Ltd and New Directions Publishing Corp.
Chris Wilson: 'Staying True to Themselves', *US News and World Report*, 8.7.2007, reprinted by permission of Wright's Media.
Although we have made every effort to trace and contact all copyright holders before publication this has not been possible in all cases. If notified, the publisher will rectify any errors or omissions at the earliest opportunity.

Course Companion definition

The IB Diploma Programme Course Companions are resource materials designed to provide students with extra support through their two-year course of study. These books will help students gain an understanding of what is expected from the study of an IB Diploma Programme subject.

The Course Companions reflect the philosophy and approach of the IB Diploma Programme and present content in a way that illustrates the purpose and aims of the IB. They encourage a deep understanding of each subject by making connections to wider issues and providing opportunities for critical thinking.

These Course Companions, therefore, may or may not contain all of the curriculum content required in each IB Diploma Programme subject, and so are not designed to be complete and prescriptive textbooks. Each book will try to ensure that areas of curriculum that are unique to the IB or to a new course revision are thoroughly covered. These books mirror the IB philosophy of viewing the curriculum in terms of a whole-course approach; the use of a wide range of resources; international-mindedness; the IB learner profile and the IB Diploma Programme core requirements; theory of knowledge; the extended essay; and creativity, action, service (CAS).

In addition, the Course Companions provide advice and guidance on the specific course assessment requirements and also on academic honesty protocol.

The Course Companions are not designed to be:

- study/revision guides or a one-stop solution for students to pass the subjects
- prescriptive or essential subject textbooks.

IB mission statement

The International Baccalaureate aims to develop inquiring, knowledgeable, and caring young people who help to create a better and more peaceful world through intercultural understanding and respect.

To this end the IB works with schools, governments, and international organizations to develop challenging programmes of international education and rigorous assessment.

These programmes encourage students across the world to become active, compassionate, and lifelong learners who understand that other people, with their differences, can also be right.

The IB learner profile

The aim of all IB programmes is to develop internationally minded people who, recognizing their common humanity and shared guardianship of the planet, help to create a better and more peaceful world. IB learners strive to be:

Inquirers   They develop their natural curiosity. They acquire the skills necessary to conduct inquiry and research and show independence in learning. They actively enjoy learning and this love of learning will be sustained throughout their lives.

Knowledgable   They explore concepts, ideas, and issues that have local and global significance. In so doing, they acquire in-depth knowledge and develop understanding across a broad and balanced range of disciplines.

Thinkers   They exercise initiative in applying thinking skills critically and creatively to recognize and approach complex problems, and make reasoned, ethical decisions.

Communicators   They understand and express ideas and information confidently and creatively in more than one language and in a variety of modes of communication. They work effectively and willingly in collaboration with others.

Principled   They act with integrity and honesty, with a strong sense of fairness, justice, and respect for the dignity of the individual, groups, and communities. They take responsibility for their own actions and the consequences that accompany them.

Open-minded   They understand and appreciate their own cultures and personal histories, and are open to the perspectives, values, and traditions of other individuals and communities. They are accustomed to seeking and evaluating a range of points of view, and are willing to grow from the experience.

Caring   They show empathy, compassion, and respect towards the needs and feelings of others. They have a personal commitment to service, and act to make a positive difference to the lives of others and to the environment.

Risk-takers   They approach unfamiliar situations and uncertainty with courage and forethought, and have the independence of spirit to explore new roles, ideas, and strategies. They are brave and articulate in defending their beliefs.

Balanced   They understand the importance of intellectual, physical, and emotional balance to achieve personal well-being for themselves and others.

Reflective   They give thoughtful consideration to their own learning and experience. They are able to assess and understand their strengths and limitations in order to support their learning and personal development.

A note on academic honesty

It is of vital importance to acknowledge and appropriately credit the owners of information when that information is used in your work. After all, owners of ideas (intellectual property) have property rights. To have an authentic piece of work, it must be based on your individual and original ideas with the work of others fully acknowledged. Therefore, all assignments, written or oral, completed for assessment must use your own language and expression. Where sources are used or referred to, whether in the form of direct quotation or paraphrase, such sources must be appropriately acknowledged.

How do I acknowledge the work of others?
The way that you acknowledge that you have used the ideas of other people is through the use of footnotes and bibliographies.

Footnotes (placed at the bottom of a page) or endnotes (placed at the end of a document) are to be provided when you quote or paraphrase from another document, or closely summarize the information provided in another document. You do not need to provide a footnote for information that is part of a "body of knowledge". That is, definitions do not need to be footnoted as they are part of the assumed knowledge.

Bibliographies should include a formal list of the resources that you used in your work. "Formal" means that you should use one of the several accepted forms of presentation. This usually involves separating the resources that you use into different categories (e.g. books, magazines, newspaper articles, Internet-based resources, CDs and works of art) and providing full information as to how a reader or viewer of your work can find the same information. A bibliography is compulsory in the extended essay.

What constitutes malpractice?

Malpractice is behaviour that results in, or may result in, you or any student gaining an unfair advantage in one or more assessment component. Malpractice includes plagiarism and collusion.

Plagiarism is defined as the representation of the ideas or work of another person as your own. The following are some of the ways to avoid plagiarism:

● Words and ideas of another person used to support one's arguments must be acknowledged.

● Passages that are quoted verbatim must be enclosed within quotation marks and acknowledged.
● CD-ROMs, email messages, web sites on the Internet, and any other electronic media must be treated in the same way as books and journals.
● The sources of all photographs, maps, illustrations, computer programs, data, graphs, audio-visual, and similar material must be acknowledged if they are not your own work.
● Works of art, whether music, film, dance, theatre arts, or visual arts, and where the creative use of a part of a work takes place, must be acknowledged.

Collusion is defined as supporting malpractice by another student. This includes:

● allowing your work to be copied or submitted for assessment by another student
● duplicating work for different assessment components and/or diploma requirements.

Other forms of malpractice include any action that gives you an unfair advantage or affects the results of another student. Examples include, taking unauthorized material into an examination room, misconduct during an examination, and falsifying a CAS record.

Contents

Introduction 6

Section 1: Why and how
1 Thinking about literature 7
2 Thinking about language 28
3 Putting it all together 44

Section 2: Language
4 Language in cultural context 83
5 Assessment in language in cultural context 134
6 Language and mass communication 157
7 Assessment in language and mass communication 199

Section 3: Literature
8 Literature: critical study 219
9 Assessment in literature: critical study 253
10 Literature: texts and contexts 272
11 Assessment in literature: texts and contexts 308

Introduction

This book has been written to provide general support and guidance for students in the IB Language A: Language and Literature course at both higher and standard level. The course is one of three options available for fulfilling the Group 1 requirement for the IB Diploma. The other two courses available are Language A: Literature and Language A: Literature and Performance (offered at the Standard Level only). All three courses are intended to be challenging, contemporary studies of language. While these courses are meant to serve students with a variety of complex language profiles, they are not English language learning courses but critical explorations of the uses of language, literature and performance. At the same time, each of these courses offers opportunities for the further development and refinement of skills with reading, viewing, listening, speaking and producing works in English. The value of the Language and Literature course goes far beyond merely meeting the requirements of the IB Diploma. This course provides students with an opportunity to acquire the skills to be successful with further academic studies and growth beyond academia. The focus is on developing skills as an informed and critical consumer of language in the analysis of a range of texts, from poetry, literature and drama to political speeches, news reporting, new media and advertising..

It must be emphasized right from the beginning that the nature of this course promotes the development of these skills rather than content competence. The nature of this course is such that there will be few set answers to commit to memory but rather a more consciously critical approach to all uses of language and literature. If you approach the passages and activities in this course companion with an open mind and some diligence, you will become more confident in your abilities to analyse and reproduce different text types, in preparation for the application of your skills to the set tasks for formal assessment.

We have included a broad range of sample extracts and examples of language usage across different media, from a wide variety of sources to illustrate their practical application and issues for analysis. The works we have chosen, then, represent those more commonly encountered among IB schools as well as texts that may be less familiar, surprising, or esoteric in an effort to broaden horizons and multiply opportunities for surveying different approaches. One of the most important skills you can develop in this course and through the use of this course companion is to be able to encounter works and topics on your own and in any situation to develop your skills of comprehension and analysis.

The Language and Literature course is designed to explore a range of topics and issues that represent the most current approaches to critical language study. The course encourages aesthetic appreciation of language and literature as well as a familiarity with literary criticism, media studies and introductory linguistics. Because of the wide focus of this course, you will encounter and explore language at its most expansive, across many different periods, forms and disciplines: from ancient to contemporary, formal to colloquial, the spoken word to digitally mediated texts and images.

Part 1 of this book begins with a section on what we believe are the foundations or underpinnings of the study of both language and literature. Sometimes, in order to study a subject, we need to know how the subject came to be: its history, it changes over time, and the assumptions it makes about both its current and future directions. The first three chapters will focus on why we study language and literature and how best to approach your study. Part 2 focuses on the language parts of the course including assessment. The final section of the book focuses on the literature parts of the course, also including assessment. There are also portions of this book that deal with cross-curricular j such as Theory of Knowledge, the use of technology and international-mindedness. We hope that the Language and Literature course naturally overlaps with the thinking you will do across all of your subjects. Language is implicated in all the thinking that you do and the way we construct knowledge and identity. Finally, in order to take most advantage of the course, you must take an active—and even interactive—role through adding to it your own enquiry and creative production. Through your participation, you will not just be preparing yourself for academic assessment, but giving to it your own authentic contribution to a living and growing body of knowledge and understanding.

We would like to thank the many teachers and students who have helped us with this book either by reading our work, giving us new ideas, or demonstrating what it means to be passionate thinkers and readers. In particular, we would like to thank all of our students who have trialed assessments, participated in discussions, and provided some of their own personal writing for this book. We would also like to thank our families, and in particular our supportive wives, as well as all our colleagues and the staff at the IB Curriculum and Assessment Centre in Cardiff, fellow IB examiners, and all of the people at Oxford University Press.

Rob Allison and Brian Chanen

Thinking about literature

What do we do with a text?

In this course, in order to study language and literature you will be looking at a wide variety of texts. Our definition of "texts" must remain fairly broad and might include advertisements, websites, poems, television shows or even stand-alone images, as in this painting called *This Place, That Place*. Perform the following activity to consider how we respond to communicative acts such as a painting.

1   Spend some time looking at the image taking into consideration both your initial feelings and reactions. Jot down these impressions including whether you find the image appealing, provocative, challenging or strange.

2   After making a note of your initial impressions, analyze some of the more particular aspects of the image, including those listed below:

   • The use of color.

   • The use of contrast, either in color, subject, text or composition.

   • The use of language in terms of meaning as well as whether you read the words as disjointed or continuous.

   • The placement of the words.

   • The subject of the image.

   • The artist's possible aims or intentions.

3   The artist who produced this painting in 2007, Kiran Chandra, was born in Kolkata, India. She has studied in Delhi, India, and Boston, USA, and worked in Florence, Italy. She currently divides her time between Brooklyn, New York City, and Kolkata. After learning more about the artist, do you have new thoughts about any aspects of the image?

4   Reflecting on your own impressions, can you identify either larger personal or cultural assumptions that have affected your reading, either as a result of experience or background? Such assumptions might include feelings about place and space, rural versus urban environments, and the lifestyle in different communities.

5   It would be impossible to account for the full variety of possible readings, or which of those we might consider more "correct" readings. It is likely, however, that many of us have recognized common aspects including the bright green countryside on the left relative to the somber, dark tones of the urban environment on the right. We may have noticed from the text that there is a juxtaposition of "places." We also may have considered the idea or significance of displacement in relation to the image.

Regardless of your final reading of the image, you have approached it from a variety of positions including your initial impressions and more extended considerations and reconsiderations. It is the focus of this course: to consider your own unique perspective and underlying assumptions as well as to come to some interesting conclusions about the meaning and importance of a wide variety of communicative acts. Before we begin, it is worth looking briefly at why such considerations are worthy of an entire course and how we go about practicing such considerations. These considerations, and more, will be discussed in this first section.

The opening activity may have surprised you. Perhaps it seems a more appropriate object of study for a course in the fine arts or even the social sciences. In this course, you will find that the approach taken is broad enough to include the use of language in a variety of formats: from the literary to the informational to even less familiar or surprising **communicative acts**. Inherent in any language and literature course must be a set of assumptions about the object and method of study. In the IB Diploma Programme, you are asked to consider why a particular area of study is interesting and valuable and how it is defined or constructed as a discipline. In this chapter, we will begin with a general discussion of several of the assumptions that we make about literature. These assumptions will not only provide background information, but will inform your future investigations.

> **Communicative act** is a term used to describe any process that demands an engagement between two or more parties involving reception, interpretation and response. One person speaking to another can be a communicative act as can a novel which waits on a shelf for a reader's response.

What is literature?

As a student, you have undoubtedly been required to complete an English (or language arts) course for every year you have attended school. Even if it was not a separate course, English has been a part of your educational curriculum and has formed a significant part of your learning. If you have only recently begun working in English, as your academic language, you have at least studied language and literature in another language. Although the aims may have been primarily toward developing more elementary literacies—such as reading or writing— "stories" or some other form of narrative have consistently been a part of these courses in one way or another. As you have progressed through different English courses, it is likely that the formal study of literature has become an even more central component of your courses. The sheer prevalence of the study of literature in formal education might suggest that formulating a definition for literature would be a relatively simple task. It most assuredly is not.

Debates over the definition of literature have been raging for centuries and show no sign of abating. Literature has meant many different things over time but also across different cultures. While one might assume it is, most basically, anything "in letters," such a definition ignores oral traditions prominent in different cultures

Activity

What is literature?

Based on your own understanding of the word "literature," which of the following would fit your classification?

Pride and Prejudice by Jane Austen

About a Boy by Nick Hornby

A Harlequin romance

Ink Heart by Caroline Funke

Into the Wild by Jon Krakauer

A biology textbook

A love letter

The film *Avatar*

An Australian Aboriginal creation story

A blog post

and in different times. At the same time, this definition allows for *all* texts such as user manuals, telephone books or advertisements to be considered literature. This might lead one to believe that literature should be defined more by its purpose than its format but, again, problems arise. Is literature about entertainment or instruction? Is it intended to be a purely aesthetic encounter or, more ambitiously, meant to incite social revolution? This still leaves us to consider whether other **text types**, such as film or the visual and performing arts, can be considered literature.

This is a long and complex debate too great in scope to settle (if that were at all possible) in this course companion. But the debate is an essential component of literature to keep in mind while you engage in the stricter parameters of the course. Awareness of this debate will encourage a continual shifting of perspective where uncertainty over what literature is and its purpose are central components for consideration. It may not be as easy as you think to classify what is (and is not) literature. For our purposes, we will consider literature as a highly developed use of language in that it is the stylized manipulation of language for larger effect (purpose) and/or affect (emotional response). The range of effect and affect may be quite wide from the visceral qualities of abstract or expressionist art to more overt and clearly stated socio-political agendas that intend to promote particular cultural viewpoints. In other words, literature may be defined as a complex and stylized use of language that is capable of both aesthetic intention and cultural critique through its representation of the worlds in which we live.

Similarly, our considerations of what kind of text may be recognized as literature will also recognize that this is a long and complex debate that involves a multiplicity of practices across different countries and cultures, and changes in the approaches to literature in the classroom over time. As with some of the implications for the study of literature, this course assumes a middle position where not just so-called "high art" may be considered but also other cultural products such as movies, song lyrics, graphic novels, television shows, etc. This is partly in an attempt to make **metacognitive** considerations of the definition of the text a central component. As a student, you should not only consider a wide variety of text types but you should consider why these text types may or may not be considered literature. Because it is a course on language and literature, multiple uses of language in performance will be considered within a broad view of reading and writing. In the sections on literature we will be considering a range of texts that might seem limited or traditional in nature— some text selections are those that are used commonly in classrooms—while others are intended to be more esoteric in order to convey the range of opportunities available. For the most part, the literature under consideration will be familiar territory: in the form of poetry, short stories, novels, graphic novels, plays, films and nonfiction texts.

A **text** is essentially an object that functions as part of a communicative act. There are obviously many types of texts, including novels, textbooks, newspapers and web blogs. Text types can include the many different types of writing as well as photographs or even dramatic performances. The term "**text types**" simply refers to the almost limitless range of texts that can be part of a communicative act.

Metacognition is, quite simply, thinking about thinking. You may be familiar with metacognition from the theory of knowledge course which asks you to think about how you "know" across a variety of academic disciplines and personal encounters. To be metacognitive, then, is to not simply perform an activity but to think about how and why you are performing that activity as well as understanding that there may be alternative approaches available.

The study of literature

In the Western tradition, reading and studying literature has been practiced formally since at least the Greeks of the fifth century BCE. Since then, the study of literature has undergone substantive change that has reflected changing attitudes toward literature's potential purpose and effect. While the following represents only a very basic and incomplete overview, some awareness of the changes over time can be useful.

Historical literary study

Philosophers like Plato and his student Aristotle debated literature (Greek poetry and drama) in reference to the imitation of life, **ontology**, **epistemology**, politics and morality. They are frequently credited with having introduced the concept of systematic literary criticism. For such early critics, literature was concerned with human behavior and its relationship with the physical world, society and ethics. They debated philosophical concerns such as "truth," "beauty" and "love" as well as the uses of literature as a form of instruction on how to behave in a civil society. The Greek plays were not only seen as moving examples of conflict between people but as guidelines for being in the world.

The Greeks, as the lengthy list of attributes above might suggest, were far from agreement in their approach to and appreciation of literature. Individual philosophers demonstrated a range of thoughts and differing perspectives over time. Plato, for instance, once railed against poets as producers of mere imitations of reality (he felt that our intuitions and emotions were themselves problematic interpretations of the world that could lead us astray). Poetry was leading us only further from the truth. Later, however, he found poets more tolerable, even beneficial, so long as their poetry was directed to the service and celebration of the state. Rather than a unified approach to literature, the Greeks signaled the rise of the kinds of debates, questions and concerns that would lead to the development of more overt literary criticism. Regardless of their conclusions, the Greeks modeled a certain behavior toward literature that requires a critical and active response. We can still join Plato in his debate over whether works of literature are trivial or worthwhile in reference to their equivalent forms in sitcoms, rap music or videos available from an online video community.

Discussion Point

High and low culture

1 What value or purposes might there be in focusing attention on literary texts such as *Hamlet* by the English playwright William Shakespeare and *Ulysses* by Irish novelist James Joyce?

2 In what ways are they different from popular culture, such as TV programs like *The Simpsons* or *The Office*? What unique qualities and/or experiences can they provide?

3 Is literature an artifact to be analyzed, understood and dissected or a construction dependent on the reader's input?

Ontology is the philosophical study of the nature of being, existence or reality.

Epistemology is the branch of philosophy concerned with the nature and limitations of knowledge.

Read

"Great" Greek literature

This extract from the *Oresteia*, a trilogy of tragedies by Aeschylus, includes the following speech by Clytemnestra. It is addressed to her husband, Agamemnon, King of Argos. He has just returned from fighting in Troy for 10 years and has brought a new bride home. Clytemnestra is intent on revenge and prepares a trap for the arrogant Agamemnon.

Clytemnestra	Now, dearest husband, come, step from your chariot.
	But do not set to earth, my lord, the conquering foot
	That trod down Troy. Servants, do as you have been bidden;
	Make haste, carpet his way with crimson tapestries,
	Spread silk before your master's feet; Justice herself
	All other matters forethought, never lulled by sleep,
	Shall order justly as the will of Heaven decrees.

As soon as Clytemnestra asks Agamemnon to step on the crimson carpet, the Greek audience understands that she is asking him to sin against the gods by assuming the position—walking on red silk—reserved for them. Agamemnon understands this. But in a very dramatic scene, he is convinced by Clytemnestra that he is truly deserving of such accolades. This would be viewed by the early Greeks as great literature because it demonstrates the very human issue of jealousy but it also clearly demonstrates the sin of excessive pride and teaches a valuable moral lesson.

Building on the Greek tradition, literary critics, even into the 18th century, concerned themselves with similar issues of social values and aesthetic standards. Literary criticism often focused on maintaining the tastes established by highly regarded writers of the past. Very simply, throughout this period, literary criticism was concerned with evaluating texts and artists for their adherence to tradition and decorum in fulfillment of common absolutes or truths. Of course, the larger aim within such policing was to maintain such values against the introduction of any cultural change. Just as a teacher in school may choose a text for study such as *Oedipus Rex* or *Agamemnon* because it is important, early literary critics were concerned with establishing what, in fact, should be considered literature at all.

Activity

Film censorship: idealism vs. realism

It may be easy to scoff at some of the aims of historical criticism as rigid, conservative or elitist on an exaggerated scale. But such concerns still abound with texts, literary and otherwise, that we encounter today. Consider film boards that rate appropriate viewing audiences for film, DVD and video games and attempt to regulate social appropriateness. Two points listed on the website for the British Board of Film Classification (BBFC) are:

> We are passionate about the moving image and balance our duty to protect with a respect for the right to freedom of expression.

> We acknowledge and reflect the cultural diversity of the UK, and anticipate and embrace change.

Source: Vision Statement, The British Board of Film Classification website. http://www.bbfc.co.uk/about/vsindex.php.

Imagine a film where these two aims are in conflict (probably a common occurrence) as, for example, in the case of a period drama from the 1950s in which the characters are smoking cigarettes. The BBFC, like historical literary critics, must debate and make decisions as to whether such a film should be valued for its historical accuracy (reality) or should be pushed toward a more idealistic view of the world (in this case, a world with fewer smokers or, at least, fewer potential smokers influenced by the mass media). This is obviously an over-simplification of a complex topic, but it is clear that debates over cultural values versus realism have not been relegated to the past.

Questions

1 Where would you stand on the issue and why? Discuss the opposing viewpoints.

2 What ultimately tips you to support one side over the other?

While the 18th century valued order, reason and appropriateness in literary texts (and beyond), the 19th century ushered in a period of literature and criticism that focused on the role of intuition and imagination in helping to perceive the world at large. Before the 19th century, much of the focus in literary criticism had been about maintaining the status quo (of *some* values). With some of the political and philosophical upheavals at the end of the 18th century (for instance, the American and French revolutions), people began to imagine evolving and better futures that relied on different kinds of encounters in the world as in works of literature.

Such encounters were, again, not necessarily homogenous. The early 19th century was associated more closely with Romanticism: that is, a belief that higher orders of human truth were possible through transcending base concerns of pure reason, politics and worldly values. This could be achieved through imaginative encounters with the world (stereotypically associated with intoxication through wine or poetic reverie, the beauty of nature and the life of ordinary people) rather than the socially constructed and controlled norms. Criticism of this era valued these transcendent issues of our "higher humanity" over the status quo. In a poem such as "The Solitary Reaper" by the English poet William Wordsworth, for example, the poet writes in the first stanza:

> Behold her, single in the field,
> Yon solitary Highland lass!
> Reaping and singing by herself;
> Stop here, or gently pass!
> Alone she cuts and binds the grain,
> And sings a melancholy strain;
> O listen! for the vale profound
> Is overflowing with the sound.

Here, the poet focuses on the everyday individual, the pleasures of rural life and emotion expressed in song. The poem does not focus on classical values or use elevated language; rather, it expresses an appreciation of individual imagination in an accessible form. Wordsworth, like many of the Romantics, believed in poetry as an expression of feeling, a reflection on everyday life and nature expressed through common language. Although this excerpt may seem traditional or even difficult to read today, it was fresh and revolutionary at the time. Wordsworth and his contemporaries were very much aware that their poetry was breaking from previous standards.

The publication of Charles Darwin's *The Origin of Species* in 1859 signaled the change from the **transcendentalism** of Romanticism to the **scientific determinism** of the Victorian era. Rather than valuing imaginative encounters with the world, science became the popular application to all questions including those of literature. Literary texts, then, became the object of scientific study and literary criticism focused on the application of the scientific method (careful observation and a systematic approach) to texts to uncover larger patterns or truths. Even if a literary text was not recognized as having its own inherent scientific value, concerns of literature's value in our human evolution continued to inform the practice of criticism.

Although Romanticism and scientific determinism may seem to have opposing aims and worldviews, both critical perspectives advocated a break from viewing literature as a phenomenon strangely divorced from ordinary life and a new recognition of literature as a function of our humanity. Whether through our imaginations or our biology (or both), literature was now seen as an organic and intrinsic part of our evolving selves and certainly worthy of attention and study.

New Criticism

By the end of the 19th century, literature was no longer understood solely as a reflection of elite culture, genteel tastes and sentiment. In the 20th century, the text itself became the main focus, as developed in the English-speaking world in the theories of New Criticism. What most distinguishes New Criticism is its focus on close reading with little to no concern for history, ideology, politics, biography or other factors outside of the text. New Critics believe that the text is a self-contained object that exists independently from all extrinsic forces, including the author. In fact, New Critics argued that the belief that a text is only an expression of an author's experiences or intentions is a fundamental error known as "intentional fallacy." Once a text has been written, it is complete in itself and its value and merit should be determined only by a close reading and analysis of its precise form and effects.

In some ways, New Criticism approaches texts like a science. New Critics attempt a close reading based on stylistic aspects—such as diction, irony and image—and views these devices as the cause of a unifying thought or intention behind the work. A "good" text is one that achieves a high level of unity of its component parts toward a singular end; a "good" reader is one suitably attentive and versed in literary techniques, allusion and language to recognize this unity and effect. But New Criticism is also decidedly nonscientific in its aims. New Criticism argues that the effect created by a very good literary text always offers us more than "simple" science can; the text provides a privileged source of meaning and value, not available through any other use of language, including the factual domain of science.

The type of unique experience suggested above is referred to as the "objective correlative" by some New Critics meaning that a literary text always speaks to an emotion or ideal that is somehow more than

Transcendentalism is a philosophic movement focusing on the value of intuition, personal revelation and conscience.

Scientific determinism is the belief that the world—objects, actions and forces—arises from clear causes that can be revealed through objective scientific inquiry.

Discussion Point

Why *this* text?
Think of any poem, novel, or play you have read in class. What is the value of reading this text? Is it valuable simply in and of itself as the expression of human imagination, thought, or emotion? Is the text meant to teach us something about the world? Why do you think you are asked to read that particular text in the class you are taking?

The answers to these difficult questions point to the ways in which critics have struggled with the nature and importance of literature.

merely the sum total of what language can convey. The early New Critics argued that it was the specific combination and use of language in literature that, while speaking of an ordinary situation, series of events, object or occurrence, manages to arouse higher emotions and intellectual meanings (an essential truth) for readers. Such is the experience of art; for the New Critics, literature assumed a place as a unique aesthetic experience performing an independent social function.

Even among New Critics, grand claims associated with the objective correlative were debated. But it is, arguably, the more practical aspects that continue to keep New Criticism a continuing part of studying literature. In a now famous story, the English literary critic I. A. Richards presented sets of poems to his students at Cambridge University without any additional information—such as the names of authors, dates of writing or publication—and asked them to write commentaries in response. While Richards probably expected common emotive readings that recognized some aspects of a larger truth (that is, closer to an objective correlative), what he encountered instead was confusion, incomprehension and difficulty in reading. This result pushed Richards to turn his attention from emotive meanings to the reading process. Richards then focused his attention on the difficulties of reading texts and developed a system for how to read a text. Whether or not one accepts the notion that studying literature can ennoble a reader (by providing access to a larger truth), the ways of approaching texts popularized by practical criticism and the New Critics have had lasting effects and continue to be a part of how literature is studied in the classroom today. When you approach an unseen text for commentary or when you read a new book in class without any kind of explicit instruction, you are most likely reading like a practical critic. Looking at a poem, you consider its title and what it suggests; you think about the subject of the poem; and you go on to consider the nuances of structure, language, and sound (for example) to get to a deeper meaning. Much of this work you do is based on the example of the New Critics from the early 20th century.

Activity

Practical criticism

Take the following very short poem by the Canadian writer Margaret Atwood and ask yourself the following questions that are typical in many English classes. To a large extent, these questions reflect a practical criticism approach.

You fit into me

You fit into me
like a hook into an eye

A fish hook
An open eye.

Questions to the text

1 What is the relationship between the title and the rest of the poem?

2 What words, if any, need to be defined (for example, are you familiar with a hook-and-eye clasping system in clothing)?

3 What relationships do you see among any words in the poem?

4 What are the various connotative meanings of the words in the poem? Do these various shades of meaning help establish relationships or patterns in the text?

5 What symbols, images or figures of speech are used? What is the relationship between them?

6 What elements of rhyme, meter or pattern can you discuss?

7 What is the tone of the poem?

8 From what point of view is the content of the poem being told?

9 What tensions, ambiguities or paradoxes arise within the poem?

10 What do you believe the chief paradox or irony is in the text?

11 How do all of the elements of the poem support and develop the primary paradox or irony?

Finally, after a thorough reading of the text, how much do you feel you have understood the higher "truth" of this poem? Has something *happened* in this reading that has allowed you to encounter aspects of your humanity beyond what you can easily or simply express in words? Is this the "true" value of literature?

Reader response

Thinking about the poem discussed in the above exercise, consider the reading that an avid fisherman might bring to the task. A New Critic would argue that such experience is irrelevant; in fact, a New Critic might be particularly concerned that such experience would negatively color a reading (that is, lead to a "wrong" reading). For instance, let us imagine that, as a result of your experience with fishing, you read the poem to be a reminder about a difficult fishing moment where, after having landed a fish in a catch-and-release-only area, you found that removing the hook was a challenge because it had gone through the fish's eye. The ensuing dilemma was that removing the hook would kill the fish and you read the poem as the emotional moment where you recognized your inability to take a step that did not involve loss of some sort.

A New Critic might argue that such a reading is overly influenced by extraneous external information. Such a reading would be viewed as incorrect. But is personal experience always a hindrance to a reading? Let us assume that a reader, the same fishing enthusiast, does not read this as a problematic episode with a fish but, more correctly for a New Critic, as a very human situation. Let us imagine that this reader has had the unfortunate experience of having a fish hook embedded in their thumb as a result of a poor cast. Such a gruesome experience may actually greatly enhance the emotional impact of the poem and might encourage more meaningful encounters with a text. A New Critic would argue that the duty of an informed reader is to be familiar enough with the denotations and connotations of the words that they would be aware of such imagery and its potential impact, without requiring the first-hand experience. All the same, a reader's personal experience might very well play a substantial role in enhancing an encounter with a text.

Richards' experiment caused him to alter his focus in the teaching of literature. As he was moved to consider how one reads a text, one can begin to detect a sizable shift in emphasis among New Critics. Traditionally, New Criticism privileges the text over and above

Why theory?

As you are reading through this chapter, it is important to know that the introduction of these approaches to literature is not intended as material that you must learn and apply in your own study. Rather, we intend to highlight how approaches to literature are not static but dynamic. It can be easy to assume that there is a standard approach to literature but, as this first section hopes to show, this is not at all the case. Not only have approaches to literature changed dramatically over the centuries, they are likely to continue changing in your lifetime. The way we view texts and interpretations of texts is always in flux.

everything else but Richards began a movement to pointedly explore the role of the reader in making meaning in a text. His work, then, was the beginning of a movement that has come to be known as "reader-response criticism." Put very simply, reader-response criticism moves the emphasis of textual analysis from a singular focus on the text to one where the reader works in concert with a text to produce an interpretation.

It is important to note that reader-response criticism implies a complementary relationship between the text and the reader. It is not enough to argue an interpretation is only based on a whimsical *feeling*; but rather, understand that the process of interpretation demands an engagement with the text that actualizes potential meanings. It implies a disciplined approach to texts that is symbiotic rather than didactic in nature, while also allowing for the possibility of multiple readings that may not only change between readers but also across cultures and over time. Again, one should be sensitive to the fact that reader-response criticism does not suggest a "free-for-all," as a purely open-ended or speculative experience, but it is important not to underestimate the significance of the change from the reader as a passive recipient to the reader as an active and equal (transactional) participant in the meaning-making process.

A quick reflection of your own learning in English classrooms may reveal a curious mix of New Criticism and reader-response criticism. It might seem foreign to ignore one's own experience and background completely when making meaning from texts but you almost certainly have been assessed in your classes on offering something defined to some degree as the correct interpretation. Assuming any extreme view is difficult if not impossible to support, encounters with literary texts tend to reverberate between these poles. Many literary critics have argued for reading as always an inherently unique experience but this has been balanced by beliefs in pragmatic recognitions of **interpretive communities,** or **horizons of expectations** that suggest general trends or likelihoods in the way groups encounter texts.

While reader-response criticism encourages new shades of meaning to the readings of texts, your own essay experience—including what will be the assessment demands of this course—is likely to reveal that encounters with literature tend to have demands beyond the purely personal and have a larger collective role to play within various social groupings.

Structuralism

Reader-response criticism has been presented above as a somewhat unified school of criticism focusing on the interrelation between text and reader but in actuality it has been less a specific school of criticism than a fundamental underpinning of a variety of critical approaches that developed throughout the 20th century. In fact, the great majority of schools of criticism developed in the last century owe a broad allegiance to reader response. Beyond this common sensitivity to the transactional nature of interpretation each approach comes with its own ideological emphasis and methodology. It is to some of these theories that we now turn.

> **Horizons of expectations** and **interpretive communities** When we encounter texts, we have expectations about what we might find: we sense what is going to come next, we know when a moment is important and we anticipate a happy or sad ending. This kind of personal response, based on literary and cultural understanding, is referred to as a **horizon of expectations**.
>
> To a large extent, our expectations and interpretations are shaped by the groups to which we belong. When we discuss a poem in class we do not necessarily argue individual opinions or memorize a teacher's opinion but come to some kind of shared agreement about the meaning and importance of the text. Meaning, therefore, comes from the **interpretive community** of a classroom.

In the next chapter, you will be introduced to some basic aspects of Ferdinand de Saussure's theory of Structuralism, with an emphasis on the study of language. For the purposes of this chapter focusing on literature, what is most significant is a mention of Saussure's work in redefining words. Before Saussure, it was commonly accepted that a word was a symbol roughly equal to the "thing" to which it referred. As with some early historical criticism, this view of words was associated with *mimesis*, the notion of a mimetic process where words have close and meaningful connections with their **referents**. Saussure proposed that words were **signs** made up of two component parts: a signifier and a signified. The signifier refers to the written or spoken form while the signified refers to the thing, idea or concept intended. The entire formula for a word is: sign=signifier/signified.

Saussure's work was both revolutionary for the time and set the scene for many changes in how the world would approach language and literature. Prior to Saussure, most linguists believed that we perceive *things* when using language because of a direct connection between words and their referents. But Saussure argued that we perceive only signs. Saussure is really claiming that all of language is arbitrary—that there is no inherent connection between any word and its referent. This concept is relatively easy to follow when considering a word like, say, "cat." Saussure argued that |cat| (this notation means the signifier—either written or spoken—as opposed to "cat" which is the sign), is merely an agreed-upon symbol, or an arbitrary signifier we adopt to refer to the signified (the furry feline, commonly domesticated). There is no real reason why |cat| means "cat"; in the development of English, it could easily have been that the signifier |rat| or even |hippopotamus| was chosen to mean "cat" instead.

What is harder to recognize and accept is when the distinctions between signified and sign are less pronounced as with, say, "meow" (the noun). Here, many students are inclined to see a link thinking that this is not an arbitrary connection but something more inherently meaningful. Though this may be somewhat onomatopoeic, |meow| is no more inherently linked to "meow" than |cat| is to "cat." For "meow" to truly be a non-arbitrary word, the *essence* of the concept of "meow" would need to be immediately understood by all people everywhere, more a metaphysical concept than a language sign (the signified and the sign would be equal with no signifier in between). In the case of "meow," the signifier is known in Spanish as |*maullido*|, for instance, and demonstrates the arbitrary adoption of signified. After all, cats don't produce a different noise as a species simply because they are born or live in a Spanish-speaking environment, or an English one!

The concept that signs are arbitrary and do not refer to objects in the world but rather to less tangible ideas is central to structuralism. The ramifications of this idea are that we don't simply discover the true nature of the world of experience but we create it through our own minds. One of the key frameworks for this is language. The structuralists show how we see the world not for how it inherently *is*, but for how it has been organized through our systems of naming—

A **referent** is the object, idea or concept to which a word is meant to refer.

A **sign** is a symbol that communicates meaning.

Discussion Point

1 Is it possible to read a text you dislike intensely? How about one that involves protagonists who are a different gender or come from another culture? How would such differences between reader and text affect interpretations?

2 What positive aspects might arise from tensions of different cultural background and understanding?

our languages. This alone suggests not only the importance of this course, but of language learning and appreciation in general.

Poststructuralism and cultural studies

Significantly, Saussure's reworking of the concept of words paved the way for the rise of poststructuralism. As the name implies, poststructuralism is the development just after the structuralism inspired by Saussure and builds upon the concepts he articulated. For our purposes, the most significant aspect of poststructuralism is the continuing evolution of the arbitrariness of language and the redesign of the meaning of words.

Poststructuralists began by affirming the notion of difference suggested by structuralists. Because language is arbitrary, we must manipulate language through a complex understanding of differences to make ourselves understood. Otherwise, the understanding of all language as arbitrary leaves us without an anchor or external reference point from which to build the rest of our language understanding. Without this reference point (what the poststructuralists called a transcendental signified) all of our use of language becomes one of negotiating not what a sign is, but what a sign is not (because there simply is no such thing as absolute knowledge of what a sign is). We *know* through difference: we do not have an absolute connection between |cat| and "cat" but rather recognize "cat" as not-"bat" or not-"rat" (and, of course, not-"hippopotamus").

This system of differences was attended to by the structuralists at the level of words (signs), but the poststructuralists recognized arbitrariness and difference even at the deeper level of signifiers and signifieds. Even concepts (this may include values or meanings that we associate with things) are unfixed and arbitrary. Think of the previous example of "meow": although we stated that we were referring to the noun, without this added information, how would you know whether we were thinking of "meow" as the sound a cat makes or a cat making a sound? As the poststructuralists were quick to point out, despite all of its pragmatic value and general reliability in allowing us to communicate language is really an arbitrary system from top to bottom: signs are arbitrary not just because signifiers are constructed, but also because signifieds, poststructuralists argue, are also without absolute authority.

This is, perhaps, an overly simplistic interpretation of interesting and challenging theoretical developments. But for our purposes it may be enough to recognize that, with the rise of poststructuralism, all of language can be said to lack any absolute meaning. Therefore, especially with literary texts, making meaning involves complex negotiations between texts and readers.

The term poststructuralism is often replaced by the term "postmodernism" in North America. The terms are not, however, strictly the same meaning. An overly reductive description of postmodernism would be that it goes further than poststructuralism to argue that even our own understanding and knowledge of ourselves is in question and **ontological certainty** itself is more

Ontological certainty A doubt in ontological certainty refers to our inability to ever know for certain who we are or the authenticity of the world in which we live.

arbitrary than fixed. Postmodernism also tends to refer to both a historical era and an artistic movement that further problematizes its usage. Yet another term that is frequently substituted for poststructuralism is deconstruction with its emphasis on texts and language *mis*-speaking, a multiplicity of meanings that emerge through interpretation and reversals of traditional **binary operations**. It is worth noting that both the overlap and the differences in all three of these terms have had an influence in the approach to literary texts during the second half of the 20th century. Again, for our purposes, the primary focus on the lack of an absolute informs the focus on ongoing and complex negotiations between parties such as a text and a reader (in other words, socially constructed meanings).

> **Binary operations** A system of conceptual oppositions where one concept is understood in light of its opposite (i.e. we know "love" because we know "hate").

Activity

Reading it two ways

Look at the following list of phrases and statements collected from newspaper headings, shop signs, advertisements, etc.

Ambiguity can create hilarious situations. Imagine the impact of the same potential ambiguity in legal documents or philosophical treatises. In fact, poststructuralists would argue that this ambiguity is everywhere, even if not in quite so obvious a manner.

As you read through the list looking for the "jokes," pay attention to what assumption you make or how your assumptions change in order to be able to "read" these statements.

We now have dress shirts on sale for men with 16 necks!

Entire store 25% off

"I once shot an elephant in my pajamas."

Hospitals are sued by 7 foot doctors

I will bring my bike tomorrow if it looks nice in the morning.

Tech support: "What does the screen say now?"
Person: "It says, 'hit enter when ready.'"
Tech support: "Well?"
Person: "How do I know when it's ready?"

Please wait for hostess to be seated

Students hate annoying teachers.

They hit the man with a cane.

SLOW CHILDREN AT PLAY

Automatic washing machines: please remove all your clothes when the light goes out

We exchange anything—bicycles, washing machines, etc. Why not bring your wife along and get a wonderful bargain?

Toilet out of order. Please use floor below.

March planned for next August

Lingerie shipment hijacked—thief gives police the slip

L.A. voters approve urban renewal by landslide

Quarter of a million Chinese live on water

Hershey Bars Protest

Police begin campaign to run down jaywalkers

Safety experts say school bus passengers should be belted

"Iraqi head seeks arms."

Local high school dropouts cut in half

"New vaccine may contain rabies."

Predictably, with the increasing recognition of the social construction of textual meanings, much attention has moved to this notion of society. If members of a common society approach a text, they do so with a shared body of tastes, assumptions and values (ideology) that is likely to lead to shared interpretations. But what about different societies approaching common texts—would there be a better or lesser reading?

An easy solution would be to allow for multiple social readings but many believe that inequitable social distributions of power and influence prevent this. If one social group enjoys much more power and influence, their reading of texts may assume a greater sway over interpretation that only further legitimizes their dominant position, cultural attitudes and tastes. For instance, if men enjoy far more power, their interpretations are going to have more influence, reinforcing the patriarchal values to maintain the status quo. The more common and influential interpretations only reinforce the values already in place in such a world.

As more diverse social groups embraced the ideas of poststructuralism and postmodernism they used these theories to offer interpretations that challenged the privileged or prevailing groups, attitudes, tastes and values. Even the most sacred of texts—literary, religious or political—are mediated in language and, therefore, both contain and are open to the challenge of addressing inequitable social orders. These groups formed multiple schools of criticism that refused to conform to prescribed **hegemonies** and instead offered divergent foci based loosely on the idea of **identity politics**. Although identity politics represented a wide array of voices that could be discordant and even in conflict with one another it did serve to promote greater inclusion of social diversity, and the different expressions of this more broadly defined view of the community. In terms of specifically literary treatment, this meant not just reinterpreting familiar, or **canonical**, texts but asking questions about what texts were chosen to be read and which authors were studied and why.

Among the many different critical schools that could loosely be organized under a cultural studies heading, for the purposes of this book we will highlight only a few. The following list represents the general approaches taken in the field.

Marxist literary criticism

Marxism is less a specific school of literary criticism than a larger critical worldview that can be used to help interpret a text. Marxist criticism starts with a central assumption that all texts contain subtexts which are extensions of historical and ideological conflict, the same conflicts being played out in real societies and not just in literary texts. For Marxist thinkers, the root of these conflicts is anchored in social class and economic differences. Groups that control the flow of money (capital) or the economic base, are able to invest in the superstructure (social institutions, such as the laws and political structure, educational and cultural institutions), in ways that advance their own values. The social classes that do not control economic capital are exploited both for their labor and by a superstructure that reinforces their servitude. Inevitably, this creates conflict.

Hegemony The ability of dominant classes to exercise social and cultural leadership or control over subordinate classes.

Identity politics Social and political interests based on the needs or desires of common identity groups. Identity, or the condition of being oneself and not another, is an idea that seems straightforward on the surface but involves a complex interplay of self and culture.

Canonical Works that have been identified as being important, significant and central to a cultural tradition. The idea of canon is discussed further in the chapter "Literature: texts and contexts."

As products of the superstructure, literary texts reveal the subtexts of this conflict. By closely paying attention to a text, a reader may discern evidence of these class conflicts and work toward egalitarian change. Interestingly, Marxist criticism argues that such change is possible because reality is material as opposed to "spiritual" (authentic and innate to our being as humans). Truths, including all values, beliefs and norms, exist in socially constructed material reality which makes them open to change and redress—the very aims of Marxist criticism.

Feminism and gender studies

Feminist criticism is, quite simply, devoted to describing and interpreting (or reinterpreting) women's experience through literature. It seeks to challenge long-standing and dominant patriarchal cultural values. Feminist criticism may approach literature with a view toward uncovering essential differences between women and men, or challenging male representations of women and society, or rediscovering previously overlooked or ignored women writers and texts or any combination of the three. It has also contributed to significant changes in the form of writing, and to questioning the point of view of all texts, and all discourses that refer to a speaking subject. In this way, feminist criticism works toward the release of all humankind from the oppression that is a result of any conscious or unconscious assimilation or subordination to a dominant cultural viewpoint. It also seeks to allow for different forms and styles of expression that may once have been looked down upon or denied through reinterpreting, for instance, hierarchies in genre alongside gender.

Gender studies can be used synonymously with feminist criticism to explore sexual identity; by extending the terms, gender studies supports an investigation of not just what it means to be a woman but also what it means to be a man. Gender studies concerns itself with questions of reproduction, sexuality, gender, family, love and marriage as well as broader social issues to challenge prevailing hegemonies, false assumptions and prejudices. Other offshoots may include Queer Theory that challenges the exclusive representation of heterosexuality (between members of the opposite sex) as the basis of all relationships. As with feminist criticism, gender studies gives people or social groups the opportunity to more fully define themselves.

Cultural poetics

Cultural poetics is a term often used to refer to trends in New Historicism in North America and Cultural Materialism in the United Kingdom. At the core of cultural poetics is a response to history as a body of knowledge. Previously, there was a common belief that history could be an accurate and objective representation of the past that would reveal the attitudes, values and worldviews of the people in that time. In literature, a knowledge of the historical background of both the content and production of a text would reveal unified truths and more "correct" interpretations. Following the same logic of poststructuralists, however, cultural poetics argues that history is not a fixed and knowable body of knowledge but rather one among many competing **discourses.** Instead of historical information

A **discourse** is a continuous stretch of language. In literary studies, it is usually an extended academic, philosophical or political discussion or a specific treatise. In many academic discussions, "discourse" is seen as a worldview or a particular perspective on beliefs and values.

providing facts that can illuminate texts, historical information is only considered valuable as one among many, often competing, discourses that can be revealed through attentive reading. Cultural poetics seeks to investigate these multiple discourses (history, law, economics, politics and even literary analysis itself) in order to explore the connections between all human activities and their role in making life meaningful.

Cultural poetics does tend to blur distinctions between literature as an artistic product and literature as a social event but not necessarily in the direction one would expect. In fact, cultural poetics looks to uncover how all of life's activities and discourses are more like art in that they work to produce metaphorical versions of reality rather than (impossible) purely analytic truths. Through such reading, we can discover not just the social realities of a text but the very social realities that affect our negotiations and interpretations of texts. Of course, this means we never get to make a correct or final statement, leaving things open-ended and dynamic.

Postcolonial criticism

Postcolonial criticism is simply defined as an approach to texts produced in colonized countries. Typically, this is in reaction to white, male, Christian and European or Western hegemony that has dominated cultural production in the past. Such studies can take a case-by-case approach (by country or region), as in the cases of Africa, Australia, North and South America, South Asia, the Caribbean and New Zealand. Postcolonial criticism derives from multiple critical approaches, through topics such as nationalism, ethnicity, language, history, and how these issues are dealt with when two (or more) cultures clash, usually with one dominant and one deemed inferior (cultural imperialism). Postcolonial criticism is concerned with investigating the social, cultural and political nature of colonialist ideologies and resistance to them. Postcolonial critics can approach a wide variety of texts from those produced by the dominant colonial cultures to the texts that represent the voices of the oppressed or marginalized. For this reason, this course incorporates a wide range of literature in translation. A postcolonial approach can offer a perspective on the clashes between cultures and the suggestion of a possibility for reconciliation between them, or ways of working across cultures.

The rise of cultural studies has been an overtly political focus in literary criticism in the wake of poststructuralist thought. Cultural studies can draw on a vast array of critical approaches and distinctions that help to broaden our approach to a text. Without question, such criticism and interpretation has been a common effort to challenge dominant cultures and, in changing literary interpretations, work toward changing societies.

Internet search

Changes in definitions of literature as well as approaches to literature have accelerated over the last century. The goal of this very brief and cursory introduction is not to overwhelm students with the rate and degree of change. Rather, it is hoped that some of the changes will be intriguing and pique your interests. To really see the range of reading and thinking opportunities, take a few minutes to explore the Internet to discover a range of resources on literary theory. You can easily use any search engine or look at some of the following sites:

- *Voice of the Shuttle* (http://vos.ucsb.edu)
- *The Postcolonial Studies Website* (http://www.postcolonialstudiesassociation.co.uk)
- *The Postcolonial Website at Emory University* (http://www.english.emory.edu/Bahri/)
- *Contemporary Postcolonial and Postimperial Literature in English* (http://www.postcolonialweb.org)
- *Postcolonial Space* (http://postcolonial.net)

Literary study today

The following short section is less about philosophical changes in approaches and attitudes to literature than an overview of some of the interesting applications of literature and literary theory today. It may be surprising to find that aspects of story and narrative have moved beyond the covers of books to the halls of justice, operating theaters, scientific laboratories and analysts' couches but thinkers and practitioners across many academic and professional disciplines are beginning to utilize these same considerations to enhance their own work.

Narrative in medicine, law and psychology

Critics have accused Western medicine of being overly "professionalist." This is not to suggest that doctors are accused of being too good and proper in their approach, but rather the term is used to imply that doctors are taught to treat medical problems as entirely independent of a patient's personal and psychological history. The emphasis in the past has been on medicine as a purely objective scientific approach, both as a way for doctors to understand and resolve the medical issues and as a means of personal protection from the often difficult or tragic conditions of an individual patient.

In the last few decades, new trends have begun to develop in medical schools that look more holistically at medicine, treating not just disease but the people involved. These trends emphasize larger narrative competence in order to be aware of the complex interactions between doctors, patients and the larger public. The Program in Narrative Medicine (http://www.narrativemedicine.org), part of the College of Physicians and Surgeons at Columbia University in New York is one of the pioneering medical school programs in narrative competence and offers the following mission statement on their website:

Narrative Medicine fortifies clinical practice with the narrative competence to recognize, absorb, metabolize, interpret, and be moved by the stories of illness. Through narrative training, the Program in Narrative Medicine helps doctors, nurses, social workers, and therapists to improve the effectiveness of care by developing the capacity for attention, reflection, representation, and affiliation with patients and colleagues.

What is implicit in such a statement is that we experience life, including illness, as story. One does not simply have illness but we construct stories about causal conditions that have led to our disease that follow very familiar narrative (story) patterns (e.g. "Well, first I was tired for two days and didn't think anything of it. Then I had a sore throat and a slight headache for a day. Now, I am bleeding through my pores!"). Understanding story and having narrative competence allows doctors to gain more thorough information and engage patients in a way that is both comfortable and inherently therapeutic. Patients enjoy being a part of the process. They want to be heard and gain more empathy and understanding from their doctors. Doctors, in incorporating narrative competencies into the therapies that they offer, are able to diagnose and analyze the problems better, and offer more holistic remedies—rather than just treating a symptom—in addition to helping to educate their patients and creating more opportunities to reflect on their own practice.

Activity

A medical narrative

Read the following short description of a patient's visit to a doctor and consider the questions that follow.

Patient Y is a 35-year-old woman with X disease. This illness is painful and has caused her to be confined to a wheelchair for most of her life. The disease runs in the family. The patient's sister, aunt, and nephews all suffer from some form of the disease. Most of her family members were diagnosed by the age of 4. Patient Y visits the doctor because she has just noticed tell-tale symptoms in her own 8-year-old daughter. "I know what this is," she states "and it is haunting me. I have been watching her for two weeks now and I can tell that she is sick. She is so energetic and funny and loud—I don't want her to change." On previous visits the patient has told the doctor how happy she is that her daughter had seemed to be spared the illness, now she is clearly devastated. "How do I tell her? She is old enough now to appreciate being well, to know what she is going to lose."

Questions to the text
1 What is your response as a reader to this beginning of a short narrative? How does the story make you feel? What kinds of emotions and possible conflicts are generated by the story?

2 How would or should a doctor respond to such a story? Is the response to this narrative a prescription for tests?

3 Why would a story that includes detail, dilemma, emotion, and even characterization be important in a formal medical conversation?

4 Would this report of an illness, *as a story*, lead to the possibility for better care?

Narrative medicine represents a great departure from "traditional" medical models of disease as problem. With a stronger focus on story, narrative medicine shifts attention from the disease to the patient and helps to validate their experiences. Sharing narratives also creates an empathetic bond between doctor and patient and encourages collaborative engagement as well as greater creativity and reflection on the personal and social aspects of disease.

Law is another field that has relatively recently turned its attention to taking a more literary approach. Judging by the proliferation of courtroom dramas on television, it is easy to see why. In the most frequently dramatized setting for legal cases in the United States—the closing arguments of a courtroom case—the climax comes as a battle between competing narratives. In one version, the defendant has knowingly planned and executed the atrocious deed; in another, they are hapless victims of circumstance and, if convicted, only add to the greater tragedy. In some versions, of course, additional entertainment twists arise as lawyers struggle internally with multiple narratives— the one they may be obligated to tell to serve their client versus the one they think they know.

The introduction of narrative is in reaction to purely formalist or doctrinal tendencies (similar to the professionalism of medicine described above). The law has been treated as an artifact or tangible product that can be known, discussed or argued in isolation from the people involved. Many believe that this is simply too limited and that other perspectives and experiences are required to get a more accurate picture. Narrative can help is realizing such aims. In particular, narrative in law focuses on the use of law and legal frameworks within larger cultural and critical contexts and the challenges of interpretation that arise as a result. Peter Brooks, a professor of law at the University of Virginia, argues that:

> Essentially, everything a lawyer produces is a story. Whether it's a contract, legal memorandum, or brief, the lawyer marshals its critical elements into a narrative that a reader must interpret, understand, and ultimately agree with. It's not a work of fiction, certainly, but the writer is making choices that tell a story about that reality. The real question, then, is what conscious or subconscious devices drive those choices? It would learn that—first of all—storytelling is not innocent. The way you go about it makes a lot of difference to the result you come up with. On the other side of telling a story is the reading and interpreting of narratives—indeed of texts of all kinds.

As in the interpretation of literature, law is a complex negotiation between the (legal) text and (legal) reader. Recognizing that there are no "innocent" readings, as Brooks suggests, has created an obvious entry portal for the valuable introduction of literary approaches and narrative frameworks within the legal world.

Psychology is yet another field to have changed as a result of approaches to literature, and changes in the approach to literature itself. There is a devoted school of literary criticism informed by psychoanalytic theory that points out how literary texts reveal the subconscious desires of authors and their larger social settings. An approach to literature with a sensitivity to these issues creates yet another interpretive possibility. But the world of narrative in psychology itself works in the opposite direction. Rather than focusing on psychological aspects of literary texts, narrative in psychology focuses on narrative and story in the construction of a psychology (in other words, how stories shape lives). Since, it is argued, we construct, define, live and convey our lives as narratives, psychology can and should use narrative in its effort to introduce, or reintroduce, modification and change in patients.

Using narrative in psychology is a way for patients to externalize their stories and explore meanings and repercussions. It also makes it possible to change or refocus stories, by introducing new interpretations that encourage participants to play an active part in authenticating and strengthening their strategies. With the introduction of narrative, the professions of medicine and law have been able to radically internalize aspects, and make stronger connections with people. Conversely, narrative in psychology has made it possible to treat problems as external realities (in which people can find themselves in a different way), providing opportunities and resources with which to make sense of a given situation to help the patient reposition themselves in respect to external problems. Of course, narrative in psychology has also drawn attention to the complex relationship between analyst and analysand, and even madness and sanity, as interesting cultural constructions.

Narrative in cognitive science

Cognitive science, brain research and neuroscience might seem even further removed from applications of literature, narrative and story than medicine, law and psychology, yet it remains a field where interesting research and utilization of literary theory is being done. The work in this arena is seen as much more symbiotic: new understandings of how the brain operates are yielding new understandings of how we read and understand narrative.

One of the central assumptions with narrative in cognitive science is that the process of narrative communication—the understanding and manipulation of lengthy, complex and detailed literary narratives—is both an enormously complex cognitive operation and one of two fundamental ways of thinking about knowledge and the human brain (the other being an operation of logic and classification). This suggests that even the roots of an understanding of self and the nature of thinking are partially tied to narrative and storytelling and thus play a truly significant role in our lives beyond aesthetic pleasure or cultural negotiation. In other words, narrative is the fundamental foundation for all of human thought and cognition.

Narrative in cognitive science looks closely at how we construct narratives of consciousness, identity and coherence both in the social and physical worlds and argues that not only do we create stories to explain all aspects of our being but we tell stories to learn how to think about and understand our being. Since story is both the "chicken" and "the egg" (we tell stories to learn how to tell stories), we gain from both approaching the understanding of stories via an idea of how the brain functions and approaching an understanding of the brain via an idea of how stories function.

A connected trend is evident in narratives of evolutionary biology. Again, if narrative and cognition—the brain—are interdependent, the traces of the brain's evolutionary developments and tendencies are to be found in story and vice versa. We can trace, for instance, the interactions of literary characters not just as culturally constructed relationships but as biologically rooted relationships aimed at developing more sophisticated designs to enhance the survival of the human species (of which culturally constructed relationships would also be a component). And, as with narrative in cognitive science, further understanding of evolutionary biology can aid in opening a text to new understandings of internal operations. Narrative as a core component of the cognitive and biological sciences is still a relatively new focus through which can be demonstrated some of the more far-reaching applications of recent approaches to literature.

Media studies

One final arena absorbed by newer approaches to literature is the field of media studies. This is potentially less surprising that in some of the fields above, as even the existence of such a discipline can be linked to changes in the ways we have thought about culture, entertainment, lifestyle, education, etc. Media studies is an academic discipline and field of study that deals with the content, history and effects of various media; in particular, the mass media and its relationship to what is broadly defined as "popular culture." As such, it signals a dramatic shift from earlier values that were concerned with only so-called "high art."

A big part of media studies has come out of structuralism and poststructuralism in the form of a new focus, semiotics. Semiotics can be defined as a science of signs, focusing in particular on how signs work as an emerging construction from a complex relationship between sender and receiver. While literature clearly focuses on signs in language, media studies includes multiple sign systems found in popular and mass culture. This might include obvious fields such as film, music, television, video games, and graffiti art but may also attend to less obvious aspects of the everyday world, such as fashion, food, conversation and social life. Media studies may include considerations of the use of literary texts but also adds consideration of additional grammars (sets of rules) focusing on visual media, sound and movement to embrace a broader appeal to the senses, and the world that surrounds us.

Conclusion

Our intention here is not to give you a history of literary theory but to suggest that our conception and approach to literature is dynamic and continues to evolve. Far from suggesting the "right way" to approach a text, this chapter has tried to encourage you to see literature and the study of literature as alive. This will encourage you to approach texts with flexibility and an open mind, but also with an understanding of the rich history of human engagement with literature.

Activity

Sign systems

It is likely that at the school you currently attend or in your local community there are multiple social groups, or cliques, that congregate around a shared set of interests, values or assumptions. It is equally likely that each of the "distinct" groups (there is probably as much overlap between groups as there is true distinction) has or employs a semiotic system to advertise its identity. List some of the groups you commonly encounter—including your own (even if your own is a distinctly anti-group group!)—and some of the signs frequently employed.

1 What sign systems are commonly used?

2 How are they used differently among different groups?

3 What ideas are suggested about sign and sign systems as a result of your observations?

Activity

What are words?

Look at this image and quickly answer two simple questions: What is this? What does it mean? Students viewing this image have come up with a wide variety of responses. Read the comments below and see if any of their ideas match your own.

- "I think it is writing in some language. At first I thought Arabic but I've seen that and it looks more like something from Asia. I have no idea what it means."

- "It is language. Whatever it is trying to say, the part in red is the most important word, or maybe something being explained."

- "It is scribbles and doesn't mean anything."

- "This is part of a document in a language I don't understand. If I knew the language I could tell you the meaning but I don't."

- "I think this is really a painting or a piece of modern art. It could mean something about confusion or about really trying to say something because it is similar to a note that was written quickly."

- "This is a picture of graffiti. It is a very long tag [a graffiti artist's signature or sign]. Or maybe the design in red is the tag, or the graffiti writer's signature."

The image is, in fact, a type of mark-making called "asemic writing" by the artist Patricia Dunn. Asemic writing resembles writing, calligraphy, or some form of alphabet but has no clear meaning. The "words" in asemic writing are not words, the "letters" are more like scribbles. At the same time, it is a work of art. The gestures on the page may suggest feelings or attitudes. Perhaps it resembles a letter, or a document from the middle ages, or an urgent note. The marks and the colors can mean something to us once we start looking at it as a work of contemporary art based on the look of writing.

Your response to this opening exercise should give you some insight into the difficulty of distinguishing between art and language, and where to draw the line between some types of mark-making that resemble pictograms or ideograms and language proper. Almost every response assumes that the image represents some sort of writing, a graphic representation of language. Even the viewers that think the image is art suggest that it is somehow commenting on or related to language. The student who saw the picture as scribbles, of course, sees it as the opposite of writing and communication, as marks on paper that do not represent language. But scribbles, we could argue, are an attempt at writing with meaning, a close imitation of written language or at least nonsense gestures based on writing we have seen before. This, in fact, is the key: the image looks an awful lot like something we have seen before, and we make judgments about what it is and what it means based on these other things.

We approach the study of language and culture with the fact that we are immersed in both. Language surrounds us every day and we know how to recognize it. Culture is the way we structure and live our lives. Because we know a lot about language and culture we automatically have a lot that we could say about the image. We know that marks on paper can be used to represent the words of language. We know that these words usually have some sort of meaning and can express an emotion. We also know that there is a lot that goes into meaning in language. Even if we could not understand the "words" in the image, the way they were written—quickly sketched, angrily marked, breezily splashed (just the way words are spoken)—adds to meaning. Because we live culture, we can also comment about how the image fits (or does not fit) in our particular culture or in another culture as we understand it. We see it as a letter, a painting, or a document because we know what these things are, and how they function in the world we live in. We see it as a foreign language because it is somewhat familiar, but not our own. As you start the language and literature course, you are in a great position because you already know the language and you already understand many things about the cultures in which the language is used (or of which it is a part).

But proximity to language and culture creates difficulties. It is hard to distance ourselves from the subject matter in order to have an objective perspective. When we talk about language or describe language, we necessarily have to *use* language to describe it. Because language and cultural objects affect us, it is sometimes hard to maintain objectivity and accurately describe how the objects—advertisements, films, books, articles, sentences, words, marks—are functioning. Part of the challenge of this course is to be aware of and use the skills you have acquired as human beings, speakers, and students over the past 15 to 19 years. At the same time, you may want to put aside some of the assumptions you have about what language is, how it operates, and the role it plays in culture.

What is language?

This is a course about language in action. You will be looking at language as it is practiced, at the evidence of language being used (as an extract of writing, a recording of speech, etc.), in order to come to some conclusions about what, how, and why language means. But it is worth spending some time defining language and looking at some of its special properties in order to understand the approaches we can take in its study. In the assessments for IB, and the assessments you will be doing in class, you will not be expected to memorize and reproduce facts about language. The following sections are meant to introduce you to current thinking and debate around language that may stimulate your own ideas.

Language, then, is a system of vocal signs through which humans communicate. To unpack this a bit, we can say that language is a system because it consists of patterns, or rules, for putting together elements such as sounds to make words and words to make sentences that when violated results in loss of meaning. Within this complex system called language there are many elements: sounds are combined according to rules in order to create words, words are put into relationship with each other (following rules again) in order to form sentences. When we follow the rules of language we can meaningfully communicate. It is, however, important to note that these rules do not limit us to a finite set of utterances. Language is open-ended and creative. Following the rules, we can make up new words in English. And following the rules, or the grammar of our language, we can combine the words to make up new sentences, some of which may have never been spoken before.

It is important to remember that language functions through a system of contrasts. The contrasting elements in language come in pairs, a property that linguists call **Duality of patterning**. Consonant sounds contrast with vowel sounds, adding "s" to a word often makes it plural, while no "s" makes a word singular. Individual, distinguishable sound units in a language, or **phonemes**, can be combined in various ways because we can distinguish the difference between them. Letters have to be distinct enough in order for listeners to be able to pick up the patterns that make up words. Some sounds may be similar—a new speaker of English may have difficulty hearing the difference between a "b" sound and a "p" sound—but it is difference that makes communication possible. By the same token, morphemes, or the smallest *meaningful* unit in language, can be combined in various ways. "Happy" is a morpheme because it can't be broken down into smaller meaningful parts. "Un" is a morpheme as well. Put the two together and you have the word "unhappy." It is amazing that we can learn such an intricate system. But the system itself is built so that differences can be recognized—language is a redundant system that guards against misunderstanding by making important parts of sound and meaning easily distinguishable to speakers of the language.

> **Duality of patterning** is the ability of language or a sign system to create distinctions between sounds, words, and units of meaning through a system of differences between two elements.
>
> A **phoneme** is the smallest contrastive unit in the sound system of a language.

Activity

Making sense

1 Which of the following nonsense words *could* be a word in English?

   pttlpp   pittle   tuckchrm   techlore

2 Which of the following word combinations are possible in English?

   John hit the ball   hit John the ball   John the ball hit

3 How much sense do these two paragraphs make?

   Tiny couches make their way slowly into the cup. The cup is completely devoid of windows so the couches are not able to see the surrounding books. The couches are more relaxed because they cannot see the books; they no longer have to fear the books' sharp teeth, their claws, their anger. This also means, though, that the books have left the dolphins outside to fend for themselves.

   This bonkoll the Potoline corporation will be introducing a predile dento to petch with the popular iToto from the seemorific Gondo group. Last bonkoll's breeo petched briefly but was eventually dintered because of its slelto fortline. Potoline shleeks that this bonkol's tolk will not klote the same todrill.

4 What do these examples tell you about the rules of language? What do they tell you about the creative possibilities of language?

> **Grammar**
>
> There are two kinds of grammar: prescriptive and descriptive. Prescriptive grammar is the set of rules we make up about how to speak and write "properly." These rules are set down based on particular groups of people (who might be educated, or of a certain class?). It is important to remember that these grammar rules can change over time and that *not* following these rules may lead to ambiguity but does not always lead to lack of meaning. Descriptive grammar is the set of rules that linguists find when studying how meaning is created in a language. These rules tend to focus on the basic structures that make meaning possible in a given language; in other words, descriptive grammar is the study of underlying systems of language.

Language is intentional

There are some other properties of language that set it apart from other means of communication or even other systems humans develop for completing certain tasks. First, language is intentional: humans use it purposefully in order to communicate facts, ideas, or emotions. Second, language, or the ability to speak or have language, is inherent: healthy humans are born with language capability (although this is still a subject for debate as we will discuss below).

Humans have many ways to communicate. If I am smiling or laughing, you may assume that I am happy. A yawn during a lecture can communicate boredom. A pained expression may, depending on the context, mean confusion or general distress. In many situations, gestures (body language) are combined with words to clarify meaning. If I say "I am so happy to be in class today" and I roll my eyes, you will know that I am being sarcastic, that I am not happy at all to be in class (although this is more likely to be the case for you, the student, than it is for me, the gainfully employed teacher … Am I rolling my eyes now?). Gestures, however, are not always intentional in the way that speaking is. Trying to catch someone's attention is an intentional form of body language. Yawning in class is, hopefully, quite unintentional. Have you ever started laughing uncontrollably at something that seems to be funny only to you? Sometimes we don't mean to communicate the things we do through our expressions and movements. It is rarely the case, even when we are in a furious rage, that fully formed words and sentences stream from our mouths without any thought, control, or moderation.

Thinking about language and intention is interesting when we consider the basic ideas about what it means to be human. Why do we speak to each other? Why are we the only animals that seem to be able to communicate in such a complex way? It is very popular today to look at how humans act and to attribute our general tendencies to the actions of early humans and to common sense notions of evolution. Men and women shop differently, some say, because early men were efficient hunters who decided what they needed to get: just traipse into the forest, kill that animal, and bring it home. Early women, on the other hand, had to spend some time at their gathering, taking a long time to find the right herbs and roots that would be healthy and heartening, as opposed to those that would poison the family. Magazines and articles on physical fitness suggest that, even if we are not the fastest animals on the planet, we are built to run for long distances. Why? Because early humans needed to tire out their prey, following the path of the speedy antelope over long distances until the antelope finally slowed and the human ultra-marathoners (long before the first marathon, of course) victoriously raised their spears. It may be very easy to say that humans developed language out of a basic need to survive, to communicate about dangers outside of the cave. Many bird and monkey species have the ability to make warning sounds but we do not often call these signs language, and the fact that animals warn each other does not explain why human language developed further.

Discussion Point

Why did we start talking?
Did humans develop language because we needed to negotiate complex relationships, or did socialization happen because of language?

When studying language development in children, many researchers have found that language is used in very interesting ways quite early in a child's development. Children learn to make sounds that correlate to a desire for something. Children very quickly learn to say something to indicate that they are hungry or thirsty, for example. This seems to fit into the pattern of theories about our communication needs that are based on strategies for survival. But researchers have also found that children at a very early age use words to communicate *something* about the world around them that gives them no apparent benefit. While a child who says "ball" may want to play with the ball, what do we say about the child who is determined to say "nose" or is equally determined to string together sounds or nonsense words that sound so much like elaborate, emotional expressions? One idea is that of theory of mind: the notion that human beings have the ability to understand that they themselves are thinking beings with thoughts, beliefs, desires and intentions that may or may not be the same as those of others. Little children might not be so good at figuring out intentions or mental states in others. This ability may, in fact, develop along with language. When you play with a three-year-old, you may laugh that when she covers her eyes she thinks *you* can't see her—not a very well developed theory of mind. At the age of six months a baby may intently observe faces and follow the gaze of a mother, indicating perhaps that the baby knows that what the mother finds important the baby may be interested in as well.

Many researchers feel we are born with this ability and that along with the acquisition of language we start to realize (by age three or four) that our thoughts are interesting to ourselves and may very well be interesting to other people. Part of the problem of talking about where language comes from, or how it first developed in humans, is to decide where to draw the historical line. If we think about intention and states of mind, we might very well ask: When did this seemingly unique human ability begin? And, here again, many theorists turn back to our needs as early humans. While many primates live together in small groups, early human groups grew in size to the point where calls and gestures simply weren't sufficient for efficient—and life-saving—social organization. This required a more complex form of communication

Activity

Who has language?

Do animals have language?

The answer is no. But this answer depends on a particular definition of language as distinct from communication. While monkeys may make specific calls to warn others of impending danger, such as fire or the approach of a lion, they may not be able to combine these signs in more reciprocal, open-ended ways. Recent research suggests that animals simply don't have the ability to guess at the mental states of others the way that humans do (theory of mind).

Decide for yourself

Research the issue of animal language on your own. What does current research indicate? Why would scientists continue to research language ability in animals if it isn't a reasonable prospect that this can be called language?

Language is inherent

The idea that our ability to communicate through language is an inherent part of being human has often been held to be true. While language ability in humans may be beyond evolution, particular nuances of language ability have certainly developed along with other human attributes. Importantly, however, language ability is now part of what it means to be human and is often considered to be in-born as opposed to learned. Charles Darwin himself noted this aspect of language, as he wrote in *The Descent of Man*, first published in 1871:

> As Horne Tooke, one of the founders of the novel science of philology observes, language is an art, like brewing or baking; but writing would have been a better simile. It certainly is not a true instinct, for every language has to be learned. It differs, however, widely from all ordinary arts, for man has an instinctive tendency to speak, as we see in the babble of our young children; while no child has an instinctive tendency to brew, bake, or write. Moreover, no philologist now supposes that any language has been deliberately invented; it has been slowly and unconsciously developed by many steps.

Darwin suggests that while a particular language needs to be learned over time, the ability or desire to speak is not learned. During the middle of the 20th century many theorists, particularly behaviorist psychologists like B. F. Skinner, preferred to look at more empirical and scientific ways of studying language acquisition and at how we learn in a rich environment of stimulus and response. But by 1957, the linguist Noam Chomsky again suggested that, based on observations such as the speed with which children pick up complex linguistic operations and the fact that humans are quickly capable of creating novel sentences that have never been uttered before, humans are born with a Universal Grammar or basic language-creating faculty.

Activity

Class debate

"Humans are born with an ability to create language" vs. "Language is a learned construct like the rules governing a sport".

It is easy to find people who disagree with the ideas of Noam Chomsky. How do we separate abilities that are inborn and abilities that are learned? What role does culture play in the development of language if we simply arrive ready to speak and create? A simple search on the Internet will find many researchers who still debate the merits of Chomskian linguistics—Chomsky himself tends to be a passionate debater.

Do some research of your own. Break up into two groups or teams to take opposing role in the debates about the inherent nature of language or grammar.

In recent years, various fields of research such as biology, neurology, psychology, and even philosophy have come together to create a new discipline called cognitive science. Advances in cognitive science have used a variety of approaches to consider the way the human mind works.

Read

The language instinct

The language instinct, as described by psychologist Steven Pinker, is closely linked to Chomsky's Universal Grammar.

Language is not a cultural artifact that we learn the way we learn to tell time or how the federal government works. Instead, it is a distinct piece of the biological makeup of our brains. Language is a complex, specialized skill, which develops in the child spontaneously, without conscious effort or formal instruction, is deployed without awareness of its underlying logic, is qualitatively the same in every individual, and is distinct from more general abilities to process information or behave intelligently. For these reasons some cognitive scientists have described language as a psychological faculty, a mental organ, a neural system, and a computational module. But I prefer the admittedly quaint term "instinct." It conveys the idea that people know how to talk in more or less the sense that spiders know how to spin webs. Web-spinning was not invented by some unsung spider genius and does not depend on having had the right education or on having an aptitude for architecture or the construction trades. Rather, spiders spin spider webs because they have spider brains, which give them the urge to spin and the competence to succeed. Although there are differences between webs and words, I will encourage you to

see language in this way, for it helps to make sense of the phenomena we will explore.

Thinking of language as an instinct inverts the popular wisdom, especially as it has been passed down in the canon of the humanities and social sciences. Language is no more a cultural invention than is upright posture. It is not a manifestation of a general capacity to use symbols: a three-year-old, we shall see, is a grammatical genius, but is quite incompetent at the visual arts, religious iconography, traffic signs, and the other staples of the semiotics curriculum. Though language is a magnificent ability unique to *Homo sapiens* among living species, it does not call for sequestering the study of humans from the domain of biology, for a magnificent ability unique to a particular living species is far from unique in the animal kingdom. Some kinds of bats home in on flying insects using Doppler sonar. Some kinds of migratory birds navigate thousands of miles by calibrating the positions of the constellations against the time of day and year. In nature's talent show we are simply a species of primate with our own act, a knack for communicating information about who did what to whom by modulating the sounds we make when we exhale.

Source: Pinker, Steven. 1994. *The Language Instinct.* New York: Penguin Books. pp. 18–19.

The emergentist perspective

Some theorists still think that there is just as much nurture involved in our language abilities as there is nature. While linguists may take a variety of perspectives on how humans develop language abilities and learn language, a current position among some linguists today is broadly labeled as the emergentist approach. Some researchers see language ability coming from rapid human learning and adaptation to the world around them so that various capabilities of the brain ranging from abilities to think, listen, remember, move muscles in certain ways, are harnessed to interact in such a way as to allow speaking and communication. In the words of the scholars Bates and McWhinney, language is a "new machine built out of old parts." According to this view, humans have certain innate abilities, but not a specific function or inborn basic grammar that could be described as language.

Without answering the question of whether or not language ability is innate, we can all agree that children have a remarkable ability to pick up the complexities of language quite quickly. It is particularly amazing to witness a young child saying something surprising or original, something that obviously has not been repeated, or shows their own thinking about the world. Based on research into the nature of language, and looking at the last sentence of the extract from *The Language Instinct* by Steven Pinker (we have a "knack for communicating who did what to whom …"), we see that no matter which language is used, we learn aspects of language use from those around us. We learn and create through language use as a social act.

Activity

The power of language

This image represents the Biblical story of the Tower of Babel. According to the story, the people of early Babylon, or of all the earth, all spoke one language. They prided themselves on being an intelligent and thriving race and set out to build a tower that would reach as high as the heavens. God was not pleased with the vanity of the people's ambitions, so he punished them by giving the people different languages, causing them to abandon their work on the tower and scatter themselves in all directions.

Questions to the text

1 What does the image, and the story, suggest about the benefits of everyone speaking the same language? What are the drawbacks?

2 What does the story suggest about the social functions of language?

3 Doing your own research or based on your own knowledge or experience, what are some other foundation narratives or early stories that deal with the origins or evolution of language? What do these stories suggest about the power of language?

The building of the Tower of Babel, from the Old English Illustrated *Hexateuch* (The first six books of the Old Testament), Canterbury, England, c. 1025–1050.

So far, we have been mainly discussing language as a mental system that determines our ability to communicate. Perhaps this is what makes language a somewhat difficult area of study to pin down. When we study language, are we concerned with the mental "grammar" that operates to organize speech? Or, are we focused on the words as they are spoken? This very division is an important area of concern for linguists. In the early 1900s, the French linguist Ferdinand de Saussure set down ways of looking at language and considering the relationship between language and thought that have influenced the study of language for over a century. In the published notes from his *Course in General Linguistics*, Saussure says that language and thought cannot be easily separated and he describes the nature of language with a striking metaphor:

> Language can also be compared with a sheet of paper: thought is the front and the sound the back; one cannot cut the front without cutting the back at the same time; likewise in language, one can neither divide sound from thought nor thought from sound …

As Saussure goes on to explain, there can be no clear, detailed thought without speech or the acquisition of **articulated language**. At the same time, sounds cannot be shaped as meaningful units without thought. This sounds like a bit of a conundrum but it leads us to another of Saussure's distinctions that may help us in the study of language in this course. Saussure posited the notion of language as a combination of *langue* and *parole. Langue*, which roughly means language, is the abstract system of signs and rules that make up the structure and nature of language. *Parole*, on the other hand, is the realization of language in practice, the words, phrases and sentences as they are actually used. For the most part, through the close study of language as it is used—the study of *parole*—we can make some conclusions about the nature of *langue* as a structured system.

Some 50 years after Saussure, Noam Chomsky had a strikingly similar idea about language, making a division between competence and performance. While Saussure thought of *langue* as a somewhat stable or set system for language, Chomsky viewed competence as a more dynamic set of abilities that the ideal speaker of a language would develop over time. The ability a human has at birth to acquire language—that universal grammar—is developed into a more complex linguistic ability, or competence. Chomsky's "performance" and Saussure's *langue* are almost interchangeable; they both refer to the way language is actually used.

Many researchers in the social aspects of language and language acquisition have broadened the idea of competence and talk about a general communicative competence. Communicative competence is the set of skills and knowledge a person must gain if they want to communicate with others in a constantly changing social environment. Communicative competence suggests that any meaning can only be understood in context. Once again, we realize that it is almost impossible to separate language from where, how, when, and why it is used. Through observation of people as they really speak, and through the study of their cultural understandings, we can try to come to conclusions both about the nature and power of language and the ways humans develop it.

Activity

Langue and *parole*

Which comes first: thought or language? Can we think without language? Is it possible that we think in images? This discussion is closely related to the debate around linguistic determinism covered in more detail in Chapter 4. At this point, it is worth considering the influence of language on thought and vice versa. Do a simple Internet search to find out what the research suggests and write a summary of some of the central debates to discuss in class.

Articulation describes the physical movements involved in modifying the flow of air to produce speech sounds.

Language and culture

Language, as a communicative act, is social. While meaning may be tied to cultural context, culture itself is shaped through our language use. These concerns will be the more specific focus of chapter 4, but it is worth noting here the close tie between what it means to be the social, cultural animals that we are and language. The more closely we consider language, the more obvious it is that it has special qualities equivalent to, or as a function of, its place in our lives.

Discussion Point

What role do languages have in your life?

Activity

Life and death in language

Read the following extracts from *On the Death and Life of Languages* by Claude Hagege and answer the questions that follow.

> Languages accompany human groups. They disappear with them; or, on the contrary, if those groups are large and quick and spread beyond their original environment, the languages can be dispersed, in their wake, over vast territories. Thus, it is from those who speak them that they derive their life principles and their ability to increase their area of usage.
>
> Nevertheless, languages are also one of the essential sources of the vital force that animates human communities. More than any other properties defining what is human, languages possess the power to provide individuals with the basis for their integration into society—that is, on a level different from one's biological framework and mental structure, meaning the very foundations of one's life.
>
> … the existence of languages is a very simple and universal means for deceiving nothingness. After all, languages allow for history, in the evocation of the dead through public or private discourse … No animal species possesses the means to evoke its past, assuming that some of them do not lack memory, or at least memories. It is humans who create the history of animals, in paleontological works in which their language allows them to relate a breathtakingly old past. ….

Through speaking and writing, languages not only allow us to trace our history well beyond our own physical obliteration, they also contain our history. Any philologist, or anyone curious about languages, knows that treasures are deposited within them that relate societies' evolution and individuals' adventures. Idiomatic expressions, compound words, have a past that calls up living figures. The history of words reflects the history of ideas. If societies do not die, it is only because they have historians, or annalists, or official narrators. It is also because they have languages, and are recounted in these languages.

Source: Hagege, Claude. (trans. Gladding, Jody). 2009. *On the Death and Life of Languages.* New Haven: Yale University Press. pp. 3–7

Questions to the text

1 Do you agree with Hagege's views on language? What does it mean when he says language "deceives nothingness"?

2 Hagege thinks it is important for people to be bilingual, no matter what two languages they speak. Why would he hold this view?

3 Can bilingualism (or multilingualism) call our attention to special qualities of language?

What is culture?

Since language is so clearly tied up in culture, and a significant part of this course asks you to look at both literature and language in relation to culture, it is worth asking what **culture** actually is. Though we could start with a basic definition for culture, it is worth looking at a variety of definitions and how our ideas of what culture is, how it operates, and how it should be studied have changed over the years and are really in a constant state of flux. It would be wrong to say that the word "culture" means the same thing to every person. In fact, your own conception of culture may vary depending on your culture.

Culture broadly defines a system of meaning for a group of people and it includes language, laws, customs, myths, images, texts, and daily practices.

Activity

Theories of culture

Read the following extracts and answer the questions that follow. As you read, think of your own ideas about what culture is. Are the views of these five notable cultural theorists mutually exclusive?

Matthew Arnold (1822–1888)

… to know ourselves in the world, we have, as the means to this end, to know the best which has been thought and said in the world.

Source: Arnold, Matthew. 1882. *Literature and Science.*

… all the love of our neighbor, the impulses towards action, help, and beneficence, the desire for removing human error, clearing human confusion, and diminishing human misery, the noble aspiration to leave the world better and happier than we found it, come in as part of the grounds of culture, and the main and pre-eminent part. Culture is then properly described not as having its origin in curiosity, but as having its origin in the love of perfection; it is a *study of perfection.*

Source: Arnold, Matthew. 1869. *Culture and Anarchy.*

Edward Tyler (1832–1917)

Culture, or civilization, is that complex whole which includes knowledge, belief, art, morals, law, custom, and any other capabilities and habits acquired by man as a member of society.

Source: Tyler, Edward. 1871. *Primitive Culture.* vol. 1.

Raymond Williams (1921–1988)

Culture is ordinary: that is the first fact. Every human society has its own shape, its own purposes, its own meanings. Every human society expresses these, in institutions, and in the arts and learning. The making of a society is the finding of common meanings and directions, and its growth is an active debate and amendment under the pressures of experience, contact, and discovery, writing themselves into the land. The growing society is there, yet it is also made and remade in every individual mind. The making of a mind is, first, the slow learning of shapes, purposes, and meanings, so that work, observation and communication are possible."

Source: Williams, Raymond. 2001. *The Raymond Williams Reader.* London: Blackwell. p. 11.

Clifford Geertz (1926–2006)

Believing [that] man is an animal suspended in webs of significance he himself has spun, I take culture to be those webs, and the analysis of it to be therefore not an experimental science in search of a law but an interpretive one in search of meaning.

Source: Geertz, Clifford. 1973. *The Interpretation of Cultures.* New York: Basic Books. p. 5.

Claude Levi-Strauss (1908–2009)

Culture is neither natural nor artificial. It stems from neither genetics nor rational thought, for it is made up of rules of conduct, which were not invented and whose function is generally not understood by the people who obey them. Some of these rules are residues of traditions acquired in the different types of social structure through which … each human group has passed. Other rules have been consciously accepted or modified for the sake of specific goals. Yet there is no doubt that, between the instincts inherited from our genotype and the rules inspired by reason, the mass of unconscious rules remains more important and more effective; because reason itself … is a product rather than a cause of cultural evolution.

Source: Levi-Strauss, Claude. 1983. *Structural Anthropology.*

Renato Rosaldo (born 1941)

Culture lends significance to human experience by selecting from and organizing it. It refers broadly to the forms throughout which people make sense of their lives … It does not inhabit a set-aside domain, as does … politics or economics. From the pirouettes of classical ballet to the most brute of brute facts, all human conduct is culturally mediated. Culture encompasses the everyday and the esoteric, the mundane and the elevated, the ridiculous and the sublime. Neither high nor low, culture is all-pervasive.

Source: Rosaldo, Renato. 1993. *Culture and Truth: The remaking of Social Analysis.* London: Routledge. p. 26.

Questions to the texts

1 Based on these brief quotes, which theorist would agree that culture is something we aspire to?

2 Which theorist would believe that culture is something outside of us that we learn or are born into?

3 Which theorist would argue that culture is something developed by humans?

4 Which definition comes close to your own view of culture?

A useful definition

A society is made up of individuals who must learn to adapt to each other and to their environment. The interactive activities humans engage in and teach, whether explicitly or by example, make up a cultural heritage. Culture may be influenced by biology—certain facial expressions may be universal (for example, a smile), and may have meaning in many cultures—but much of culture is arbitrary and its features are only meaningful to a particular group of people. Culture is a system of meaning for a group of people and it includes language, laws, customs, myths, images, texts, and daily practices. Culture allows humans to function in the physical world and organize their social lives. At the heart of culture, language is what allows humans to socialize and to create a store of inherited knowledge about the world.

Activity

Symbols in art

Art 1

A Byzantine icon of St Nicholas.

Art 3

Seven Miles a Second, a mixed media work on paper from 1988 by US artist David Wojnarowicz.

Art 2

A Soviet poster commemorating May Day, 1950.

Questions to the texts

1 Consider these three works of art in terms of their use of symbols that may have cultural significance. How are the symbols different in all three pictures? How are they similar?

2 How do stylistic considerations, such as the use of color or composition, contribute to our reading of the imagery?

3 How much do you need to know about another culture to really understand the symbols? How does the last painting call attention to the arbitrary or changing nature of symbols?

What is high culture?

The Victorian attitude toward culture, as expressed by Matthew Arnold and implied by Edward Tyler, is rejected by anthropologists today but it is not necessarily rejected in everyday use. Mention of the word "culture" can call to mind classical music, the opera, art museums, and learning Latin. Appreciation of this notion of culture may be part of the reason some people think you have to study Shakespeare in school. Because the Western notion of high culture can be exclusive and elitist, it is closely tied to what some people call Culture with a capital C: these forms or expression are part of a society's inherited system of meaning and interaction. And remember, culture is both implicitly and explicitly taught. Society at any given time decides that an artifact, myth, or story is important and passes it down to the next generation. What should be kept in mind is that what society values changes over time and notions of high and low are always changing. One example of the changing status of a work of literature is Shakespeare's play *Titus Andronicus*, which was very popular throughout the Elizabethan era. After this, the violence and gore of the play encouraged many critics to believe that it could not possibly be the work of Shakespeare. It remains one of the less commonly set texts in schools these days. In 1999, *Titus Andronicus* was rehabilitated in the movie *Titus* directed by Julie Taymor, as one of the many Shakespearean dramas recently popularized through film. In this course, when we talk about culture we are talking about the broader, anthropological definition of culture even though some of the works we study fit with our notions of high culture. While the notion of high culture may lead people to the mistaken idea that one person can somehow have more or better culture than another, in our conception of culture, everyone "has" culture and contributes to the diversity of culture by the simple fact of being a member of society.

Cultural boundaries

Is culture an integrated whole—a system that stands above individuals, organizing their actions and beliefs—or is it something that is made up of as many parts as there are people? One way to look at culture is similar to the grammar in language. All languages share basic ways of representing the world (no matter the actual word chosen—every language has a words for colors, words to describe degree, words to indicate relationships etc.). In the same way, cultures around the world often develop systems within similar realms (individual cultures have ways of dealing with law, marriage, food, and celebration, for example). Culture is like the rules of the game we need to know in order to play along. Although the rules of the game are both arbitrary and tightly constructed, that doesn't mean we don't play by them and it would certainly be hard for one person to change the rules.

Another view of culture is that it is a more dynamic mix, a *bricolage*, or gluing together of ideas and objects that are "tested" by different groups over time. When people felt basketball games were being dominated by the slam dunk, eventually the culture, and the rules, changed in order to create the three-point line. The answer to how much influence we have on culture, and how it molds us as we mold it, passing it on to the next generation as somehow modified or

Bricolage is a term that is often used in art and literature to refer to works that have been created through the literal or metaphorical pasting together of various found objects. *Bricolage* assumes the role of artist to be that both of original creator and agent who borrows from the culture at large.

expanded, provides much room for critical interpretation. And, in our increasingly globalized world, the boundaries of one culture and another are often blurred. It is important in understanding culture that we do not see an individual culture as a monolithic structure in which everything and everyone is the same—within cultures there are differences too. At the same time, we need to recognize small cultures: less powerful societies that have come to share common beliefs or traditions. Culture is like a lens for examining the way groups create meaning in their social lives and when using this lens we understand that the views we have on a group's values, ideologies, or norms, may be distorted.

Cultural relativism

Understanding culture or the idea of culture can be a guard against racism or ethnocentrism. Cultural relativism is the idea that all of the elements of our culture are learned and that those elements of our culture—our beliefs, values, myths—are also arbitrary. Our cultural norms did not *have to be*, they just *are*. If we understand this, the obvious next step is to understand that the same is true for other cultures. The conclusion is that no one culture has the "right" answers to the organization of society. A particular worldview or practice cannot be wrong, it is just different. In a positive sense, cultural relativism leads us to a way to accept a wide variety of cultures and beliefs; it is a form of openness to the world.

But cultural relativism has its complexities. What if a theoretical culture believes that women should not be educated past the age of nine. If, on the one hand, we believe in some form of universal human rights, we would say that this cultural practice is wrong and should be changed. But, in order to respect a culture, should we not be allowed to have an opinion on the matter? Although this debate can be carried on in classes in many IB courses, it is enough to say here that many people feel that belief in the superiority of one's own culture is much more dangerous than the most extreme relativism. But, when we do begin to question cultural practices, even for humanitarian reasons, it is important to do so only while truly trying to understand its context.

Discussion Point

You are what you eat

What assumptions do we make when we think about the foods from different cultures? What, if anything, does this picture tell you about a culture? Can you guess the culture from the food pictured here? What does this particular food suggest about the values of a culture? Can we make generalizations about the people in a culture based on this image or our assumptions about its meaning or importance?

What if I told you that many people from this culture don't like hamburgers and would rather eat sushi or *gaeng kiew wan*, would you say that they are not part of this culture?

How do we describe a culture?

It is difficult to define culture; it may also be difficult to describe a culture. Where do you begin if you want to start talking about what is important in Italian culture? Do you describe the food? Or, do you start with the importance of family life? If so, how do you make distinctions between Italian food and family life compared to another culture? As soon as we start talking about our own culture, we sometimes more clearly see the difficulties of defining *any* culture. While these examples may suggest that we are well on the way to describing a culture, we always have to be aware of whether or not we are describing something accurately or whether we are dealing with available and common stereotypes. An Italian newsweekly, for example, may publish a study suggesting that Italian family life and eating habits have been changing in the 21st century. By the same token, if we were to describe the nature of an Italian family would we be suggesting that this family life is qualitatively different from family life in India or Togo? Cultural description is a difficult process that even trained anthropologists undertake with care.

Just try explaining the rules of baseball or cricket to someone from a country where neither sport is played. Try explaining that everyone in your culture knows these rules. But is that even true? Baseball is a part of the culture of the United States, but if I don't know the rules of baseball, am I then less a part of North American culture?

What determines who a person is: biology? family? culture? personal will? All of these concerns do not make it pointless to study our own and other cultures. In fact, the understanding of our different positions within and outside various cultures makes it important to consider the ways in which we clarify our speaking position, and avoid being complacent about our knowledge and understanding of the world around us.

Beyond a celebration of culture

An understanding of the complexity of culture and identity, and of defining our speaking positions within a cultural context, leads us to further analyze the way we identify ourselves and our cultural affiliations. To say we appreciate culture is no easy statement to make. The celebration of culture through "international days," multicultural fairs, or world celebrations can be fun but often does not lead to a more critical understanding of identity. A critical approach to culture takes into account the power of culture over an individual, and the ways in which we express our individual differences. A critical perspective understands that a single identity can include a hybrid mix of cultures. One of the goals of this course is not just to investigate culture on its own, but to investigate the ways in which language conveys, defines, or reflects culture. When considering different forms or practice, works of art or literature, including emails, newspaper articles, and recorded speech, it becomes clear that the cultural context of the producer as well as the reader or intended audience becomes crucial. When reading a work from another culture we might look for broad human themes that seem to transcend cultural differences—it is easy to be swept away by the feelings of guilt in *The Kite Runner* or camaraderie in *To Kill a*

Mockingbird. Reading these same texts, however, we may succumb to just relegating what we don't understand to cultural difference, as something foreign or irreconcilable to our own beliefs—such as the Taliban policies and their ultimate cruelty in *The Kite Runner*, or the racism in *To Kill a Mockingbird*, both examples arguably being from a time and place that (for the majority of readers) is not our own. A more critical perspective, one that both attempts to understand culture while continuously acknowledging the difficulties of pinning down culture, keeps moving between the poles of emotional response and critical understanding. It *is* possible to discuss elements of cultural difference without either erasing difference or retreating to nationalism.

We study cultural context in order to help us understand the meaning and effect of the words and images around us. Consider the hamburger again. What does the hamburger mean or represent? I guess it is just fast food to eat. But your reaction to the picture or what it means to you certainly depends on your own cultural context. If this is a meal you eat every week then you probably just shrugged at this very ordinary meal. As suggested above, someone with ethnic origins in the Asian subcontinent or who eats a Mediterranean diet every day may have quickly regarded the meaning of the picture as "junk food." Context matters. By the same token we need to consider the contexts of production. Is this from an advertisement trying to convince us to eat at a particular restaurant? Is this from a government pamphlet talking about unhealthy diets? And even the intended audience versus the actual audience matters. If this is an advertisement, it certainly was not produced to be put in a text book and analyzed, it was meant to appeal to a certain group of people who might be thinking about where to go eat.

Studying language

It may be useful to think about how researchers and academics view the study of language in order to understand the approaches you can take in this course. Language as a field of study is very broad and has undergone many changes through the years. In many ways, you may find that the language and literature course fits neatly into contemporary ways of looking at language and culture in colleges and universities. A close look at the course components for language in cultural context and language and mass communication puts you in a good position for further study in a broad range of subject areas. Your job in this course, and throughout the rest of this book, is simply to be multi-talented, cross-disciplinary, a sensitive critic of language and cultural context and someone who enjoys the challenge of the text in its various forms and modes of production.

Putting it all together

In the first two chapters, we have focused primarily on approaches to literature and language. As a result, you have hopefully developed more of an understanding of how literature and language have been defined over time, including contemporary views on the subject and even hints about future possible directions. The language and literature course is not, however, intended to instruct you in a specific body of content through an awareness of terminology, intellectual and critical movements and aspects of linguistics or anthropology. Instead, the course is intended to be one of active engagement and performance. You are being asked to approach language as literature and as a means of recording, promoting, challenging, defining, thinking and being, as well as by offering up evidence of your intellectual engagement across a variety of media. The following chapter, then, begins to explore how one goes about using an understanding of literature and language to more broadly and deeply engage in its various manifestations as well as demonstrating the conclusions that you reach along the way.

Reading critically

The intention of this course is to make you a more critical reader. You are essentially working to become a critical consumer of all the messages that surround you in the world. This may sound easy enough—you have probably been told to "think critically" before. But what exactly does it mean to be a critical reader? Readers in Australia and New Zealand might be familiar to an approach to texts called "critical literacy," that calls for a skillful judgment (not necessarily a severe judgment) of what one reads or writes. In the United Kingdom, North America, and other areas of the world, you may have been asked to take a careful, critical stance with media works such as films or advertisements or you have engaged in "discourse analysis." In this course you are meant to take a critical stance in relation to all texts. This practice, however, might not be as easy as you think. Below, we will outline some assumptions that come from a tradition of critical literacy and that are modified here so that you can apply these basic (but not necessarily easy) techniques to all texts in the course.

Critical literacy is a result of trends in poststructuralism and the theories that developed in its wake. As you will recall from chapter 1, there were some strong statements that, although primarily focusing on literary texts, will form the basis of our approach to all communicative acts. The following points suggest ways we can always question a text:

- **There is no perfect or model language or act within a language** We will consider a wide variety of texts in this course and all are open to discussion and interpretation. There is never an assumption that one language act or type of language use (say, for example, the way language in used in 19th-century British poetry, or the language of Shakespeare) is the model for all language use that follows.

- **All cultural practices are sign systems, much like language itself** This implies that there are no inherent, *natural* meanings in anything. All meaning is constructed through a complex relationship between arbitrary signifiers and signifieds. Sign systems are not just in language; they also inform our value and belief systems, our practices and social mores and even our ethical judgments. These sign systems develop for a number of reasons, some of which are out of our control. Our job is to analyze how these sign systems are used.

- **No language act is unbiased or innocent** This implies that reading, viewing, speaking, writing or any engagement—regardless of how actively or passively we pursue it—involves assumptions and agendas that are ideologically motivated. Not all motivations are even consciously recognized but we encounter all communicative acts with worldviews that are constructed by our cultural context.

- **There are many possible, often conflicting, interpretations of a text** Many different interpretations of a text or language act are possible. The bigger implication here is that there are no absolute truths or even more inherently correct interpretations or *best* practice. All we can do is *agree to* a tendency of interpretation or a way to approach things that enjoys wide support.

These critical assumptions are often taken one step further, calling attention to the fact that many communicative acts are political. It is important to recognize that there are reasons why people communicate, and one of the reasons to publish, post, or broadcast our thoughts is to influence people. This desire to influence, persuade or gain (and maintain) power, is worth considering when trying to determine the meaning or significance of a work.

What all of the above points assume is that no text represents some higher truth. Some critics note that they don't want to "love" books but to question them: that is, to find their bias, or figure out what they are trying to show the reader about the world. Most importantly, the points suggest that we should never be passive consumers of what we read. In a sense, we can build upon the old saying "don't believe everything you read."

What this simply means for going about your work in this course is a focus on active engagement rather than passive encounter. As meanings and purposes are not always clear, simply experiencing a language act and expecting to receive a complete knowledge and understanding of the author's intentions is not only impossible but potentially even dangerous. Paying attention to the complexities underlying all communications, and what they reveal about human society and identity, is not just an academic exercise in critical thinking, but a way of participating fully in the social world.

A useful checklist

Following are a set of simple questions to ask yourself in response to any text/language act to encourage active rather than passive encounters. Hopefully, these simple steps will support a wide range of the possible variables.

- Whose views are being represented?

- What or whose interests are being served?

- What are the intentions behind the message?

- What reading or speaking position are you being invited to take up? Are we being asked to see the situation from a particular point of view?

- What cultural assumptions are being taken for granted?

- What or who is absent that one might expect to find?

Analyzing an image

Look at the relatively straightforward image of a handshake here. While you could dismiss this image with little thought, you may find that closer examination reveals a variety of possible narratives. What could this image mean or suggest? How do you react to it? Try applying the questions for critical analysis to this image and then, as a challenge, write a one-page response discussing why what appears to be a simple handshake is rich with complexity.

Appreciating beauty

New Criticism was introduced in chapter 1 to highlight some of the value in close textual analysis and the attention to stylistic effect, as well as providing a general model for looking at a work of art or literature as a unified idea. It may seem like an antiquated approach to criticism, but skill in being able to make a close reading for content and form is still assessed in this course. (In paper 2, for instance, you will need to demonstrate knowledge of the texts you have studied. While examiners will be open to multiple possible *readings,* any that clearly indicate a candidate has not, in fact, understood or closely read the text in question will not be given high marks, regardless of how clever your essay is in embracing the topicality of the narrative.) Careful attention to texts and other communicative acts is also valuable in that it calls attention to construction, style and the beauty of an aesthetic or emotional response.

Focusing only on biases and intentions might imply that the only approach you should assume with communicative acts is one of a cold, cynical picking-apart of texts. The purpose of this section, however, is to both assure you and encourage you not to limit yourself to this aim. We want to emphasize both the value and necessity of continuing to be open to aesthetic experience with all communicative acts. We all have had encounters with art and music, a book or a television program that truly moves us. It is possible that you have encountered an advertisement for a holiday on an island paradise and even knowing about some of the political, economic and environmental implications of such a visit does not change your desire to experience that beautiful place or location first-hand. We want to emphasize in this section that such a *feeling* is valuable in and of itself and needs to be acknowledged even as we approach the text with a critical eye. Even if, for instance, what one understands as beauty is a cultural construct, the effect of beauty on the beholder is still real and of interest and value in this course.

And although we mention the careful attention to communicative acts in New Criticism, as a movement that particularly valued the philosophical or scientific approach over and above the emotional and aesthetic, we do not want to limit you to this school of criticism. In addition to the critical assumptions listed above, we ask that you approach this course with the additional aesthetic assumptions that directly challenge the New Critical model. Some points to consider:

- **The emotional, sensory, and affective nature of texts is as important as the intellectual** This assumption implies that we *know* the world around us through a variety of means and not just the intellectual. Although we may still strive to question the source of our initial *feelings* (emotional, sensory or affective), it is not at the cost of outright denial. Something that is funny or beautiful or gory is an encounter with the world around us that needs to be both recognized and explored.

- **The individual voice of an artist is valuable** Communicative acts—even those we do not automatically assume are creative in intention—often arise from strong emotion or passion, or commitment to an aesthetic idea based on a personal response. In this course, we can recognize the fact that an individual, through language, can express a unique and particular experience.

In adding these assumptions, the intention of this text is not necessarily to value the individual over the larger social group or the emotional over the intellectual experience, but rather to argue the need to consider all sides. It would be a shame to read books with no concern for the sheer pleasure they bring just as it would be to approach art or film or music or even advertisements without any concern for the emotional, sensory and affective beauty they can offer. In fact, we argue, it would not just be a shame but a detriment to larger understanding.

Activity

Aesthetic experience

Let's take some time to appreciate an aesthetic response to a work. All texts and images can have an aesthetic value just as all texts and images that may seem purely aesthetic can have an intellectual, social, or political purpose. Thinking about beauty and responding to a work based on feelings or emotional response, write down your impressions of the two paintings below.

Art 1

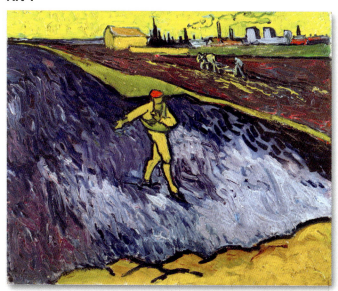

The Sower (also known as "The Reaper") painted by the Dutch artist Vincent Van Gogh in 1888 when he lived in Provence in the south of France.

Art 2

A mural by Diego Rivera about the Mexican Revolution at the National Agricultural School in Chapingo, Mexico, from the 1920s.

Further Steps

Now research the context for the works of art further. Where were they painted and why? What did these works of art say about the lives of the people they depicted? Think about the relationship of the form to the content to also help you in your critical evaluation. Does your initial response still inform your revised critical response?

Ultimately, your aim and the goal of this course, is to approach all communicative acts with an eye toward both purposes: a critical analysis of the intellectual and political nature of a communicative act and an appreciation, almost regardless of politics, of its aesthetic and personal value. That is, to approach all communicative acts with a sensitive combination of both skilful judgment and an awareness and appreciation of the very real emotional, sensory and affective impacts such language acts have upon us, and the creators of the works themselves. One should also be able to recognize assumptions and subtle manipulations in the use of print advertisements, for instance, but also be open to the reasons why these images are genuinely pleasing. These aspects need not be in opposition but rather act in concert and as interrelated components of a common enterprise toward a more full and rich understanding. Again, there are a few points to consider about the value of looking at the aesthetic side of texts:

- **Pleasure often enhances our experience with language**
  In other words, when we enjoy a work of art the emotion generated by it often increases our engagement. It is important to remember to both enjoy and keep a critical eye open.

- **Aesthetic responses inform our cultural values and belief systems** When we understand the aesthetic value of a text, and when we think about *why* we enjoy or feel emotion because of a certain language act, we begin to examine our own cultural values or the cultural values of the creator of the text.

● **An aesthetic experience can help us to understand how form and content come together to create meaning or emotion** A feeling of sadness or awe when listening to Beethoven can lead us to thinking about how particular notes, played in a particular way, can create such emotion.

Consideration of the aesthetic value of a work of art, music or literature also gives rise to a demand to consider more critical aspects; looking at cultural context and point of view (whose position or values we are being encouraged to adopt), and who (or what) is left out in a work of art can provide more insight as to the nature of the aesthetic and its positive and negative impact. In the end, no language act would be as rich or as interesting without a consideration of both. While it is true that no language act is innocent, a concern with only the aesthetic would be naive and a concern with only a critical awareness of our consumption of language would be an extreme limitation. The first step, then, in putting it all together is to recognize the existence of the wide range of experiences we can have with a text and the number of ways we must analyze both the experience and the work itself.

Activity

Writing a response

Examine the two texts that follow and consider the following questions in relation to *both* texts:

Taking a critical literacy approach:

● Whose views are represented?

● What are the intentions behind the message?

● Whose interests are being served?

● What cultural assumptions are being made in relation to the content of the piece? In relation to the assumed audience?

● Whose assumptions are taken for granted?

● What voices or perspectives are left out of the piece?

Taking an aesthetic approach:

● What is your impression of the piece?

● What is the tone or atmosphere of the piece?

● What is the effect of the particular imagery, diction, metaphor, color, or layout?

● What feelings are stirred in you by the content of the piece?

● What ideas or feelings does the creator wish to convey? How are these ideas suggested or presented?

Text 1

A Marlboro Man cigarette advertisement from 1970.

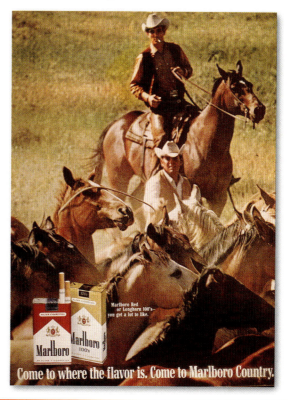

Text 2

Following is an extract from the short story "Brokeback Mountain"
by Annie Proulx.

Ennis, high-arched nose and narrow face, was scruffy and a little cave-
chested, balanced a small torso on long, caliper legs, possessed a muscular
and supple body made for the horse and for fighting. His reflexes were
uncommonly quick and he was farsighted enough to dislike reading
anything except Hamley's saddle catalog.

The sheep trucks and horse trailers unloaded at the trailhead and a bandy-
legged Basque showed Ennis how to pack the mules, two packs and a
riding load on each animal ring-lashed with double diamonds and secured
with half hitches, telling him, "Don't never order soup. Them boxes a soup
are real bad to pack." Three puppies belonging to one of the blue heelers
went in a pack basket, the runt inside Jack's coat, for he loved a little dog.
Ennis picked out a big chestnut called Cigar Butt to ride, Jack a bay mare
who turned out to have a low startle point. The string of spare horses
included a mouse-colored grullo whose looks Ennis liked. Ennis and Jack,
the dogs, horses and mules, a thousand ewes and their lambs flowed up
the trail like dirty water through the timber and out above the tree line into
the great flowery Meadows and the coursing, endless wind.

They got the big tent up on the Forest Service's platform, the kitchen and
grub boxes secured. Both slept in camp that first night, Jack already
bitching about Joe Aguirre's sleep-with-the-sheep-and-no-fire order, though
he saddled the bay mare in the dark morning without saying much. Dawn
came glassy orange, stained from below by a gelatinous band of pale
green. The sooty bulk of the mountain paled slowly until it was the same
color as the smoke from Ennis's breakfast fire. The cold air sweetened,
banded pebbles and crumbs of soil cast sudden pencil-long shadows and
the rearing lodgepole pines below them massed in slabs of somber
malachite.

Source: Proulx, Annie. 1999. "Brokeback Mountain." *Close Range: Wyoming Stories.*
New York: Scribner, 2000. p. 356.

After responding to this image and extract, you may well find that the critical
literacy or discourse analysis approach works well with the advertisement and
the more aesthetic approach works well with the passage from the Proulx's
short story. At the same time, you can probably see how these techniques
overlap or complement each other, how the one might inform the other, and
how you might be able to take a variety of approaches to texts in this course.

Theory of knowledge

In these initial chapters we are asking you to consider the way we
build knowledge in a field and how we make conscious decisions
about *what* and *how* to study. This practice is intimately tied to work
you will do in your theory of knowledge course. The primary
intention behind the theory of knowledge (TOK) as a core component
of the IB Diploma Programme is to encourage students to be
conscious and aware of knowledge issues that are addressed both
across and between disciplines. As you will explore in your TOK
study more explicitly, "knowing" and "understanding" can mean
different things in different fields of learning. What is and may be
construed as true in one subject may be very different from what is
construed in another. And, perhaps ironically, at the very moment of

realizing that knowledge and understanding are not static but dynamic, one begins to also appreciate their common pursuit in seemingly disparate disciplines. In other words, just as you learn that knowledge and understanding are constantly changing and dependent on context, you also begin to appreciate their common enterprise both in your academic subjects and in your general approach to life.

Inevitably, there are significant and substantial links between the theory of knowledge and the language and literature course. This course is focused very explicitly on questions of knowledge, truth, understanding and meaning. While the language and literature course does have some parameters around the literary texts chosen for study, the aims and objects are less concerned with understanding a particular body of content and more concerned with a method (or methods) of engaging, questioning, performing and reflecting on an almost infinite array of communicative acts. Because of this, questions about the nature of knowledge and understanding are virtually built into the course and it is quite likely that you will identify knowledge issues and make overt connections with topics covered in theory of knowledge.

Language as a way of knowing

In more common variations of the TOK diagram (see two examples on the following page) "Ways of knowing" is the first "plane" into which the individual learner passes as a means of engaging with and entering into knowledge and understanding. Comprised of sense perception, language, logic and emotion (the order is listed at random here), our ways of knowing may also be a way of expressing how the human brain essentially encounters the world. Somehow, these four ways of knowing account for our encounters with and reactions to a variety of stimuli (both physical and intellectual). As one of the four ways of knowing and a very central concern of this course, language and considerations about its relation to knowledge and understanding will be common to both a theory of knowledge course and a language and literature course, to the point at which they become indistinguishable. In both courses, you will explore language as a sign system that represents and helps us understand our world. You will also explore language as both a tool for expressing knowledge and as a foundation for primary understanding and knowledge. Consider the following questions:

- Does language merely communicate knowledge or does it, rather, create it?
- What is the relationship between written and spoken language? Between written and spoken and visual language?
- What is the relationship between language and technology?
- What role does language play in individual experience compared to broader social experience? (How does language shape understanding of the self? Of others?)
- Can language be free from subjectivity?

In exploring such questions, but within a course very much devoted to language, there is an added inherent metacognitive element. Perhaps more than in any other course you might take as part of your IB Diploma Programme studies, in language and literature you will be aware that you are exploring the role and meaning of language in knowledge and understanding *through language*.

A common expression is "language is slippery" which means that sometimes it is hard to pin down the exact meaning of words or the exact meaning of a speaker. How difficult is it, then, to use language to describe the role of language in knowing?

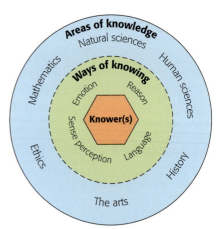

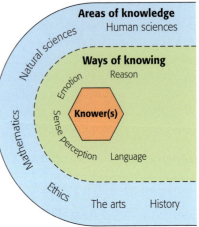

Diagrams showing the ways of knowing from the IB *Theory of knowledge guide*.

Discussion Point

Thinking through signs

Do you think in signs? That is, do you think in images or abstractions? Language can be a fantastic tool but it also defies common knowledge. Look at the cartoon below as an example of how language can be a slippery tool for communicating common understanding.

What does it mean when a two-way conversation comes up with the following mental pictures, triggering a different response?

With such varying approaches to knowledge, language is only ever approximate rather than definitive. Consider how this may be both a strength and a weakness as a way of knowing. Perhaps one of the most interesting aspects of language is that it is creative.

Denotation versus connotation

We have spent a lot of time looking at language as an essential tool that is nevertheless rooted in uncertainty. Even if we ignore, for the moment, some of the implications of poststructuralism (specifically, its argument for the absence of a universal signified), the challenges become clear when we try to pin down meaning in a single word or term. Generally speaking, when trying to explain a term in language we rely on either denotative or connotative associations. Denotative associations are those based on dictionary definitions, implying a "correct" answer and usually, by association, a meaningful word as opposed to gibberish (a meaningless word). But any use of a dictionary will immediately reveal problems with denotations, in the form of multiple possible uses of a term, and a reliance on even more words, that themselves require denotative investigation. Dictionary meanings, then, involve a circularity of logic where one definition is only understood through another definition that can only be understood via further definitions *ad infinitum*. Denotations are, after all, only marks or references to other marks rather than truly denuding truth.

Connotations are even harder to pin down and are, very simply, popular associations—often emotional—with words that go beyond their dictionary definitions. Connotations are familiar to you primarily through popular slang although connotations that have been used for long enough can enter into the realm of denotation and actually become part of a dictionary definition (in the process, revealing the limitations of denotation even further). Common examples may include words like "cool" or "sick" but there can also be multiple connotations with seemingly "neutral" words such as "love" or "school." It probably stands as self-evident (as much as anything in language can be self-evident) that connotation makes certainty in language that much more difficult.

Regardless of certainty, however, there can be no denying that we utilize denotation and connotation all the time and very frequently toward a desired and anticipated effect. There is, it seems, some level of pragmatic usage that fuels itself and makes language, despite its imperfections (and there are many imperfections), a meaningful and valuable way of knowing.

The use of metaphor

Another challenge in the recognition of language as a way of knowing is the use of metaphor in communicative acts. It is likely that you have already encountered this term. You will perhaps recall that a metaphor is a substitution of one idea or object for another to suggest resemblances, similarities or common connotative qualities between the two. But for the purposes of this section of this text, we use the term metaphor to refer much more broadly to a larger body of figures of speech that involve comparison, either direct or indirect, as well as non-real or nonliteral association. To say that we describe only what an idea or a thing is like or similar to, rather than what an idea or a thing is in and of itself, brings up many issues. To think that we believe we have knowledge and understanding that occurs through statements that are not literally true (but only metaphorical) is a curious notion indeed. Still, on occasion, a well-chosen metaphor is just what is required to most adequately convey meaning.

Activity

Creating a spectrum

Read the list of terms referring to "a young person" below and note the diverse range of connotations associated with each term. Rearrange the terms to reflect a spectrum of most favorable through neutral to least favorable.

developing human, youngster, child, kid, little one, small fry, dependent, brat, urchin, juvenile, minor, tyke, pre-pubescent, immature person

Unintentional connotations

On a billboard I encountered recently, I noticed an advertisement for an insurance plan. One of the smaller-print disclaimers warned potential investors to read the "investment scheme" for details including liability. Given the attention devoted to the challenges for the world economy over the last year or two, "scheme" struck me as a curious term, almost too laden with distractive connotations. In fact, "scheme" is a common, if slightly jargonistic, term in the insurance industry though arguably not necessarily the most apt for a larger publicity campaign.

Keep your eye out for examples of such contextual clashes (insurance and advertising, in this case but you could find them anywhere) where terminology that inspires contradictory connotations creates challenging scenarios for full knowledge or understanding.

Activity

Metaphorical or imprecise language

Read the following newspaper article on a winter storm that recently affected New York City and the larger northeastern coast of the USA. Circle or note all of the metaphorical language used, including terms that are inherently vague, ambiguous and euphemistic.

- How does the use of metaphor add to or enhance the clarity of this article?
- How does the use of metaphor impede the clarity of this article?
- Is the use of metaphor appropriate? Why or why not?

As an extension, rewrite the gist of the article using as little metaphor as possible. After doing so, compare the versions and discuss the relative strengths and weaknesses of both.

- How does such a comparison enhance your understanding of language as a way of knowing?

Storm Batters East, Closing Schools and Halting Flights

New York. 10 February 2010

A blustery snowstorm, the second to sweep across the Northeast in less than a week, swaggered into the New York area on Wednesday morning, closing schools, courts and the United Nations and threatening to play havoc with the rhythms and routines of everyone who did not simply stay home.

New York City had gone through a slow windup after days of forecasters' warnings — and after largely missing out on the storm last weekend that stopped much of the rest of the East Coast in very deep tracks. By the time most New Yorkers turned out the lights and went to bed on Tuesday, only light snow was falling — a tease for what the meteorologists insisted was coming. But by 7 a.m., thick, wet flakes were sticking, even in places where snow almost never accumulates, like Times Square. By 8 a.m., the wind was swirling and the streets were glistening, as what had been slush flirted with turning slippery — and treacherous.

"It's here," said Brian Ciemnecki, from the National Weather Service, and as early as 7 a.m., the measurements backed him up. He said 5.5 inches had fallen in Elizabeth, N.J., 1.5 inches in Central Park and between 2 and 4 inches on Long Island.

He said that New York would see 12 to 15 inches by day's end — a lot, to be sure, but less than had piled up in places farther south during the storm last week. In New York itself, the worst was expected later in the day, potentially creating a nightmarish commute home. Some transit lines planned extra service for early afternoon, figuring that workers who made it into the city in the morning would abandon their desks before the regular quitting time.

Source: Barron, James. "Storm Batters East, Closing Schools and Halting Flights." *The New York Times*. 10 February 2010.

Jargon and specialist language

Later in this course companion, as we discuss language in cultural contexts in more detail, we will introduce jargon more fully. As with metaphor, we refer to jargon in a broader sense than the more denotatively accurate specialized language and terminology associated with unique social and professional groups. Instead, we mean all language that is for a specialist purpose or intended toward specialized effect whether positive, negative or neutral. This is not just professional argot, but could include stereotyping, labeling and the emotive use of language.

Jargon, in this sense, can have real value in enhancing understanding. It is preferable, for example, that in an operating theater a surgeon may ask for a unique tool that goes by a rather esoteric name not widely known outside of the medical profession rather than relying on metaphorical description and vagueness ("the no. 10 scalpel" instead of "the tool that cuts … the small one …with the long handles"). Names, exact terms, and technical language of a particular community can serve a valuable purpose for communication in specific contexts. But this knowledge and specificity of terms is obviously highly specialized and less significant as a way of knowing outside of the specialized community. On the other hand, stereotyping, labeling and emotive language can have significant impact on knowledge, but not always for good. With familiar labeling, we may know what to expect but also expect what to know. If we meet a new student who has been labeled as brilliant and a substantial addition to the intellectual rigor of a community, we will develop a kind of knowledge without ever having actually encountered this person face to face. Not only will this color our encounter but it can have, obviously, larger repercussions on continued engagements with this person (which may be good or bad depending on whether they live up to their labeling or not and our individual response to that label).

Stereotyping and emotive language are more likely to be associated with negative attributes as a way of knowing through language. To be a "terrorist" or a "martyr," for instance, have very different connotations, but are both highly reactive terms in our era. To use either term will necessarily cloud knowledge and give it a distinctly doctrinal overtone. Some terms, such as "genocide," are so laden with emotional imperative that the United Nations has pledged that "an act of genocide" must be prevented and punished, using force if necessary. But what constitutes prevention and punishment is not always readily agreed upon—perhaps another language issue. In all of these cases, whether good, bad or neutral, it is clear that language has a dynamic relationship with knowledge.

Activity

Job titles

Over the last decade, many occupations have been renamed to enhance their prestige and accommodate a growing number of specialized professions, roles and duties across a broad range of occupations. Take a look at the following list and try to determine the job description.

Barista

Education Centre Nourishment Consultant

Front Line Customer Support Facilitator

Media Distribution Officer

Coin Facilitation Engineer

Gastronomical Hygiene Technician

Petroleum Transfer Engineer

Beverage Dissemination Officer

Colour Distribution Technician

Field Nourishment Consultant

Domestic Technician

Highway Environmental Hygienist

Vice President

Further steps

● **On your own** Do some research on the Internet to find interesting or obscure job titles. What kind of job do they describe? Can you think of an alternative job title?

● **In your group** If you are working in a group, try the following exercise: each person think of a common profession and make up your own interesting title for the job with more positive or negative connotations. See if your partner or other group members can figure out what the job is.

Language is powerful. Language is arbitrary. Language describes knowledge. Language determines knowledge. In truth, these are all statements of fact, and this simultaneously makes language an integral part of any consideration of knowledge and understanding. What is more singular is that language—including its positive attributes, its negative shortcomings and its neutral realities—is an integral part of the way we come to terms with our world.

Language as an area of knowledge

Another link between theory of knowledge and language and literature is the fact that literature is also considered an area of knowledge within the arts. It is both a way of knowing and an area of knowledge simultaneously. As an area of knowledge, the arts can articulate a very personal encounter and a unique kind of knowing and understanding that may be quite different to socially-constructed knowledge (after all, beauty is in the eye of the beholder). However, they should not be treated without some critical awareness of the cultural context. It is possible, for instance, that culture has such a significant effect on us that even our unconscious sense of beauty is not wholly our own.

With literature, an interesting aesthetic moment occurs in the conflict zone between the singular and individual aesthetic encounter and larger social influences. Much of our literary tradition is involved in the identification of meanings and associations, as well as broader social constructs. At the same time a literary text may be primarily about generating a more direct aesthetic response. As an example, the following poem by the American poet Larry Eigner, associated with a group called the Language Poets, employs these more visceral and immediate forms of expression, using language in a way that demonstrates its almost physical impact *before* the mind gets to an intellectual interpretation:

the knowledge of death, and now
knowledge of the stars
there is one end
and the endless
Room at the center
passage / in no time
a rail thickets hills grass

The example of Language Poetry tries to challenge our desire for more literal meaning, and in doing so reminds us not only of the inherent ambiguity of language but also its aesthetic nature (when we concern ourselves with the sounds of the words, or the pictures and the free associations it creates).

Activity

Finding knowledge or truth

Art has the ability to shine a light on our everyday encounters with the world. Things we may take for granted as ordinary and mundane—and therefore that we may tend to ignore—are suddenly made the objects of our attention and can lead to new understandings and insights.

Text 1

Read the following poem by the 19th-century American poet Emily Dickinson. Note your initial impressions and the way she approaches her subject.

> Tell all the Truth but tell it slant—
> Success in Circuit lies
> Too bright for our infirm Delight
> The Truth's superb surprise
> As Lightning to the Children eased
> With explanation kind
> The Truth must dazzle gradually
> Or every man be blind—

Dickinson suggests that truth can never be experienced directly and wholly but should only be "revealed" in small amounts and from different perspectives. Truth and knowledge can, and perhaps should, take us by surprise.

1 Why is truth a surprise?
2 How is it revealed to us?
3 Why is it kinder to be indirect?
4 Which different perspectives does Dickinson draw on?

Text 2

Untitled, 2009, by Priti Kahar.

Look at these mixed media works of art by the Indian artist Priti Kahar. The curator of the exhibition said of Kahar's work that it draws "attention to things we use daily but barely notice," inviting us to look more closely.

1 How does the artist make us see the object differently?

2 How is language used in this work of art?

3 What links exist between this work of visual art by Kahar and the poem by Dickinson?

4 What do these works of art and literature reveal about the advantages and limitation of language as a way of knowing? As an area of knowledge?

Literature in translation

One of the most popular aspects of all of the group 1 options in the IB Diploma Programme is the focus on literature in translation. This component of the course allows students to take a more global view of trends in literature. It has, of course, become commonplace to read texts in translation. It may be that we tend to overlook this reality; in fact, even in this text we have used terms like "language" and "texts" in a rather monolithic plural sense (suggesting a variety of uses of the English language as synecdoche for all communicative acts); we are aware that English is only one of many possible paroles. Similarly, we often treat literature translated into English as primary documents rather than more subtle approximations of an original. It certainly is an advantage to have translations available. But the act of translation is itself fraught with challenges that are probably not too difficult to anticipate.

With a literary text in particular, the act of translation is frequently referred to as an "art" in and of itself. This process involves a complex balance of the denotative and connotative aspects of language, the latter in reference to extended metaphor, tone, cultural context and even interpretive intention. Translators must constantly make decisions and compromises to balance out these objectives as the translation is necessarily the sum of these component parts. A denotative translation of one word may, for instance, detract from the emotional intelligence of a sentence and the mood of the work as a whole. To rectify these issues, a translator would use an alternative term that may be less literally correct, but more metaphorically apt.

There is probably little need to belabor the challenges of translation. The following exercise demonstrates how different two translations can be, and we would assume (unless we speak Russian and can read the original) that both are different again from the original. But translation is also an asset in its endeavor to bridge cultural and language gaps; and, of necessity, demonstrates all of the challenges of knowing in any language by drawing attention to itself.

Read

Translating Dostoyevsky

Read the two translations of the first page of Fyodor Dostoyevsky's *Crime and Punishment* first published in Russian in 1886. The first translation is by Constance Garnett, a well-known translator of Russian novels published in English in the middle of the 20th century. Garnett's translations have been criticized for their similarity of voice in her translations of numerous Russian authors. Here it is compared with a more recent translation by Richard Pevear and Larissa Volokhonsky.

What affect do some of the differences in the choice or words and sentence structure have in helping to describe the character of the main protagonist, set the scene and establish the critical tensions? Does each translation have a distinct flavor? What criteria would you use to judge the best translation?

Translation 1

On an exceptionally hot evening early in July a young man came out of the garret in which he lodged in S. Place and walked slowly, as though in hesitation, towards K. bridge. He had successfully avoided meeting his landlady on the staircase. His garret was under the roof of a high, five-storied house and was more like a cupboard than a room. The landlady who provided him with garret, dinners, and attendance, lived on the floor below, and every time he went out he was obliged to pass her kitchen, the door of which invariably stood open. And each time he passed, the young man had a sick, frightened feeling, which made him scowl and feel ashamed. He was hopelessly in debt to his landlady, and was afraid of meeting her.

This was not because he was cowardly and abject, quite the contrary; but for some time past he had been in an overstrained irritable condition, verging on hypochondria. He had become so completely absorbed in himself, and isolated from his fellows that he dreaded meeting, not only his landlady, but any one at all. He was crushed by poverty, but the anxieties of his position had of late ceased to weigh upon him. He had given up attending to matters of practical importance; he had lost all desire to do so.

Nothing that any landlady could do had a real terror for him. But to be stopped on the stairs, to be forced to listen to her trivial, irrelevant gossip, to pestering demands for payment, threats and complaints, and to rack his brains for excuses, to prevaricate, to lie—no, rather than that, he would creep down the stairs like a cat and slip out unseen.

Translation 2

At the beginning of July, during an extremely hot spell, towards evening, a young man left the closet he rented from tenants in S——y Lane, walked out to the street, and slowly, as if indecisively, headed for the K——n Bridge.

He had safely avoided meeting his landlady on the stairs. His closet was located just under the roof of a tall, five-storied house, and was more like a cupboard than a room. As for the landlady, from whom he rented this closet with dinner and maid-service included, she lived one flight below, in separate rooms, and every time he went out he could not fail to pass by the landlady's kitchen, the door of which almost always stood open to the stairs. And each time he passed by, the young man felt some painful and cowardly sensation, which made him wince with shame. He was over his head in debt to the lady and was afraid of meeting her.

It was not that he was so cowardly and downtrodden, even quite the contrary; but for some time he had been in an irritable and tense state, resembling hypochondria. He was so immersed in himself and had isolated himself so much from everyone that he was afraid not only of meeting his landlady but of meeting anyone at all. He was crushed by poverty; but even his strained circumstances had lately ceased to burden him. He had entirely given up attending to his daily affairs and did not want to attend to them. As a matter of fact, he was not afraid of any landlady, whatever she might be plotting against him. But to stop on the stairs, to listen to all sorts of nonsense about this commonplace rubbish, which he could not care less about, all this badgering for payment, these threats and complaints, and to have to dodge all the while, make excuses, lie—oh, no, better to steal catlike down the stairs somehow and slip away unseen by anyone.

Using technology

In this section, we will suggest why technology is important in the Language and Literature course and how you might use technology either on your own or in school. Throughout the rest of the book, our basic philosophies around technology will be reflected in the activities and suggestions for further research. Depending on how well your school is resourced you will have varying access to technology. Your school may have a small computer lab or provide access to computers in the library. You may be learning in a classroom where every student has their own wireless laptop. No matter what your situation, however, you undoubtedly know that digital technology is an important part of education in the 21st century. Not only do many of us use computers as word processors, but we also use them to go online to access the World Wide Web (the Internet). What other digital resources do you use? Think about this question as you read through this section.

Activity

Online resources

At its most basic level, technology offers the student of English an endless number of resources. The web-based or online resources you have available may depend upon your school or local library. These resources may include:

- professional and organizational websites
- online magazines
- quick access to a variety of images, film, video and sound recordings
- databases for literary or scholarly research, including Wikipedia, Project Gutenberg and commercial or higher education-based reference libraries such as JSTOR, EBSCO, Project Muse private blogs and social networking sites
- Online search engines.

How many of the following online resources do you regularly access?

- A private blog or personal website
- An online newspaper, such as the *New York Times* or *The Independent* (UK)
- A student study guide and support site, such as *IB Survival* (www.ibsurvival.com) or *Sparknotes* (www.sparknotes.com)
- Wikipedia (www.wikipedia.org).

Evaluating a resource

On your own, or in a class group, evaluate the Internet-based resources listed above.

1 What are the values and limitations of a private blog? What about a blog that is part of an online newspaper?

2 How has the Internet changed the way we do creative research and scholarship?

3 What are the values and limitations of an Internet search engine?

Misconceptions about technology

Technology changes quickly and it sometimes seems like there is a "next big thing" every six months. One minute we are using laptops and the next we are thinking about buying a portable tablet that stores all of our entertainment and connects us to the Internet on the go. As a secondary school student, you have grown up in this type of quick-changing digital environment. But just because you may have been born to a world of mp3 players, and your teacher may have listened to a wax recording powered by a crank, this does not mean that new media is always a superior form for the distribution of ideas and cultural material, or that you have nothing to learn in relation to technology. Teachers today are working hard to marry digital technology with important concepts and skills in their courses in support of maintaining a critical perspective on our use of online and other digital resources. You might also be inspired to take the lead in introducing a new (or old) form of technology to the classroom, and lead a class discussion on how it can best be used, as well as its implications for the field of creative producers and audiences or "readers."

Activity

Changes in the technology of production

Think about the role technology plays in the writing process. (Why do some writers, for example, still rely on pen and paper?) How would the following technologies have changed the way we communicate, create literature, or present our findings about literature? Think about the advantages and disadvantages of upgrading from one technology to the other. Discuss in your group what happens when people upgrade their modes of production, using the following examples:

- cave painting to handwriting
- quill pens dipped in ink to fountain pens (or other pens) with an internal supply of ink.
- handwriting to the personal typewriter.
- the typewriter to the word processor.
- word processing on a personal computer to Google Docs.

Take any one of these pairings to use as a topic for a class debate.

Technology in this course

In this course, technology is often part of the object of study, not just a tool to use to do your work. Although much of the reading you will do is on the printed page, you are constantly surrounded by text in a digital environment. You read text messages from friends, emails, website content, or search engine results. At the same time you are also producing language using technology—from word processors (like Microsoft Word) to postings on someone's "wall" on Facebook, much of your writing is mediated through digital applications. The close relationship between language and technology in today's world raises a number of questions that can be addressed in the course. How does the layout of a website affect our approach to the content on a website? How are website-reading practices different from print-reading practices? Do these practices, in turn, affect the way writers organize text? How does texting change the way you use language? Does email encourage or discourage clear communication? What is the effect of our ability to communicate with people in different parts of the world?

Because of technology, there are also new forms of audio-visual media to facilitate interactions as well as new ways to post and exchange information and files. While blogging may be similar to writing an editorial and email resembles a letter, we may need to find new ways of approaching the study of audio-visual media. Technology changes have brought about genres such as hypertext fiction (stories written on a multilink, web-like, platform), SMS poetry, and ebooks that incorporate images, sound, and text.

Activity

Creative intervention

Machinima (www.machinima. com) is an art form that uses an existing platform to create a new work of art. A writer, player, or artist uses the graphics-generating capability of an existing video game in order to create a modified version or an extended narrative that might, for instance, more closely resemble a story or a film rather than a game.

Machinima at its most basic could involve playing through an interesting or innovative sequence on a video game, recording it, and then adding new music or text afterwards to create a new product or version. What genre would you call this? Would a Machinima production be an original work of art? Does it infringe on the original creator's rights? Do some web research to find out how it works.

Alternatively, find other file-sharing networks to explore interventionist forms of practice and how they contribute to an online creative community.

Technology can be used in all kinds of creative ways to analyze language use for research purposes. The literary scholar Franco Moretti uses literature as data to map out stylistic, thematic, and even plot-related trends in the European novel as well as literature from across the globe. In what he mischievously calls "distance reading," Moretti uses the publication data, for example, to graph changes in the development of the novel over time (through the work of different authors). His reading is based on the collation of data rather than a close reading of the text. Moretti also uses maps to plot character interaction in stories, offering a graphic representation of events in a story that may suggest new meanings or interpretations.

After studying a large number of novels that are set in Paris, Moretti mapped the locations of the male characters (their names are listed

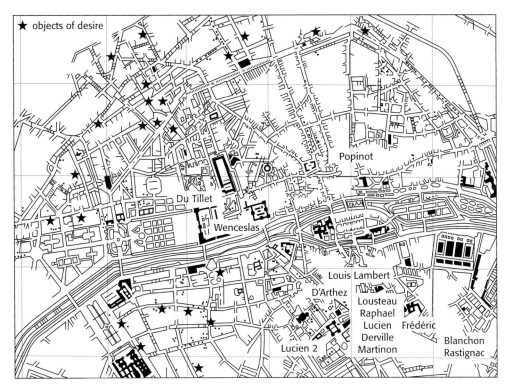

A map of protagonists from various French novels and their locations relative to their "objects of desire."
Source: Moretti, Franco. 2005. *Graphs, Maps, Trees,* New York: Verso, 2005. p. 55.

on the right side) and their objects of affection (represented by the stars). He found that a pattern emerged. He saw from his own map that the men lived in the *Latin Quarter*, an area known for its bohemian nature, as many young, creative people lived there, taking advantage of the cheap rent and the vibrant atmosphere, even to the extent of celebrating its run-down qualities. The "objects of desire" (the women they were in love with) on the other hand, lived in more affluent parts of the city (as indicated by the stars). Moretti was interested in exploring the patterns that emerged. This kind of map presents a different type of analysis than one derived from the close reading of an individual text.

Some scholars analyze texts to look at particular forms of language use, such as grammatical structures in literature. Researchers from all fields are taking advantage of current programming advances to create more interesting graphic representations of information in texts. In linguistics, scholars use large databases of language examples to analyze how language is used today and how it is changing over time. All of these changes don't even take into account the changes to scholarship that are happening because of increased access to information online, and the ease of sharing research as it progresses. The content of this course, the information that comes from the study of language, is possible because of technology.

Activity

Graphic representation

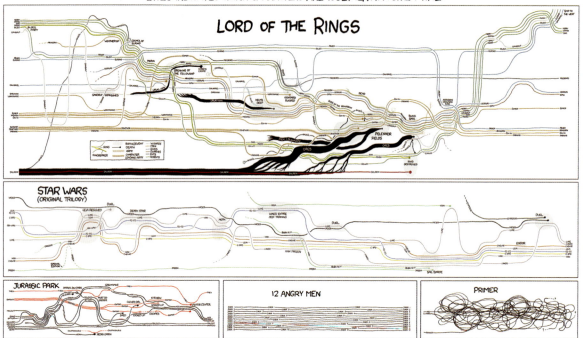

THESE CHARTS SHOW MOVIE CHARACTER INTERACTIONS. THE HORIZONTAL AXIS IS TIME. THE VERTICAL GROUPING OF THE LINES INDICATES WHICH CHARACTERS ARE TOGETHER AT A GIVEN TIME.

A movie narrative chart by Randall Munro.

The image above is a graphic representation of character interaction in various films. With the aid of computer technology, critics are more easily able to compile data and come up with interesting ways of displaying it. In some literature classes, students are encouraged to use Google Earth to create dynamic maps that trace the routes that fictional characters have taken on their journeys. A text can also be represented, for instance, as a "word cloud" that displays words from a text on the page in various font sizes related to the frequency with which they appear in a work.

Your turn

On the Internet, research "graphic representations of texts" and see how many ways you can find to represent literature graphically using available technology. See if you can find a tool that you can use with a text you are currently studying. Consider, as well, the practical aspects. How are current graphic representations any different from simply drawing a map based on your reading of a novel?

Read

Emily Dickinson's papers

Because of digital technology and ease of communication through the Internet, we now have access to a wider variety of texts in most classrooms. Digitization projects such as the British Library digital initiative, Project Gutenberg and the growing collection at Google Books allow access to hard-to-find texts and in some cases allow access to reproductions of original manuscripts. We no longer have to go to a rare book library to see a Shakespeare folio. The Emily Dickinson archive is an interesting example. Many critics feel that Emily Dickinson's poetry is best understood in relation to her idiosyncratic use of punctuation, spacing or the general material nature of her text. With the help of technology, we are better able to study not only rare texts but the effects of very early technologies (the paper and the pen) on creative writing.

Is this frostier?

Springs – shake the Sills –
But – the Echoes - stiffen –
Hoar – is the Window – and
numb – the Door –
Tribes of Eclipse – in Tents
of Marble –
Staples of Ages – have
buckled – there –

Dear Sue –
Your praise is good –
to me – because I *know*
it *knows* – and *suppose* –
it *means* –
Could I make you and
Austin – proud – sometime – a
great way off – 'twould give
me taller feet –
Here is a crumb – for the
"Ring dove" – and a spray,
for *his Nest*, a little while
ago – *just* – *"Sue"* –

Emily

Source: Dickinson Electronic Archives.
http://www.emilydickinson.org

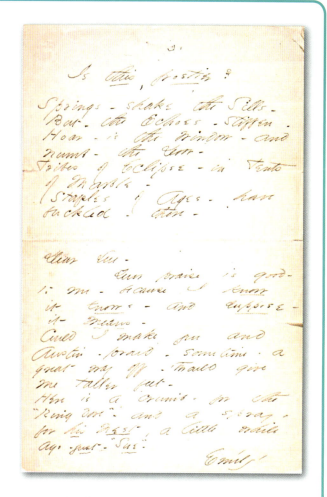

In the case of this poem and correspondence, new technology lets us consider the importance of old technology (handwriting and exchange of letters) to the creative process. Popular stories of Emily Dickinson portray her as a recluse, writing her poetry only for herself. This manuscript, however, suggests that her poetry was more collaborative than is commonly thought. The image of the manuscript also shows Dickinson's original script, capitalization, and spacing. Are these elements a side effect of the technologies Dickinson was using? Or, are they somehow as inseparable from the meaning of the poem as rhyme and rhythm?

Digital software

Some digital tools are so second nature today that it is hard to imagine that the first personal computer (the Altair 8800) went on sale in 1975, and the first computer software program (Microsoft BASIC created by Bill Gates and Paul Allen) was launched in 1976. The World Wide Web as we know it was not even invented until 1989. Very few people had access to email before the mid-1990s. So the digital revolution is still relatively recent (and still very much evolving).

Think of how this has affected our access to software applications. How many of the following tools have you used?

- Presentation software
- Movie-making software
- Voice recording/podcast creating software
- Video recording
- Digital imaging, photo manipulation, and drawing programs
- Blog software
- Digital filing systems and e-portfolios

Discuss in your group how knowledge of these systems and applications has assisted you in your creative projects and research.

Technology as enhancement

By now you will have a fair idea of the digital resources available. But what do these tools do for the study of English? Technology certainly makes the job of a teacher easier: we can save lesson plans in a folder, post assignments on a digital classroom portal, store all student work in an e-portfolio, record student grades online (which means, never having to calculate averages, or write on a report card), and more. Speed and efficiency may be sufficient justification for the use of technology, but can there be too much speed and efficiency? Sometimes the information we glean from the World Wide Web can be overwhelming—there is so much out there it is hard to find the best information, or hard to focus our attention on the most salient facts. Speed can also lead to sloppiness, such as relying too much on a spell checker. Along with speed and efficiency, through technology, especially with the advent of Web 2.0 and beyond, there is an added focus on interactivity and creativity. Use of an electronic forum allows you to have a discussion with your peers even when you are not in the classroom. An "SMS" chat gets you quick responses to niggling homework questions. With this interactivity comes both increased productivity and greater opportunities for creative collaboration.

Activity

Back-channeling and the Google jockey

In some experimental classrooms and conferences, teachers or organizers set up a "back channel" or a live chat on a website that can be accessed while a lecture is being given or a discussion is being led from the front of the classroom. Participants in the back-channel chat are essentially engaged in a whispering discussion—we hope relevant to the work at hand.

In a somewhat similar scenario, a student may be delegated the role of "Google jockey" for a day's discussion. During class it is the student's responsibility to search for relevant background information, commentary, or images. In a class with a projector these findings are projected on a screen.

What are the chances that activities like these would be productive in your classroom? Get your teacher to write a roster, and nominate yourself to be a Google jockey!

Activity

Chart the interactive process

Participating in a class on online forum adds an important ingredient to a traditional journal: interactivity.

- How would you describe or chart the nature of interactivity? Draw a model of the lines of communication, like a data or mind map, of a group of forum users.
- Consider the frequency of the communication between users, and the people who played the most central role in attracting contributors to the discussion.
- Give the digital names of the forum users and provide digital portraits or icons to distinguish them. Compare notes and discuss your graphic models in class.

Transforming technologies

As modes of production, dissemination, consumption, and analysis change, so too do the nature of the practices themselves. What difference does it make if you read a book on an e-reader or in the more usual print format? We can speculate, but the answer is that we do not really know what the future holds and what developers will come up with next. What is more important: quick access to books, and ephemeral files, or close attention to the detail of an individual printed text, read over and over again? Are these two approaches mutually exclusive? What works better: flipping to a section of a book we remember and jotting down notes, or digitally marking-up a page? What matters more: access to all the published and out-of-print resources in the world, or accessing an original object and printed edition of a work of literature that is important to your culture? Is it possible for the World Wide Web to provide resources for both?

What we can say is that there are current processes, as we have shown above, that may change the nature of the study of language and literature. No one knows for sure what the broader sociological changes will be. Judging by recent advances, academic activities are likely to change fast.

Discussion Point

Have you ever wondered what the future holds for e-books and their applications? While a dedicated e-reader offers access to a vast number of books and the ability to carry a 4,000 volume library in your bag (a phenomenal development in reading, mobility and scholarship!) new tablets may offer other exciting additions to the reading experience, including access to audio-visual material?

How will this encourage creative research and greater access to entertainment, culture and news media? Will this change the nature of reading itself?

Activity

Class debate

Google vs. the publishing industry

"The agreement limits consumer choice in out-of-print books about as much as it limits consumer choice in unicorns," says Google co-founder, Sergey Brin. The main objection to the Google Books settlement is that it will give Google a monopoly on out-of-print, or orphan books, that are otherwise only available in large research libraries.

In your group, get into teams to research and debate the right for Google to digitize and publish all out-of-print books online, without paying copyright to authors or publishers. Google Books has digitized more than 10 million books for its Google Book Search Library project, but is currently being challenged by a number of publishing concerns to make distribution of these resources illegal. What are the broader implications of a Google Books monopoly? Weigh up the advantages and disadvantages of the proposed initiative.

Activity

Technology and the word

As a final reflection on the importance of technology to the study of the humanities, viewed historically, consider these short passages by the scholars Walter Ong and David Crystal.

Text 1

Most persons are surprised, and many distressed, to learn that essentially the same objections commonly urged today against computers were urged by Plato in the *Phaedrus* … and in the *Seventh Letter* against writing. Writing, Plato has Socrates say in the *Phaedrus*, is inhuman, pretending to establish outside the mind what in reality can be only in the mind. It is a thing, a manufactured product. The same of course is said about computers. Secondly, Plato's Socrates urges, writing destroys memory. Those who use writing will become forgetful, relying on an external resource for what they lack in internal resources. Writing weakens the mind. Today, parents and others fear that pocket calculators provide an external resource for what ought to be the internal resource of memorized multiplication tables. Calculators weaken the mind, relieve it of the work that keeps it strong. Thirdly, a written text is basically unresponsive. If you ask a person to explain his or her statement, you can get an explanation; if you ask a text, you get back nothing except the same, often stupid, words which called for your questions in the first place. In the modern critique of the computer, the same objection is put, "Garbage in, garbage out". Fourthly, in keeping with the agonistic mentality of oral cultures, Plato's Socrates also holds it against writing that the written word cannot defend itself as the natural spoken word can: real speech and thought always exist essentially in a context of give-and-take between real persons. Writing is passive, out of it, in an unreal, unnatural world. So are computers. …

One weakness in Plato's position was that, to make his objections effective, he put them into writing, just as one weakness of anti-print positions is that their proponents, to make their objections more effective, put the objections into print. The same weakness in anti-computer positions is that, to make them effective, their proponents articulate them in articles or books printed from tapes composed on computer terminals. Writing and print and the computer are all ways of technologizing the word. Once the word is technologized, there is no effective way to criticize what technology has done with it without the aid of the highest technology available. Moreover, new technology is not merely used to convey the critique: in fact, it brought the critique into existence.

Source: Ong, Walter. 2004. *Orality and Literacy: The Technologizing of the Word.* London: Routledge. pp. 77–79.

Text 2

Txting: The Gr8 Db8

… There are several distinctive features of the way texts are written that combine to give the impression of novelty, but none of them is, in fact, linguistically novel. Many of them were being used in chatroom interactions that predated the arrival of mobile phones. Some can be found in pre-computer informal writing, dating back a hundred years or more. The most noticeable feature is the use of single letters, numerals, and symbols to represent words or parts of words, as with b "be" and 2 "to". They are called rebuses, and they go back centuries. …

Similarly, the use of initial letters for whole words (n for "no", gf for "girlfriend", cmb "call me back") is not at all new. People have been initialising common phrases for ages. IOU is known from 1618. In texts we find such forms as msg ("message") and xlnt ("excellent"). Almst any wrd cn be abbrvted in ths wy …. But this isn't new either. Eric Partridge published his Dictionary of Abbreviations in 1942. It contained dozens of SMS-looking examples, such as

agn "again", mth "month", and gd "good"—50 years before texting was born. English has had abbreviated words ever since it began to be written down. Words such as exam, vet, fridge, cox and bus are so familiar that they have effectively become new words. When some of these abbreviated forms first came into use, they also attracted criticism. In 1711, for example, Joseph Addison complained about the way words were being "miserably curtailed"—he mentioned pos (itive) and incog (nito). And Jonathan Swift thought that abbreviating words was a "barbarous custom". What novelty there is in texting lies chiefly in the way it takes further some of the processes used in the past. All conceivable types of feature can be juxtaposed—sequences of shortened and full words (hldmecls "hold me close"), logograms and shortened words (2bctnd "to be continued"), logograms and nonstandard spellings (cu2nite) and so on. …

There are also individual differences in texting, as in any other linguistic domain. In 2002, Stuart Campbell was found guilty of the murder of his 15-year-old niece after his text message alibi was shown to be a forgery. He had claimed that certain texts sent by the girl showed he was innocent. But a detailed comparison of the vocabulary and other stylistic features of his own text messages and those of his niece showed that he had written the messages himself. The fact that texting is a relatively unstandardised mode of communication, prone to idiosyncrasy, turns out to be an advantage in such a context, as authorship differences are likely to be more easily detectable than in writing using standard English.

Source: Crystal, David. "Txting: The Gr8 Db8." *The Guardian.* 5 July 2009.

Questions to the texts

Use your own knowledge and ideas from the above extracts to answer the following questions.

1 Does technology change the way we think?

2 How does each new change in our communication habits, compare with those that have gone on before?

3 How differently have people throughout history responded to new technological developments? Why do you think some of the same arguments come up again and again?

4 Consider the point of view of these two authors on the inevitability of change in language usage. What is reassuring, or disturbing about the conclusions they reach?

Reading, listening, and viewing

No matter where you are, what approach your teacher takes in class, or which sections of the course you study first, everything you do in this course will focus on reading, listening to, and viewing various communicative acts or texts. You are certainly expected to read carefully, actively, and critically, but you will find that much of the best reading (and from now on, we will assume, listening and viewing as well) does comes naturally. Later in this book you will find specific ways to approach types of texts. You will also learn some tips for producing types of written and oral assessments. But in all honesty, the best tip we can give you is to read, re-read, and trust your instincts. No matter what advice we give, no formula will serve you better than a fresh, close engagement with a text. That being said, it is worth looking at what a critical reader does.

Active reading

In chapter two we said that New Criticism, the school of theory that brought our attention more fully to the text itself, has had a profound influence on our reading and critical practices. The fact of the matter is that we always turn to the text to find meaning or, in a discussion, to support our ideas. When we look closely at a text we begin to see how it functions, how various technical aspects work together to create meaning or affect the reader. Being an active reader, however, also has a lot to do with later theorists who suggested that much of the power of a text, while it lies in the structures of the text itself, also lies in the mind of the reader. Far from just uncovering the thoughts and intentions of an author, as a passive recipient, the reader has a much more creative role to play in the investigation of a text.

Read

The death of the author

Consider the following excerpt from an influential essay entitled "The Death of the Author" (1968) by the French literary theorist Roland Barthes.

> Once the Author is distanced, the claim to "decipher" a text becomes entirely futile. To assign an Author to a text is to impose a brake on it, to furnish it with a final signified, to close writing. This conception is quite suited to criticism, which then undertakes the important task of discovering the Author (or his … society, history, the psych, freedom) beneath the work: once the Author is found, the text is "explained," the critic has won; hence, it is hardly surprising that historically the Author's empire has been the Critic's as well, and also that (even new) criticism is today unsettled at the same time as the Author. In multiple writing, in effect, everything is to be *disentangled*, structure can be followed, "threaded" (as we say of a run in a stocking) in all is reprises, all its stages, but there is no end to it, no bottom; the space of writing is to be traversed, not pierced; writing constantly posits meaning but always in order to evaporate it: writing seeks a systematic exemption of meaning. Thereby literature (it would be better, from now on, to say *writing*), by refusing to assign to the text (and to the world-as-text) a "secret," i.e., an ultimate meaning, liberates an activity we may call … properly revolutionary…

Source: Barthes, Roland. (trans. Howard, Richard). *The Rustle of Language*. Berkeley, USA: University of California. pp. 53–54.

While the new critics certainly suggested that the text itself is more important than what the author may or may not have intended, the French literary theorist Roland Barthes pushes this a little further by recommending the metaphoric death of the author and even, it seems, the death of any possibility for pinning down meaning. Throughout this book we will suggest many ways of thinking about the meaning and importance of a text. We will also suggest many ways to look at details and consider the effects of particular features. We may even (going against the advice of Barthes) think about an author's intentions or the role that context plays in the meaning of a text. But, for now, it is worth embracing the power Barthes gives to the reader in the role of constructing meaning. Rather than looking for some "secret" that can be found locked in a text, we should think about the text as a bottomless space to be "traversed." An active reader explores, wonders, disentangles, reworks and assembles an always imperfect meaning that can always be revisited, and is potentially revolutionary!

The basics of reading

An initial approach to a text

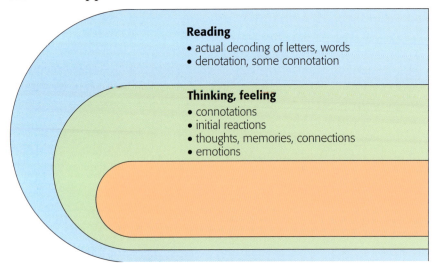

Moving to critical reading

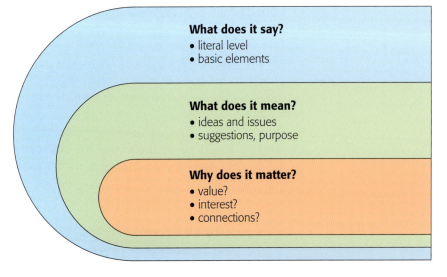

The creative act

We often talk about the intention of the author or a text. We study language in action and language as a communicative or intentional act. Therefore, we always make the assumption that an originator of an utterance, a novel, a picture on a cave wall, or an advertisement, had some purpose in mind. It is always a good idea to think about the intentions of the artist or author. But as we see from the new critics all the way to Roland Barthes and his "Death of the Author," it is problematic to talk about an author's intention as the sole basis for an interpretation.

Is there anything to be gained from a discussion of the creative act? What useful insights can we get from an interview with an author? Can't we also look at a large body of work by an artist and see that the artist was clearly working through particular themes or ideas, or the refinement of a particular technique? Also, realistically, can't we look at a text and at least surmise some relevant approach to intentionality? A practical way of looking at intention, or at the role that is played by the author that we have in our minds, as we read a text, is what the Italian literary critic Umberto Eco calls "hypothetical intentionality." When we read we imagine what an author's intentions or purposes *may* have been, based on what we read and our (imperfect) knowledge of contexts.

As previously discussed, the main concern of someone who studies language and literature is to approach a text or language act critically. You have learned what it means to question a text, to look for bias, to look at intentions, and to look for what a text leaves out. You have also considered the ways in which a text can be approached as an aesthetic object. These steps can be summed up in three questions you can ask yourself about any text:

● What does it say (what is going on, what is it about)?

● What does it mean (what does it suggest, imply, explain)?

● Why is it valuable (or interesting, important, or engaging)?

If you ask yourself these three questions in relation to every book or article that you read, any newscast you listen to, or any advertisement you view in a magazine, you are practicing for this course. From here on in, everything is just refinement and added experience. But these three questions are not always easy to answer. You may already be thinking about texts that you have read that evade the second question ... or maybe even the first. Look at the following three short passages and try to answer the three questions as simply and as directly as you can: What does it say? What does it mean? Why does it matter?

Text 1

The Auckland SPCA [Society for the Prevention of Cruelty to Animals] has warned its inspectors will take a police escort to close down an arcade game involving live crayfish if it does not get co-operation from pub managers. The SPCA said today it would close down several games in pubs in Auckland where patrons paid to try to catch live crayfish in a tank using a metal claw.

Source: "SPCA blocks contentious crayfish game." *New Zealand Herald*. Tuesday, February 9, 2010.

Text 2

My sister, Mrs. Joe Gargery, was more than twenty years older than I, and had established a great reputation with herself and the neighbours because she had brought me up "by hand." Having at that time to find out for myself what the expression meant, and knowing her to have a hard and heavy hand, and to be much in the habit of laying it upon her husband as well as upon me, I supposed that Joe Gargery and I were both brought up by hand.

Source: Dickens, Charles. 1861. *Great Expectations*. New York: Alfred A. Knopf. 1992. p. 6.

Text 3

You see, they have no judgment.
So it is natural that they should drown,
first the ice taking them in
and then, all winter, their wool scarves
floating behind them as they sink
until at last they are quiet.
And the pond lifts them in its manifold arms.

Source: Glück, Louise. "The Drowned Children." 1980. *The First Four Books of Poems*. New York: HarperCollins, 1995.

Your response to these extracts should tell you something about the elements of reading that come easily as well as the wonderful play of texts and the potential subtleties of meaning, effect and ultimately the value you see in them. While the first two texts, a newspaper article and a novel, seem to be clear in what they are literally saying, it may be somewhat hard to determine meaning. What is being suggested in the brief clipping from the newspaper? Is this clearly showing a victory for the SPCA as crayfish games are made illegal, or is it suggesting that the police are overstepping boundaries? Is the piece completely neutral? Reading this text critically we can appreciate its possible irony or even humor and may find some value in it beyond the purely informational. What may have first been read quickly for the details turns out to be something that can be enjoyed for its humor or even viewed as an interesting snapshot of our cultural concerns. The second passage, from the novel *Great Expectations*, engages our interest more personally and introduces us to both the narrator and two important characters in the novel, as well as the relationship between them. Although we may not yet be able to say definitively what this passage means in relation to the rest of the novel, we are drawn to the descriptions and the personal narrative. We may be captivated by the combination of humor and naiveté in the voice. Finally, the third passage presents us with a more suggestive story about someone or something in a cold climate, and a pond that presents a very real threat. The precise nature of the event is, however, a bit obscure. Upon reading this last text, a work of poetry, we may allow for or expect some ambiguity but, just as we may be surprised by a closer reading of the newspaper, we may find that the lyrical poem has its own sense of a literal story. Close reading should reveal myriad possibilities to explore in a text.

Steps toward being critical

The following diagram suggests some very practical ways of moving from your first reading of a text to a more formal analysis (that might result, for example, in an essay, commentary, or a presentation).

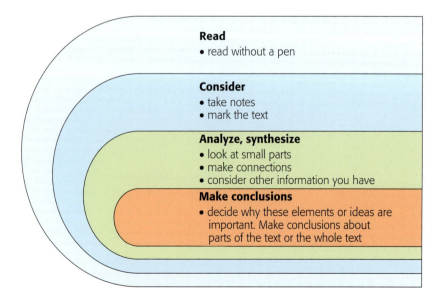

Here are some ways to be an active reader:

- **Make notes** We will talk about this more later.

- **Question the text** Note sections, sentences, or words that you do not understand. Take guesses at the meanings of ambiguous elements.

- **Allow for the ambiguity** If something has more than one possible meaning, or is unclear, make several hypotheses to start. Narrow ideas based on evidence throughout the piece.

- **Be attentive to the "rules of notice"** All texts call attention to themselves in some ways: they use surprising or difficult words, they make interesting allusions, they use colors or images that become the center of focus and/or they contain repetitions. Think closely about the elements you notice, you are probably *meant* to notice them.

- **Know when to look for help** Use a dictionary, the Internet, the library, a teacher, a parent or even the back of the book. You never know where you are going to find information that will nudge in the right direction. Sometimes, as in an exam, we are on our own with a text. At other times, we have some help. Just do not let the help substitute for your own close reading and ideas.

A list of features to consider

What should you consider beyond the literal meaning of a text? How do you start to talk not just about what is happening but about how the text is put together by an author, designer, or creator? The elements you need to look for in a text are essentially the building blocks for any communicative act. In reality, the list is endless and it is impossible to put together a simple checklist of elements to consider in a literary or informational work. You may be encouraged to look at setting, for example, in a work or passage where setting seems to have little significance. On the other hand, there may be a particular feature of a given text—maybe an odd use of font in a visually striking poem—that would never be covered by a checklist. This list of features, then, is an attempt to get you thinking about the fact that any communicative act is purposeful and created and that many elements come together in a work to create meaning. It is your job in understanding and interpretation to consider how individual elements combine to make meaning. We are trying to take what is normally subconscious in reading and make it concrete. Beyond thinking about what the text is saying and what it seems to be about (this would include literal meaning along with issues, ideas, or themes suggested by the work), you should consider the following elements in relation to both texts and images:

- **Narrator or speaker** Who is speaking in the text? Is the narrator the same as the author? Does the speaker have a particular voice? In an informational piece, does the writer have an individual voice or a voice that is more "institutional"?

- **Perspective** Who seems to be doing the "seeing" in the work? Sometimes a third person narrator clearly explains events and emotions through a particular, often central character. In a work of art, we automatically view content from a particular point of view. Where, or from whose perspective, is the subject approached?

- **Setting** This would include the time and place of a scene from the very general (France in the 1800s) to the very specific—the afternoon in a small, greasy kitchen in a side street just off the Boulevard de Montparnasse (May 12, 1839, the day of the Paris uprising) …

- **Characters** Who are the main characters? Which other characters have an important role? Do they speak or are they silent? How are they described? How much do we know about them? Some works of literature are all about the subtleties about the relationships between the characters and what happens to them. In other texts the identity of the main protagonists might seem secondary to the machinations of the plot.

- **Structure** This can be a very difficult to pin down, as it involves the development or form of the work. If the work is a poem, structure is an important compositional element, and can include the length of lines, the separation of stanzas or even the use of punctuation. These elements can help to create movement and emotional effect as well as propelling the narrative to its ultimate conclusion. In prose, structure can refer to sentence and paragraph length, but it can also refer the division of chapters and the overall pattern or order of the telling of the story (maybe every chapter starts with a description before launching into the action at hand, perhaps every third section of the work begins and ends with a flashback …). In an image, structure consists of elements such as balance and contrast in the formal elements of the work (such as line and color).

- **Vocabulary and diction** The formal vocabulary and diction (the choice of words in a literary text) can make a difference. Are the words simple? Are they complex? Does the writer use a lot of adjectives and flowery language? Is there a lot of technical jargon? How important is the sound of the words and phrases (as in poetry). In art, vocabulary could include images "borrowed" from other sources (like advertisements or reproductions of older art) or the formal elements such as the choice of colors, quality of line, textures and forms.

- **Imagery** How do the words or images create pictures or associations in your mind? Does the author use metaphors, similes, or hyperbole to evoke a particularly strong image or effect? In visual art, as in literature, there is potentially a reference to a theme or the repetition of certain symbols, forms or subjects. These can be quite abstract like the way the seventeenth-century Dutch painter Johannes Vermeer captures the effect of light on the lip of a ceramic jug to focus on the distinction between materiality and immateriality.

- **Tone and atmosphere** Tone comes from the combination of elements such as diction, action, dialogue, and description that lean toward a particular attitude or emotion. Atmosphere is perhaps better described as the general tone of the setting. A dark atmosphere may be conveyed through the description of a haunted mansion or a stormy sky in a landscape painting. A light touch as in an impressionist painting, or the dancing quality of a poetic description, might convey a more lighthearted approach to life.

- **Tension or conflict** A famous critic once said, "The cat sat on the mat is not a story. The cat sat on the dog's mat is." Conflict or potential conflict is often what drives a narrative from a short story to an editorial blog. Tension, or the feeling that comes from the potential for conflict, can also be portrayed through terse dialogue, sound effects or contrasting images in a film. A visual artist might use jagged forms and unsettling, abrasive colors, or incorporate text and other elements to disrupt a simple reading of the image.

- **Other relevant features** These could range from the particular genre, text type, or style, to specifics like assonance, alliteration, font size, rhythm, or rhyme. A story within a story, overlapping narratives, or a sense that something is going on outside the visible field in a film or photograph are just some of the devices that a work of art in any form might use to propel the story or capture our attention. Sometimes, works of art and literature (like people) play tricks on us just to show that what is going on (like events in real life) is not always clear on first reading.

You may find it useful to refer to a dictionary of literary terms. Your teacher may give you an alternative list, focusing on some of the most commonly occurring features. No list of features will cover all aspects of a critical analysis, and/or how to apply them, but sometimes the very act of naming them will inspire you to come up with an appropriate range of responses.

Activity

Applying your analysis

Using some of the steps suggested, consider the list of the many possible features in a text. Write a one-page commentary on the two texts below, also in response to the following questions:

- What is being shown or said in the texts? Why are the texts interesting?
- What do you think and feel about the texts?
- What particular elements in the texts have led you to your conclusions?

Text 1

A film still from *Fallen Angel* (Dir. Otto Preminger, 1945).

Text 2

I went quickly away from her down the room and out and down the tiled staircase to the front hall. I didn't see anybody when I left. I found my hat alone this time. Outside, the bright gardens had a haunted look, as though small wild eyes were watching me from behind the bushes, as though the sunshine itself had a mysterious something in its light. I got into my car and drove off down the hill.

What did it matter where you lay once you were dead? In a dirty sump or in a marble tower on top of a high hill? You were dead, you were sleeping the big sleep, you were not bothered by things like that. Oil and water were the same as wind and air to you. You just slept the big sleep, not caring about the nastiness of how you died or where you fell. Me, I was part of the nastiness now. Far more a part of it than Rusty Regan was. But the old man didn't have to be. He could lie quiet in his canopied bed, with his bloodless hands folded on the sheet, waiting. His heart was a brief, uncertain murmur. His thoughts were as gray as ashes. And in a little while he too, like Rusty Regan, would be sleeping the big sleep.

On the way downtown I stopped at a bar and had a couple of double Scotches. They didn't do me any good. All they did was make me think of Silver Wig, and I never saw her again.

Source: Chandler, Raymond. 1939. *The Big Sleep*. Knopf/ Doubleday, New York, 2002. pp. 231–32.

What does it mean?

Faced with a difficult text? A confusing abstract image? An advertisement that you just don't get? Try picking one line or one element (such as a sentence, or a symbol) in an image or text to think about.

- What is striking, interesting, confusing, strange, emotional or funny about it?
- What *could* it mean in relation to the whole work?

You may be on your way to thinking about what the text is saying, why it is interesting, or how it has been put together in an original way.

Marking a text

Taking notes while reading is one of the best ways to ensure that you are being an active reader. If you are working from a photocopy, or print-out, or your own personal copy of the book, you can mark-up the text, or write notes in the margin. If you wonder what something means, write a question in the margin. If you ask something like "How is the short sentence related to what the character said before?" you are forcing yourself to make connections and to push to conclusions. If you ask a number of questions, the next logical step would be to come up with possible answers. Marking a text can also involve simply underlining or highlighting particular passages that you wish to return to later.

If you are in the habit of marking-up a text you will find that your system can get quite elaborate. One benefit of always reading with a pen is that when you have a good idea or are inspired about a possible writing topic, you can write it down immediately. Some students find that a structured method of color marking can help them when approaching a passage. You could highlight all of the adjectives in one color (hopefully in a small passage) and the verbs in another, or a more specific object that they might refer to. Color-marking elements that relate to your topic can help you when it comes to pulling out quotations from a document that takes up many pages. As with all systems for literary analysis, be careful not to pre-judge what you are looking for, and cloud an authentic reading by trying to adhere too closely to your plan. It is not great to highlight elements of setting if this is the least important element in the narrative. Highlighting an adjective is useless if you are not considering the particular effect of the word in its role as a carrier of the emotional expression or descriptive power of the subject or scene in question.

Marking-up texts

Below are three passages for comment that have been marked-up by student readers. Read the passage and examine the marking and comments in the margins. Is it possible to recognize what the person was thinking through the evidence of their marking and other notations? How useful does this marking look to you? What would you add or change in your own notes to the texts? You may want to take some notes while you read through the passages.

Example 1

I quickly straightened my collar and tie, licked my hair flat to show off my part, <u>because</u> <u>I knew that in these circumstances a straight line on the side of one's head was not devoid</u> <u>of meaning</u>. The line, God knows why, <u>was something modern</u>. As I crossed the dining room I picked up a toothpick from the table, and I appeared before her (the phone was in the anteroom), emerging nonchalantly on the threshold, and, leaning with my shoulder against the door, I stood there. I quietly bent forward with my entire being, still chewing on the toothpick. <u>A modern toothpick</u>. Don't think that it was easy to stand there, a toothpick in my mouth pretending that I was at ease while everything within me was still paralyzed, to be aggressive while inwardly remaining deathly passive.

    In the meantime, Miss Youngblood was talking to her girlfriend.

    "No, not necessarily, hell, sure, go with her, no, not with him, the photo, what fun, I'm sorry—wait a minute."

    She put down the receiver and asked me:

    "Do you want to make a phone call?"

She said this in a sociable, cool tone, quite as if it wasn't me she had kicked. I shook my head. I wanted her to realize that I was here for no other reason than: <u>"it's just you</u> <u>and me, I have the right to stand in the door while you're making a phone call</u>, I'm your comrade in (modernity) and your (contemporary), <u>and, do understand, Miss Youngblood,</u> <u>that any explanations between us are superfluous, that I can join you, standing on no</u> <u>ceremony, it's as simple as that</u>." I was risking a great deal because, had she asked for an explanations, I would have been hard pressed to explain anything, and this horribly artificial situation would have immediately forced me to retreat.

Source: Gombrowicz, Witold (trans. Borchardt, Danuta). *Ferdydurke*. New Haven: Yale University Press. p. 120.

Comments

This student didn't do too much in terms of marking. But it is clear that he or she has noticed some possibly interesting or troubling attributes in the passage. There are two further steps for the student to take: first, look for a pattern in what has been highlighted—a question about the difference between modernity and contemporary would be good. More detailed notes about the obvious features of the passage might help: notes to explain what is going on, the attitudes of the characters, or the point of view of the narrator. Sometimes we underline out of habit or instinct because we have noticed something odd or interesting. We must consider what called our attention to them and how they relate to the work or passage as a whole.

Example 2

I quickly straightened my collar and tie, licked my hair flat to show off my part, because I knew that in these circumstances a straight line on the side of one's head was not devoid of meaning. The line, God knows why, was something modern. As I crossed the dining room I picked up a toothpick from the table, and I appeared before her (the phone was in the anteroom), emerging nonchalantly on the threshold, and, leaning with my shoulder against the door, I stood there. I quietly bent forward with my entire being, still chewing on the toothpick. A modern toothpick. Don't think that it was easy to stand there, a toothpick in my mouth pretending that I was at ease while everything within me was still paralyzed, to be aggressive while inwardly remaining deathly passive.

In the meantime, Miss Youngblood was talking to her girlfriend.

"No, not necessarily, hell, sure, go with her, no, not with him, the photo, what fun, I'm sorry—wait a minute."

She put down the receiver and asked me:

"Do you want to make a phone call?"

adjective all
focus on attitude
narrator
wants to have

She said this in a sociable, cool tone, quite as if it wasn't me she had kicked. I shook my head. I wanted her to realize that I was here for no other reason than: "it's just you and me, I have the right to stand in the door while you're making a phone call, I'm your comrade in modernity and your contemporary, and, do understand, Miss Youngblood, that any explanations between us are superfluous, that I can join you, standing on no ceremony, it's as simple as that." I was risking a great deal because, had she asked for an explanations, I would have been hard pressed to explain anything, and this horribly artificial situation would have immediately forced me to retreat.

- *Narrator unsure in actions*
- *Girl doesn't care – we can tell from her speech*

Comments

While this marking is somewhat limiting as it focuses only on adjectives and verbs, there are a couple of interesting thoughts in the margin. This is a good case of where more thinking and note-taking would have been more helpful than sticking rigidly to a system. The adjectives do suggest some interesting things about the narrator and the character of the girl. The actions of the narrator are also telling. But the notes could deal with other attributes of the passage and could also differentiate between the types of adjectives, what they are being used to describe, and how they relate to other elements in the passage.

Example 3

Appearance or totally planned

matters that this is a modern novel?

Is he commenting on his own attitude as an artist?

Or more about youth and inexp.?

Modern or mean?

I quickly straightened my collar and tie, licked my hair flat to show off my part, because I knew that in these circumstances a straight line on the side of one's head was not devoid of meaning. The line, God knows why, was something modern. As I crossed the dining room I picked up a toothpick from the table, and I appeared before her (the phone was in the anteroom), emerging nonchalantly on the threshold and, leaning with my shoulder against the door, I stood there. I quietly bent forward with my entire being, still chewing on the toothpick. A modern toothpick. Don't think that it was easy to stand there, a toothpick in my mouth pretending that I was at ease while everything within me was still paralyzed, to be aggressive while inwardly remaining deathly passive. Contradiction?

In the meantime, Miss Youngblood was talking to her girlfriend.

"No, not necessarily, hell, sure, go with her, no, not with him, the photo, what fun, I'm sorry—wait a minute."

She put down the receiver and asked me:

"Do you want to make a phone call?"

Idea of Modernity: nonchalance, coolness, natural (actions done without thinking)

Contradiction between his will of appearing modern that makes the narrator uneasy and the concept of modernity

She said this in a sociable, cool tone, quite as if it wasn't me she had kicked. I shook my head. I wanted her to realize that I was here for no other reason than: "it's just you and me, I have the right to stand in the door while you're making a phone call, I'm your comrade in modernity and your contemporary, and, do understand, Miss Youngblood, that any explanations between us are superfluous, that I can join you, standing on no ceremony, it's as simple as that." I was risking a great deal because, had she asked for an explanations, I would have been hard pressed to explain anything, and this horribly artificial situation would have immediately forced me to retreat.

Comments

This is the most-developed mark-up of the three examples. The colors seem to make some clear distinctions, and the connections being drawn are more obvious. The remarks in the margin articulate more directly questions about the meaning and importance of the passage. There still, however, may be elements worth noting beyond this marking.

Now it's your turn!

Look at some of the notes you have taken on your own. Now go back to some of the lists or suggestions earlier in the chapter. Are there other elements in this passage that you might consider? What stands out for you? Try writing a brief response to the passage, and how you went about analyzing it and prioritizing your concerns.

A creative response

Write your own version of an awkward situation or encounter. Perhaps you experienced a similar situation at school or in another setting.

● Decide on the mannerisms and habits of your two main characters and the nature of the confrontation. How do they react to each other?

● What do our perception of gesture and the tone or manner in which people speak reveal about a person's thoughts or feelings?

Developing your skills

The best way to develop your skills in critical awareness is to be attentive to all of the language that surrounds you. It is important to read, view, listen and consider the way the text is approached. Even thinking about a TV show that you frequently watch can help you to develop your skills as a reader and thinker. If a show is funny, think about what *exactly* made you laugh—was it the focus on a character's reaction? The way a line was said? Was it the peculiar manipulation or distortion of familiar words and expressions? If you think of the first funny movie that comes to your mind, and think of one particularly amusing moment, you are sure to see that it is not only what is said but how it is said in a particular context that matters.

When thinking about any communicative act, an important part of the process of thinking is responding. It is difficult to clarify ideas or emotions surrounding a text if we do not somehow try to articulate them to another person. Luckily we often have friends or family with whom to share our experiences of a film. Compare notes with your friends, by discussing articles, or your responses to the texts you encounter in a journal or in a blog. Reading and responding, and participating in group discussions will help you become a more active reader.

From reading to writing

Responding to a work goes hand in hand with critical reading. But it is very difficult to think clearly about a work or to evaluate it if we do not organize our thoughts and put them into words. There are a variety of ways to respond to a text. Making notes is a first step. A further step, a more formal response, is to respond by writing down your thoughts in a journal or a blog, or participating in class discussions. You can respond to a text in an essay or a letter, or take a more creative approach by responding in kind with another story or image of your own devising to make further links. Study the charts below to help you to clarify the elements that go into critical reading and writing.

Showing critical reading in your writing/speaking

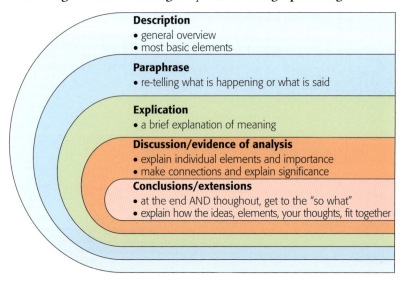

Description
- general overview
- most basic elements

Paraphrase
- re-telling what is happening or what is said

Explication
- a brief explanation of meaning

Discussion/evidence of analysis
- explain individual elements and importance
- make connections and explain significance

Conclusions/extensions
- at the end AND thoughout, get to the "so what"
- explain how the ideas, elements, your thoughts, fit together

Writing for purpose and clarity

First, it is important to always aim for clarity. Some student writers feel a need to write as if they have swallowed a thesaurus and this can sometimes lead to a lack of clarity rather than impressive variation. While it is important to use words as exactly as possible and it can be important to use correct literary or linguistic terms, it is much more important to communicate your ideas to a reader. Simple words used correctly are more effective than "big words" used incorrectly or in a way that obfuscates rather than clarifies. In this same vein, it is important to use good diction, or a general register of terminology that is appropriate for the type of text you are writing and the supposed audience of your text (in an essay this might be an examiner or a teacher but often your audience is your peers or an imagined audience). Using complex language to appear smarter often has the opposite effect, if you don't fully understand the concepts. Consider the following advice from Sheridan Blau:

> My own cautionary rule for students … is to 'try to sound as dumb as you are.' It's a maxim that can work well … because it functions as a therapeutic double bind. That is, if you try to sound as dumb as you are, you won't really have to try at all. You will simply trust your own voice and not give any attention to trying to sound any particular way. Your attention will then be free to focus on your ideas and getting them straight and clear and not on how they sound. And if that's where you put your focus, you'll surely produce prose that is a good deal smarter than it would be if you were trying to sound smart. By trying to sound as dumb as you are, in other words, you allow yourself (without trying) to also sound as smart as you are. And that is as well as any of us can do.

After choosing a type of production, consider the general "rules" of the text type chosen to establish your purpose. We will consider this at greater length in later chapters but essentially you should consider models in your writing, speaking, and producing. Are you going to give a mock political speech? Then listen to some actual speeches by politicians. Are you writing a short story? Are you attempting to make a film trailer for a hypothetical movie version of a work you have read? Take some notes on the format you will need to follow.

Plan, plan, plan, outline, and plan again. In all types of production, effective planning achieves results. The hardest part of writing is thinking about what to write and considering approaches. If you are actively reading and taking notes, part of your job is already done. You will need to decide how much time you have to complete your assignment but once you consider these time constraints, you should immediately start brainstorming. Even if you are in an exam situation, your careful reading of a question or passage should lead right into a period of planning before putting words on the page. Every type of work can benefit from an outline whether you jot down a few main points before an exam essay or create an elaborate storyboard for a film.

A nonfiction text can usually be broken down into an introduction, body (or main section), and conclusion. This applies to all types of writing. Let the reader or viewer have an idea of what you are trying to do or where you are trying to go (introduction), then take us through the development of your idea, argument, or story (body), and then let us know that you are finished (and have not just left the work suddenly incomplete). Reread and revise the text on completion. Spend some time looking over what you have produced. Once again, you are aiming for clarity and precision. In terms of organization you should also try to determine if the order of your argument or presentation makes sense or progresses logically. You should also be sure that there is a smooth transition from one idea to the next.

Conclusion

This last section of the chapter was meant to be a way for you to move from very broad theoretical considerations in the study of language and literature to the practical concerns of approaching texts and communicating your findings. The theoretical underpinnings and the simple, practical base prepare you for the more focused work ahead. We hope that the discussions here have prepared you both to think about your study metacognitively as you would naturally do in a theory of knowledge course, and to quite directly get the work done. We hope that the following chapters will be fun to explore and offer a sound approach to the language and literature course as a whole.

The use of first person

Why is it that some teachers tell you not to use "I" in an essay or other formal writing? While in some disciplines it may be considered inappropriate to use the first person (think of a science lab report), this is not unusual in a literature course. Forcing yourself to use an artificial, supposedly academic tone can often hinder communication and lead to awkward constructions. One simple reason some teachers suggest not using "I" is that its overuse can become repetitive and writing "I think" over and over again can be a case of stating the obvious. But as the scholar and teacher Sheridan Blau has noted the rule against the first person is usually regarded as a "misguided" secondary school practice and is almost never taken up by university instructors. In addition, Blau has noted that even a brief survey of professional literary criticism will reveal that a majority of scholars employ the use of first person.

Reading for cultural context

Ganga or Gayle: Who Will Lead the Windies

By Tony Cozier

It is a fitting irony that Daren Ganga should have, in the space of a couple of weeks, suddenly returned as a credible candidate as West Indies skipper through his leadership in the shortest form of the game, even more so since the principal claimant to reclaiming the post is Chris Gayle. The two are closely linked in the ever changing story of the captaincy.

Ganga, based on his influence in bringing Trinidad and Tobago from near bottom to the top in regional cricket within a few years, was placed to lead West Indies 'A' teams on tour and in two Tests in England in 2007 when deputy to the injured Ramnaresh Sarwan before Gayle came into the picture.

Gayle was first elevated for the three ODIs on the same England tour only because of Sarwan's absence and Ganga's perceived inability as a limited-overs batsman. Even then, Gayle's nomination by the selectors was initially rejected by a West Indies Cricket Board (WICB) executive committee dubious of his suitability. In the end, under pressure, it had to make an embarrassing U-turn.

Now, on the eve of a tour of Australia for three Tests, the two Gs, so different in every way, are again the names most prominent among the public's short-list of who should be at the helm.

Gayle was the incumbent before he and all those players originally chosen for the series against Bangladesh walked out two days before the first Test to press the West Indies Players Association (WIPA) case in its long-running disputes over contracts with the West Indies Cricket Board. Through a tenuous agreement that had to be brokered by Caricom politicians, the issues are now supposedly settled and the aggrieved players are all once more available for selection.

Gayle has asserted that he is ready to resume his role, stating that 'it is always an honour to captain the West Indies'.

Ganga has sensibly made no mention of such ambitions. He has simply once more come to the fore following his universally-praised leadership during Trinidad and Tobago's advance to Friday's final of the global Twenty20 Champions League final in India, paradoxically the kind of cricket that cost him the West Indies captaincy in the first place. He is now being promoted, inside and outside of Trinidad and Tobago, as the one needed to instill the same discipline, unity and pride shown by his team in India.

There can be no doubt that he has special qualities of leadership. As astute a judge as Ian Chappell alluded to it in the television commentary. Given the responsibility at whatever level, he will hardly shirk from it ...

Source: Cozier, Tony. "Ganga or Gayle: Who Will Lead the Windies," *The Trinidad and Tobago Express.* October 25, 2009.

Questions to the text

1   What are the main points of the article?
2   Are there ideas or concepts that are difficult for you to understand?
3   Do you know the sport being played? The particular sporting terms?

4   Regardless of the sport or your knowledge of it, do you understand the main concern?

5   For whom is this article written?

6   Are there nuances that this particular audience would understand that you wouldn't?

7   Are there particular words or terms you don't understand? How could some of these have significance to the intended audience?

8   Do you think this is an important issue? Is this issue important to the audience? Why do you think so?

9   Did individual words or terms make it difficult for you to understand this article? What were these words? Were they all related to cricket?

10 Were there references in the article that you didn't understand? Were they related to cricket? A particular nation? A team? Particular people?

11 Now consider what aspects of your own background and language use may have made this article either relevant and interesting or perhaps confusing and foreign: nationality, personal interests or hobbies, race, gender, class etc.

The purpose of this chapter is to examine the ways in which language and culture are interconnected. It is often difficult to isolate the study of language from social practice. After all, language is a discursive practice—it is our means of communicating with other people and so in many ways it can be viewed as a social act, an act that has the power to shape culture. Start with the above activity. When you have read the newspaper article, answer the questions that follow. It may be helpful to do this activity, like all of the activities in this book, with a partner or class group.

In your study of language there are times when you will be called upon to look at the minutiae of the text. In the classroom you may consider the ways in which sounds are made in speech, or the grammatical differences between different dialects of English. You may also be studying language from a broader perspective, considering the history of English or regional variations in the language. Some of your reading will directly address more social and cultural aspects of language, covering any number of issues from language acquisition in children to the uses of language in political campaigns. In addition to this specific study of language, or academic theories of language usage, you will also be looking at a wide variety of texts—including speeches, songs, newspaper articles, diaries, blogs, SMS chats, essays, photographs, posters, restaurant menus, and billboards. In your reading, you will be asked to do two jobs: to interrogate the opinions of others in relation to language and culture; and, by examining language in context, to come to your own conclusions about the way language is used.

While the Latin term most commonly used for humans is *homo sapiens*, we are also rightly known as *homo loquens*. We think, define ourselves, make ourselves known, and relate to others through language. It is important to consider how language is used in interesting and special ways in different types of texts. It will be important to consider individual words, terms, and patterns, as well as the use of language as a communicative, social act, aimed at a particular audience. The texts you will read in this book, in class, along with those you encounter in everyday life, may require you to examine multiple viewpoints, or to consider viewpoints not represented. Communication acts are also about establishing power relationships. In this section you will work towards the following understandings in relation to language:

- **Language changes in relationship to time and place**
  Language is not only a broad and challenging subject to study but is an intriguing area of study partly because of its wide variation. In this section you will be asked to consider language that is very familiar to you and varieties of English that might be unfamiliar or even surprising. At any one given point in time, language can vary significantly from place to place and person to person, as it has throughout history and across different cultures.

- **Language, culture and context determine the ways in which meaning is constructed in texts** Language can be seen as the most basic tool for social interaction. It is not only a means for describing culture, but is part and parcel of the customs, traditions, and beliefs that we call culture. If something—from a poster for a circus, to a bottle of wine, to a short story—has meaning, it is because it is somehow related to a time, place, and language that we can at least partially understand.

- **Meaning comes from complex interactions between text (or speech, or image), audience, and purpose** Language is necessarily communicative. Even if you are alone in your room talking to yourself or sitting quietly composing a blog entry, you are communicating with yourself, thinking though language, modelling your ideas on something or someone else, or preparing to present them to your intended audience. Because, for most of us, language is an almost seamless connection between thought and our interaction with others, the words we use and the statements we make in speech and writing tell us about who we are or want to be, and can give us insight into the workings of our minds. By considering the ways in which language is both "sent" and "received" you will hone your abilities to interpret the wide variety of texts in your world.

The language and literature syllabus covers a broad range of topics related to cultural issues that involve language or are, in fact, created by language use. Your teacher may use topics suggested in the guide or design their topics around the specific interests of your class or group, or broader areas of investigation relevant to your cultural context. You will find that issues in one area overlap with issues in another. Is it possible, for example, to talk about identity as an area of investigation without considering ethnicity or gender? In addition, a specific area of investigation (as in environmental studies) may require you to analyze the way the news media has picked up on certain terms that reflect current sensitivities or topical issues.

For the purposes of this book, we have decided to give examples of ways in which you may approach a broad area of investigation. We have intentionally picked important, perhaps overarching, areas so that you may find that areas you have studied in other courses are reflected in the topics we have chosen. Along the way, we have also tried to make some suggestions about how your own study can be broadened. While we have presented in this section texts about particular subjects other than language itself (as in the news article on cricket that you have just read), we have purposefully chosen passages that are also specifically about language issues and debates in society. From thinking about the ways in which language and knowledge are connected, and looking at issues that are closely connected to theory of knowledge, we will move to language and communities. Community takes us naturally to issues of identity, covered in the next section of readings.

Language and knowledge

Language is not an abstract construction of the learned, or of dictionary-makers, but is something arising out of the work, needs, ties, joys, affections, tastes, of long generations of humanity, and has its bases broad and low, close to the ground.

Walt Whitman

When we study human language, we are approaching what some might call the "human essence," the distinctive qualities of mind that are, so far as we know, unique to man.

Noam Chomsky

Among linguists, philosophers and biologists, the possession of language, perhaps more than any other attribute, distinguishes humans from other animals. In other words, we become "human" because we know language. Our ability to express emotions, maintain friendships, develop intellectual and social interests and even professional occupations are all rooted in language. But as our humanity is directly associated with language, it does beg the question of how, or how much, our knowledge of ourselves and the world around us is dependent upon or affected by language.

By now, you are very aware of some of the shortcomings of linguistic determinism. Our thoughts and perceptions are not determined only by the words or grammars that we know: we are not preprogrammed by whatever language we speak. Recent studies do, however, point toward a clear *influence* that language has on our cognition. Advertisements point to "new and improved" products that powerfully affect our purchases of products even as we believe we are conscious and aware of such marketing tactics. Politicians refer to "welfare" for the people or "hand-outs" depending on what values they wish to convey. Even as students, you use a different language when producing a formal essay in your English class that may be inappropriate in a more personal discussion on the same topic (such as love) with friends, recognizing also that discussions on different kinds of knowledge and the relationship to lived experience require different kinds of language. All of these cases suggest a connection between language and knowledge, as well as social context. This idea is carried further in the work of George Lakoff and Mark Johnson who argue that language is directly related to experience through metaphor. On the very first page of their book *Metaphors We Live By*, Lakoff and Johnson begin with the following:

Metaphor is for most people a device of the poetic imagination and the rhetorical flourish …We have found, on the contrary, that metaphor is pervasive in everyday life, not just in language but in thought and

Key questions about language and cultural context

The following questions do not necessarily have an answer, but they may guide your approach to this section of the course:

- Is the ability to acquire language innate or learned?
- Are some languages more or less difficult to learn than other languages?
- Is class a more important factor in language variation than geography?
- Are changes in language directly related to the power of a group of language users?
- Can the biases towards particular language usage be unlearned?
- Does language shape culture or culture shape language?
- If language is an integral part of knowledge, can we really know and understand language?
- Can we understand texts that are written for different audiences in different times or cultures?
- Does the language of new media corrupt communication and culture?
- Should minority languages be saved from extinction?
- Should governments have a language policy for a particular nation?
- Does language define our identity?
- Do our beliefs influence our language use?

action. Our ordinary conceptual system, in terms of which we both think and act, is fundamentally metaphorical in nature.

The concepts that govern our thought are not just matters of the intellect. They also govern our everyday functioning, down to the most mundane details. Our concepts structure what we perceive, how we get around in the world, and how we relate to other people. Our conceptual system thus plays a central role in defining our everyday realities. If we are right in suggesting that our conceptual system in largely metaphorical, then the way we think, what we experience, and what we do every day is very much a matter of metaphor

Language and knowledge, as a suggested topic in the language and literature course, also clearly introduces central concerns intrinsic to this course of study in the widest possible sense. Any knowledge one possesses that involves abstract thought relies on language. Thus, consciously or not, we are all engaged in producing, consuming and critiquing the world around us in language. Considerations about either knowledge or language are interwoven in symbiotic fashion requiring that any consideration of one demands questions of the other. The answer to questions such as "Who are you?" or "What do you do?" necessarily involve multiple social identities and each identity has consequences for the kind of language (or metaphors) we use. As David Crystal notes, "it is usually language which is the chief signal of both permanent and transient aspects of our social identity." Beliefs, values, understandings and occupations are just some of the myriad identities and knowledges constructed in and around the language or languages that we use.

Jargon and argot

In some cases, certain subsets of knowledge (e.g. law, science, politics, sports) overtly develop their own specialized language or terminology, sometimes called **jargon** or **argot**. Reasons for such specialization range from a desire to belong to a larger social or professional group to the need for clarity in communications. Jargon may be considered a type of slang or a type of specialized technical language, particular to a social group. For instance, while "spaced out," "hang" or "lol" may be widespread and easily understood by people of a certain age group or social clique, this "teen argot" is viewed as slang while the arguably even less-penetrable "sjuzet," "diegesis" and "metalepsis" are recognized as technically appropriate terms for professional literary theorists. However, whether viewed as slang or more formally accepted (proscriptive) language, even these two examples highlight the interrelationship between social and knowledge issues. In an extended version of the argument, two teenage friends emailing one another using the professional discourse of literary theory become, in fact, not just "teenage friends" but professional colleagues. Finally, although there is a tendency to draw clear distinctions between specialized terminologies (and social identities/knowledge), of course language is always shifting and jargon is subject to change: jargon terms pass into standard usage as they come to be embraced and understood by a larger segment of a population.

For the purposes of this chapter, we will focus on language and knowledge issues in relationship to a few specific areas of specialist

Jargon is the vocabulary peculiar to a particular profession or group.

Argot is a specialized vocabulary particular to a class or group, especially one devised for private communication.

knowledge (using the examples of medicine, law and sport), although it should be evident that these are just selective examples of topics that could be covered. You are encouraged to consider language and knowledge issues in your own life and throughout the course regardless of the specific topics covered here.

Legal language

An interesting case study for the relation of language and knowledge is in the use of legal language. Legal language is meant to be clear statements of rules to regulate the behaviour of members of society and to protect the rights of those members. Legal language affects the way we conduct relationships, the way we come to understand our roles and the way we formulate our values because it quite literally puts these aspects in writing. Law is an act of language that has been given official status by a governmental system. Because laws are meant to be binding and regulatory, legal language attempts to be as clear and specific as possible. On the other hand, legal language is also always open to interpretation and debate because it can never be as clear, precise and concrete as it is intended to be. As David Crystal points out in *The Cambridge Encyclopedia of the English Language,* legal language is unique in being required to respond to a variety of contradictory demands and functions:

> Legal language is always being pulled in different directions. Its statements have to be so phrased that we can see their general applicability, yet be specific enough to apply to individual circumstances. They have to be stable enough to stand the test of time … yet flexible enough to adapt to new social situations. Above all, they have to be expressed in such a way that people can be certain about the intention of the law respecting their rights and duties. No other variety of language has to carry such a responsibility.

Many factors of legal language highlight its complicated role in knowledge and understanding:

- **Legal language is conservative** Authority in law requires relying on legal statements that have already been accepted by governing bodies and tested in the courts. This may encourage the continued use of archaic language that no longer holds meaning for the general public. Because of this, it is not easy or often desirable to create or dismantle laws.

- **Legal language employs highly technical terminology** The use of specific legal terms facilitates communication within a very particular group but this can undermine accessibility to the general public that it is meant to serve.

- **Legal language often has strategic aims** Law can be used to further political, economic or social aims of powerful groups. While insurance laws, for example, may protect the consumer in difficult times, certain laws may be constructed to protect financial interests of insurance corporations. These aims can sometimes be in conflict. This can even be true in a courtroom where attorneys may use language to argue less about law and legal transgressions than creating sympathy or simply convincing a judge or a jury.

- **Legal language is inherently adversarial** Legal language attempts to solidify one particular side of an argument and therefore can always be argued against.

Discussion Point

Different voices

An element that we sometimes look for in lively, engaging writing is voice. Voice can be described as the tone, attitude, or even personality of a writer revealing itself in a piece. Do you think voice is a function of personality or word choice or both? How easily can you change your voice and how desirable is this?

Consider the varieties of writing you produce in an average day or week. In what ways do you have a common *voice* across different language mediums (e.g. in the comparison between text messages and class essays, or emails you write to teachers in comparison to emails you send to friends)? In what ways is your *voice* different? In what ways can you recognize yourself as essentially *the same*?

What does the idea of common or separate voices suggest about who we are in the world, and how we adapt our language usage?

All of this is to say that the law affects what we know and understand. Legal language attempts to inscribe our beliefs and values but because it is *language*, law is never a completely firm grounding for knowledge and understanding.

Read the following sample disclaimer for the use of company email, an example that is probably similar to many other messages we ignore on a regular basis.

> Communications on or through [company department] may be monitored or recorded to secure effective system operation and for other lawful purposes. Unless otherwise agreed expressly in writing by [company], this communication is to be treated as confidential and the information in it may not be used or disclosed except for the purpose for which it has been sent. If you have reason to believe that you are not the intended recipient of this communication, please contact the sender immediately. No employee or agent is authorized to conclude any binding agreement on behalf of [company] with another party by e-mail without express written confirmation by [company].
>
> Employees of [company] are required not to make any defamatory statements and not to infringe or authorize any infringement of copyright or any other legal right by e-mail communications. Any such communication is contrary to organisational policy and outside the scope of the employment of the individual concerned. [Company] will not accept any liability in respect of such a communication, and the employee responsible will be personally liable for any damages or other liability arising.

Is this legal language meant to protect the individual? Protect the company? Does the language clarify rights and expectations? What specific penalties could result from transgressions?

Activity

Mother Goose hires an attorney

1 Take a nursery rhyme such as "Jack and Jill" or "Humpty Dumpty" and parody it by rewriting the account in legal language.

2 Take a simple issue and debate, working hard to attend to all present and future possibilities, to accurately reflect the standards of scientific research.

3 Find a sample of legal language from an historical document, disclaimer or brief. Does meaning become clearer or less clear in legal language? How?

4 Find a simple advertisement and recreate it as three different versions using the languages of sport, the law and a scientific laboratory. How do they compare?

Scientific language

Similar to legal language, the language of medicine and science can be highly technical: facilitating understanding within a professional community but possibly confusing the general public. Considering the discussion of legal language above, look at the following examples from medicine and science and explore the ways in which the language highlights both precision and ambiguity. Like legal terminology, medical and scientific language can be unintentionally mystifying and adversarial.

Advances in medicine

Read the following two articles concerned with medicine or medical advances.
What are the intentions of the two texts? What does the language used tell you
about the nature of the findings, the advances, or medicine in general?

Text 1

Following is a text by an agency of the US government health department on the condition known as Fibromyalgia

---

| Home | Health Information | Research | Funding | News & Events | About Us | Portal en español | | Search |

You are here: Home > Health_Info > Fibromyalgia > Fast Facts About Fibromyalgia

Health Information

Fibromyalgia

Find a Clinical Trial

Journal Articles

What Is Fibromyalgia?

Fast Facts: An Easy-to-Read Series of Publications for the Public

Fibromyalgia is a disorder that causes muscle pain and fatigue (feeling tired). People with fibromyalgia have "tender points" on the body. Tender points are specific places on the neck, shoulders, back, hips, arms, and legs. These points hurt when pressure is put on them.

People with fibromyalgia may also have other symptoms, such as:

- Trouble sleeping
- Morning stiffness
- Headaches
- Painful menstrual periods
- Tingling or numbness in hands and feet
- Problems with thinking and memory (sometimes called "fibro fog").

What Causes Fibromyalgia?

The causes of fibromyalgia are unknown. There may be a number of factors involved. Fibromyalgia has been linked to:

- Stressful or traumatic events, such as car accidents
- Repetitive injuries
- Illness
- Certain diseases.

Fibromyalgia can also occur on its own.

Some scientists think that a gene or genes might be involved in fibromyalgia. The genes could make a person react strongly to things that other people would not find painful.

How Is Fibromyalgia Treated?

Fibromyalgia can be hard to treat. It's important to find a doctor who is familiar with the disorder and its treatment. Many family physicians, general internists, or rheumatologists can treat fibromyalgia. Rheumatologists are doctors who specialize in arthritis and other conditions that affect the joints or soft tissues.

Fibromyalgia treatment often requires a team approach. The team may include your doctor, a physical therapist, and possibly other health care providers. A pain or rheumatology clinic can be a good place to get treatment.

What Can I Do to Try to Feel Better?

There are many things you can do to feel better, including:

- Taking medicines as prescribed
- Getting enough sleep
- Exercising
- Eating well
- Making work changes if necessary.

Source: "Facts about Fibromyalgia," NIAMS (National Institute of Arthritis and Musculoskeletal and Skin Diseases), part of the National Institutes of Health, Department of Health and Human Services website. Updated 2009. http://www.niams.nih.gov/Health_Info/Fibromyalgia/fibromyalgia_ff.asp. Accessed 04/03/2011.

Text 2

This is from a newspaper article published in the *International Herald Tribune*.

Successes fuel hope for gene therapy resurgence

Not long ago, gene therapy seemed troubled by insurmountable difficulties.

After decades of hype and dashed hopes, many who once embraced the idea of correcting genetic disorders by giving people new genes all but gave up the idea.

But scientists say gene therapy may be on the edge of a resurgence. There were three recent, though small, successes …

But given the history of gene therapy, some, like Mark Kay, a gene therapy researcher at Stanford, were careful to avoid promising too much.

The field was dealt a blow when the first gene therapy success, reported six years ago, turned out to be a problem. Eighteen of 20 children with a rare genetic disease were cured, but then three of the children developed leukemia and one died of it. Researchers and gene therapy companies became skittish.

"I like to be really cautious," Dr. Kay said. But now, he added, "there is a lot of reasonably cautious optimism."

The latest encouraging news arises from a paper published Friday in the journal Science. An international team of researchers is reporting the successful treatment of two children with adrenoleukodystrophy, or A.L.D., in which the fatty insulation of nerve cells dengenerates. A result is progressive brain damage and death two to five years after diagnosis.

Scientists say they believe they avoided the cancer problem by using a different method to get genes into the children's DNA. Two years have gone by, and the children are doing well.

The children were not cured, but their disease was arrested. And gene therapy was as good as the standard treatment, a bone marrow transplant. In this case, the children could not have a transplant because they did not have marrow donors who were genetic matches.

In addition, a paper last month in the journal Lancet reported that a different method of gene therapy, which did not involve inserting a new gene in DNA, partly restored the sight of five children and seven adults with a rare congenital eye disease, Leber's congenital amourosis. People with the disease have a mutated gene that prevents them from making a retina protein.

And a paper in The New England Journal of Medicine a year ago reported that 8 out of 10 patients with a rare immunological disorder were cured with gene therapy. The method was the same as the one that led to leukemia, and Dr. Cornetta and scientists were still studying why it did not cause cancer in those children. The paper in Science was accompanied by an editorial by Dr. Naldini titled, "A Comeback for Gene Therapy."

Source: "Successes fuel hope for gene therapy resurgence." *International Herald Tribune*. November 7–8, 2009.

Comparing terminology

In comparing the two texts, both can be said to offer medical opinions presented in a furtive or guarded manner.

- Make a list of the different terms each text uses to describe uncertainty. What different rhetorical strategies can you detect in these two texts?

- What is the overall difference in the tone and effect of the language employed?

Discussion Point

The language of the science lab

An experiment is only as good as the lab report that describes it.

Anonymous

Science also employs a specific style of language. The specialized nomenclature and technical jargon is intended to provide objective information in a manner straightforward enough to be shared by a specific community of people. In other words, while frequently written for an audience with some specialized knowledge, it is also intended to be understood by everyone within that audience.

Consider science lab reports you have written in the past. In what ways do they rely on a unique argot and style? How do these traits enhance the experiment? Why or why not would this be inappropriate as a way of discussing a poem in English class?

Discussion Point

Language and the environment

The way we talk about an issue such as global warming affects the way we feel about the issue. Look at the chemical equation for the creation of carbon dioxide from methane and it's more creative rendering as an image.

Which version is more scientifically useful? Which one makes the stronger statement? Which version is most meaningful to you? Do either or both of these seem to meet the demands of scientific language? Why or why not?

$$CH_4 + 2O_2 \rightarrow CO_2 + 2H_2O$$

Language in sport

Quite clearly, we encounter the world beyond intellectual engagement. Sport, for instance, offers a physical and emotional way of knowing and understanding the world. While it may seem obvious to translate our thoughts about morality, values and rights into language (as we do in the realm of law), translating the action of sport into language may not be so easy. Consider, for instance, an interview with a tennis player just after winning a major tournament:

Interviewer	After double-faulting on double-match point, you seemed to take some speed off your second serve going for a lot more spin and just getting the ball in. Though a gamble, was that just to calm your nerves and get back into the point and the game?
Player	No ... I don't know.
Interviewer	But even though you did miss on the serve, you seemed like you were trying to slow the game and control the tempo.
Player	At that time, I wasn't thinking about the point or the moment. I just hit the ball, believing I could hit it like I have many times before.
Interviewer	But then you missed it. Surely you were worried about another double fault.
Player	Of course! After that, I hit the ball in. But when he was out of position for the backhand, I knew I had won.

The athlete here may have a difficult job explaining clearly the nearly mechanical movements that they are able to perform so well on a regular basis. The interviewer's job, however, is to seek to put into words a clear understanding of the often dramatic tensions that comprise at least part of the movement. The language of sport can incorporate contrasting challenges. On the one hand, it can attempt to almost scientifically describe the actions, strategies and expertise in the movements of a game. On the other hand, the good sports journalist understands that the language of sport may need to capture some of the emotional intensity behind and beyond the action.

The language of sport offers both precise analysis and emotional translation. In sports commentary, these poles are frequently recognized and institutionalized in the role of *analyst* and *colour commentator*. An analyst is responsible for technical description of movement and strategy. Most commonly, analysts are former coaches or athletes with substantial insight and knowledge. A colour commentator, on the other hand, is responsible for providing the human interest side. A colour commentator's job is to give background information, describe stories and create an emotional and distinctly human backdrop against which the actions are performed. Perhaps the most interesting aspect of the language of sport, then, is that it combines these two often contradictory aims and intentions.

Read

The most decorated athlete

Consider the introduction to this article about Michael Phelps. Although it describes a highly emotional moment, how does the language rely on metaphors about competition or sport in general to convey effect?

> Down in a basement corner of the Water Cube, everything was chaos. Michael Phelps had just won his eighth gold medal, in the 4 × 100 medley relay, and the world's press was sardined into the mixed zone, a low-ceilinged concrete gauntlet through which swimmers pass after a race. At best the mixed zone is an uninviting place; on this historic Sunday morning it was a mosh pit of outstretched hands holding cameras and voice recorders, of bodies jammed against barricades, a media Olympics in which the main sports were pushing and shoving. And the prize? A glimpse of Phelps after he exited the pool, still dripping water and fresh with victory. Hopefully he would stop for 30 seconds and say something, anything, to answer this question: How on earth did you pull this off?

The Australian relay swimmers came first, in full-relaxation mode, their suits pulled down from the shoulders. The Russians followed, and the great Japanese breaststroker Kosuke Kitajima strolled by, and the crowd pressed forward as Phelps arrived in the narrow passage. Walking next to a woman holding a microphone, trailed by a television crew, he was six feet, four inches of relief, fatigue and quiet joy. His shoulders curled forward, rolling him into the question-mark posture that happens to swimmers when the back muscles take on a life of their own. Asked how it felt to be the first person to win eight gold medals in a single Olympic Games and the most decorated athlete of all time, he smiled and shrugged. "I don't know," he said. "So much emotion going through my head. … I kinda just want to see my mom."

Source: Casey, Susan. "We Are All Witnesses." *Sports Illustrated*. August 25, 2008. pp. 68–73.

Activity

How fast can she go?

Read the following article about the training and progress of a young runner.

Desiree Davila Targeting Chicago and a Fast Time This Fall <<<

Halfway into the 2009 world marathon championship in Berlin, Desiree Davila sat 42 seconds off the lead pack in 1:14:21 and 28th place. No scooter-mounted cameras fed her every stride to dissecting commentators. To the few who observed her—other than her coaches, who knew better—she appeared out of the race, an anonymous Team USA marathoner clicking off solo 5:38 miles.

"She has a quiet confidence about her," says coach Keith Hanson who, with brother Kevin, has coached Davila over her six years as a member of the Hansons-Brooks Distance Project, based in Rochester, Mich. "She doesn't say something she doesn't believe."

Before Berlin, Davila laid down the verbal gauntlet, announcing goals of running a 2:28 and finishing in the top 15, an ambitious prediction considering her PR was 2:31:33 and only one other U.S. woman, Deena Kastor, had placed as high in a world championship or Olympic marathon in the previous decade. But Davila had her reasons.

Earlier that spring, Davila set PRs at 3,000m, 5,000m, and 10,000m. With these accomplishments in her back pockets, Davila and the Hanson brothers were confident of her capabilities.

"It's been almost predictable: If we do x and y, we will achieve z," says Kevin Hanson on how track segments feed the bigger goals of Davila's marathon performance. "Whatever you train her to, she's going to run. [She] comes to the starting line saying, 'I know I can do this well.'"

It's this level of mutual trust and confidence, slowly built over a professional career, that makes Davila and the Hansons an effective team.

Starting at the half of the world championships marathon, Davila launched an assault on the field, negative-splitting the course and gobbling up international competition en route to running 2:27:53—a PR of over 3 and a half minutes—good for 11th in the world, just one place and 5 seconds behind Kara Goucher.

As fall marathon season approaches, Davila eyes another breakthrough performance, but to get to the streets, the Hansons again steered Davila to the source of her previous success, the track.

Since Berlin, Davila has set PRs at 3,000m (8:51), 5,000m (15:29), and 10,000m (32:06), even somewhat improbably donning the Team USA uniform again at the 2010 indoor world championships in Doha, Qatar, where she made the 3,000m final.

"You're not developing if you're racing two marathons a year," Kevin Hanson says. "As soon as you're recovering from your last race, you're starting the next segment. It's why so many marathoners become stale. People sometimes get themselves pigeon-holed in one event. When you do that, it affects your overall development."

The Hanson brothers use track or cross country segments to break up marathon training for their athletes, following a rule of no more than three marathons every two years. For Davila, it has meant the difference between a 2:31 marathon and a 2:27.

"The goal is the 2012 trials," Davila says, unequivocally. "But you have to be well-rounded, and competitive throughout the range of distances."

Davila's track season concluded after the 10,000m at the outdoor national championships on June 24, where she placed 3rd behind Amy Begley and Lisa Koll, and July 3's Prefontaine meet. Then her training shifted toward a fall marathon. Her accomplishments during the spring track season point to another breakthrough marathon, and Davila and the Hansons have decided that nowhere offers a better opportunity to display her fitness than on the flat and fast course of the Chicago Marathon on Oct. 10.

How fast can she go?

"When we chart her progress on the track as we have in the past, we're looking at a couple-minute PR in the marathon," says Kevin Hanson.

"We look for her to be competitive in the 2:25 range," says Keith Hanson. These are tall claims—breaking 2:26 would make Davila the fourth-fastest American in history, behind only Kastor, Joan Benoit Samuelson and Goucher—but so were Davila's predictions for Berlin. Davila isn't one to guess about races; she performs at the level to which she's trained.

"If [my coaches] say 2:25, I know I'll be ready to run it. We'll go after it, and Chicago is a great place to do that," says Davila.

The formula Davila followed to her Berlin race is rolling toward a dynamic performance in the fall, and when it happens, no one will be less surprised than Davila herself.

Source: Gugala, Jon. "Desiree Davila Targeting Chicago and a Fast Time This Fall: Fast Times on the Track Indicate Good Potential on the Roads." *Running Times*. September 2010.

Questions to the text

1 What does the discussion of a technical and planned approach to training suggest about the nature of sport?

2 Is there language in this article that appeals to the emotion in sport?

3 Would you argue that the focus of this article is the athlete, the competition or the training?

How language affects knowledge

This brief section on language and knowledge has focused on a couple of specific jargons. As will have become apparent, certain kinds of knowledge attempt to employ specific kinds of language for a variety of reasons. The reverse can also be true: specific kinds of language engender certain kinds of knowledge. Although there can never be a truly clear line distinguishing knowledge and language, it is important to recognize and consider how understanding, knowledge and intention affect language and how language affects understanding, knowledge and intention.

Activity

Is truth social?

What might be the strengths and limitations of living in a world where "you" are the truth, and the origin of the production of knowledge.

Truth is Social: Humans have always wondered what makes something true. We have imagined truth to come from what the ancients wrote, what our ancestors believed, what repeatable experiments established.

But truth became social—truth as what we collectively think it is, with the most important truths being those about us. The idea of professionally produced, neutral, paid-for-information about situations not related to the self suffered. Blogs, YouTube, Facebook, crowd-sourcing, Wikipedia and Lonely-Girl15 filled the void.

Public and private happenings traded places: the former seemed to bore a new generation. Exhibitionism become a mainstream ethic. "Yes, You," Time Magazine said when it made "you" the person of the year in the middle of the decade. "You control the Information Age. Welcome to your world."

While the "Information Age" may involve information in many forms, there is clearly a link between language and what is argued above as the new knowledge of truth. What might be strengths and limitations to living in a world where one's own production of language becomes truth/knowledge in the world?

Source: Giridharadas, Anand. "Reflections on the start of the 2000s." *International Herald Tribune.* December 5–6, 2009.

Questions to the text

1 What is exhibitionist about the way people behave on social networking sites?

2 Is the focus of attention on everything we do or say empowering or disempowering, or both?

3 What, as Giridharadas asks, might be the strengths and limitations of living in a world where one's own production of language becomes truth/knowledge in the world?

Activity

Researching sports coverage across different sporting cultures

Consider how language is used differently in different sports. For example, what might be the impact of referring to "all-out war" during a boxing match in comparison to "gentlemen's singles" in tennis?

Find a newspaper article on a sport popular in your region. What terms, metaphors and connotations are reflected in the article? Grouping these together, what picture do they describe in terms of the participants, fans and role the particular sport plays in your community. Is it a popular or an elite sport? Where else is it played in the world?

Discussion Point

The medium affects the message

In an era of multiple communication channels, it is not just the language used that can affect knowledge but possibly even the medium of transmission of that language. Does email, for instance, have the same effect as a certified legal document even if the content is the same?

Consider the variety of media in which you communicate and how they affect the language you use. What specific features are unique to differing media and how do they enhance the impact of communication? What effect would mixing communication protocols across different media have?

Politically correct language

Language use can have a powerful social effect. For example, if we treat each other with respect by using more polite language in the classroom we might encourage greater tolerance and risk-taking in the exchange of ideas; the reverse approach would be to treat each other sarcastically and mock attempts to grow and change. To what degree this is true is a far more complex issue than presented here, but we have probably all had experience where politeness and rudeness have created very different environments. How hard did you try to make sure *not* to use an offensive or politically incorrect term when referring to other people?

The use of gender neutral or more politically correct language is directly related to the idea that the language we use may shape our understanding of, or relationship with, the world around us. If a book consistently uses "he" or "man" as a generalization for any person, the unintended effect is to exclude half of the reading public. The use of more precise or neutral language is an attempt to correct sexist, racist or potentially offensive terms being used. While some have argued that the movement to use correct language can seem a bit clinical, or lacking in expression, for the most part, these more politically correct terms have replaced outdated, inaccurate and old-fashioned conventions in language use. Often people use incorrect terminology without fully understanding the nature of the prejudice implied. The term Asian, for example, replaced the term "Oriental," because the former implied geographical location only in relation to a European worldview. And, instead of using the word "man" as an archetype, "people" or "human beings" would do just as well if you want to refer to all of the human race (including women and children). You might, however, still have to negotiate the term "man" in reference to a universal human subject in a historical text, so it is important to understand the distinctions between current and past usage.

Discussion Point

Think of terms or expressions you use that might seem offensive to others. Can you change your own attitude and relationship to other people by changing your language?

If you use offensive language when describing a particular group as a joke, is it surprising that some people might react to this critically? How can resisting the use of restricting labels and offensive terms show what you know about the world? If you think in a racist way, could you theoretically change your own view of the world by working to change your language?

Language and community

Humans are social animals and we tend to gravitate towards people who share our interests. A group of people can not only share interests but also foster healthy debate about particular differences within the group. We all belong to a number of communities, both large and small, ranging from a nation to a neighborhood. But the types of communities are infinitely variable and can include sports teams, schools, churches, Internet groups, clubs, or organizations. Sometimes, in fact, we are members of a community without ever really contemplating our involvement, or signing up for it. A formal definition of community, in fact, may be a group of people that share the same customs, interests, laws or traditions, and language. Communities can be amorphous and hard to define—like the large informal community of people who love a particular type of music, or a sport. A community can be quite small, exclusive, and rules based—like the Canadian Warmblood Horse Breeding Association. Regardless of group profile, language plays an important role in the formation, nature, and dynamic activity of communities. Language, as a way of knowing, is a means of describing or capturing what we know. A community is something that we as people create to *produce* knowledge, authority, and language.

Language, then, as a whole or as it is generally spoken, is itself a type of community. No matter where you are now or what your other languages may be, you are able to read this book because you are part of a large and diverse community of English speakers. Your language community may be even a bit more specific. If you are reading this book as a Portuguese speaker in Brazil who attends an English language school you belong to a community that may use English in different and interesting ways—you may be part of a community that ranges from Andorra to Zimbabwe that goes to school in one language and speaks another at home. You may be a student in Southern California, who despite not being a surfer, belongs to a particular, if stereotypical, language community of teenage "surf-ese." You might live in London, but you could be a member of a large Polish community.

Besides being a community in and of itself, language is also one of the key elements that makes a community distinctive. A professional organization for surgeons would use a particular shared vocabulary— one that I wouldn't understand—to communicate with its members. Of course, the language of a group is often distinctive because this group shares common interests, but beyond that, communities have the power to shape their language, not only through word choice but through the creation of new vocabulary. A surgeon knows what "brachytherapy" means. Without access to an encyclopedia, you may not know that it is a form of radiotherapy used in the treatment for some common forms of cancer, and is much in demand all over the world. From your knowledge of teen movies, however, you are more likely to be able to pick up that a "dude" can go from the beaches of California to a locker room in New England and eventually wind up in a Bollywood film. By considering different groupings of people— small and large, formal and informal—it is possible to see that language helps define community and that at the same time communities can influence language.

Activity

List your communities

How many communities do you belong to, either formally or informally? List as many as you can.

Do any of your communities use language in a particular way? Sometimes we are aware of vocabulary we may use with some groups but not with others. List some of the words (excluding, perhaps, the expletives) that you use in a particular community and not another.

Activity

The English language

The development of the English language and its expansion throughout the world is a captivating story. From family origins in Indo-European languages to early Anglo-Saxon dialects, through the influence of Celtic and Roman borrowings, then on through its later manifestations into a broad range of regional variants, the development of the language has many twists, turns, nooks, and crannies that are interesting to investigate and compare.

Look at the following word chart and select from each row the term or the spelling that is most familiar to you. Which countries do you think they come from?

aeroplane	airplane	
railway	railroad	
petrol	gas	
tyre	tire	
centre	center	
lorry driver	trucker	truckie
move (to a new house)	move (to a new house)	shift
trainers	sneakers	takkies
ghost	ghost	duppy

Analyzing your choice of words

If you chose the words in the left column of the chart you are most likely speak some version of British English. At the same time, you could be from a place where for some reason the English language was more heavily influenced by British English because of earlier imperialism or migration.

If you circled words from the middle column, you are probably speaking American English. American English is a variation of English that began its development almost as soon as the British colonized North America. Patterns of immigration, geography, and regional influences all play a role in developing the different strands of continental variants of English.

If you circled words in both the left and middle columns you may be speaking either Canadian or Australian English (if you circled "truckie" this would help to define you as Australian). Obviously, the English in these two countries branched directly from British English but in both cases the languages were influenced by their own changing demographics, or make-up of peoples and cultures. In addition, the English in both countries is strongly influenced by American English through the pervasiveness of US culture and the sheer distance from the British Isles, and in the case of Canada in particular because of proximity to the border.

Finally, if you circled "shift" you are probably speaking Indian English, while if you chose "takkies" instead of "trainers" or "sneakers" you may be speaking a South African variation of English, while "duppy" would reveal your Caribbean origins. While the English in all of these areas was strongly influenced by British English, all three varieties developed separately. Currently, Indian English in particular is varied and robust because of the size of the English-speaking population, the size of the country, and its growing influence on English outside of the country's own borders through migration and the influence of its entertainment industry.

Sociolinguistics and Corpus Linguistics

Sociolinguistics is a subfield of linguistics that studies language as it is used in a wide variety of social contexts. While some linguists are primarily concerned with language and the brain, the formation of sounds and the more "scientific" side of language study, sociolinguists may cross over into fields such as anthropology, sociology, education, or any field that concerns itself with the effect that language has on society or vice versa.

Corpus Linguistics is the study of a wide but delineated database of language as it is used for the purpose of studying language variety and structure in detail. An example of a corpus might be a massive collection of magazines published in the 1800s or, in a more contemporary example, the writing posted on a large number of blogs. Today, digital technology and the ease of both collecting and analyzing data from a corpus is accelerating both the particular insights of corpus linguistics and the possibilities for studying language in a variety of social contexts.

Activity

Which English is that?

There are as many variations of English as there are countries in the English-speaking world, and varieties of English spoken elsewhere. Research the particularities of vocabulary, grammar, and accent in any of a number of countries from the islands of the Caribbean, to Ireland, to Kenya, or to New Zealand.

Membership in a community is, of course, a lot more complex than identifying with a list of words. Not only are individuals members of a number of different communities, but the groups themselves take on different identities and go in different directions based on the concerns or needs of their members. A broad language community is subject to pressures and conflicts just as a student club or a hockey team might be. The large communities of common-language speakers (often multilingual communities called nations), exist in a push and pull relationship. A nation changes the way a language is used while the use of a particular language changes the way a nation defines itself. Also, powerful groups have the ability to change language. Language, in turn, has the power to influence and change communities. Read the two newspaper editorials in the next activity and compare the attitudes the writers have about language, nation, and the changing nature of both.

Activity

Language and nation
Text 1

A Language Without Limits

By Deena Kamel

Hinglish, Chinglish and Arabizi among variations as spoken English undergoes a revolution in the GTA [Greater Toronto Area]. That eve-teasing man thinks he's such a ranjha, but he's really a badmash. Chi-chi. In other words: "The man who sexually harasses women thinks he's such a Romeo, but he's really ill-mannered. Ick." That sentence, with its Hindi-English mix, might have folks at Merriam-Webster scratching their heads.

But all around the GTA, if you listen carefully, you'll hear English increasingly spiced with flavours from foreign languages. Hinglish, Chinglish and Arabizi are just a few of the variations. With its ethnic neighbourhoods, Toronto is the perfect city for a revolution in spoken English, historically an "absorbent language." The language we are hearing today will be very different from the English we will speak in future, as we borrow more words from dominant languages like Hindi or Chinese.

Academics call this mid-conversation and mid-sentence hybridization "code switching." It is disliked by some native English speakers, but not by language experts. "It is perfectly normal and linguistically fascinating, but people sometimes find it embarrassing," says Jack Chambers, professor of sociolinguistics at the University of Toronto. "They think it is a sign of incompetence when it is really a sign of resiliency and creativity."

Siham Ben, 27, a Moroccan medical student, came to Canada when she was 7. She switches between English and Arabic, producing a hybrid dubbed by Jordanian youth as Arabizi—a slang term for Arabic and "Inglizi" or "English" in Arabic.

"I don't feel it when I'm doing it," says the Toronto resident. "I don't pay attention to it." Ben, code-switching is a way of maintaining her identity. "I feel Moroccan first, then Canadian second. If I don't use Arabic first, I don't feel true to myself. It's a way of coping with life here."

Zina Alobaydi, 20, is a telecommunications sales representative living in Scarborough. "I feel my head is a dictionary," she says, as she thinks in Arabic and speaks in English. Alobaydi speaks the Iraqi dialect with her parents, as a sign of respect to them, but uses Arabizi with her friends. Alobaydi uses more Arabic, with its richness and depth, to express emotions that cannot be conveyed as well in English.

"Take the word 'bahr' for example," she says letting the word for 'sea' roll in her mouth. "It gives you the feeling of a big, unlimited space. It has an echo. It rhymes in your head and stays there." But she uses English when talking about culturally taboo subjects, such as dating, which are harder for her to convey in Arabic.

Hinglish, a lively hybrid spread quickly by the Internet and satellite channels, is the language of globalization. In 2004, David Crystal, a British linguist at the University of Wales, predicted that the world's 350 million Hinglish speakers may soon outnumber native English speakers in the United States and United Kingdom.

About eight years ago, Telus started to run Hinglish ads as part of a campaign to reach out to Canada's growing South Asian communities. The ads appeared in South Asian and ethnic print and broadcast media including Can-India News, Voice Weekly, and Hindi outlets abroad as well as Omni Television, according to Telus spokesperson A.J. Gratton. But with the popular mixing of Hindi and English, we may even be seeing Hinglish ads in Canadian mainstream media in future, says Telus marketing director Tracy Lim.

Pepsi ran a campaign in India with the slogan 'Yeh Dil Maange More!' (this heart wants more) and Coke followed with 'Life Ho To Aisi' (life should be this way).

A dictionary of the hybrid, The Queen's Hinglish: How to speak Pukka, was compiled in 2006 by Baljinder Mahal, a teacher from Derby in England.

Rena Helms-Park, an associate professor of linguistics at the University of Toronto, Scarborough, says code-switching creates a "rapport" that unifies the community. It can also be subversive. In post-colonial countries speakers are trying to reclaim English in their own way, to create a new national identity. "It's not a lesser English, it's one type of world English," Helms-Park says.

Indian writer Raja Rao writes: "We cannot write like the English. We should not. We cannot write only as Indians. Our method of expression therefore has to be a dialect which will some day prove to be as distinctive and colourful as the Irish or American."

English has always been a sponge language. Since it was written down in the year 700, it has adopted words from Norse, French and Latin, among others. English now has up to 700,000 words—more than almost any other language, according to Chambers. "That's a direct consequence of international scope, the fact that English has travelled so far around the world and mixed with so many other cultures and has absorbed influences from all those other cultures. It has been an amazingly tolerant language." Now there is an explosion in English vocabulary comparable to the development of its syntax in the 1400s and 1500s, when the printing press was invented.

"Some people feel threatened because the standard isn't adhered to across the board," Helms-Park says. "There are lots of purists out there." But times change, and with them, language. "In a sense it is a true reflection of the 21st century where immigration of groups, permanent crossing of national boundaries, is one of the constants of our lifestyle. The English language has a head start over lots of other languages because it already is so cosmopolitan in its constituents," Chambers says. Peering into the future, Helms-Park said written English will remain stable, but we will see a "melting pot of Englishes" in Canada rather than pockets of Hinglish or Chinglish. "What we end up with is more local colour."

Shoofihada, mezeiwan. LOOK AT THIS, IT'S NICE. Ahlain, Keefak? HI, HOW ARE YOU? Dim ah lei? HOW ARE YOU?

Source: Kamel, Deena. 2008. "A Language without Limits." *Toronto Star.* 19 August 2008.

Text 2

English grows into strange shapes when transplanted into foreign soil

By Ben Macintyre

LAST WEEK THE THINK-TANK DEMOS came up with a revolutionary new approach to the language —given the spread of hybrid forms of English, instead of insisting that new arrivals to this country learn standard English, it said, they should be taught such variations as Spanglish (Spanish-English), Hinglish (Hindi/Punjbi/Urdu-English) and Chinglish (Chinese-English).

Foisting a dollop of post-colonial guilt on to the mother tongue, the report argued that British attitudes to the language are "better suited to the days of the British Empire than the modern world". Rather than regard English as a uniquely British invention to be defended, the British should see themselves as "just one of many shareholders in a global asset".

I love the strange shapes into which English grows when transplanted into foreign soil, and the varieties of words that we import from the subspecies. "Chuddies", the Hinglish for underpants, is only one of the most recent adoptions from India, following a long and honourable tradition of pyjamas, bungalows and kedgeree.

"Long time no see", now standard English, was once a literal translation from Chinese to English. But to leap from an appreciation of English in all its hybrid forms to the notion that these should be accorded equal status with standard English in England seems faintly perverse, and a misunderstanding of the organic way in which language evolves.

Latin provided the root for a multitude of languages. The same is undoubtedly true of English. But I don't recall any Roman thinker suggesting that the bastardised and regionalised forms of the language spoken in such outposts as, say, Britain, should be taught in Roman schools.

Maintaining and preserving a standard form of English is not merely "Little Englishism": employers and governments need to know that there is a correct way to use English, as do new learners. Demos suggests abandoning the Oxford English Dictionary as the repository of true English, and replacing it with a website to which anyone could contribute "English" words and definitions. Such a project would be fascinating, but not English: the outcome would be an informal lingua franca, a sprawling form of communication derived from English, but hardly a language.

English is spreading faster, and in a richer variety of ways, than any language in history. French schoolchildren refer, not just to "le weekend" and "le MacDo", but use words of much more recent vintage: "le reality TV", "le hoodie" and "le handsfree".

Millions of Chinese use English as a second language, with the result that the largest proportion of new words being coined in everyday English are Chinese in origin. Some have been adopted into Mandarin: "drinktea", meaning "closed" and derived from a Mandarin word, "torunbusiness", meaning "open". Where once such terms might have been absorbed slowly, the internet means that they circulate with astonishing speed. In the 1960s, there were some 250 million English speakers, mostly in the US, Britain and former colonies; today there are approximately the same number of Chinese with at least some grasp of English.

One of the most fertile and gorgeous English adaptations is Indian-English, a vigorous hybrid with its own syntax and vocabulary. English use is expanding more rapidly in India than at any time since its arrival on the subcontinent, fulfilling the novelist Raja Rao's prediction that Indian-English is "a dialect which will one day prove to be as distinctive and colourful as the Irish or the American". There is a delightful internal rhythm to Indian-English. Rather than wash one's hair, an Indian may take a "headbath"; sexual harassment is "eve-teasing", a word at once less clinical and more suggestive than ours. In English we can only postpone an event; in India, we can "prepone" it, to bring it forward.

Lee Knapp, of Cambridge University's English for Speakers of Other Languages examinations, argues that new forms of English (like the old) will have a gradual impact on the standard tongue. "The varieties (of English) are an expression of human communities," he says. "It's more likely they will be no different to the colloquial language of the UK, providing words and language use which will change the dictionaries over time."

Applauding the adaptation of English in other countries should not mean abandoning a sense of where it comes from, or insisting that all forms are equal in this country. One cannot postpone the adoption of foreign forms of English—but there is no need to prepone it either.

If Chinglish must be taught in English schools, then teachers should also instruct pupils on playground patois, internet argot, Glasgow patter or any of the countless subsidiaries into which English has evolved. These are all interesting and valuable children of the mother tongue, but children nonetheless. To put that another way, there may be many shareholders in the English language, but there is only one CEO—Shakespeare.

Source: Macintyre, Ben. 2007. "English grows into strange shapes when transplanted into foreign soil." *The Times*. March 24, 2007.

For further discussion

Consider the following questions in relation to these articles. Write a brief summary of the situation in your country, in response to some of the main points discussed.

1 In what ways do the articles above celebrate language diversity?

2 Are the articles critical of language diversity? Language blending? Language change?

3 What are the possible reasons for people who "code switch" to feel self-conscious about using language combinations in public?

4 Why would linguists be interested in studying language change?

5 What are the possible reasons for wanting to slow or stop the change of language use in a particular country?

6 How should public education, in a given country, handle the instruction of the dominant native language? How should educators approach language variations?

Activity

Do a language-use survey

On your own, with a partner, or with an entire class, carry out a language-use survey. What are the various languages spoken by students, parents, teachers, or others in your community? If English is widely spoken, what regional variations of English are spoken? What other variations of English are spoken and why? What is the reason for variations within a single community that you have chosen to survey?

Activity

Research into IB language policy

The IB has a "language policy" and takes a stance on issues ranging from support to students with "complex language profiles" and mother tongue entitlement.

Find documents related to IB language policy. How do these policies define the nature of the IB community? How could this policy itself be part of the debate over language, community, and power? Creative ideas for a written task could follow from your research.

Region and dialect

It is almost impossible to think of a monolithic, easily described community such as "nation" or "English language speakers" without starting to see the variations at work within these groups. Regional variation and social variation play a great role in creating communities and subcultures within larger states. Many cultural variations in language also serve to identify or unite—for good and bad—particular communities. As we have seen even in the articles about changes in the English language, difference in the form of dialect, accents, and word choice stand out and we tend to make judgments about these differences. Speakers of one dialect may look at another dialect from what many critics call the deficit model, or a way of viewing certain language variations as somehow inferior of deficient. From judging an accent it is a small step to broader prejudice.

The use of African American Vernacular English (or AAVE) in the United States is a good example of the complex role language plays in a culture. The United States still struggles with the legacy of slavery and the disadvantage among African American communities; this is reflected in the naming of the particular dialects spoken by many African Americans (which was recently more often referred to as Black Vernacular English). In the following activity, a series of short readings and questions, the existence and use of AAVE and issues concerning African Americans as a community and their relation to other communities, the importance of language in terms of community cohesion and identity, and the role of education are further discussed.

Activity

Dialect, identity, and power

Read the following passages, taking notes as you go along, and consider any guiding questions. Interrogate the texts, trying to uncover interesting features, ideas, and attitudes towards language and particular communities. At the same time note any interesting linguistic features or patterns.

Text 1

In 1993, the African American writer Toni Morrison was awarded the Nobel Prize for Literature. In its press release, the Nobel committee noted Morrison's narrative experimentation, the human spirit of her novels, and the range and quality of her work. The committee also made special mention that her work: "delves into the language itself, a language she wants to liberate from the fetters of race."

Read the following passage from her novel *Beloved* in which Morrison, through the eyes of one of the main characters, Suggs, describes the singing—and language—of another character, Paul D.

> And wouldn't you know he'd be a singing man.
>
> > *Little rice, little bean,*
> > *No meat in between*
> > *Hard work ain't easy,*
> > *Dry bread ain't greasy.*
>
> He was us now and singing as he mended things he had broken the day before. Some old pieces of song he'd learned on the prison farm or in the War afterward. Nothing like what they sand at Sweet Home, where yearning fashioned every note.
>
> The songs he knew from Georgia were flat-headed nails for pounding and pounding and pounding.
>
> > *Lay my head on the railroad line,*
> > *Train come along, pacify my mind.*
> > *If I had my weight in lime,*
> > *I'd whip my captain till he went stone blind.*
> > *Five-cent nickel,*
> > *Ten-cent dime,*
> > *Busting rocks is busting time.*
>
> But they didn't fit, these songs. They were too loud, had too much power for the little house chores he was engaged in—resetting table legs; glazing.
>
> He couldn't go back to "Storm upon the Waters" that they sang under the trees of Sweet Home, so he contented himself with mmmmmmmmmm, throwing in a line if one occurred to him, and what occurred over and over was "Bare feet and chamomile sap,/Took off my shoes; took off my hat."
>
> It was tempting to change the words (Gimme back my shoes; gimme back my hat), because he didn't believe he could live with a woman—any woman—for over two out of three months. That was about as long as he could abide in one place. …

Source: Morrison, Toni. 1987. *Beloved,* New York: Vintage International. 2004. Kindle position 743–61.

Questions to the text

1. How would you describe the language and diction of the narrator?
2. How is the implied diction or vocabulary of the character Paul D. conveyed?
3. Why does he sing one kind of song as opposed to another?

Discussion Point

- What do you think it means to liberate language?
- How might language be enslaved, captured or restricted?
- Can a language be as enslaved as a person?

Text 2

In this excerpt from her 1993 Nobel Lecture, Toni Morrison describes the thoughts of a wise old woman trying to impart a lesson to young children while she contemplates language and the way it is "susceptible to death."

For her a dead language is not only one no longer spoken or written, it is unyielding language content to admire its own paralysis. Like statist language, censored and censoring. Ruthless in its policing duties, it has no desire or purpose other than maintaining the free range of its own narcotic narcissism, its own exclusivity and dominance. However moribund, it is not without effect for it actively thwarts the intellect, stalls conscience, suppresses human potential. Unreceptive to interrogation, it cannot form or tolerate new ideas, shape other thoughts, tell another story, fill baffling silences. Official language smitheryed to sanction ignorance and preserve privilege is a suit of armor polished to shocking glitter, a husk from which the knight departed long ago. Yet there it is: dumb, predatory, sentimental. Exciting reverence in schoolchildren, providing shelter for despots, summoning false memories of stability, harmony among the public.

She is convinced that when language dies, out of carelessness, disuse, indifference and absence of esteem, or killed by fiat, not only she herself, but all uses and makers are accountable for its demise. In her country children have bitten their tongues off and use bullets instead to iterate the voice of speechlessness, of disabled and disabling language, of language adults have abandoned altogether as a device for grappling with meaning, providing guidance, or expressing love. But she knows tongue-suicide is not only the choice of children. It is common among the infantile heads of state and power merchants whose evacuated language leaves them with no access to what is left of their human instincts for they speak only to those who obey, or in order to force obedience.

Questions to the text

1   Who is Morrison speaking to?
2   How would you describe her use of language and vocabulary?
3   Is the language academic? Literary? Inventive?
4   How would someone's language be stolen?

Text 3

DeAndre Cortez Way, better known by his stage name Soulja Boy Tell 'Em, or simply Soulja Boy, is an African American rapper and record producer. Following are the song lines from his 1998 single "Turn My Swag On."

Turn My Swag On

Soulja Boy tell 'em!
Hopped up out the bed,
Turn my swag on,
Took a look in the mirror said what's up
Yeah I'm getting money (oh) *[x2]*

Turn my swag on,
It's my turn, now turn it up
Yeah, yeah
I put my team on, and my theme song
Now it's time to turn it up
Yeah, yeah

I got a question why they hating on me,
I got a question why they hating on me
I ain't did nothing to 'em, but count this money
And put my team on, now my whole clic stunning
Boy what's up, yeah
Boy what's up, yeah

When I was 9 years old I put it in my head
That I'm gonna die for this gold

(Soulja Boy tell 'em)
Boy what's up, yeah
Hopped up out the bed
Turn my swag on
Took a look in the mirror said what's up
Yeah I'm gettin money (ooh) *[x2]*

I'm back again,
I know a lot of you all thought I wasn't coming back …
Yeah, yeah
I had to prove them wrong,
Got back in the studio and came up with another hit
Yeah, yeah
I told the world my story, the world where I'm from
Souljaboy X L dot com, boy what's up
Yeah, yeah

Now everytime you see me spit
Every time you hear me rhyme
Everytime you see me in your state or town
Say what's up
Yeah, yeah

Hopped up out the bed
Turn my swag on
Took a look in the mirror said what's up
Yeah I'm gettin money (ooh) *[x2]*

Source: Soulja Boy Tell 'Em. 2008. *iSouljaBoyTellem*, ColliPark Music/Interscope Records.

Questions to the text

1 How much of the vocabulary do you understand in this song?

2 Does this song belong to a particular community or to a variety of communities?

3 For whom is this song written or performed? To whom is this song marketed? By whom?

4 Does this song go against a dominant community, or along with it?

Activity

Image analysis: comparison and contrast

The novel *Uncle Tom's Cabin* by Harriet Beecher Stowe was first published in 1852 to promote the anti-slavery movement. The book was extremely popular throughout the century. While the novel is at times credited with helping the effort to abolish slavery in the United States, the portrayal of the characters in the work itself and the plays and musicals based on the original, are often seen as promoting negative stereotypes of African Americans. How do the images on the poster juxtapose with the images on the quilt created by Harriet Powers, an African American artist, active in the same time period?

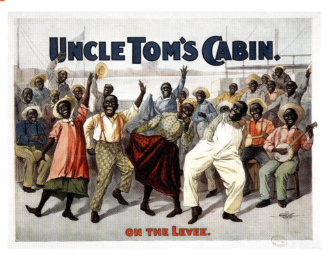

A lithograph from 1899 promoting the stage show of Uncle Tom's Cabin.

A quilt by Harriet Powers, 1895–98.

Discussion Point

Many of the concerns raised in a discussion of regional variation, dialect, class, and the multiplicity of communities are related to the decisions we make about belonging.

1 How limited are we by the languages that we are able to speak?

2 How is our membership in a community tied to identity?

3 How is our identity tied to language?

4 How flexible is our identity? You will have the chance to explore some of these questions in the next section of this chapter.

Activity

Class project

Study the English language and literature of a particular dialect or region

Explore the use of a particular regional variation or dialect of English and the issues that surround its use. Try to find the widest variety of texts that either use that particular dialect or comment upon it. Some further questions you might consider to support your research:

● How is this dialect primarily used? Is its use related to region? Race? Gender? Class? In what form is it usually expressed? Is its use primarily oral? Literary? Or, does it more frequently come across in popular culture, such as traditional folk songs?

Write an opinion piece on the value of these texts for further research and analysis.

Activity

Create graphs, maps, and trees

Graphic representation may be one of the best ways to make sense of language development and change, and the complexity of diverse community languages. A map with different colors can be used to show language variation across a country or within a city. A venn diagram can show the ways in which our membership in different communities bring us into contact with diverse registers and vocabularies. A tree diagram can show how aspects of an older language—for example, Celtic—have survived in modern English. Choose one aspect found in this chapter—nation, region, dialect, subculture—and think about how you could research and compile data, and represent it graphically.

Online communities

Discussion Point

"On the Internet, nobody knows you're a dog."

"On the internet no one knows you are a dog." Cartoon by Peter Steiner, first published in The New Yorker on 7 May 1993.

What is funny about this cartoon?

- Is it "true"? Can we be anyone we want on the Internet?
- What are the limits to this freedom? What are the dangers?
- Can we be identified by our use of language on the Internet?
- Do digital communities or social networking sites have a language of their own?

By 2008, both the Pew Internet and American Life surveys and the Office for National Statistics in the UK reported that over 90% of teenagers regularly went online. One can only imagine that if that number isn't growing, then certainly the amount of time spent on the Internet in a variety of activities must be increasing. This massive access to the Internet is necessarily changing our relationship with reading, communicating, and language use in general. Simply being familiar with words such as "LoL", "poke", or "friend" (in its new digital connotation) places many people within the linguistic influence of the expanding Internet. For most young people, the Internet is a regular place to communicate, interact, and network.

It is hard to talk about the Internet as a community in and of itself. The communities found on the Internet or through email are at least as numerous and just as complex as those found in the "real" world. Many digital communities mirror communities already established between people in face-to-face environments. Classes at school, for example, might exist both in the classroom and *virtually* on a class website (through discussion on an online forum). Parents at your school may find they communicate more often with other parents and the administration at school through an Internet portal that mirrors the larger school community. But this is where the boundaries of communities get fuzzy again. Is an online presence simply an extension of an already existing community? Can we separate communities by the way they communicate? One thing is for sure: more than ever before, we now have the option of participating in an almost overwhelming number of communities.

Activity

Online research into community languages

Slang is a language that rolls up its sleeves, spits on its hands and goes to work.

Carl Sandburg

Net speak is just one kind of slang or new use of language. What are some slang words or inventive vocabulary used in your peer group? In what ways does this language "go to work" as Sandburg says?

Find curious examples of the vernacular that you know about. What typical slang words do communities you know about use? Think of slang words that are common to a distinct language group (like Australia or Scotland). Can you find any on the Internet? How is vernacular language promoted or overtaken by more global forms of communication?

Online communities
Text 1

From a blog post on www.thefragmatica.com

THEFRAGMATICA.COM

HOME	ABOUT	BLOGS	WEB	CONTACT	NEWS

Gaming without language

Posted on 02 August 09 by Broken Luck

First off, we need to recognize that there is a semi-universal vocabulary related to gaming which allows for a relatively high level of inter-player communication. Furthermore, within the greater gaming language, there are a series of dialects spoken by certain subsets. You need only drop a console gamer into a pre-raid *WoW* meeting to understand this. Gamer culture is, in fact, steeped in acronyms and slang (frag, noob, RPG, etc.). And, even beyond that, we have basic terms relating to the rules of a game (class, hit point, skill tree) which can be applied across series and even genres. This cross-game translation is possible because these terms are part of a vocabulary based squarely within acknowledged, written rules. These are words we must have just to play the game. What we, the general gaming public, are lacking is a way to talk about video games on a higher level.

But where are we limited in our current vocabulary? Anthony's example of the classic pre-boss fight loadup of weapons, ammo, and mana is a good one. This is a well known gaming trope appearing across platforms and genres, yet we have no universal term for it. Similarly, is there a term we can apply to the acquisition of key weapons/spells/techniques, such as when you receive the Master Sword in the *Zelda* games or your Big Daddy suit in *BioShock*? Or, on an even more mechanical level, what do we call the new interactive loading screens like those featured in *Assassin's Creed*?

Even better, let's consider genre names for a moment. What do we call games like *A Kingdom for Keflings* or *Pikmin*? They're not exactly sims, nor are they real time strategy games (because the emphasis isn't on combat, which is what the term RTS implies). *Pikmin* has some slight puzzle/platforming elements, but to describe it as a platformer would be highly inacurrate.

As a community, we simply don't have the words to effectively describe our hobby. It seems to me that this is a major failing and is, in some ways, preventing an intellectualized look at video gaming. If we're lacking the vocabulary, how are we supposed to approach video games in an academic way? Is it even possible? We wonder why literature and films are given high praise while video games are vilified. It may be, in part, that language allows other artforms to be studied and dissected, while ours remains amorphous and unapproachable.

The real question, then, is what do we do about this? Who is responsible for creating this language? Is it up to the industry insiders — the developers, producers, and marketers? Or, do we go to the few video game scholars like James Paul Gee and demand that they build us a vocabulary? Or, is it up to you and me, the average gamers, to find a way to talk about all this? Unfortunately, there doesn't seem to be an easy answer. We can hope, however, that as the gaming community grows and becomes more culturally and ecnomically significant, we will see the creation of new, game-specific language to help us establish a legitimate place in artistic discourse.

View the original article here

Posted in Uncategorized | Leave a comment

Questions to the text

- Who is the audience for this blog post?
- Does the author assume a particular language use among the readership?
- How are the blogger's views about language variation similar or different from views expressed in earlier passages?
- Do you think people ever consciously make up a language?

Text 2

The following opinion piece was posted on the *New York Times* online edition.

Teenagers' Internet Socializing Not a Bad Thing

By Tamar Lewin

Good news for worried parents: All those hours their teenagers spend socializing on the Internet are not a bad thing, according to a new study by the MacArthur Foundation.

"It may look as though kids are wasting a lot of time hanging out with new media, whether it's on MySpace or sending instant messages," said Mizuko Ito, lead researcher on the study, "Living and Learning With New Media." "But their participation is giving them the technological skills and literacy they need to succeed in the contemporary world. They're learning how to get along with others, how to manage a public identity, how to create a home page."

The study, conducted from 2005 to last summer, describes new-media usage but does not measure its effects.

"It certainly rings true that new media are inextricably woven into young people's lives," said Vicki Rideout, vice president of the Kaiser Family Foundation and director of its program for the study of media and health. "Ethnographic studies like this are good at describing how young people fit social media into their lives. What they can't do is document effects. This highlights the need for larger, nationally representative studies."

Ms. Ito, a research scientist in the department of informatics at the University of California, Irvine, said that some parental concern about the dangers of Internet socializing might result from a misperception.

"Those concerns about predators and stranger danger have been overblown," she said. "There's been some confusion about what kids are actually doing online. Mostly, they're socializing with their friends, people they've met at school or camp or sports."

The study, part of a $50 million project on digital and media learning, used several teams of researchers to interview more than 800 young people and their parents and to observe teenagers online for more than 5,000 hours. Because of the adult sense that socializing on the Internet is a waste of time, the study said, teenagers reported many rules and restrictions on their electronic hanging out, but most found ways to work around such barriers that let them stay in touch with their friends steadily throughout the day.

"Teens usually have a 'full-time intimate community' with whom they communicate in an always-on mode via mobile phones and instant messaging," the study said.

This is not news to a cluster of Bronx teenagers, gathered after school on Wednesday to tell a reporter about their social routines. All of them used MySpace and instant messaging to stay in touch with a dozen or two of their closest friends every evening. "As soon as I get home, I turn on my computer,"

said a 15-year-old boy who started his MySpace page four years ago. "My MySpace is always on, and when I get a message on MySpace, it sends a text message to my phone. It's not an obsession; it's a necessity." (School rules did not permit using students' names without written parental permission, which could not be immediately obtained.)

Only one student, a 14-year-old girl, had ever opted out—and she lasted only a week. "It didn't work," she said. "You become addicted. You can't live without it."

In a situation familiar to many parents, the study describes two 17-year-olds, dating for more than a year, who wake up and log on to their computers between taking showers and doing their hair, talk on their cellphones as they travel to school, exchange text messages through the school day, then get together after school to do homework — during which time they also play a video game—talk on the phone during the evening, perhaps ending the night with a text-messaged "I love you."

Teenagers also use new media to explore new romantic relationships, through interactions casual enough to ensure no loss of face if the other party is not interested. The study describes two early Facebook messages, or "wall posts," by teenagers who eventually started dating. First, the girl posted a message saying, "hey ... hm. wut to say? iono lol/well I left you a comment ... u sud feel SPECIAL haha." (Translation: Hmm ... what to say? I don't know. Laugh out loud. Well I left you a comment ... You should feel special.) A day later, the boy replied, "hello there ... umm I don't know what to say, but at least I wrote something ..."

While online socializing is ubiquitous, many young people move on to a period of tinkering and exploration, as they look for information online, customize games or experiment with digital media production, the study found. For example, a Brooklyn teenager did a Google image search to look at a video card and find out where in a computer such cards are, then installed his own.

What the study calls "geeking out" is the most intense Internet use, in which young people delve deeply into a particular area of interest, often through a connection to an online interest group. "New media allow for a degree of freedom and autonomy for youth that is less apparent in a classroom setting," the study said. "Youth respect one another's authority online, and they are often more motivated to learn from peers than from adults."

Source: Lewin, Tamar. 2008. "Teenagers' Internet Socializing Not a Bad Thing." *New York Times*. 20 November 2008. http://nytimes.com.

Text 3

The following article from the UK's Daily Mail, also accessed online, provides a different view on the risks attached to an increasingly online life.

How using Facebook could raise your risk of cancer

Daily Mail Reporter, *The Daily Mail*, February 19, 2009

Social networking sites such as Facebook could raise your risk of serious health problems by reducing levels of face-to-face contact, a doctor claims. Emailing people rather than meeting up with them may have wide-ranging biological effects, said psychologist Dr Aric Sigman. Increased isolation could alter the way genes work and upset immune responses, hormone levels and the function of arteries. It could also impair mental performance.

The number of hours people spend interacting face-to-face has fallen dramatically since 1987 as electronic media use has risen. This could increase the risk of problems as serious as cancer, strokes, heart disease and dementia, Dr Sigman says in Biologist, the journal of the Institute of Biology. Social networking sites such as MySpace and Facebook allow people to keep in touch with friends over the web. They can swap pictures, play games and leave messages which explain how their day is going.

But even though they are designed to bring people together, Dr Sigman said they were actually playing a significant role in people becoming more isolated.

Interacting 'in person' had effects on the body not seen when writing emails, Dr Sigman claimed. Levels of hormones such as the 'cuddle chemical' oxytocin, which promotes bonding, altered according to whether people were in close contact or not. 'There does seem to be a difference between "real presence" and the virtual variety,' Dr Sigman added. Some genes, including ones involved with the immune system and responses to stress, acted differently according to how much social interaction a person had with others.

Dr Sigman added: 'Social networking sites should allow us to embellish our social lives, but what we find is very different. It's not that I'm old fashioned in terms of new technology, but its purpose should be to provide a tool that enhances our lives.' Dr Sigman told the Press Association: 'Social networking is the internet's biggest growth area, particular among young children. 'A quarter of British children have a laptop or computer in their room by the age of five and they have their own social networking sites, like the BBC's myCBBC. It's causing huge changes.'

Studies had shown that children taught via video broadcasts or DVDs did not learn as well as they did when given lessons by a real teacher. Dr Sigman said 209 'socially regulated' genes had been identified, including ones involved in the immune system, cell proliferation and responses to stress. Their activity may account for higher rates of inflammatory disease and other health problems seen in socially isolated individuals. Electronic media was also undermining the ability of children and young people to learn vital social skills and read body language, said Dr Sigman.

'One of the most pronounced changes in the daily habits of British citizens is a reduction in the number of minutes per day that they interact with another human being,' he said. 'In less than two decades, the number of people saying there is no one with whom they discuss important matters nearly tripled. Parents spend less time with their children than they did only a decade ago. Britain has the lowest proportion of children in all of Europe who eat with their parents at the table. The proportion of people who work at home alone continues to rise. I am worried about where this is all leading. Social networking sites should allow us to embellish our social lives, but what we find is very different. The tail is wagging the dog. These are not tools that enhance, they are tools that displace.

Questions to the texts

1 What are the opinions expressed by the researchers in texts 2 and 3?

2 What are the differences in the ways the researchers view community?

3 What kinds of distinctions do the researchers make (or not make) in relation to communication?

Your turn

Considering the ways we communicate through language, is there any difference in actual communication, between members of an online community and a physical world community? If you communicate with your friends online, do you use different types of language to the way you communicate face to face?

● Write a brief response reflecting on your own views about communication, types of communities, and the variety of ways you use language.

Language and identity

Turn back to the *New Yorker* cartoon of the dog on the computer. Now, assuming this could somehow be real, consider the cartoon in relation to language. What language would the dog speak on the Internet? If the dog can only write "bark" wouldn't he somehow tip off his identity? Wouldn't he at least be viewed as a strange person who wants to be seen as a dog? What if this dog is communicating on the Internet in a multi-modal environment, using video downloads, online social networks with pictures, and lists favorite tunes and movies. Once he posts Snoop Dogg, and a few photos of himself partying with friends, wouldn't he have the opposite problem? Wouldn't, in fact, absolutely everyone—including college admissions officers—know exactly who he is? Or maybe the dog could manage to post judiciously, writing in an English variation that sounds BBC and Harvard rolled into one, and perform to such an extent that he is no longer the dog we once knew.

As is evident from the previous readings and discussions of language and community, the way we communicate is closely tied to the formal and informal groups to which we belong. While we join some of these communities by choice, we belong to others because of our families, our educational background, or the coincidence even of proximity. As individuals we have the power to change communities but communities also strongly influence what we believe, how we act, and how we present ourselves to others. When we think about individual identity we come to realize that, in a similar way to community membership, who we are is both a product of our environment, a product of our genes, and a product of our own conscious choices. In that we make choices about who we are, and can modify those choices, our identities can be said to be performative. And a large part of our performance of identity—the way we want others to see us and how we want to see ourselves—is tied to language.

Every individual's use of language is unique. First, the sound of a voice, from intonation to volume, can be influenced by the size and shape of our bodies. Accent is affected by the area we live and the places we travel. Diction is affected by family and education. Our language patterns or quirks can be shaped by the types of movies we watch or even by a single book we read. Sometimes a person might be subconsciously influenced by the language of a celebrity, and at other times a person might purposefully imitate someone who represents some personal goal. Again, it is obvious that we can control some of our language choices and not others and that at times we would like to be judged by the language we use and at other times we are subject to prejudice because of the particularities of individual language use.

Linguists who study individual differences in personal language use have formally studied some of the above phenomena. One of the most common language variations, code-switching, was discussed in the previous section on language and community. Obviously, although, the frequency, type, and extent of code-switching, varies greatly from

Activity

Language and identity

Before starting this section, write a reflection on the way identity can be tied to language.

Activity

Talking Tom

"Talking Tom" by the software developers Outfit7 is an "app" that features an animated cat who responds to touch and has the ability to repeat words and phrases spoken by the user. A simple toy that speaks when squeezed might entertain a child for a lazy afternoon. But "Talking Tom" seems to reduce people to fits of laughter. There is something about hearing your own words with the same intonation spoken through the screechy voice of a cat. It is as if the cat has, indeed, "got your tongue!"

Try the "Talking Tom" app yourself. What effect does it have on you? Is this application effective because it deforms personal attributes of language? Is it important that it maintains certain aspects of personal language? Why is it sometimes disconcerting to hear your own recorded voice?

individual to individual. Linguists have also formulated the Communication Accommodation Theory, another interesting variation in language use that affects the way idiolect is shaped. The theory states that people bend or shape their language either towards or away from their communication partner's. In an amicable conversation with a friend, or with someone with whom we would like to be friends, it is natural for speech patterns, diction, or pronunciation to converge. Again, this convergence can be subconscious or may be a purposeful act on the speaker's part. The theory also suggests that at times we may want to differentiate ourselves from others, elevating or lowering our diction slightly, or accentuating an accent. On a visit to North America, a British student may want to highlight her differences—out of pride or any number of feelings—through her speech, highlighting an accent rather than playing it down. This type of language accommodation may in fact be related, as some linguists suggest, to what happens to children who learn language at the same time they are learning to negotiate various social contexts ranging from school and the playground, to the family and visitors to the home. Anyone who has a younger sibling (or has watched a movie that features a cute, precocious kid) has laughed when the innocent pre-schooler uses a bad word heard at home in front of the teacher.

The development of our own language use, our own individual idiolect, takes a long time and is not without hiccups ranging from the wrong word used in a particular situation, to a mispronunciation of a word we have only read. A relatively noticeable aspect of an individual's language are often, in fact, the occurrence of small errors or the use of filler words that have nothing to do necessarily with the development of language so much as the natural workings of human language production. Sometimes it is difficult to know if you are using "um" all of the time when speaking in front of a group, but it is easy to realize that someone else is doing it. But what does "um" or "ah" and even small grammar mistakes—like saying "who" instead of "whom" after a preposition—actually indicate about a person? The use of filler words may be due to the simple fact that speaking is often a spontaneous and difficult task that involves quickly translating thought to audible sound: "um" is a kind of halfway point in the thought-into-language, speaking process. The sticking point with fillers and blunders, however, is that they are a marker of our speech and these markers can be interpreted by others. The way we interpret language quirks depends on their type, frequency, and the way in which society has passed judgment.

Sometimes we make grammar mistakes that the "wrong people" notice, like a teacher or a prospective employer. Correct grammar may be subjective and situational, but how do we "learn grammar" so that we communicate in a way that the groups we want to join (and thrive in) will understand us? While many English teachers would say that fluent use of language comes through reading, speaking, and writing on a regular basis, others might say that a more focused study of grammatical construction, grammatical errors, and sentence fluency is needed to guide language use.

Activity

Grammar

Brainstorm your own ideas about grammar instruction and write a brief reflection on whether or not grammar instruction is important.

Activity

Personal vocabulary

Do you have any private words? Maybe you made up words with a friend when you were young and you still use them with that friend today. Do they ever slip into your everyday speech? Many families have their own words, sometimes for actions like using the washroom, or behaving a certain way at dinner. When I was little I used to say that I hated the "brickle" (pulp) in orange juice. It wasn't until I was 40 that my parents told me I made the word up myself.

- Interview a family member and see if you can come up with any words from a personal or family vocabulary.

Activity

Um and other disfluencies

In the following excerpt from his book *Um: Slips, Stumbles and Verbal Blunders, and What They Mean*, author and linguist Michael Erard discusses the development of attitudes towards fillers, a particular aspect of idiolect. In this passage he contemplates the possible origins of the prohibition against using "um."

> It may be that "uh" and "um" became the emblem of a disorganized self. If the aesthetic of umlessness applied only to public speaking, one might say that orators were most concerned with pleasing their listeners by leaving out such disfluencies. Yet umlessness was taught as the norm for private and intimate spheres of life. The only rule left unwritten was "don't say 'um' when you're talking to yourself."
>
> This persistence suggests worries were attached to "uh" and "um" uniquely. For the last century, sociologists have argued that identity is neither essential nor fixed in complex industrialized societies. The modern identity, they say, is performed. Individuals must navigate a variety of settings, interact with many different people, and play diverse roles to achieve a shifting set of goals. The aesthetic of umlessness may have emerged as a response to this demanding modern conception of self. Perhaps saying "um" was a sign that a person couldn't keep their social performances in order and thus wasn't fit for this social world. "Um" represented a breakdown of the bureaucracy in your head.
>
> Umlessness isn't a natural preference—left to our own devices, we naturally ignore most "ums." People began to prefer umlessness in public speaking and conversation around the same time they began to value order, organization, planning, and efficiency in an increasingly complex and urbanizing society. People worked hard to keep control of how they performed socially, and they prized and admired others who did the same. We prefer in speakers what we prefer in ourselves.

Source: Erard, Michael. 2007. *Um: Slips, Stumbles, and Verbal Blunders, and What They Mean*. Pantheon, New York. pp. 133–34.

Questions to the text

1 Have you ever been told not to use "um" while giving an oral presentation in class? Why do you think it is better not to use "um." What are the consequences of using it?

2 What quirks or mistakes do you notice in your speech or the speech of others? Are these "disfluencies" considered bad? What do you think about the speaker who makes these slips?

3 How conscious are you of your own language use? Does this make speaking and communication easier or more difficult for you?

4 To what extent do you agree or disagree with the final sentence?

Grammar by committee

Prescriptive grammar gives us the rules we are supposed to follow when using a language. Descriptive grammar is a linguist's attempt to record, explain, and describe the language structures as they are commonly used. In a sense, there is no right or wrong in grammar as much as there is clear and unclear communication that is accepted or frowned upon. If a mistake is made consistently by a wide variety of speakers—if "who" and "whom" are mixed up all the time by a large number of speakers of English, increasing over the next century or more—eventually the grammar of a language changes based on common usage. Major dictionaries, in fact, have "usage committees" who judge the appropriateness of various issues of language use and grammar. The committee consists of large numbers of scholars, linguists, journalists, writers of fiction, poets, and even talk-show hosts who vote on particular grammar rules. You can do some research about these committees and find out which rules seem to be set in stone, and which may be on the verge of change.

While it may seem unfair to judge people by their use of language, we clearly take it into account. We can also use language to influence the way other people think of us. There may be aspects of identity such as emotions, attitudes or general intentions that others can infer from our use of language. The way I say "shut the door" can communicate impatience, anger or even the prospect of a juicy secret to be shared. In the same way, the choice of metaphor-rich language and the use of colorful expressions ("Whew! That stink could drive dogs from a meat wagon," my father-in-law likes to say) may rightfully represent a creative or exuberant personality.

The Internet is an interesting laboratory for the study of language and identity. In fact, it has been a boon to linguists who can use the proliferation of different types of writing on the Internet to explore global social interactions and trends. As the Internet moved from a collection of sites meant primarily for information and commerce to what is known as Web 2.0, or a place for interaction and creativity (and commerce), the construction of language and identity and the way the two are interrelated has been made more apparent to millions of users. New technology has also meant that the Internet allows for complex interaction between spoken and written words and images, further foregrounding the human attempt to be a self-actualized, active communicator.

Read

Language and identity

Read the following passages that are based on the language laboratory that we call the Internet. Based on these articles, how strong is the connection between language and identity?

Text 1

In 2007, Joan Morris DiMicco and David R. Millen, researchers at IBM, conducted a study to investigate the ways in which employees manage social networks and self-presentation on the social networking site Facebook. In their study, they identified three distinct types of Facebook users at IBM: those who had just exited college, those who had been at the company for a few years and were moving away from college friends, and those who had worked at the company for a more significant period of time and tended to be in their late 30s to early 40s. The following passage describes some of the habits of the Facebook users.

> The members of the *College Days* group described above appear to be carrying over the identity they crafted during the early use of Facebook on university campuses. The personal information disclosed in profiles is full of hobbies, quotes, favorite books and activities (e.g., college fraternity/sorority or athletics). Members of the *College Days* group represent themselves in their main profile photos with quite playful and varied images. In our survey of 30, we saw images of motorcycles and cars (3), images with friends and family members (8), images of movie/

television characters (2), pets (1), dancing (2) and a piece of computer hardware (1).

The personal status messages and wall postings are typically informal as well. Examples of status messages, which are authored by Facebook users and intended to show timely status of the current activity, are: 1) *is ready to party like a rockstar in the A!!!!!!* 2) *is asking people to pls pls sponsor her even just a little on www.justgiving.com* and 3) *is headed to Michigan!!* The interest groups that this user segment join include political groups, social clubs, friend (and insider joke) groups, religious organizations, and sexual orientation groups.

The clues about online identity for the *College Days* group are fairly typical for many social network sites. Of interest is the emergence of some professional or work identity within the profiles of this group … many members of this group have "friended" people in their corporate network and have provided some job-related information (title, description or start date) in their profile. A small number (6) also provide their corporate email address within their profile and a small number are part of job related groups. We believe that these users post information about their job because they want their non-work friends to know what they are doing with their lives, in contrast with a professional networker who might want to use a social networking site to keep in touch with current colleagues. The very limited discussion of work on their profiles is with outsiders. For example, someone may post on the user's wall asking how the job is going or offering congratulations on a new job assignment. The second group of Facebook users, the *Dressed to Impress* group, is more conservative and professional in their use of Facebook. Eight (of 14) members of this group provided no information in the "personal" section of the Facebook profile … On the other hand, 12 of 14 provided some job-related information. The main profile photo image was much less playful. Twelve of 14 were single person images, three people were wearing ties, and two were in a work setting.

Source: DiMicco, Joan Morris & Millen, D. 2007. "Identity Management: Multiple Presentations of Self in Facebook" Conference Supporting Group Work, Proceedings of the 2007 International ACM, Sannibel Island, Florida, USA.

Text 2

The following article suggests that psychological evaluations of the content of social networking pages and of the subjects of themselves reveal many correlations. Are you surprised by the initial conclusions drawn in the magazine article below?

Staying True to Themselves

Student Facebook profiles, it turns out, match the real thing. Personality used to be a one-per-customer deal: like it or not, you were who you were, and lying to a pen pal was about the closest you could get to having an alter ego. That was then. With the advent of MySpace, Facebook, and other social networking sites, a second, carefully crafted identity is now available to anyone with an Internet connection. And that has psychologists wondering: just how well do these online personalities match the person sitting at the keyboard?

The answer, it turns out, is pretty well. In a recent study of 133 undergraduates with Facebook profiles, University of Texas psychologist Samuel D. Gosling measured the correlation between personality tests online and off and found—contrary to the assumption that kilobytes can't capture one's essence—that the students represented themselves quite faithfully.

Gosling polled the group on a standard five-point personality test, which measures extroversion, agreeableness, conscientiousness, emotional stability, and openness to new experiences. Then researchers rated the same subjects based only on their Facebook profiles, which usually included photos and lists of interests, from academic majors to favorite books and movies.

The researchers found a correlation between assessments in four of the five categories, with emotional stability as the only attribute showing no significant results across personal and online assessments. (Gosling says he was not surprised at the latter, since emotional stability is something that people are good at concealing across most media.)

While extroversion showed the highest correlation, the research suggests that "openness to new experience" is perhaps better conveyed online than in person. A fan of Mendelssohn and Metallica, for example, can communicate a breadth of interests much more quickly online than he can face to face.

Judith Donath, an associate professor at the Media Laboratory at Massachusetts Institute of Technology who reviewed Gosling's research, divides the content of social networking sites into "signals" and "unintended cues."

"Facebook users don't tend to put a lot of hyper-personal information on their pages," she says, so someone who posted touching personal anecdotes, for example, might come off as oversharing without intending to.

In short, says Gosling, Facebook users aren't generally using the site as an image buffer, a resume enhancer, or a separate self (though he found scattered evidence of self-enhancement in two categories). "They just use it as a medium for social life," he says.

Source: Wilson, Chris. *US News and World Report. July 8, 2007.* www.usnes.com/usnews/news/articles/070708/16facebook.htm.

Activity

User-profile

A social networking page or site can serve as a complex way of communicating identity with a broader community. How do you "read" a Facebook page and think about the identity of the user? If you have a social networking page, try to investigate it from someone else's point of view. Look at some of the pages of your friends and look at them with a new eye (not as a friend but more as a critic or investigator). Looking at a variety of social networking pages, consider the following questions:

1 How would you describe the personality of the user?

2 What do the profile pictures suggest about the user?

3 How is language used in the user's own posts?

4 How is language used by others who post on the site?

5 How does a profile or other information add to your perception of the user?

6 How do these various elements work to construct a person's identity?

Activity

Monitoring yourself

Look at some of your own writing in a variety of media—online, in a class assignment, in a formal essay. How does your language use differ from one type of writing to another? Are there certain words that you use only in one form of communication? Are there particular words that you use in all your writing? Do you think the use of these words may be particular to you as an individual?

Use digital tools to further analyze your own writing. You can use "search" and "find" functions to look for particular words in various documents. You can also find online "text mining" sites that will allow you to cut and paste pieces of writing into a window, allowing a program to analyze word occurrence and frequency.

You are probably already very aware of the different types of language you are required to use in different situations. You are able to speak and act one way with teachers, and another way with your friends, and still another in front of your parents. In terms of language use, the difference is probably most clearly highlighted when you sit down to write: there is a clear difference between the way we communicate in writing in a formal essay (appropriate register?) and the way we write in an email or a Facebook wall post. In terms of managing, negotiating, or otherwise constructing identity, you are also most likely involved with rather important pieces of linguistic performance that indicate who you want to be and who you would like to be in the eyes of others: the college or university application essay. The following series of passages consists of an actual application essay, an online forum homework assignment, and a brief Facebook conversation, all written by the same student. As you read the following in order to consider language and identity, you most likely will not be able to resist forming an opinion about the identity of the writer (and forming an opinion about the desired impression the writer is trying to create).

Activity

The many texts of student X

Following are excerpts from a Facebook conversation by student X.

Text 1

> **PM** whaaat are you doing in cali? GYLC? having fun? :D
> okkkkkk happy indonesian independence day my dear
> everything is great! :)
> how are you?
> xxx

AP Hun I'm in Cali now, so fat chance we'll be on at the same time. Heading back to India on the 19th, so we shall Skype then okay? =) how's everything otherwise love?

♥ xx

PM waaaaahhh okay
skype you as SOON as i get home
i have heaps to tell you as well!

♥ ♥

AP well didn't that take long enough -__-
skype soon? Come to Dubai womaann!!
I've been amaazzziiing, so much to tell! I'm thinking that's mutual?

♥ xx

Text 2

Following is an online forum response for an English class (not graded) by student X.

I chose this passage because I found it to be very interesting. This passage is essentially depicting the innermost feelings of a young adolescent living in a "divided house." The feelings that Aurora is feeling can be applied to any child living in a broken home even today. It is interesting to see how Rushdie depicts a scene from that era that could very well be a scene in the lives of young adolescents today. Aurora da Gama is the mother of the main character in this book, Moraes Zogoiby, but in this particular passage Aurora is shown as the child. She waits on Cabral Island for a magician to come and whisk her and her friends off their feet with his tricks and spells. Magic is an important theme in *The Moor's Last Sigh*; strange events are depicted throughout the book which are not possible at all, but are written with such a matter-of-fact tone that they almost seem to be possible. For example, in this case the magician "made fish swim out of the young girls' mouths and drew live snakes from beneath their skirts." These are definitely not common tricks and certainly not those that can be done by a street magician roaming from island to island, therefore the only explanation for it can me real magic. Now this real magic elicits many different reactions from different members of the Da Gama family; Epifania is horrified, Carmen and Aires are disapproving, and Belle and Camoens are delighted to see such fantasy in their daughter's eyes. Epifania's horror shows the tension starting to build between her and Aurora; she cannot just be happy for her grand-daughter. This tension reaches its climax in the family church when Aurora sits idly while she watches her grandmother die (albeit of natural causes) in front of her. Carmen and Aires' disapproval shows their jealousy of being "still-childless." Belle and Camoens are giggling excitedly as they see their only daughter finally understanding the importance of magic, just as Rushdie is trying to explain it to us. Aurora understands that all she needs is a "personal magician" who could fix all the problems in her life. The problems in her life are depicted with a melancholy comparison to a war zone with all the allusions to "chalk lines drawn across its floors, like frontiers" and "spice-sacks…as though they were defenses." The obvious comparison to a war-zone serves to show the conditions in which a young 10-year-old Aurora found herself in, and how much she needed her knight in shining armor, or her "personal magician" to come and fix it all for her. Similarly every child in a broken home today wishes for somebody to come save them.

Text 3

This application essay by student X forms part of a package for a UCAS application—an application to a university in the UK. (You may want to keep in mind that there may be a different style of essay demanded in the UK compared to what is commonly written for a college in the United States. One college counsellor explained the difference: "the US wants you to tell an interesting story that will somehow reveal who you are, while the UK wants the facts about what you have done and why you may be qualified to take a particular course." It is fair to say that in both cases a student is trying to show something about themselves to a faceless committee.

Brought up in developing countries across the world, I always wondered why the roads were better built in other countries or why it took me 2.5 hours to cover a span of 15kms. I wondered why the government coming into power reiterated the problems with infrastructure time and again, but why nobody *really* did anything. As I grew older, I started to recognize potential in each of these countries and realized that it was lack of infrastructure holding them back from becoming a developed country. Infrastructure is what would increase the standard of living for each individual, ensuring economic growth and development for the country as a whole. That's when I decided I want to bring about that change in infrastructure; I want to be a Civil Engineer.

My academic interest in the area soon ensued; I started to become fascinated by the way Mathematics and Physics could be applied to the real world. I saw how I could solve problems concerning population using Maths or find the speed of a car reaching the bottom of an inclined plane using Physics. My passion for the two subjects is exemplified in my hard work and dedication towards the classes that have resulted in my high grades. I took them both at the highest level and continue to excel in them. Another class that I believe will also help me understand the issues facing Civil Engineers is Economics HL. This will help me understand the implications of my actions upon an economy in the long run.

Aside from academics, my activities range from Choir to Student Council. Having attended over 10 international Model United Nation conferences in The Netherlands, Singapore and China, I was exposed to many socioeconomic problems that our world is currently facing. Civil Engineers often work internationally and understanding these issues from the perspective of other countries helps me understand and prepare for possible repercussions. My other activities include National Honour Society. After being selected based on the four pillars of the NHS, character, scholarship, leadership and service, I attained the position of Treasurer in my very first year. In my second year I became President of the National Honour Society implementing changes that made the society more active and involved in helping the community around us, much like I plan to do through the course of my career. In my first year on the basketball team I was awarded Most Valuable Player. This motivated me to play hard, be dedicated and committed in our next season resulting in my Coaches Award for that season. Basketball has taught me to be aggressive and determined; important skills needed to see my projects as an engineer all the way through from feasibility to design and finally, implementation.

My 3 weeks of work experience with an engineering and construction firm sparked my interest in how engineering plays a vital role in the development of a society. In this time, I learned how to use innovation in order to combat problems such as repetitive and unsafe use of "bamboo" formwork to construct buildings. Through the review of several prospective projects, I was exposed to various solutions to poverty and housing problems in metropolitan areas. I discerned that in order to eradicate slum areas and provide the poor with adequate housing and sanitary conditions, it is necessary to construct fast-track, multi-story and precast buildings. Similarly, to combat the lack of portable water available to the poor, these buildings were fitted with rain harvesting mechanisms and solar panels to provide energy...

Questions to the texts

1 Are there differences in the words used in the three passages? What accounts for these differences? What does this reveal about student X?

2 Are there grammar differences in the different passages? Why?

3 If the formality of a writing situation affects language, does it affect personality? Identity?

4 How do the formalities of presentation such as paragraphing, introductions, use of punctuation inform our analysis of the text?

5 How does the choice of language in the broader sense than word or grammar usage reflect the different situations, intentions and context for which each text was written?

When you write a paper for your English class, an application for a job, or a college personal statement, who checks your work? If a college counsellor, a teacher or even a peer edits your work, is it still your work? Professional writers have editors. Isn't it logical to have someone check our language use? Words matter and there are many pressures to force us to conform to the standards imposed on us, or that we impose on ourselves. Is it ever appropriate to put aside such standards? Do we ever censor ourselves? Read the following opening section from an article in the *New Zealand Herald* that announces the very public apology of a public figure. Without knowing the full details of the incident, consider the sentiment expressed about the need for self-censorship alongside the motivation to express strong feelings, like deep-seated political views.

> Hone Harawira knew his words were wrong minutes after sending an email that included bad language and racist comments. Mr. Harawira has apologised for the language that he used in an email but not the sentiment. He told a press conference at the University of Auckland Waipapa Marae this afternoon that there was no pressure from Maori Party leadership to apologise and his apology was genuine.
>
> Mr. Harawira said a meeting later this week with party leadership could result in disciplinary action. He said he had the support of his electorate of Te Tai Tokerau who had voted for a "rebel to be their spokesman."
>
> Mr. Harawira said his wife saw the email shortly after it was sent and told him that he should not have sent it. "What I should have done is ask her to look at it first before I sent it," he said. Asked if she was angry, Mr Harawira said: "love conquers all." ...

Activity

Play the language switch game

As an exercise in class, take a sample of writing and switch the language, the dialect, or the register. What happens if you take a college application essay and write it in everyday slang? How would a formal, academic tone sound on a social networking site? What is the effect of rewriting a passage from a novel in a different dialect? Some of these switches can draw attention to cultural differences, power differences, potential conflicts, and other tensions in language use.

Language and gender

You are probably familiar with the climactic moment in a wedding scene frequently staged in film and television dramas when a couple exchanges marriage vows. Even if you have never been to a wedding, the narrator or screenwriter expects that their audience knows something of the wedding oath and the moment we hear "I now pronounce you … " a cultural lexicon is activated. In fact, the traditional conclusion to this pronouncement is "man and wife." It is frequently changed to "husband and wife" or some other variation of the participants' choosing but the variations are recognized as "redirections" from the traditional "man and wife." Very obviously, the use of language here displays several social attitudes and assumptions, and a specifically gendered form of language. While the word "man" promotes an active state of being and identity, the word for woman, "wife", is recognized only as a function of marital status in relation to "man" (and, of course, this is why it is frequently altered to create more equality in the terminology and, one hopes, the partnership). What is clear is that the use of language is, at the very least, being used to promote a male-oriented view of the world and a lesser status for women in society.

Today there is considerable awareness of the more overt gender biases within language such as the one illustrated above. Some of the most important linguistic changes affecting English since the 1960s have arisen from the way society has come to look differently at the practices and consequences of sexism. There is now a widespread awareness, which was lacking a generation ago, of the way in which language covertly displays social attitudes towards men and women. The relation between language and gender continues to be an issue worthy of our attention, and an important component in the continuing evolution of language.

Biology and sociology

When speaking of language and gender, multiple questions come to mind: Do men and women *speak* differently (use languages that are different phonologically and morphologically)? Or, do men and women *use* language differently (language as practice, and as a distinct culture)? Or, is it some combination of the above? Larger questions of language and identity arise as a result of these queries and we are naturally compelled to follow up with asking whether language shapes who we are or whether it reflects who we are by nature and/or social conditioning. As yet, no absolute answers have emerged but the questions are worth exploring in any critical perspective on language.

Biologists now recognize that the language function of the brain develops differently in girls than in boys. But the repercussions of this knowledge are less certain and do not necessarily mean that women and men ultimately have different languages. Similarly, anthropologists have noted how some languages have phonological and morphological differences in women's and men's language (e.g. women may pronounce vowel sounds slightly differently from men or use more pronouns and intensive adverbs than men). But such sweeping conclusions about separate languages remain difficult to verify.

Activity

Using "Find" and "Replace"

Choose any text—a poem, a piece of prose, an excerpt from a blog—on the Internet and cut and paste it into word. Read the piece and see if you find words or types of words that are repeated. You could even use a text mining tool from the internet to calculate word use and frequency.

Now, use the find and replace function in Microsoft Word to change the text around. What happens, for example, when you change "he" to "she"? Sometimes these changes are more striking when we look at a document or passage with the actual changes made.

Robin Lakoff, for instance, noted differences like the above but concluded that such speech differences suggested not disparate languages but rather disparate powers in society. She argues that because men wield greater power, the language women use tends toward "powerlessness." For example, in her book *Language and Women's Place* (1975), she suggests that women frequently qualify opinions with phrases like "sort of" or "a little bit." Others have attributed this less to powerlessness and more to an attempt to elicit greater involvement by their conversation partner. Still other researchers, Deborah Tannen for instance, believe differences in the use of language might suggest distinct female and male cultures. But this view, too, has been challenged by critics who worry over any attempt at essentializing as a result of gender and believe differences in language usage are preferences as opposed to fixed categories.

What is more certain is that there have been noticeable changes in social attitudes regarding gender that have impacted on how we use language, particularly in writing. Whether it is measured in terms of the significant grammatical change in English over the last 60 years or the recommended use of nonsexist language, awareness of gender has had a tremendous impact on language awareness and the subtle prejudices behind communications. Issues around gender, like race and ethnicity, significantly inform the way language helps to construct identity. In the following exercises, we will explore these ideas further.

Read

The language of men and women

The social linguist Deborah Tannen wrote the following article to highlight the different ways in which boys and girls express themselves on the playground and on the playing fields. Have you noticed these differences yourself? To what extent do you think that these differences relate to social pressures or the different relations to power that men and women have had throughout recent history?

The Talk of the Sandbox; How Johnny and Suzy's Playground Chatter Prepares Them for Life at the Office

BOB HOOVER of the Pittsburgh Post-Gazette was interviewing me when he remarked that after years of coaching boys' softball teams, he was now coaching girls and they were very different. I immediately whipped out my yellow pad and began interviewing him—and discovered that his observations about how girls and boys play softball parallel mine about how women and men talk at work.

Hoover told me that boys' teams always had one or two stars whom the other boys treated with deference. So when he started coaching a girls' team, he began by looking for the leader. He couldn't find one. "The girls who are better athletes don't lord it over the others," he said. "You get the feeling that everyone's the same." When a girl got the ball, she didn't try to throw it all the way home as a strong-armed boy would; instead, she'd throw it to another team member, so they all became better catchers and throwers. He went on, "If a girl makes an error, she's not in the doghouse for a long time, as a boy would be."

"But wait," I interrupted. "I've heard that when girls make a mistake at sports, they often say 'I'm sorry,' whereas boys don't."

That's true, he said, but then the girl forgets it—and so do her teammates. "For boys, sports is a performance art. They're concerned with how they look." When they make an error, they sulk because they've let their teammates down. Girls want to win, but if they lose, they're still all in it together—so the mistake isn't as dreadful for the individual or the team.

What Hoover described in these youngsters were the seeds of behavior I have observed among women and men at work.

The girls who are the best athletes don't "lord it over" the others—just the ethic I found among women in positions of authority. Women managers frequently told me they were good managers because they did not act in an authoritarian manner. They said they did not flaunt their power, or behave as though they were better than their subordinates. Similarly, linguist Elisabeth Kuhn found that women professors in her study informed students of course requirements as if they had magically appeared on the syllabus ("There are two papers. The first paper, ah, let's see, is due … . It's back here [referring to the syllabus] at the beginning"), whereas the men professors made it clear that they had set the requirements ("I have two midterms and a final").

A woman manager might say to her secretary, "Could you do me a favor and type this letter right away?" knowing that her secretary is going to type the letter. But her male boss, on hearing this, might conclude she doesn't feel she deserves the authority she has, just as a boys' coach might think the star athlete doesn't realize how good he is if he doesn't expect his teammates to treat him with deference.

I was especially delighted by Hoover's observation that, although girls are more likely to say, "I'm sorry," they are actually far less sorry when they make a mistake than boys who don't say it, but are "in the doghouse" for a long time. This dramatizes the ritual nature of many women's apologies. How often is a woman who is "always apologizing" seen as weak and lacking in confidence? In fact, for many women, saying "I'm sorry" often doesn't mean "I apologize." It means "I'm sorry that happened."

Like many of the rituals common among women, it's a way of speaking that takes into account the other person's point of view. It can even be an automatic conversational smoother. For example, you left your pad in someone's office; you knock on the door and say, "Excuse me, I left my pad on your desk," and the person whose office it is might reply, "Oh, I'm sorry. Here it is." She knows it is not her fault that you left your pad on her desk; she's just letting you know it's okay.

Finally, I was intrigued by Hoover's remark that boys regard sports as "a performance art" and worry about "how they look." There, perhaps, is the rub, the key to why so many women feel they don't get credit for what they do. From childhood, many boys learn something that is very adaptive to the workplace: Raises and promotions are based on "performance" evaluations and these depend, in large measure, on how you appear in other people's eyes. In other words, you have to worry not only about getting your job done but also about getting credit for what you do.

Getting credit often depends on the way you talk. For example, a woman told me she was given a poor evaluation because her supervisor felt she knew less than her male peers. Her boss, it turned out, reached this conclusion because the woman asked more questions: She was seeking information without regard to how her queries would make her look.

The same principle applies to apologizing. Whereas some women seem to be taking undeserved blame by saying "I'm sorry," some men seem to evade deserved blame. I observed this when a man disconnected a conference call by accidentally elbowing the speaker-phone. When his secretary re-connected the call, I expected him to say, "I'm sorry; I knocked the phone by mistake." Instead he said, "Hey, what happened?! One minute you were there, the next minute you were gone!" Annoying as this might be, there are certainly instances in which people improve their fortunes by covering up mistakes. If Hoover's observations about girls' and boys' athletic styles are fascinating, it is even more revealing to see actual transcripts of children at play and how they mirror the adult workplace. Amy Sheldon, a linguist at the University of Minnesota who studies children talking at play in a day care center, compared the conflicts of pre-school girls and boys. She found that boys who fought with one another tended to pursue their own goal. Girls tended to balance their own interests with those of the other girls through complex verbal negotiations.

Look how different the negotiations were:

Two boys fought over a toy telephone: Tony had it; Charlie wanted it. Tony was sitting on a foam chair with the base of the phone in his lap and the receiver lying beside him. Charlie picked up the receiver, and Tony protested, "No, that's my phone!" He grabbed the telephone cord and tried to pull the receiver away from Charlie, saying, "No, that—uh, it's on MY couch. It's on MY couch, Charlie. It's on MY couch. It's on MY couch." It seems he had only one point to make, so he made it repeatedly as he used physical force to get the phone back.

Charlie ignored Tony and held onto the receiver. Tony then got off the couch, set the phone base on the floor and tried to keep possession of it by overturning the chair on top of it. Charlie managed to push the chair off, get the telephone and win the fight.

This might seem like a typical kids' fight until you compare it with a fight Sheldon videotaped among girls. Here the contested objects were toy medical instruments: Elaine had them; Arlene wanted them. But she didn't just grab for them; she argued her case. Elaine, in turn, balanced her own desire to keep them with Arlene's desire to get them. Elaine lost ground gradually, by compromising.

Arlene began not by grabbing but by asking and giving a reason: "Can I have that, that thing? I'm going to take my baby's temperature." Elaine was agreeable, but cautious: "You can use it—you can use my temperature. Just make sure you can't use anything else unless you can ask." Arlene did just that; she asked for the toy syringe: "May I?" Elaine at first resisted, but gave a reason: "No, I'm gonna need to use the shot in a couple of minutes." Arlene reached for the syringe anyway, explaining in a "beseeching" tone, "But I—I need this though."

Elaine capitulated, but again tried to set limits: "Okay, just use it once." She even gave Arlene permission to give "just a couple of shots."

Arlene then pressed her advantage, and became possessive of her property: "Now don't touch the baby until I get back, because it IS MY BABY! I'll check her ears, okay?" (Even when being demanding, she asked for agreement: "okay?")

Elaine tried to regain some rights through compromise: "Well, let's pretend it's another day, that we have to look in her ears together." Elaine also tried another approach that would give Arlene something she wanted: "I'll have to shot her after, after, after you listen—after you look in her ears," suggested Elaine. Arlene, however, was adamant: "Now don't shot her at all!"

What happened next will sound familiar to anyone who has ever been a little girl or overheard one. Elaine could no longer abide Arlene's selfish behavior and applied the ultimate sanction: "Well, then, you can't come to my birthday!" Arlene uttered the predictable retort: "I don't want to come to your birthday!"

The boys and girls followed different rituals for fighting. Each boy went after what he wanted; they slugged it out; one won. But the girls enacted a complex negotiation, trying to get what they wanted while taking into account what the other wanted.

Here is an example of how women and men at work used comparable strategies. Maureen and Harold, two managers at a medium-size company, were assigned to hire a human-resources coordinator for their division. Each favored a different candidate, and both felt strongly about their preferences. They traded arguments for some time, neither convincing the other. Then Harold said that hiring the candidate Maureen wanted would make him so uncomfortable that he would have to consider resigning. Maureen respected Harold. What's more, she liked him and considered him a friend. So she said what seemed to her the only thing she could say under the circumstances: "Well, I certainly don't want you to feel uncomfortable here. You're one of the pillars of the place." Harold's choice was hired.

What was crucial was not Maureen's and Harold's individual styles in isolation but how they played in concert with each other's style. Harold's threat to quit ensured his triumph—when used with someone for whom it was a trump card. If he had been arguing with someone who regarded this threat as simply another move in the negotiation rather than a non-negotiable expression of deep feelings, the result might have been different. For example, had she said, "That's ridiculous; of course you're not going to quit!" or matched it ("Well, I'd be tempted to quit if we hired your guy"), the decision might well have gone the other way.

Like the girls at play, Maureen was balancing her perspective with those of her colleague and expected him to do the same. Harold was simply going for what he wanted and trusted Maureen to do likewise.

This is not to say that all women and all men, or all boys and girls, behave any one way. Many factors influence our styles, including regional and ethnic backgrounds, family experience and individual personality. But gender is a key factor, and understanding its influence can help clarify what happens when we talk.

Understanding the ritual nature of communication gives you the flexibility to consider different approaches if you're not happy with the reaction you're getting. Someone who tends to avoid expressing disagreement might learn to play "devil's advocate" without taking it as a personal attack. Someone who tends to avoid admitting fault might find it is effective to say "I'm sorry"—that the loss of face is outweighed by a gain in credibility.

There is no one way of talking that will always work best. But understanding how conversational rituals work allows individuals to have more control over their own lives.

Source: Tannen, Deborah. 1994. "The Talk of the Sandbox; How Johnny and Suzy's Playground Chatter Prepares Them for Life at the Office." *The Washington Post*. December 11, 1994.

Tannen brings up interesting points about the relationships between language use and the rituals of everyday life. She notes that it is important to at least be aware of the communication differences between men and women and to theorize about the possible causes. It could also be argued that it is important to think about the consequences of these different ways of expressing hopes, fears, concerns and criticisms. In society at large, or more particularly in the workplace, these differences along with gender biases, can lead to very real discrimination that translates into lack of promotion, lower salaries, and even a lack of political representation.

A related issue is the way stereotypes and differences are communicated or exploited. It is worth considering the role of the media and advertising in relation to gender roles and the ways in which media language itself communicates differences or social expectations. Consider the following advertisement that is clearly directed at a female consumer. Try to consider this advertisement from a variety of positions: how would you read this as a girl? A woman? A female athlete? A man? A male athlete?

Discussion Point

Advertising and gender

Nike advertisement, created in 2005 by Wieden and Kennedy (Nike in-house advertising firm).

Look at the language, images and design components of the Nike advertisement. How does it challenge gender stereotypes? Are there aspects of the ad that paradoxically reinforce or play into these same stereotypes? Is this ad ultimately liberating? How does the text of the advertisement either complement or work against the image?

A response to gender bias

The academic investigation of the role of women in society and the study of both production by women and the representation of women in the arts and media can broadly be allied with feminism. Feminism can be defined as a political perspective or a call to action for the recognition of the rights of women, and as a general commitment to greater social equality and opportunities for women.

In fact, any social endeavour can be investigated through a feminist lens either because it directly concerns women or purposefully neglects them, and their point of view.

Much like a study of the relationship between race and language, the study of language and gender can involve the consideration of texts ranging from an ancient work of literature in which women arguably may play secondary roles in relation to men as characters in the drama (Homer's *The Odyssey*) or a more pivotal and morally questionable role reflecting a male point of view (*Medea* by Euripedes) to contemporary works by female authors and cultural producers.

Activity

Feminist aesthetics

The work of early feminists was often pragmatic, pushing for women's suffrage or equal protection under the law. At the same time, in the academic and literary worlds, many feminists were closely investigating the power relationships between men and women and the different ways in which women express and position themselves in discourses like psychoanalysis and the study of classical texts.

Text 1

The following excerpt from "The Laugh of the Medusa" by the French literary theorist Hélène Cixous, uses as a reference point the ancient Greek and Roman myth of the medusa, one look from whom—or so the legend goes—could turn you to stone. Cixous's response to the threat of a direct gaze into the eyes's of a powerful woman, was to suggest that "You only have to look at the Medusa straight on to see her. And she's not deadly. She's beautiful and she's laughing." Tackling issues like theoretical castration and the physical aspects of the feminine body, as signs of her difference to the masculine subject, Cixous was one of a group of influential French feminists to introduce the concept of "*écriture feminine*," or a feminist aesthetic in women's writing.

> I write this as a woman, towards women. When I say 'woman', I'm speaking of woman in her inevitable struggle against conventional man; and of a universal woman subject who must bring women to their senses and to their meaning in history. But first it must be said that in spite of the enormity of the repression that has kept them in the 'dark'— that dark which people have been trying to make them accept as their attribute—there is, at this time, no general woman, no one typical woman. What they have *in common* I will say. But what strikes me is the infinite richness of their individual constitutions: you can't talk about *a* female sexuality, uniform, homogeneous, classifiable into codes—any more than you can talk about one unconscious resembling another. Women's imaginary is inexhaustible, like music, painting, writing: their stream of phantasms is incredible....
>
> I wished that woman would write and proclaim this unique empire so that other women, other unacknowledged sovereigns, might exclaim: I, too, overflow; my desires have invented new desires, my body knows unheard-of songs. Time and again I, too, have felt so full of luminous torrents that I could burst—burst with forms much more beautiful than those which are put up in frames and sold for a stinking fortune. And I, too, said nothing, showed nothing; I didn't open my mouth, I didn't repaint my half of the world. I was ashamed. I was afraid, and I

swallowed my shame and my fear. I said to myself: You are mad! What' the meaning of these waves, these floods, these outbursts? Where is the ebullient, infinite woman who, immersed as she was in her *naiveté*, kept in the dark about herself, led into self-disdain by the great arm of parental-conjugal phallocentrism, hasn't been ashamed of her strength? Who, surprised and horrified by the fantastic tumult of her drives (for she was made to believe that a well-adjusted normal woman has a ... divine composure), hasn't actually accused herself of being a monster? Who, feeling a funny desire stirring inside her (to sing, to write, to dare to speak, in short, to bring out something new), hasn't thought she was sick? Well, her shameful sickness is that she resists death, that she makes trouble.

And why don't you write? Write! Writing is for you, you are for you; your body is yours, take it. I know why you haven't written. (And why I didn't write before the age of twenty-seven.) Because writing is at once too high, too great for you, it's reserved for the great—that is for 'great men'; and it's 'silly'... Besides, you've written a little, but in secret. And it wasn't good, because it was in secret, and because you punished yourself for writing, because you didn't go all the way, or because you wrote, irresistibly... Write, let no one hold you back, let nothing stop you: not man; not the imbecilic capitalist machinery, in which publishing houses are the crafty, obsequious relayers of imperatives handed down by an economy that works against us and off our backs; and not *yourself*. Smug-faced readers, managing editors, and big bosses don't like the true texts of women—female-sexed texts. That kind scares them. I write woman: woman must write woman. And man, man. So only an oblique consideration will be found here of man; it's up to him to say where his masculinity and femininity are at: this will concern us once men have opened their eyes and seen themselves clearly.

Source: Cixous, Hélène. (trans. by Cohen, Keith & Paula). "The Laugh of the Medusa." *Signs: Journal of Women in Culture and Society*. 1976. vol. 1, no. 4. pp. 875–77.

Questions to the text

1 How does Cixous link the physical and social qualities of women's identity and sexuality to suggest a new approach to writing?

2 How could such an approach to the literary establishment help to bring about change?

3 How do such discourses of liberation also free up men to write differently about themselves?

Text 2

Read the following excerpt from an interview with the artist Barbara Kruger. Note the ways in which Kruger attempts to consider the roles of culture at large, the producer of art and images, and the role of the viewer in particular. What does Kruger suggest about the forces that influence both our views of gender and our roles as consumers? What does Kruger suggest about her job as an artist?

Mitchell Do you think of your own art, insofar as it's engaged with the commercial public sphere—that is, with advertising, publicity, mass media, and other technologies for influencing a consumer public—that it is automatically a form of public art? Or does it stand in opposition to public art?

Kruger	I have a question for you: what is a public sphere which is an uncommercial public sphere? I live and speak through a body which is constructed by moments which are formed by the velocity of power and money. So I don't see this division between what is commercial and what is not commercial. I see rather a broad, nonending flow of moments which are informed if not motored by exchange.
Mitchell	But do you see yourself as "going with the flow," as they used to say, or intervening in it?
Kruger	Again, I think that the word oppositional becomes problematized because it is binary. It has to do with anti's and pro's, or whatever, and basically I feel that there are many of us who are working to make certain displacements, certain changes, who are invested in questions rather than the surety of knowledge. And I think that those are the ways that we displace that flow a little or redirect it.
Mitchell	When someone feels like they're either intervening or redirecting a flow like the circulation of capital or publicity, I want to ask what they have to push off against that allows them to swim upstream or to make eddies against the current. I realize we're speaking figuratively here, but you're awfully good with figures. Is it a sense of solidarity—you said others are also engaged in doing this sort of thing, trying to disrupt the flow, intervene in the circuits in some way? Is it the fact that there are others that gives you some way of having leverage?
Kruger	Yes, in that one hopes to make a space for another kind of viewer. But I think that there are those of us who don't see ourselves as guardians of culture. We hope for a place which allows for differences and tolerances. What we are doing is trying to construct another kind of spectator who has not yet been seen or heard.
Mitchell	You mean a kind of innocent spectator, who hasn't been seduced yet?
Kruger	Oh, no, I didn't say anything about innocence.
Mitchell	You said it was someone who hasn't been approached yet?
Kruger	No, I said someone who in fact has not had control over the devices of their own representation. Now to me that doesn't have anything to do with innocence or morality or anything like that. I'm just saying that we have always been represented rather than tried to represent ourselves.
Mitchell	Would you say the issue, then, is empowerment rather than innocence?
Kruger	Well, the question certainly is one of the constructions of power and how they work and what perpetuates them and what trips them. Sure. Absolutely.

Source: Mitchell, T.J. "An Interview with Barbara Kruger." *Critical Inquiry* 17 (Winter 1991). pp. 434–36.

Text 3
The following work of art by Barbara Kruger has been shown in art galleries and on billboards in the United States. For this work, Kruger appropriated the image of the boy and girl from a painting by the

American realist painter Norman Rockwell (1894–1978), whose illustrations often featured on magazine covers, and were popular if sentimental and idealized images of small-town American life.

Barbara Kruger, *We don't need another hero*, 1987.

Questions to the text

1 Why do you think Kruger uses such old-fashioned images of gender stereotypes? How do they help to subvert or maintain the status quo?

2 How does Kruger's image work to displace our reading of such images and the type of representations you might expect to see on a billboard?

3 Do you agree with Kruger's comments about the commercialization of public space?

4 What responsibilities do we have as spectators and consumers? What responsibilities might we have as cultural producers?

Activity

Reading, speaking and writing

As a final activity, read the following texts which offer perspectives on the relationship between gender roles and reading, speaking, and writing. In the first text, the storyteller, poet and essayist Gloria Anzaldua discusses her relationship to language as a young Hispanic girl living in the United States. The second text is from a collection of graphic short stories by Megan Kelso, in which the a brief exchange between a daughter and her hard-working mother is juxtaposed with the story of a squirrel mother who makes plans to abandon her children and start a new life.

Text 1
How to Tame a Wild Tongue

"We're going to have to control your tongue," the dentist says, pulling out all the metal from my mouth.

Silver bits plop and tinkle into the basin. My mouth is a motherlode.

The dentist is cleaning out my roots. I get a whiff of the stench when I gasp. "I can't cap that tooth yet, you're still draining," he says.

"We're going to have to do something about your tongue," I hear the anger rising in his voice. My tongue keeps pushing out the wads of cotton, pushing back the drills, the long thin needles. "I've never seen anything as strong or as stubborn," he says. And I think, how do you tame a wild tongue, train it to be quiet, how do you bridle and saddle it? How do you make it lie down?

Who is to say that robbing a people of its language is less violent than war?

Ray Gwyn Smith

131

I remember being caught speaking Spanish at recess—that was good for three licks on the knuckles with a sharp ruler. I remember being sent to the corner of the classroom for "talking back" to the Anglo teacher when all I was trying to do was tell her how to pronounce my name. "If you want to be American, speak 'American.' If you don't like it, go back to Mexico where you belong."

"I want to speak English. *Pa'hallar buen trabajo tienes que saber hablar el ingles bien. Que vale toda tu educación si todavía hablas ingles con un* 'accent,'" my mother would say, mortified that I spoke English like a Mexican. At Pan American University, I, and all Chicano students were required to take two speech classes. Their purpose: to get rid of our accents.

Attacks on one's form of expression with the intent to censor are a violation of the First Ammendment. *El Anglo con cara de inocente nos arranco la lengua.* Wild tongues can't be tamed, they can only be cut out.

Overcoming the Tradition of Silence
Ahogadas, escupimos el occuo.
Peleando con nuestra propia sombra
el silencio nos sepulta.

En boca cerrada no entran moscas. "Flies don't enter a closed mouth" is a saying I kept hearing when I was a child. *Ser habladora* was to be a gossip and a liar, to talk too much. *Muchachitas bien criadas,* well-bred girls don't answer back. *Es una falta de respeto* to talk back to one's mother or father. I remember one of the sins I'd recite to the priest in the confession box the few times I went to confession: talking back to my mother, *hablar pa' 'tras, repelar. Hocicona, repelona, chismosa,* having a big mouth, questioning, carrying tales are all signs of being *mal criada.* In my culture they are all words that are derogatory if applied to women—I've never heard them applied to men.

The first time I heard two women, a Puerto Rican and a Cuban, say the word *"nosotras,"* I was shocked. I had not known the word existed. Chicanas use *nosotros* whether we're male or female. We are robbed of our female being by the masculine plural. Language is a male discourse.

And our tongues have become
dry the wilderness has
dried out our tongues and
we have forgotten speech.

Irene Kepfisz

Source: Anzaldua, Gloria. 1987. *Borderlands/La Frontera: The New Mestiza.* San Francisco: Aunt Lute Books. pp. 53–54.)

Text 2

Source: Kelso, Megan. 2006. *The Squirrel Mother*. Seattle: Fantagraphics Books, 2006. pp. 11–13.

Questions to the text

1   What do these texts suggest about societal norms and expectations in relation to reading, writing and speaking?

2   How do these texts demonstrate the transformative power of reading, writing, and speaking?

3   What do these texts suggest about the relationship between language and gender?

4   Considering identity more broadly, how do these texts relate to passages you have read in earlier sections of this chapter?

In conclusion

In the text from the previous activity, Gloria Anzaldua learns, through the social pressures that surround her, that her language is both a strength and a liability. As a writer, she investigates the role language plays in her schooling, her home life and in what she sees as her identity. The title of her book, *Borderlands/La Frontera*, suggests the ways in which we define ourselves within various social, cultural, and geographical borders and, as well, define ourselves by crossing these borders. The study of language in cultural context is also meant to be an exploration of borders—the borders of language and self, community, and the practice of everyday life. The readings, images and ideas in this chapter are a good starting point for you to continue your own varied explorations.

Assessment in language in cultural context

The most important task for you as a student in the language and literature course is to read and think. If you are engaged with the texts you study and participate in class at your school you will learn and improve as a consumer and student of language in all forms. At some point, however, you have to learn to improve your own production and use of language—your communication skills. In this chapter, and in each assessment chapter throughout the rest of this book, we will provide further advice on how to improve your writing and speaking in general and in relation to specific IB external assessments.

In all of the "assessment" chapters you will find the following advice and helpful examples:

- A description of and suggestions for types of writing and speaking you might do in your own school.
- Tips for practicing writing and speaking on your own.
- A description of the IB assessments that will be completed in relation to this section and eventually submitted to the IB.
- Suggestions for the types of topics you might develop.
- Examples of student work.
- Examiner comments on the student samples.
- General ideas and tips from examiners who have marked a wide variety of assessments over the years.

The best advice we can give you is to remember that the IB assessments have been designed to give you a chance to demonstrate what you have learned. The assessments are not meant to be tricky, impossible tests; they are opportunities to explore ideas as much as they are tests of knowledge. The best way to learn how to generate ideas, organize your thoughts and write or speak more effectively and convincingly is to practice. You should understand that there is no one model or correct way to approach many of these assessment tasks. When you look at examples and tips below, think of them as general guidelines or nudges in a possible direction. Ultimately, your best writing is bound to be fresh, personal, and based on your own discoveries that have occurred throughout the course. When you read on, think to yourself, "How would I have approached this topic? Which elements are worth imitating? What would I have done differently? Whose advice is important for me as a writer? What advice have I already incorporated in my work?"

Formative and summative assessment

The work that you do in a course really serves two purposes. In the first instance, a writing assignment such as an essay demonstrates where your skills are at the moment and what you know about the material you have studied. These writing tasks indicate how well you have understood the material and often serve as your grades in a course at school or, when formally submitted, as part of your IB grade. These assessments are called "summative" because they are meant to indicate all that you have learned after going through a particular course of study. Ideally, by the time you work on your IB assessments you have participated in class discussions, listened to lectures, and practiced on your own so that you are ready to demonstrate what you know.

Other work you do in class serves not only to indicate what you have learned so far and helps teachers understand where you need further practice, but gives you the hands-on practice you need to improve your skills. Every time you read, think, and listen, you take steps in learning the material of the course as well as learning how to read and respond to the texts in your world. This type of writing (or speaking) helps you learn and also, once again, helps teachers to think about where you need to go next. This type of work, "formative" assessment, checks your learning and more importantly acts as a catalyst for your learning. Formative assessment, assessment *for* learning, can seem very basic. Think about a class discussion: this kind of performance indicates to the teacher where you are in your thinking process in relation to a text, but it also gives you the practice you need to come up with ideas on the spur of the moment, formulate a quick response, and speak in front of others in a way that is convincing, interesting, or provocative. Participating in class discussion will help you to become a more critical reader and thinker. There is a very short distance between responding in a class discussion and writing an essay response on an exam. In fact, writing and speaking often helps us in the act of thinking. It is relatively easy to read a text and keep our ideas to ourselves. Our initial thoughts about a text may be vague or based upon gut instinct. To take these thoughts to the next level, by writing a few notes, raising your hand, and making a point (especially one that uses the text as an example), makes you work that little bit harder. As well as being good preparation for assessment, it also encourages the kind of critical reading, thinking and responding that you can use in almost any academic or professional context.

You should try to think of every opportunity to speak and write as an opportunity to practice thinking. Over the years, examiners have frequently noted that the best exam answers and the best written tasks reflect an engaged, informed, personal response. What this means is that the candidate has studied the text at hand or considered a question, has re-read, thought, taken notes, and then stepped out on a limb and attempted to communicate those thoughts in a logical way to another person (in this case, an anonymous examiner). Every time you write, speak, and respond, you are both doing and practicing the real work of the course.

Have you ever been given an assignment and not known where to start, frantically searching on the Internet for a model of a comparative essay or the "correct" format for a research paper? The best advice we can give is to strive for clarity. It may be worth reviewing some of the basic tips we have given you in chapter 3 of this book. Throughout these assessment chapters, the student samples and examiner notes can serve as models or suggestions for ways to approach assignments. Before approaching any writing or speaking assignment you should consider your work as an exploration of a text or issue. Writing is an opportunity for you to consider an idea or problem, elaborate on your own thoughts, or explain a complicated issue you have encountered in a text. Reading naturally leads to reflection and thinking. Reflection can lead to a collection of notes, comments, and questions. These initial considerations can lead to a more developed attempt to share your thoughts: an essay, a written task, a commentary, or an oral presentation.

Activities along the way

In class and on your own, you can practice for assessment by responding in speech or writing to the language you encounter in your everyday activities. These activities could be as basic and obvious as going to a movie with your friends and then talking about your reactions. At a slightly more formal level you could create your own blog where you review movies you have seen or books you have read. This course companion is an attempt to give you opportunities to read, engage, and actively reflect. The activities throughout the chapters will help you to apply your skills and practice self-assessment at the same time.

One of the best ways to both analyze language use and improve your own skills is to imitate the texts that you see. How is it that a five-year-old knows how to write a fairy tale about their favorite stuffed animal ("Once upon a time, the princess browny bear …")? How do we know how to talk like a sports commentator? The answer is obviously that we naturally imitate the language use that surrounds us. If you want to improve your essay-writing skills you may want to read examples (as provided below) of the very special genre of student essay writing. In addition, you could expand your horizons and your capabilities by reading essays in newspapers or magazines or even academic journals. You could read an essay on an issue in social linguistics and then try to write an essay with a similar format and in a similar register on an issue related to your own study. And while these examples may help you to improve your essay-writing skills (or to expand your repertoire of available strategies) you can also read and imitate other types of writing. Try reading a short story and then writing one. You can read a variety of blogs and then create your own. The more often you read and imitate, the more likely you are to become fluent in a variety of types of writing.

There are many types of activities that can help you to develop your writing and speaking skills while at the same time allowing you to refine your thinking or demonstrate your understanding of an issue. Here are some activities that you can use to push yourself in the right direction:

- A reading log to record your reflections on personal reading.
- A blog that includes book reviews for texts you read both in and out of class.
- A personal blog that records your thoughts on issues, movies, readings, or interesting ideas you have encountered on the Internet.

- An email newsletter to friends and family reflecting on trips, school sports, activities, or outside interests.

- An essay that imitates an opinion column from a magazine or newspaper such as *Harper's, The Atlantic, The Guardian, The Economist, Al Ahram,* or websites such as www.slate.com or www.aldaily.com.

- Create your own podcast or vodcast to speak your ideas, opinions, reviews, or even experiences to friends, family and others. A podcast or vodcast is a great way to practice for oral commentaries or further oral activities.

Written task 1

What is it?

Written task 1 is an opportunity for students to demonstrate understanding and explore issues in language and literature in an imaginative way. By "imaginative," we do not necessarily mean creative writing—as with all reading and writing in this course, you are expected to demonstrate an intellectual engagement and understanding of the texts studied. The written task offers a more open opportunity to consider different methods for conveying that engagement and understanding. Writing a traditional essay is a familiar and perfectly fine method for demonstrating your understanding of a text or issue but it is perhaps a misnomer on the part of students, teachers, schools and entire educational systems that this is considered to be the *only* way to have a profound intellectual experience with a work. After all, beyond your formal education, you may never write or read another essay in the style of what you are often asked to produce in school. This is not to suggest that there is no role for the formal, traditional essay (you will be writing these as part of the assessments in this course), but written task 1 does represent an opportunity to experiment with several other options. This may range from a more familiar kind of writing such as an editorial, a blog or a pamphlet to a more creative text such as a pastiche, a poem or a dramatic script.

What are the rules?

- First and foremost, written task 1 is not an essay (there may be some very rare circumstances where an essay is acceptable but, in general, it will not be appropriate). Beyond this, you will be looking to find an appropriate text type to use as a model. Again, this is not meant to imply unlimited creative opportunity. It might not be appropriate to convey an overview of the effects of an Internet usage policy in your school, for example, in the form of an epic poem. It may be appropriate, however, to approach the topic by writing a blog, informational pamphlet or newspaper editorial depending on your critical intention.

- Written task 1 must be between 800 and 1000 words only.

- Written task 1 must include a rationale. The rationale should be between 200 and 300 words which do not count toward the written task word count. The rationale should explain the nature of the chosen written task including purpose, formal conventions, relationships to aspects of the course and any other pertinent information as to the aims and objectives of the task.

When is it done?

Written task 1 is likely to be part of your ongoing assessment. Formally, you will be completing at least three (standard level) or four (higher level) written tasks, and submitting one (standard level) or two (higher level) for external moderation. You should be completing written tasks for different parts of the course with at least one referring to the language component of the course (parts 1 and 2) and one referring to the literature component of the course (parts 3 and 4). The exact breakdown and numbers of written tasks will vary from school to school and classroom to classroom. Written task 1 should be an integral and useful writing option for a variety of critical approaches to the works you study. Optimally, written task 1 will be a critical approach that can be used as part of both your formative and summative assessment in this course.

How is it marked?

Very simply, there are four criteria used to assess written task 1:

- **Rationale** Does the rationale adequately explain your work for the written task and how it is linked to the course topic?

- **Task and content** Does the written task convey more substantially developed understanding of the work or topic; is the content appropriate to the task chosen and are the conventions of the text type understood?

- **Organization and argument** Is the structure and organization coherent and sustained? Has the word count been met (two marks will be deducted from tasks that exceed the word count)?

- **Language and style** Is the use of language and style effective and appropriate to the task chosen?

As with any assessment task, whether formative or summative, examiners are looking for a strong understanding of the work or topic and a thoughtful critical engagement. Organized and polished writing is an asset but remember that this is most realized with careful thinking and preparation as well as consciously writing within your own abilities (use your own voice; do not try to *sound* sophisticated, but be honest and open in your engagement with the text).

For part 1, on language and cultural context, there are many written task 1 possibilities that explore interesting overlaps between language, purpose, and audience. The following student samples are based on a simple prompt from a class that has been exploring the use of English in different, traditionally non-English, cultural contexts. The first sample chooses to explore the decision to move to English as the medium of instruction in a Korean university and does so through the form of an editorial. The second sample chooses to debate the merits of forcing signs to be written in Marathi rather than English in the multicultural and multilingual Mumbai through a more personal blog.

Student sample 1

Rational This editorial talks about the English Bilingual Policy that has been embraced by Pohang University of Science and Technology (POSTECH). The policy is about adopting English as an official language at POSTECH. I welcome the policy since it is the monumental first step for Korean colleges to be internationally competitive. However, in this editorial I stand like an antagonist and point out some weaknesses embedded in the policy to let POSTECH know there is a need of change in its plan.

Why is this?

Some facts suggest POSTECH rushed into the decision. POSTECH gives Hong Kong University of Science and Technology (HKUST)'s success model as an example. However, it is an immature decision that did not consider the difference between Korea and Hong Kong. Also POSTECH did not review how many universities struggle with providing a quality level of English. In addition, this decision is toadyism in the point that it will never use Korean anymore just to gain fame internationally; it did not take account of losing identity as Koreans.

Is this really the issue? Are there broader cultural concerns for this editorial?

A bit more on track here. The language is a bit awkward in this section.

After I point out all the potential problems, I give some suggestions and conclude with prospect for the future of POSTECH.

An editorial

POSTECH's English Bilingual Campus Policy

Pohang University of Science and Technology (POSTECH), considered as the best science and technology institute of Korea, announced its English Bilingual Campus Policy which took effect right from this school year. This new policy applies to not only lectures but also conferences, seminars, papers, administration documents and regulations; students should use only English in the campus. "An English Bilingual Campus Policy is inevitable to become a global university," said Baek Seong Gi, the president of POSTECH. He continued, "The background of the rapid advancement of Hong Kong University of Science and Technology (HKUST), which was modeled from POSTECH, was the inspiration behind its bilingual policy."

Why does he have this position? Also ... you will need to reread this, perhaps out loud, for fluency.

Unlike other aspiring global universities that provide only English lectures, POTECH's decision is a breakthrough in the point that it uses only English in the whole campus. Actually such a breakthrough was anticipated for a long time, but no one expected POSTECH, the best Science institute of Korea, would be the one brave enough to announce an "English dominated" university first.

Why brave, and why a breakthrough? How is this good or bad? You need to explain.

POSTECH is faced with many problems these days: conflicts with students, falling in the college rankings and a big leap of Ulsan National Institute of Science and Technology. There is some indication that POSTECH rushed the decision as a reaction to these issues and just to save its skin from these inconvenient conditions; questions remains as to whether these changes have been made for real developmental reasons or rather only as a reaction to these other issues.

Still vague on the issues. How would English help? What are the other concerns?

Furthermore POSTECH did not make it clear why it wants to be global. Why would one of the best universities in Korea move toward globalization in exchange for the risk of losing its cultural identity? Please do not say because it is a trend. Although Mr. Baek gives the improvement of HKUST after adapting a bilingual policy as an example, what he has to be aware of is that Hong Kong has English as its official language while Korea is a country where people spend more than 8 billion dollars every year for English education but do not use English as a primary language of exchange of any kind.

Yes, I think more on this cultural shift here would be important to your editorial.

Mr. Baek may want to justify POSTECH's "globalization" by suggesting that a country like Korea, which has small natural resources, has to focus on raising students to be global leaders by competing them with international students. However, Makoto Kobayashi, 2008 Nobel Prize recipient in physics, cannot speak English at all and did not even have a passport until he had won the prize. It implies what is needed for scientists who have reached a certain level is a good environment for their research, not the ability of speaking English. If a student with an extraordinary potential in science cannot speak English so that he/she even could not give a try for the best science university in Korea (POSTECH), what else in the world can be a bigger loss than that?

A good point.

In addition POSTECH should examine the case of universities that have already started providing English lectures. So far, it is hard to say it is the only path to success. Not all professors have an experience with overseas study and are able to provide quality education in English. In spite of six months of time for preparation that Mr.Beak kindly provided for those who need it, it remains doubtful whether they can overcome the language problem in that short period.

It is not only professors; students also struggle with this change. At the current level of command of English, only a small number of the students would be able to understand lectures that even feel difficult with Korean talking profoundly about subjects. Views that students should have no problem in speaking English to be successful at POSTECH would only give passionate Korean moms an opportunity to increase the expense on private English educations that is already a threat to family budgets.

This is getting a bit particular, and is at the expense of some of the more interesting cultural points you hinted at above.

English is clearly the global language now. So without discussing whether it is toadyism or not, something should be done for universities about English education. The critique above does not mean POSTECH's policy is wholly bad. There are distinct advantages: students' accessibility to up-to-date papers, mostly written in English, would increase, and if the policy adapts successfully, Korea would possess an internationally well-reputed college for the first time. The only obstacle is the impatience of POSTECH officers. The quick change will result incompetent students taught by murmuring professors which will eventually discourage foreign students to come and study at POSTECH. Therefore the gradual increase in the rate of English usage, for example, using English text books first and then starting English lectures later when students get used to it, is preferable along with

But ... to whom are they "toadying"? Is English making inroads in other Korean schools?

continuative investment on Korean culture lectures and campaigns. Only in this way can POSTECH raise trained students who will grow its reputation as well as go for a global university without losing its identity.

This policy, announced after another shocking announcement—using the admission officer system firstly for everyone who applies to POSTECH, will be a chance for POSTECH to re-establish its stable position. However, it must make sure that the drive toward globalization is not through absolute English usage, but through a review of the old (Korean) with enhancements from the new (English).

A bit confusing here.

Examiner comments

Rationale The rationale starts with a relatively straightforward sense of purpose and direction and the topic, of the switch to English at POSTECH, seems an interesting and appropriate focus for a Written Task 1 assessment. Unfortunately, after this the rationale is quite short on detail. Though the candidate apparently welcomes the decision, it is not clear why. The candidate suggests that they will assume a critical position and does try and offer a kind of organization with the rebuttal but again the points lack detail. Cultural differences, challenges to a wholesale switch to an English medium and cultural autonomy all seem valid but are only offered in the vaguest terms here. The final point is weak and vague, reading as an addendum rather than an integral part of the task. Given the length of the rationale, there is room to offer a little more clarity and speak to issues such as the decision to write an editorial and to make more specific connections between this language issue and cultural context.

The decision to write an editorial, however, does seem a reasonable approach to the issue. Though there is a lack of detail and much work is required on the part of the reader, it remains clear that this is an appropriate approach to the task.

The language is clear. Though there is a lack of true sophistication with the language, it is clear and straight forward. The student is writing within their abilities and attempting to use an authentic voice.

Written task The candidate does introduce the topic in the introduction but the larger thrust of the editorial remains uncertain. Even the second paragraph fails to fully identify the primary argument of the writer but only seems to offer a summative overview: that this university is adopting/has adopted an English usage policy. More direct attention toward the larger purpose and the larger ramifications of the primary issue would be helpful here. The language is accurate but as with topic, there is a lack of precision.

The body begins more promisingly than the introduction with a list of some issues relevant to language and cultural context. In particular, this candidate focuses on some questionable assertions by the university and begins to note some ideas more editorial-like. Though this still would have been stronger if it had followed a clearer and more precise introduction, the main body begins with more promise.

A potentially strong point regarding cultural identity as created through language is badly missed here. Though it is mentioned, it is not at all developed or explained. This could well have provided the primary material of the written task—and does seem a significant issue—but is treated too briefly here. This begins a larger trend toward touching on ideas but not expanding or developing them fully. Again, cultural differences and distinctions of both Hong Kong and Korea are cited but not explored as are examples of contributions outside of the English-speaking academe. Other issues, from family budgets to "mumbling" professors to "toadyism" are suggested but not adequately developed.

There is an attempt to offer knowledge of the opposing viewpoint and to respond to it with a more softened compromise position. Unfortunately, this compromise seems to have arisen out of nowhere rather than a rational editorial-like argument. The position adopted in the final paragraph or so again seems slightly underdeveloped and surprising for it. As with much of the piece, there is a lack of detail and detailed development.

The piece does attempt a degree of organization though the points do need further development. The language used is appropriate but can lack precision. The text type adopted—the editorial—is well-chosen but not wholly successfully implemented in this written task. This work suggests a sound foundation but would greatly benefit from further revision with attention to much more development, detail and explanation.

Student sample 2

Rationale In 1995 in Maharashtra state, the Hindu nationalist Shiv Sena party came to power and abruptly called for abandoning foreign names and reverting back to Marathi-language names. Though this affected street names, restaurant signage and billboards, nothing was bigger than changing Bombay to Mumbai. In the last 15 years, Mumbai is accepted the world over though many Mumbaikers still call it Bombay. A common joke is that Bombay is only Mumbai in Delhi.

You may still need a bit more background information here.

Since 1981, the American School of Bombay has been operating as one of the easily recognized international schools in the city. It made a conscious decision not to change its name in the 1990s, arguing that its own independent and international brand identity were more important than local political issues. Though the Shiv Sena is currently not in power in Maharashtra, the school is said to still receive "visits" from members of the party "suggesting" that the school support these changes. The school continues to politely refuse.

Why? Are we getting a sense of the issues here?

In 2008, a small group of terrorists arrived in the city unleashing enough carnage to garner international notice. The school, in concert with the US Consulate in Mumbai, has decided to alter all signage to a simple "ASB" thus avoiding potential violent encounters as a result of the word American.

Another tricky point. We now have a couple of very different reasons for changing or not changing a name. Do you want to focus only on the Marthi issue in this paper?

The issue of the name of the school remains complex. Should the school hold on to its own identity in the face of criticism, or support more autonomous local identity? Should we "hide" our identity in the face of danger, or boldly state who and what we are? I have decided to explore the issue in the form of a blog. On the one hand, a blog is an intensely personal medium and allows me to share feelings about an intensely personal issue: identity. But the issue is also controversial enough that it often isn't covered in more mainstream media like news and newspapers (for fear of violent reprisal by the Shiv Sena) and a blog offers the kind of forum free from the constraints other media may face. The combination of controversial subject and personal and opinionated perspective makes the blog an idea format for thinking about what is in a name.

Some good reasons here for choosing the blog format.

A blog

What's in a name? I know you can never totally trust the rumors that spread through the halls, but at school today the buzz was about the Shiv Sena. Personally the party bugs me. The city can't build a new airport because the SS thinks the new space is on sacred Hindu ground. Every time I go through the airport, it is clear the city needs something new to be the truly global and cosmopolitan place it claims to be. I want to be sensitive to Hinduism (I am Hindu) but can a statue of Ram really not be moved to accommodate the growth and the times?!

Nice tone in first lines here.

Anyway, the SS supposedly "visited" the school to "ask" us to change the name to American School of Mumbai instead of American School of Bombay. Whenever I say I go to American School of Bombay, people ask me why we are called that instead of American School of Mumbai. It just is. It has always been American School of Bombay. I admit when I first came here in ninth grade, I thought it was strange. Maybe even insensitive. But now I feel like I am a part of this school and it is American School of Bombay. Plus the threats of Shiv sometimes make you want to react against them. Their argument that the city needed to throw of the shackles of its colonial past seems good. But when they make the push so hard to incorporate threats and actual violence—like they do so often—the logic is compromised.

Also, the city and the school are more heterogeneous than that. This city and this school are emblems of internationalism. Even if renaming the place is a good idea, the extremism of the Shiv Sena feels like just the other end of a repressive, colonial mindset. This seems like reverting backwards to a less international, less inclusive and more repressive place. I think if the Shiv Sena weren't so extreme, changing the name would be good but ironically, refusing to change to American School of Mumbai feels like the best action toward a more inclusive, international and modern identity. This affirms both the "Indian-ness" of the city and the place as part of a larger global society. I'm proud that the school resists the party's calls to change the name. We probably don't face the same pressures that local merchants and restaurants do to switch to Marathi but I think our resistance is good for everyone. BTW: the school does acknowledge the place of Marathi in the city and the state even if we don't change the name. We have our mission printed in English, Hindi and Marathi all over the school.

But as soon as I developed this pride in American School of Bombay, I found an email notifying the school about new safety measures taken after the November terrorist attack. The school has decided not to use any signs that say the full name any more but just announce itself as ASB. They are worried that the word "American" might attract the wrong kind of attention in a world where attacks are becoming more common and often directed against anything associated with America. Once again the name of the school, the name we use to refer to ourselves, seems to carry much more complicated aspects of identity and a place in the world. Against the Shiv Sena, American School of Bombay seems freeing and expansive but against potential terrorist threats, the same name is limiting and imprisoning. The "American" has come to represent something far more than we are: a political, military, religious and cultural identity that transcends either Bombay or Mumbai.

The truth is that I feel like American School of Bombay represents a notion of Bombay more than of America. We are an international

Keep in mind that a blog doesn't have to be just personal reflection ... how about responding to other blogs or articles about the same issue?

Can you unpack this a bit? Explain exactly why it would be insensitive?

This is an interesting issue that potentially needs more focus and explanation.

How significant is this? Is it the same as recognizing a broader culture?

Interesting. What might be some arguments both for and against retaining the name, even in this instance? Does it suggest that we change in the face of violence?

school that represents a global world of exchange and compromise and I have been proud that the name suggested that. But now the name has been taken to represent something else and I am again stuck with a name that acts more as a limiting label than a true identity. The fact is that the neither is totally accurate but reminds me of the power of names, labels and language. How do I refer to my school and myself in a way that truly reflects what I believe and what to express? Since language and names are both public and unfixed, there is no way to guarantee meaning or identity. I suppose the Shiv Sena has as much right to interpret the name as I do though it makes it impossible for me to ever claim a name myself. Maybe I was naive to think that the name American School of Bombay could represent a resistant or idealistic ideal. But clearly names have enough power to provoke intense response from many sides. I guess I see that pride or anger are both equally probably responses to either Bombay or Mumbai, American or other. I guess I see that because all sides are equal responses, what's in a name can be both everything and nothing.

I wonder what value the name has to the school in the first place? I still wonder about the connection to Bombay as a name …

It's not likely that we will give up having a formal name for our school regardless of what it actually is. But whatever the name is or will be, it's probably sure to cause pride and outrage, stability and change. Maybe that's what always really in a name.

Examiner comments

Rationale This rationale is well written, using precise terminology and varied vocabulary to clearly lay out the basis for the task to follow. The choice of a blog as a text type is somewhat problematic. Many students will choose to write a blog because it may seem like a relatively easy type to imitate. The justification here, though, is reasonable, in that the issue chosen is both appropriate to the section of the course while being of personal and local interest. A blog seems like it would be a logical medium for offering an opinion on these language issues.

Written task One of the most interesting aspects of this task in terms of the writing is that it differs in tone and register so completely from the rationale. The student has clearly attempted to imitate the more casual language of blogs and the use of texting or internet slang such as "BTW," because we have already seen the language use in the rationale, is obviously purposeful and successful. Another strong point of this piece in general is that despite the casual language the student manages to clearly express opinions on a sensitive and complex issue.

The strengths and weaknesses of this task are tied to the language topics that it addresses. The student is clearly engaged with an important issue of language and culture that happens to be tied to her home and school. The blog post is informed and makes references to clearly identified linguistic issues. In attempting to remain an informal blog post, however, a few of these issues are touched on rather lightly. A couple of better explained examples about the influence of nationalists and language policy may have been helpful. In addition, the focus splits part way through the essay when the student begins to discuss the issue of "American" in the school name. In a similar way, the "post" is also complicated by external factors that are briefly discussed such as the terrorist attacks in the city.

Overall, this is an informed, fresh, engaged response that shows knowledge and personal response.

Suggestions for topics

Topics to explore in written task 1 for part 1 of the course (Language in cultural context) are almost unlimited and will be largely focused through the particular topics and issues chosen by your school. You may be exploring issues of gender, for instance, and comparing writings and speeches both about and by women over time in a particular culture. If such a topic were to be of particular interest to you, it could be appropriate to write your own speech in the style of some of the works you have studied or a series of diary entries exploring different challenges and perspectives you have encountered in the texts you have studied. What is important to remember is that you are not asked to write a critical, persuasive essay but to be open to further exploration of a topic while conveying some understanding through your competent manipulation of different text types.

Deciding on a particular text type may be a challenge. You will want to select a text type that is of interest to you but that also matches the topic selected. You will need to articulate why you have selected a particular text type and then demonstrate your mastery of the type in performance. It might not be appropriate, for example, to choose to adopt a humorous tone in a personal diary or work on a multimedia project that employs extensive, wordy and lengthy paragraphs of text. Regardless of the text type you choose, remember that although the topics may involve any number of cultural and social issues the focus of the assessment and of the course is on how language is used to critically reflect on and inform these issues. Following is a brief list of potential written task 1 text types:

- **Editorial** An opinion piece that conveys a critical, personal point of view using a generally formal (persuasive) tone.

- **Advertisement** A clearly promotional piece focusing less on argument and more on positive reinforcement. This will likely include a mix of language and other design features.

- **Mixed media** A collage or mix of formats and media that express a number of possibilities through the juxtaposition of different styles and material elements.

- **Pamphlet** An informational text that seeks to instruct or inform the reader. Can possibly be used to persuade but is more intentionally informative.

- **Blog** An electronic format that is often highly personal, and critical. Can have similar intentions to an essay but is generally less formal with less requirement to substantiate arguments in reference to external sources.

- **Website** A nonlinear format of information presentation with multiple strands branching off from a common point. Generally shorter or more succinct than a more formal text but also with an emphasis on inter-connectedness with a variety of other subject matter, media or text types.

● **Diary entry** Similar to a blog in style but with an emphasis on a more personal response. The audience is also the writer and this encourages more open, honest and personal testimony in reflections on a particular topic.

Written task 2 (higher level)

What is it?

Written task 2 is an opportunity for students to demonstrate their understanding and explore issues in language and literature in a slightly more detailed manner. Unlike written task 1, written task 2 is meant to be a more traditional persuasive academic essay, as a formal critical response. Although you will ultimately decide on the topic, you are asked to respond to one of six set questions, with two questions coming from each of the following three areas of study:

● Reader, culture and text.

● Power and privilege.

● Text and genre.

Written task 2 assessments are meant to be between 800 and 1,000 words. With this assessment task, you will be asked to also provide an outline for your essay. Details about both the outline and the prescribed questions will be provided by your teacher.

What are the rules?

Written task 2 must:

● address one of six possible questions with two questions coming from three distinct areas of study.

● be between 800 and 1,000 words.

● include a written outline.

● be based on material studied in the course.

● include a bibliographic record of all materials used or referred to in the essay. Copies of any material should not be submitted with the task.

When is it done?

This is entirely dependent on the organization of your class. Your teacher will decide when higher level students will focus on written task 2 or if you will perform multiple written task 2 assessments. Written task 2 may be used for any or all parts of the course.

How is it marked?

Very simply, there are four criteria used to assess written task 2:

● **Outline** Does the outline adequately explain, define and highlight the focus of the essay?

● **Response to the question** Does the written task convey a developed and sophisticated understanding of the expectations of the question? Does the essay respond to the question or seek only to summarize information? Is the essay supported by well-chosen and thoroughly explained examples?

- **Organization** Is the structure and organization coherent and sustained? Has the word count been met (two marks will be deducted from tasks that exceed the word count)?
- **Language** Is the use of language effective and appropriate to the task chosen, including an appropriate style and register?

As with any assessment task, whether formative or summative, written task 1 or written task 2, examiners are looking for a strong sense of understanding of the works and topics studied as well as a thoughtful critical engagement. Organized and polished writing is an asset but remember that this is most effectively realized through careful thinking and preparation and writing to your own ability and level of engagements (use your own voice; do not try to sound sophisticated).

Samples of student work with written task 2 can be found in chapter 11.

Further oral activity

What is it?

The further oral activity is an opportunity for students to demonstrate understanding and explore issues in language and literature through any number of methods. It must, of course, be an oral presentation of some sort and addresses the relationship between language, meaning and cultural context. Although this may focus on a heightened awareness of your own cultural practices, it may also focus on an understanding of other cultural practices. Topics and activities will be developed in consultation with your teacher in relation to your aims and objectives and you will conclude your further oral activities by making a short reflective statement on your performance, challenges and progress as measured against personal goals.

What are the rules?

- Further oral activities must include an oral element but may be highly interactive in nature. This means, in particular, that you should not simply be reading from a pre-prepared text.
- You must complete the reflective statement at the conclusion of your further oral activity.

When is it done?

Further oral activities will hopefully be part of your ongoing tasks for assessment. Formally, you will be completing at least two further oral activities, and submit one for external moderation. You will complete at least one further oral activity based on part 1 of the course and one further oral activity based on part 2 of the course. The exact breakdown and number of further oral activities will vary from school to school and classroom to classroom. The intention, however, is that you are consistently approaching the texts throughout the course with a careful and critical reading and through making the most of opportunities to speak about the works. The further oral activity should be an integral part of your approach to study. Ideally, the further oral activity will be used as part of both your formative and summative assessment in this course.

How is it marked?

Very simply, there are four criteria used to assess the further oral activity:

- **Knowledge and understanding of the text(s) and subject matter** Does the presentation adequately convey knowledge and understanding of the works referred to and their larger meaning and cultural significance?

- **Understanding of how language is used** Does the further oral activity convey specific understanding of the way language, style and format are used to create meaning and/or effect?

- **Organization** Is the structure and organization coherent and sustained?

- **Language** Is the use of language effective and appropriate to the task chosen?

As with any assessment task, whether formative or summative, examiners are looking for a strong sense of understanding of the work or topic and a thoughtful critical engagement. Organized and polished speaking is an asset but remember that this is most realized with careful thinking and preparation as well as consciously writing within your own abilities (use your own voice; do not try and sound sophisticated).

The further oral activity is one where you can exercise quite a bit of choice to exploit your own intellectual and creative talents and interests. You may have an opportunity to act out a role, create interactive websites, sing or dance, bring in paintings or art works; or lead discussion, debate and seminars. The further oral activity allows for and encourages exploration and experimentation. However, there is also room to do more traditional oral presentations. A brief list of potential formal oral activities for part 1 (Language in cultural context) of the course includes the following:

- An exploration of the lyrics of the songs used in the musical *Fela!*, also in relation to the presentations through dance and costume.

- A role play of a fictional overheard conversation between Clifford Geertz and Raymond Williams at a coffee shop on the role of language in the construction of culture.

- A formal debate arguing for and against the use of domain names in non-Roman alphabets and the effect on the common production of knowledge.

- A role play demonstrating a pitch by a public relations firm explaining its new print campaign on an environmental issue.

- A consideration of the way children are presented in the movies *Home Alone* and *Stand By Me*.

- A comparison of different responses to an oil spill from the perspectives of the oil corporation, the local government, the local business community, the local residential community and an environmental group.

Exam paper 1: comparative textual analysis (HL); textual analysis (SL)

What is it?

The comparative textual analysis/textual analysis is the first paper of the IB exam that is taken at the end of the two-year Diploma Programme. The marks on paper 1 make up 25% of the overall IB mark. Although paper 1 is not tied to any one part of the course, the skills you develop in "Language in cultural context" are clearly relevant to the task. This exam paper is a challenging activity that asks you to be an independent critic of language in action—the main task of the course as a whole.

At the higher level, paper 1 will consist of two pairs of previously unseen texts for comparative analysis, one of which will be chosen for analysis. The pairing could include two nonliterary texts or one literary and one nonliterary text. One of these texts may also be a visual text. The pairs of texts will be linked in terms of themes, issues, content, or techniques so that you will find clear avenues for comparison and investigation. At standard level, you will select one text for analysis from a choice of two. The texts will be nonliterary only and although they may contain an image or images, they will not consist of an image alone. Extracts may include a variety of text types, such as the following:

- advertisement
- opinion column
- essay
- electronic text such as a blog
- brochure
- memoir, diary, or autobiography
- poem
- screenplay
- novel or short story
- press photograph
- satirical cartoon.

What are the rules?

At higher level you will have two hours to complete the exam, while at standard level you have one-and-a-half hours. During this time you will be expected to read the texts, select one/one pair on which to write a commentary, then produce a continuous, well-organized written response. The analysis needs to consider structure, language, style, text type and/or genre, as well as a discussion of content issues. Ultimately, the essay you write should demonstrate your understanding of the text/texts as well as an understanding of the way language functions for a variety of purposes. Your written response should never be a basic list of attributes, similarities and differences or features but should be a developed essay that makes observations, uses sections or quotes from the texts/texts as support, explains ideas, and elaborates on significance.

You will have opportunities to practice this comparative textual analysis in class. Almost all of the activities in this book are essentially asking you to read, think, make comparisons and somehow comment on language in action, so the comparative textual analysis should never feel like a unique or particularly complex task.

How is it marked?

Examiners are looking for a well-written, coherent commentary that demonstrates an understanding of the text/texts and their relationship to each other (at higher level). Examiners will mark the paper in relation to understanding of the texts, understanding of the use and effects of stylistic features including the features of visual texts, organization and development, and language. At higher level, essays must make comparisons between the two exam texts. The following is a summary of what examiners consider in each category:

- **Understanding and comparison of texts (HL)/Understanding of the text (SL)** Is there an understanding of the content, ideas, and possible purposes of the texts? Where appropriate, is there an understanding of possible contexts? At higher level, has the analysis shown the similarities and differences between texts?

- **Understanding of the use and effects of stylistic features** Does the analysis show an awareness of how stylistic features such as language, structure, tone, style and technique are used to construct meaning? Does the analysis show the possible effects of these features on the reader?

- **Organization and development** How organized, coherent, logical and purposeful is the analysis? At higher level, how balanced is the analysis (does the analysis give an equal amount of attention to each text)?

- **Language** Is the register, style and terminology appropriate to the task at hand? How accurate is grammar and vocabulary? Is the language clear, concise and precise?

How should I approach the task?

The comparative textual analysis/textual analysis should be approached in the same way that you would read and analyze any texts in class. Here are some suggestions for a way to handle the analysis:

- Read all passages, perhaps first without making notes or marks. Try to get a general sense or feel for all texts.

- Re-read the text/texts, this time noting difficult aspects, moments where you have questions, or elements that you think are most important.

- Read the text/texts again making more extensive notes and, at higher level, being sure to note similar and different aspects or relationships between the texts.

- Begin to organize your notes. What is most important? What is less important but still worth mentioning?

- Be sure not to leave out substantial parts of the text/texts in your notes or discussion.

- When preparing to write you may wonder how to organize your essay. While you should obviously have an introduction, body, and conclusion, you need to consider other elements. Your introduction may make reference to the most basic content or aspects of the text/texts. Your introduction will have a main point, thesis, or focus but may be somewhat broad to allow you to discuss all aspects of the text/texts.

- At higher level, while it is fine for your essay to concentrate on one text for a few paragraphs followed by a discussion of the next text, you will have to be careful to remember that you are making a comparison. You do not want to write what seems like two independent essays on different texts. Sometimes transition or comparative words can help here ("while in text one the tone is …. text 2 uses …") but it may be even easier for each paragraph to focus on an idea or technique and to discuss both texts together.

Sample of a comparative textual analysis

Look at the following example of an exam question for a comparative textual analysis along with a sample student response. When reading these two texts, keep in mind the issues you have considered in the previous chapter. How might your knowledge and skills come to bear on this activity? What important features or ideas do you notice? Remember to think critically even when reading the student response. What do you like about the response? What do you find problematic? Has the student left anything out? Are there areas where the student could better explain ideas? How could you do it differently or even better?

Comparative textual analysis

Compare and analyze one of the pairs of texts below. Include comments on the similarities and differences between the texts and the significance of any possible contexts, audience, purpose, and the use of linguistic and literary devices.

Text 1

A United Fruit Company travel poster from 1922.

Text 2

Squatters Take on Developers

October 15, 2007 Miami Herald, The (FL) Edition: Final
Section: Business Monday
Page: 12G
Author: BENJAMIN SHORS

ISLA CARENERO, PANAMA—In the late 1980s, Nicasio Jiménez built two listing shacks with mangrove beams, a roof of scavenged tin, and rough floor planks that allowed Caribbean breezes and tsetse flies to flit through the cracks. Jiménez, a 61-year-old retired banana pruner who earned $1 an hour, did not own the waterfront land. Like hundreds of other low-income people living in Bocas del Toro, a stunning archipelago once relegated to some of Panamas poorest residents, he instead relied on "squatter rights" written into the country's law.

Now, as foreign investment transforms these languid islands, Jiménez family faces eviction from a Naples developer who claims he bought the property from a third party.

"Before, nobody wanted this land," said Feliciano Santos, Jiménezs 36-year-old son-in-law. "You didn't need documents. This was a garbage disposal area. We are the ones who cut our feet and got dirty working the land."

For centuries, this Caribbean island has been a beautiful place to be dirt poor. But in recent years, a booming real estate market has brought American entrepreneurs into direct conflict with Afro-Caribbean and indigenous Indians who occupy these once-isolated isles.

Now, developers have targeted an emerging demographic: retirees from America and Europe.

Although American expatriates have been a part of the funky vibe in Bocas since the 1990s, they remained a relatively minor note in the Caribbean town. But as development in Panama City boomed—construction permits last year topped $1 billion—investors pushed into more remote reaches of the country.

Now, critics say, the size of the new developments threaten to displace hundreds of low-income island residents, many of whom live on prime oceanfront real estate.

In the past year, the conflict has spiraled. Armed private security guards patrol disputed beaches. A powerful union of construction workers has leveled charges of "colonialism" against several developers. Homes have mysteriously burned and been torn to the ground.

"There is this tremendous lust for the coastline," said Osvaldo Jordan, executive director of the Alliance for Conservation and Development, a Panamanian nonprofit group based in Panama City. "Developers and speculators will use any means necessary to get the land from the people.

Sample student response

Text 1, a cruise line advertisement from 1922, and text 2, a newspaper article from 2007, both offer unique perspectives on the Caribbean and on tourism in the area. The advertisement attempts to convince people to have a holiday in the beautiful tropics while the newspaper article explains how tourism and development are affecting local people and causing them to lose their homes. It is interesting that both pieces talk about the beauty of the Caribbean but while the newspaper article sees tourism as exploitation, the advertisement is maybe an example of how exploitation begins or how we may not even consider the local people when we look for a luxurious vacation.

A nice, clear introduction although this last sentence might need more explanation. Also, does it matter or is it worth mentioning the different time periods here?

First aspect we can note about the two texts is that they have different purposes. This is inherently obvious as newspapers and advertisements generally do not target the same audience, nor are they built for the same purpose. The advertisement is trying to persuade the audience and the newspaper article is trying to inform the audience and support its bias. The audience in question for both is also different. The newspaper is targeting a more general audience while the advertisement is targeted at a more specific audience that can be likened to the people noted in the newspaper text—"retirees from America and Europe" and other holiday goers. The advertisement notes, near the top, that "only first class passengers are carried." The advertisement wants the viewer to think of himself as first class and maybe that he deserves such a nice vacation. The reader of the newspaper article is more likely to put themselves into the position of the people quoted in the text, the Jimenez family members, and to think that the holiday goers and developers are insensitive.

Watch language in this sentence.

Is it trying to support a bias? Is this the best way to put this?

Could be clearer and more specific.

This may be true, but how does the language in the text push the reader to do this?

The linguistic devices that each use are different to serve these purposes. For example, in the advertisement only uses words with positive denotations such as "delightful" and "noteworthy for excellence". This is obviously to convince the people looking at the advertisement to use the services detailed, because nobody would want to go to on a holiday to a place that is "unpleasant" and "insignificant for its achievements". This serves the advertisements purpose which is to persuade the audience to use their services over other competitor's services. The advertisement also takes advantage of the name of the cruise line and the image. "The Great White Fleet" sounds impressive and I also think that it is interesting that the people reading this advertisement in 1922 were most likely rich Caucasian people. It seems as if these people are the wealthy white colonialists being taken down to the "brown" Caribbean. The image itself shows light skinned people dressed in expensive clothing, enjoying their cruise. The advertisement emphasizes the "cool" temperatures and the "comfort" of the ship and the passengers seem almost dressed for winter. I think the Caribbean is shown to be an exotic place but almost too hot and uncomfortable for a wealthy passenger. If we compare this to the newspaper article, which has a bit of bias in it towards the squatters, we can see that it too uses words with positive denotations— "stunning", "beautiful" and "Caribbean breeze" – but each of these words are followed by words with a negative denotation—

Need a better transition here.

An interesting reading.

"relegated … poorest", "dirt poor", "tsetse flies". This contrast is used to display the already unpleasant conditions that the squatters live in, and that the development will take them into an even deeper level of poverty and depression. When the author writes that the Caribbean is a "beautiful place to be dirt poor" the reader is bluntly reminded of how we normally view the islands as tropical paradise but that this view may be ignorant of the sometimes sad conditions. This is helping to serve the newspapers aim, which is to inform the audience by being descriptive about the topic at hand, but it also shows some bias in favor of the local people. Even the title of the article makes the reader root for the underdog as the "squatters take on developers." The developers in the article are similar to the passengers in the advertisement because they come to the Caribbean and change it to meet their needs rather than becoming part of the local culture.

Good point.

Is this the goal?

OK … but is this worse? Better? Why?

We can see that the size of the overall text is different for each text. The advertisement is just a small snippet of 3 paragraphs while the newspaper article is a detailed look into the event at hand, with the newspaper being substantially larger in text size than the advertisement. This again is to serve their respective purposes. The advertisement has to have small and short text because it does not have a static audience. Unless the audience is forced to read the poster, as they are in elevators and waiting for buses etc, they will not stop their lives just to read an advertisement that probably won't affect their lives. This audience is a chance audience, because you cannot specifically force the audience to read the advertisement. It is up to the audience's discretion to read the advertisement and so this is why the text is so small—so that all pertinent information can be communicated quickly without any distracting or unnecessary text. This is in stark contrast to the newspaper article, but it still serves the purpose the newspaper was aiming for. Since the newspaper is trying to be informative it has a larger amount of text to convey as much information as possible to its audience. Also it is serving the secondary purpose of the newspaper which is to support its bias. With a larger amount of text there is more space for the newspaper to support its bias.

Does not seem like a very significant point of comparison here.

The voice in each text is different. The advertisement has a much stronger, persuasive voice than the newspaper which is aiming for a more neutral, formal voice. The advertisement seems to portray a much more personal voice by talking to "you" in the first person. This conveys a much more personal connection with you the audience, thereby making you want to use the services that they provide because they make themselves seem more like a friend than as a salesperson. This is in contrast to the newspaper which has a more authoritative but less personal voice and tries to stay in the third person at all times. This is to serve its purpose because it is trying to stay in the informative tone and it doesn't need a voice to show its bias so having no personality is fine for the newspaper because it doesn't detract from the purpose.

Not so sure … you need some more specific supporting evidence here.

Show this with evidence from the texts.

In the end, the most interesting aspect of both texts is that they somehow have very similar audiences but the authors and purpose vary greatly. We can assume that both the advertisement and the article could be found in a newspaper. The advertisement, though, convinces somewhat wealthy people to visit and take advantage of the islands. The authors of the piece are really the "United Fruit Company" that we can assume is a company that has ships going into the Caribbean because they have fruit exporting business there. They might be a company that can be seen as exploiting the Caribbean and attempting to make money from business and tourism. The author of the newspaper article is convincing a very similar audience that tourism has to be more sensitive to the people who "got dirty working the land." The owner of the shack on the Caribbean beach even works as a banana company which is ironic when compared to the advertisement text created by a fruit company.

Yes … could you do more with this in comparing and contrasting the different time periods?

In conclusion I think that both these texts are effective in their methods of achieving their purposes. The advertisement was short and well made for the average passerby to get the gist of what was trying to be conveyed and the newspaper clearly stated its stance on the squatter vs. development issue in Panama and still managed to give an informative assessment of the situation. The advertisement sells beauty and comfort to people who want to be rich and relaxed and probably leads to ignorant exploitation while the newspaper article attempts to convince a similar type of audience that trying to relax in the Caribbean might have some serious side effects.

Examiner comments

This candidate has written in a clear, straightforward way that demonstrates an understanding of the main content and techniques of the two texts. At the same time, the candidate has managed to convey a sense of the cultural issues at play in the texts and the possible relationships between author, purpose, and reader.

The introduction is clear and also focuses attention on an interesting and relative originally perspective on the relationship between the two texts and the way the audiences, separated by many decades, share some similarities. While the first body paragraph is relatively basic or underdeveloped it does identify the main purposes of the texts. The paragraph could be improved, perhaps, by how purpose might affect what is portrayed or even left out of either text. The second body paragraph, while somewhat long and disorganized, calls attention to particular linguistic features and how they might affect the reader.

The fourth body track goes off track in that it speculates without much evidence and the issue discussed, the relative size of each text, doesn't seem to be an issue. At the same time, the idea that an advertisement is meant to attract attention quickly and with shorter, perhaps bolder, images and statements, is not really mistaken. The paragraph could have been redeemed by a closer focus on the type of language and images used because of the compressed space in the advertisement or the types of arguments and support used in the longer, more developed article.

The penultimate paragraph gets back on track with a nice observation about the authors/producers of the two texts. The connections made in relation to the role of the fruit company are perceptive.

Conclusion

It is important to remember that the assessment for part 1 (Language in cultural context) of the course—and for all parts of the course for that matter—is not intending to measure your mastery of any particular body of content. Instead, throughout the course you are asked to demonstrate understanding and critical exploration of issues around language and literature. The assessments, as a result, are attempting to gauge your skills and abilities with *approaching* works and issues. In truth, you will always be reading, thinking about and presenting ideas about language and literature. To borrow terms from the theatre, formal assessments represent only those "live performances" where you present the same material you have been rehearsing but in full-costume and make-up. The assessments, then, are not unique or distinct tasks but rather the natural culmination of your ongoing hard work and practice throughout the course.

6 Language and mass communication

Activity

Ad analysis

Look at this advertisement, and jot down your general reflections on its purpose, meaning and effect, before answering the questions below.

- Who created this advertisement?
- Is this advertisement attractive or enticing? What particular techniques are used to get attention, affect emotion, or entertain?
- What values are represented in this advertisement?
- What point of view is left out in this advertisement?
- What is the purpose of this advertisement?

"Arcade," by the ad agency Lowe Bull, Johannesburg.

Analyze the advertisement on this page before you start reading further. After completing this brief activity, you might notice two things: the types of questions we ask in relation to advertising and other forms of mass communication are similar to the types of critical approaches we take throughout this course, and some forms of mass communication have more obvious objectives than others (capturing your attention, making money, influencing choices etc.). In addition, you may have noticed that the "texts" we consider when studying mass communication can be as complex and subtle, employing a variety of techniques, as a text that we may more commonly study as a work of literature. In this section of the course you will pay particular attention to the products of mass communication in order to understand how they are produced and consumed: their purpose and assumptions. You will also pay focused attention to the role language plays in mass communication and the way a media product participates in a language or sign system with a set of rules and purposes.

The focus on language

In this book we have often stressed the point that language surrounds us and that it is an integral part of culture and identity. While many of our communicative acts take place in a face-to-face environment or at least appear to be personal (reading a book, for example, can have the feel of an intimate conversation), much of the language you encounter comes to you through a variety of media and is often "sent" not only to you, but to a wide number of people through books, magazines and mp3s, as well as via the Internet or through film or television. While there are many courses that choose to focus on the study of media and media institutions or the critical study of their messages, this course has a particular focus on the specific relationship between language and mass communication through a variety of **media**. When you have completed this chapter, you should feel comfortable analyzing a wide variety of media and the ways they convey meaning.

Media is the plural of medium.

The media offers us easy access to a wide set of data when considering the importance of language in society. Because of the availability of the media and mass communication at the click of a switch, linguists not only have different examples of language use at their fingertips, but this language use is easily recorded. The study of these examples gives us insight into general language use and additionally suggests differences between the use of language in one **medium**, a newspaper for example, and another, like a website (although, these could also be the same, now that most print media is also available online). From the study of language across a variety of media, questions begin to arise about the effect of the different media on language. For example, how are news stories communicated differently on television, in a major newspaper, or through its online platform? Is our level and duration of attention different when approaching different media? Does this, in turn, affect the construction of a message in the first place? Is there a difference in language use when it is accompanied by images, moving pictures, or sounds? These are some of the linguistic concerns in relation to mass communication.

Medium is the means or instrument of communication such as a newspaper or television. Society at large often refers to "the media" as the broad collection of institutions that, through a variety of media, communicate information to the public.

The study of language use in a given medium over time (for example, in the comparison between print advertising in the 1950s to print advertising now) and the comparative study of language use across different media (for example, in the comparison between an interactive e-book and a traditional print book) leads to cultural insights as well. We can see that different media incorporate a wide variety of signs and sign systems in order to convey messages. Over time, different types of media also begin to establish ways of communicating that become familiar to a wide audience. Society at large is influenced by the media to such a large extent that we seldom stop to consider its particular importance or effects. A close engagement with a variety of media messages allows us to at least attempt to step back from our cultural assumptions and examine the complex relationships between identity, community, language, and powerful modes of production and communication (including the institutions and individuals active within them).

Definition of mass communication

Before we go any further, it is important to make a few distinctions about the focus of study in this section of the course. For instance, what exactly do we mean by mass communication, compared to other forms of communication? Back and forth communication that takes place between individuals or among a group of people is traditionally called reciprocal or dyadic communication. Mass communication takes place between an agent in the center and a large group on the periphery. In other words, mass communication is a language act that is "one way" and is sent out to an often incalculably large number of people. It is easy to think about a radio broadcast taking place in a studio and being sent out over the airwaves to a large number of people. Other typical forms of mass communication include a newspaper that is printed in one place and distributed to a large readership located elsewhere, or even a live speech that is amplified by speakers heard by a mass assembled audience. Often, when we talk about studying media, we are essentially saying that we are studying traditional forms of mass communication.

The digital age has, of course, complicated the definition of mass communication. Lines are now blurred between reciprocal and mass communication. Media that formerly was used only for one-way communication can now involve interaction (personal media devices can help the individual to enter into the realm of mass communication). Think of an earlier example, such as the telephone. The telephone is a form of technology- or medium-assisted interactive communication. But with recording, automated dialing, and other advances, the telephone can be used for mass communication: advertisements and political messages can be "broadcast" (sent to a large number of people). More current examples clearly complicate our traditional ideas of mass communication and the production of technology-assisted messages. Individuals can post their own writing, audio, and video productions on the Internet. Politicians, in a live speech to a television audience, can watch and respond to videos submitted by individuals. The distinction between one-way communication to a large audience and conversations among a group of individuals has got more complicated.

The division between the great mass of people and the individual is closely linked to the division between the public and the private. Typically, we think of media or mass communication as a somewhat anonymous, public affair. When we think of the language of news broadcasts, for example, the language that comes to mind is somewhat formal, addressed to a large audience, and intended to serve a variety of tastes and interests in a general way. When it enters our homes and personal life, we can either pay attention to it or turn it off, something the sender has no control of, although they may monitor our listening and viewing habits. Again, digital advances are complicating our ideas of the public/private boundary. Social networking makes it possible to share previously private information with a large group of people, often anonymously. Blogging is a form of mass communication that can use a private style of writing and address a large audience, but perhaps an audience, unlike that for a major news programme, with particular tastes. These examples don't even begin to approach the media blending that happens today with video sites on the Internet, targeted "infomercials" on television, and "reality" programs such as "Big Brother."

The medium that mediates

Some things we know about the world have come to us from first-hand experience. If you have run a long-distance race, you probably know the feeling of excitement and exhaustion that overwhelms you as you near the finish line. Most information, however, comes to us through some other channel, through something that stands in the middle, or to use the latin term *medius*, mediates between us and the

Public? Private? Reciprocal? Mass?

Have you ever received a "phishing" email? These emails, designed to find your personal and financial information, sometimes involve viral computer programs and other times involve individuals simply trying to convince you to give private information.

Peter Rabinowitz, a literary scholar and professor at Ithaca College in the United States has received these emails and turned them into an interesting media and writing assignment that calls attention to the roles of sender and receiver, the private/public boundary, and mass versus private communication as well as other language issues related to literature such as the complex relationships between author, narrator and reader. Rabinowitz and his class participate in "baiting" by responding to a phishing email and attempting to engage the sender, the attempted fraudster, in a long conversation that involves fictional stories, misleading information, and sometimes other participants. While Rabinowitz notes that the assignment has some risk involved, the students keep their real identities a close secret and they learn a great deal about the complicated roles of modern day digital mass communication.

actual experience. People can act as a medium of communication: a person gives you information that you have not received first hand. If your friend tells you what she learned the day before in physics class, she acts as a medium between you and the actual experience of sitting in the class and taking notes. Of course, individuals have a limited potential to reach a wide audience and so often so we use a variety of formats to communicate information. One of the oldest media devices is the book. With the advent of the printing press in the late 1400s more people had access to events they could not experience themselves through the new communication medium. The history of the modern era can be conceived as the history of changes in the variety of media (the plural of medium) available to us and the ease of access to these media. The list of modern technological media includes the book, the telephone, television, film, and the Internet. Every medium serves as a channel for communication and each medium also filters or alters the message in some way before it reaches its audience.

Communication models

In the late 1940s information theorists Claude Elwood Shannon and Warren Weaver described what has come to be known as the Shannon-Weaver model of communication. This basic description of language transmission often serves as a starting point for studying the various stages of sending and receiving a message. The writings of Shannon and Weaver are quite complex and delve into detailed issues of encoding/decoding and the nature of noise, or those elements like poor satellite reception that affect the quality of the reception of information. The usefulness of the model is also complicated by current developments in technology that make the roles of participants and various technologies less clear. Here is a rough drawing of the model:

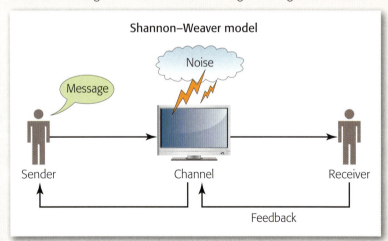

Also in the late 1940s, the political scientist Harold Lasswell developed a formula for the study of communicative acts. This model is similar to the Shannon-Weaver model and suggests possible areas for analytic attention.

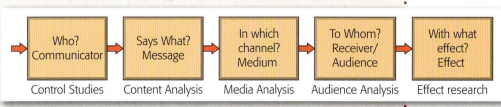

The mass media, that can be discussed as a conglomerate or plural mode of transmission, is the form of communication technology and its business interests that enables communication. While these technologies have changed over time, the technologies do not necessarily die; rather, they develop in relation to each other, and in relation to both technological developments and economic and social demands. The following is a basic list of the major categories of communication media in the order that they were developed (the list doesn't consider the telephone and telegraph, as these were initially meant to be only for one-to-one communication):

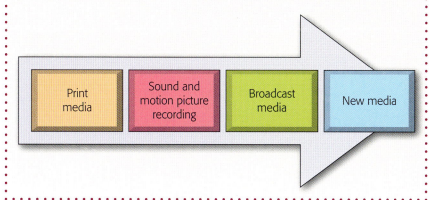

As part of this course, it is important to reflect on the use of language in the mass media categories presented above. It is also interesting to consider the ways in which these media environments influence each other. A brief overview here can give you some ideas to consider as you begin to analyze media messages.

Print media

Modern mass communication started with the birth of print media following the invention of the printing press by Johannes Gutenberg in 1450. Before the printing press, texts were copied by hand and these manuscripts could not be widely disseminated. The printing press enabled the relatively inexpensive reproduction of texts for a larger audience which, in turn, led to an increase in information available to a significant proportion of society. With the increased availability of information in print came the societal focus on the importance of literacy for educated members of society which, in its own way, spurred the widening variety of texts available in print. Literate life developed from a small number of people reading, for the most part, religious texts, to a wider general public with access to works of fiction and nonfiction, and eventually more ephemeral forms of writing promoted through newspapers and magazines.

The history of print media is complex and is worth considering in greater detail in relation to the study of media institutions in the second half of this chapter but it is important to note here that the print media has not remained stagnant and is, in fact, facing some of its greatest changes today. As a particular media gains attention and value it can also be used to influence people or to gain power. Print naturally attracted investment that led to the development of publishing firms and newspaper organizations. Newspaper and magazine production saw a steady rise from the late 1800s until the 1970s. The number of books printed continued to increase. But what do you think caused the decline in newspaper and magazine circulation? One answer is television. As mentioned earlier, the advent of new media often replaces older media or forces them to change. Newspapers may have been forced to highlight particular qualities, such as more detailed, in-depth reporting not suitable for a short news broadcast for example, or to downplay others, such as the ability to report news as it happens. What changes are happening to newspapers with the advent of the Internet? Considering print media more broadly, how has the Internet or the development of e-readers had a positive or negative impact on print media? And how are e-books different to print publications? What will become of book shops and lending libraries in the digital era? These questions are all worth considering and the answers may offer insights into the ways in which language is affected by the media interface.

Sound and motion picture recording

In the late 1800s, Thomas Edison invented separate technologies for the recording of sound and of moving pictures. The development of these technologies led to the 20th-century rise of recording industries. First silent film and then in the 1920s sound film created the opportunity to record the spectacle of events—ranging from gatherings and fairs to political speeches—and present them to a large audience. The technology was also used to display fictional representations much like plays. Audiences no longer had to rely solely on local or traveling theater groups for their entertainment. Similarly, the development of sound-recording technology gave birth to the record industry and, while access to music and recorded performance increased, the reliance on sheet music and live performances began to decrease.

With changes in technology and modes of distribution, these technologies were involved in a mutual exchange and development with the times. As camera technology has become less expensive and cumbersome, more individuals are apt to do their own "motion picture" recording. The same goes for audio recording. And with development of personal recording devices, and the ability to distribute films in other formats such as DVDs (starting from tape, to CD, to DVD, and now to digital formats), both industries continue to change.

Broadcast media

Broadcast media refers to those technologies that allow for the transmission of images and sound over long distances to a wide audience. Film (as opposed to video technology) can record but not play live to audiences, similar to traditional audio recording devices (records, tapes, and cds), making some form of time delay necessary between production and communication. Broadcast technology makes it possible for live or recorded messages to be sent over the airwaves directly, with or without editorial intervention. In the era of television, and before that radio, people could experience communicative acts as they happened in real time, as well as previously recorded time, from the ringside seat of their own. And going back a bit, the era of the microphone made it possible to project a voice through loud speakers, enabling the first forms of mass communication as a live presentation; none of this would

Discussion Point

Consider the following question about media change:

1 What effect would video recording and distribution have on the film industry?

2 How would radio and television negatively affect film and record sales? How could the development of radio and television be used to boost film and record sales?

3 How has digital technology and the increased use of the Internet affected film and sound recording? How has the Internet had an effect on distribution?

4 What distinctions can we make between professional film and sound productions and personal or amateur use? What role do they both play, and are these roles interchangeable?

have been possible without the amplifier, and its subsequent modification into the dual role of speaker system and recording system. And, while the popularity of radio may have suffered with the rise of television, both media remain in wide use today, providing us (in still distinct ways) with great access to news, information, and entertainment. But broadcast media, too, is undergoing change in the 21st century. First, the ubiquity of digital technology and the ease of access to a wide variety of television and radio channels (through satellite, cable, and the Internet) have resulted in the fragmentation of audiences. While mass media still reaches large numbers of people, individuals with particular tastes can search through a wide variety of media transmissions to find the information or the entertainment that most interests them. There is no need to listen to a wide variety of music on a single radio station when the Internet allows you to access a specialist radio station. Similarly, you can watch the fashion channel, if that is a major interest, or just sit down the national broadcaster for general news and information and a wide variety of programming. Recording devices, and the ease of distribution of film and sound recordings in disc or mp3 format, have also affected and directed broadcast media organizations to look at a broader range of platforms to facilitate access for consumers. Not only do these devices allow people to avoid live broadcasts (and the advertisements that go with them) but television shows are now created with a different type of consumer in mind. When producers and writers know that consumers will eventually purchase shows like *The Office* or *Grey's Anatomy* in a box set, they may also plan more carefully for longer, interconnected narratives over a number of episodes as opposed to small independent blocks of stories.

New media

The final category of media is the most contentious and difficult to pin down, but is where the newest developments are happening, and already making broadcast media providers themselves willing participants in multi-channel platforms for broader access and distribution. New media, an admittedly somewhat amorphous term beyond a purely literal meaning, can be broadly defined as any means of transmission that utilizes digital or computer technology. This includes the Internet, the World Wide Web, digital imaging, sound and voice recording and playback, via all forms of hand-held, or computer-based accessories such as web-cams, cell (mobile) phones, and the small tablet computers that combine to provide music storage, e-readers, Internet browsers and a wide selection of applications for home use or while you are on the road.

If it sounds like the idea of new media is ill-defined, or that new media technology actually crosses the boundaries of many of the above media, then you have noted the important notion of **convergence** in the current digital age. Boundaries between media are being blurred and many forms are coming together so that one technology can serve many functions. Mass/Dyadic, Sender/Receiver, Print/Recording/Broadcasting, are flipped, mixed, and confused in this era of accelerated convergence.

Convergence refers to the tendency for disparate technological devices, as they develop, to perform similar tasks. Today, for example, you may buy a tablet that functions as a computer, a phone and a television. In addition, **media convergence** refers to the ability of a single device to stream very different types of signals from voice and video to simple texts and data.

Multimedia and multimodality

The above section should make it clear that media and mass communication has the potential to affect language in many ways. It should also suggest that language acts in the digital age take advantage of a variety of media and modes of transmission. In this course, you will find it increasingly difficult to focus on one medium—and only on reading, or viewing, or listening, or speaking at a given point in time—when the language is transmitted or transmissible through a variety of media platforms concurrently (you can, for instance, watch a short video on YouTube while reading subtitles that a viewer has added for comedic effect, or an audio commentary), blurring the lines of the medium as well as its authorship. While medium refers to the technology of transmission, modality commonly refers to the nature of the data to be consumed and our potential to interface with it. In other words, is the communicative act something to view like an image, something to read, or something to hear, feel, or even talk back to? It is fairly common to find multimedia and multimodal confused and, in fact, sometimes it is hard to separate a type of data from the way it is transmitted and received. What is important is to gain some insight into the effects on language and communicative acts.

Remediation

One further issue to consider in relation to media before looking at specific concerns related to language is the idea of remediation, a concept introduced by the media scholars Jay David Bolter and Robert Grusin. As we have discussed, stories, ideas, and information are rarely communicated through one medium these days. In fact, we very often find that the stories we encounter are remediated—they are taken from their original medium and re-presented in a new form. The most obvious example would be a narrative text that is turned into a graphic novel or a film. In this case, for example, a story originally told in print, is transferred to the medium of the storyboard (as film), and then back into the storyboard print format (as a graphic novel) or vice versa. The changes that take place in a story and in the reader's experience (the audience) through its presentation shed light on the effects media can have on communicative acts and the importance of language across different forms of cultural production.

How many times have you heard people say, "the movie was great, but I prefer the book." Why is this? Apart from the issue of the creator or originator's genius, the difficulty of adaptation can highlight how the medium of print is more well-suited to the lengthy development of intricate plots, or the complex inner thoughts of a character in a novel. Another element of the book that some readers enjoy is the simple ability to enjoy a long story over an extended period of time. On the other hand, films have certain advantages over print: exotic and exciting images as well as the fast pace of an action sequence, filled with crashing sound effects, might well win out over the static nature of the page. Whatever the case, the process of remediation sheds light on the significant impact the use of media can have on presentation, meaning and emotional effect.

Discussion Point

Language, media, and mobility

Current media technology strives to be light and mobile. With a device that fits into your pocket you can watch movies, surf the Internet and go to your Facebook page, listen to music, call a friend, or send a text. This obviously changes the nature of both interpersonal and mass communication. It can also change the nature of how we use language.

1 What does it mean to always be within inexpensive and easy communicative reach with almost anyone?

2 How do you use language in these various environments?

3 How do individuals and large institutions attempt to take advantage of changing media to communicate with you?

4 How do we, as individuals, control how much and with whom we communicate?

These questions and more can be considered in the sections for further study in the second half of this chapter.

Just as the digital environment tends to encourage multimedia and multimodality, it also encourages the frequent, sometimes circular, transition of stories from one medium to another. An old oral epic like the *Iliad* can be taken out of its live communicative environment and reworked on the printed page, perhaps taking away the element of intimate person-to-person storytelling. The movie *Troy* may be seen as a corruption of Homer's original *Iliad*, written down as verse, but it may create something visually new that in the process restores some of the experiential aspects of a community sharing a story told with sound and fury. How would we retell the story of Troy on the Internet? In a graphic novel? Upon what modes would the story most heavily rely? How would the story have to be changed, and what added dimension would be brought to it? What would be different about an Internet-based rendition, with its infinite possibilities of linking us back to a multitude of documents, historical relics, maps, re-created images and accounts, to make sense of what happened there?

Register and style

A close examination of language in different media reveals linguistic similarities within and across media, as well as certain restrictions particular to the media, and style rules that are there to be followed or broken. In previous chapters of this course companion, you learned about regional and cultural variation in language and the ways people use and consume language in different contexts. Most individuals have the ability to switch between dialects or to use a different register, a different level of formality, when they are communicating with different groups or communities. Various media formats—and individual genres within a format—also have their own register and style depending on the nature of the sender, the purpose, and the audience. Register is best described as language choices based on the situation, the information being communicated and the target audience. Style, which is closely related to register, refers to the individual linguistic choices that make a communicative act distinctive. Register and style is sometimes easier to recognize than it is to define. Just as you can easily recognize the difference between a student writing a text message to a friend, participating in a class discussion, or writing a formal essay in a history class, you are probably able to distinguish between genres or text types like a television news update, a newspaper editorial, a celebrity profile in a fashion magazine, and a blog post. Linguistic evidence—such as the use of description, tone, diction, or imagery—help to establish the particular register and style that determine media genres. The next important question around register and style is: how does the recognizable linguistic nature of a genre shape communication, and how does it help us to critically approach the communicative act?

A textbook is a text type or genre within the category of print media. A variety of elements help to make a textbook recognizable. Just look at this course companion: textbooks tend to have straightforward titles and headings; they closely follow a logical course structure; they strive to inform, define, and guide. But what

Activity

Remediating a rhyme

Read the following rhyme and then consider the picture:

Bah, Bah a black Sheep,
Have you any Wool?
Yes merry have I,
Three Bags full,
One for my master,
One for my Dame,
One for the little Boy
That lives down the lane.

First printed in *Tommy Thumb's Pretty Song Book*, 1744.

Questions

1 How is the tone different in the two stories?

2 What are the limitations of telling a story only with words?

3 If you saw the image without the rhyme, what would you say are the limitations of image as a means of storytelling?

4 Must a story always change when transferred from one medium to another?

does a textbook sound like? Are the register and style of a textbook recognizable? Look at the following example—a textbook written by a 10-year-old—and note the diction, tone, register, and purpose.

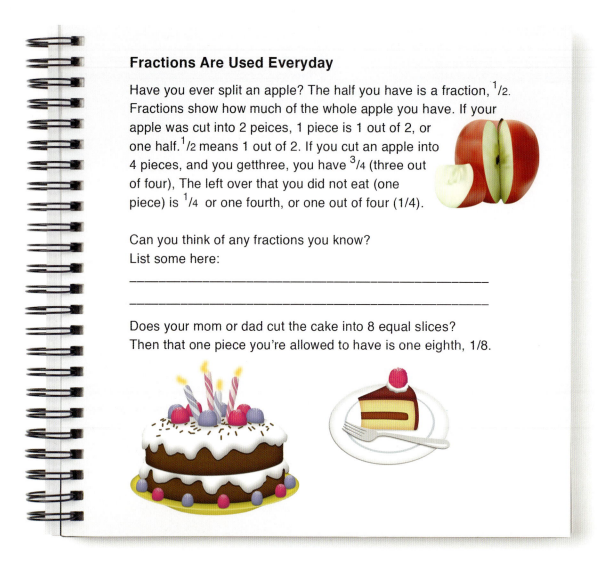

Fractions Are Used Everyday

Have you ever split an apple? The half you have is a fraction, $^1/_2$. Fractions show how much of the whole apple you have. If your apple was cut into 2 peices, 1 piece is 1 out of 2, or one half. $^1/_2$ means 1 out of 2. If you cut an apple into 4 pieces, and you getthree, you have $^3/_4$ (three out of four), The left over that you did not eat (one piece) is $^1/_4$ or one fourth, or one out of four (1/4).

Can you think of any fractions you know?
List some here:

_____

_____

Does your mom or dad cut the cake into 8 equal slices?
Then that one piece you're allowed to have is one eighth, 1/8.

This creative attempt to write a book for younger students clearly indicates that we are aware of media register at a young age, and keen to participate in the process. Exposure to media allows us to function as both consumers and creators of media. Register and style alone, in this short piece, alerts us to the fact that we are being taught and that the information, if not necessarily correct, is at least striving to be helpful and informative. You should also note that there are certain constraints attached to any particular genre. While we use an informal register in this book (in order to communicate in a more casual, approachable manner), on occasion (when walking through a difficult theoretical concept, for example), we may be more formal. But we can't go too far in either direction. We must choose a style that is understandable to a wide audience; we need to use examples that are from a wide variety of cultures and English-speaking areas, and we have to be careful that our examples do not offend. The appropriate register and style of a textbook can be positively defined as "balanced and accessible" but may more often be described as "bland."

Dialect, jargon, pronunciation

Dialect, jargon and pronunciation play important roles in the overall register or style of a communicative act. These major elements help to determine genre and set audience expectations for the nature of the content. Television newscasters, for example, tend to use a formal register, a vocabulary that seems educated but not too highbrow or full of jargon to exclude people. They also tend to avoid a dialect and pronunciation that would identify them with a particular region or community. Sometimes, particular pronunciations or dialects add interest or variety to a newscast and are purposefully chosen: a US sports channel may like the fact that their soccer (or football) expert speaks with an English accent; a reporter in conversation with people "on the streets" may speak in a less formal-sounding vernacular. In general, however, while there is variety within a medium or genre, certain attributes of dialect, jargon, and pronunciation create an impressions of media genre.

Activity

Standard desirable attributes

How fitting would the use of jargon, dialect, nonstandard pronunciation, irony or sarcasm, informality, loose dialogue, loosely structured narrative, descriptive or personal touches be to the following genres.

A television news report

A television opinion piece

A newspaper editorial

A political columnist's blog

A celebrity profile in a magazine

A sports broadcast

A political speech

An advertisement

Speech versus writing

It is sometimes hard to discuss an attribute like dialect when making comparisons between genres, such as the difference between a speech-based medium and a print-based medium. The difference between speech and writing is in and of itself a significant element of register and style. What these differences are, and how they relate to audience perceptions are sometimes difficult to describe and open to debate. First of all, some genres are an odd combination of speech and writing: what can we say, for example, about the written script of a film? Is this writing or speech? The same could be said for a speech that has been carefully crafted and then read from a teleprompter. Analysts of linguistic differences between written and spoken language have suggested that speech has a tendency to be informal, interpersonal, unstructured, grammatically simple, and concerned with the present context whereas writing tends towards the opposite of these. Various media often fall along a continuum between attributes we normally attribute to speech and those we attribute to written communication.

Activity

Subverting assumptions

List as many genres or text types as you can that usually take place as oral or written communication. Where do these acts fall in relation to the attributes used to describe oral communication? How many communicative acts seem to subvert our assumptions about oral and written communication?

Activity

Analyzing a news broadcast in a foreign language

Go online and look for television news programs broadcast in a language that you do not understand. Watch the show and try to determine the following: when are the newscasters presenting a serious news item? When are they presenting a "human interest" story? When are the newscasters offering editorial opinion? When are they speaking off-the-cuff to each other? When on the show do the newscasters advertise themselves, their network, their guest's product or another program?

This type of analysis offers some insight into the ways we filter for intention, bias, and significance starting with the most basic elements of communication. While you are at it: what other elements of presentation beyond the tone of voice, helped you to decipher intention?

Ad analysis

Analyze the advertisement below. Write a brief response describing its style and register. What is the general tone of the text? How do both words and images contribute to the tone? What is the style and register of the text? How is this style and register related to genre? How does this text take advantage of our expectations or knowledge of genre? What words and images point to the first level of the text's humorous or superficial intentions? What words and images point to the real message of the text?

Product recall.
Volkswagen Golf Type I, 1974 model

It has been shown that, due to vibration, the **closing mechanism of the glove compart-ment** can be subject to wear. In the long run, in some cases, this might result in a more difficult handling of this mechanism. Even though no complaints have been registered, Volkswagen is making Golf Type I owners aware of this, as a precaution.

As this is not in line with the high standards of quality that Volkswagen has for its products, owners of the above-mentioned model are requested to go to www.volkswagen.nl/recall before 12 January 2008.
If necessary, Volkswagen will have the closing mechanism **replaced free of charge**. Volkswagen regrets any inconvenience caused. This is why Volkswagen offers dissatisfied customers **free servicing** for their car as compensation.

Volkswagen emphasizes that this only applies to the Volkswagen Golf Type I, 1974 model.

Once again, Volkswagen offers its apologies for any inconvenience caused.

Pon's Automobielhandel B.V. (Volkswagen importer)

Volkswagen Golf print advertisement, "Product Recall." Agency DDB Amersterdam.

Discourse genres

In the previous discussion we gave you a very general definition of genre: that is, a type of text within a given medium. Genre is a term used both in media studies and in the study of literature and some other art forms to mean type, or a group of works sharing similar characteristics. There are many genres within every media category. Examples of genre range from action and adventure, comedy, romantic comedy, and the thriller in feature films to a news program, situation comedy, reality show, and sports broadcast on television. As soon as we begin to classify texts as a particular genre, however, we begin to see that there are many genres, and sub-genres, that by definition are never completely fixed. As such, they are often in the process of subverting expectations and evolving further. Genre is necessarily a broad way of categorizing texts across and within a particular art form or discourse.

If genre is a difficult and somewhat limiting way to describe texts or language acts, what is the use of genre and why should we study it? First of all, people tend to group items and compare and contrast them in order to manage large amounts of information. Identifying and understanding the typical attributes of a type of text can aid a reader or audience member to make conclusions about the meaning and purpose of a text. Even if we did not name genre, as we begin to build a list of attributes and similarities in a certain type of work, we can get more comfortable in our predictions. Take, for example, horror films. This is one of the easiest examples of how genre expectations work because audience members are quickly attuned to the ways the movies build suspense and the games they play. Audiences look out for certain "codes" in the genre. At the beginning of the film, when there is scary music and a disturbing noise behind the door … it is only the family pet. We know it is a mistake to go outside alone and check on a noise. Couples should never split up and go out into the woods … (the list could go on and on). Genre helps us to understand what we are watching quite quickly. Most of us can turn the channel to a film in progress and know within a few seconds if it is a horror film. Understanding the codes of genre helps us to establish a comfortable relationship to the text, and build on our enjoyment of appraising how the conventions are developed and subverted.

Classification of texts by genre can also give us insight into the way media products are produced and consumed. Institutions are intent on genre. The success of *Harry Potter* pushed both publishing firms and the movie industry to find other works within the genre that would stimulate the audience (and stimulate sales) in the same way. We can also see, in relation to genre, how audiences both look for and get bored by established conventions. While an audience might turn again and again to a reality television show, this can only go on for a time; after a while, the audience wants something fresh from the genre and looks for those moments when a work crosses new boundaries, either twisting the existing genre, or creating a new one. Sometimes, as consumers, we become critical of the constant supply of the same. (Why create another story along the same lines as so many other thrillers you have seen? Why do another "buddy cop"

Activity

Film genres

Write down the name of five films you have seen recently. How would you classify the genres of these films? What elements of each film helped you to decide upon the "correct" genre? Were any of the films difficult to classify? Why?

movie?). Some creative producers purposefully try to avoid categorization within a particular form for this reason. The study of what gets created in particular genres, how audiences react to those texts, and the ways new genres develop offer great insights into creative practice and society more broadly.

A friend tells you that he watched a great show on television last night. He doesn't remember what it was called, but it was really funny. In a scene, he saw three young couples, maybe married, maybe friends, sit in a small restaurant and get into a humorous argument. If you were to try to find this show on television the next night, what would you expect to find? What would you hope to find? How long would one episode of the show last? Where is it likely to take place? How old are the characters? How serious are their arguments? What types of topics will they discuss? Does knowing, or thinking you know, the answers to these questions increase or decrease your potential enjoyment of the show?

As a society we come up with generic classifications on our own based on the linguistic or more broadly communicative aspects of a work. These classifications, in turn, influence the production of and our understanding of other works. It is worth thinking about how we go about classifying texts by genre because the elements we look for in classification are those that matter in the way a text communicates with a mass audience. In general, the following elements help to distinguish genre: mode of address (does the broadcaster speak directly to the audience, or are we meant to be overhearing someone else's conversation, for example?), structure (from number of lines in a poem, to the length of a film), theme or topic, and anticipated reader response (broadly speaking, for example, an advertisement might play on fear, sympathy, excitement, etc.). Ultimately, the classification of texts by genre and the study of the boundaries of the genre we have created give us insights into how media operate in terms of complicated relationships between producer, audience and the message itself.

Rhetorical strategies

Apart from media forms that have the primary intention of entertainment, media products can be broadly classed as those that attempt to inform and those that are meant to persuade. Through close attention to elements such as register, style and genre a consumer can often intuit the intention behind a media product. Frequently, however, communicative acts blur the boundaries between information and persuasion. While a political speech during an electoral campaign is clearly aimed at persuasion, how is a speech given by an elected official during a crisis meant to be interpreted? While the speech may be informative, the nature of politics and election campaigning may suggest that the desire to persuade is never far below the surface. Equally possible, a news broadcast may have a primary intention to inform, but bias may lead to a subtle form of persuasion. The boundaries become even more complex online and in cross-media formats, where styles and registers seem to be blended easily and where an individual, facing a mass of information, must make decisions about purpose and intent on his or her own. The study of media rhetoric is the study of the styles and strategies media products use to indicate, or sometimes hide intentions and hold sway over an audience. The close study of media language helps to understand the calculated construction of both informative and persuasive works.

Rhetoric itself, as it is understood today in the Western tradition, originated with the ancient Greeks who saw rhetoric as the study and practice of the art of persuasion. For Aristotle, rhetoric consisted of the ability to see what is persuasive in an act of communication and this skill was seen as a necessary part of determining the truth or validity of an argument. While the Greeks developed intricate systems to both describe and learn the art of rhetoric, Aristotle's basic distinctions in regards to how speakers manage to persuade still function as a good base for media study today. In *Rhetoric*, Aristotle described how a speaker can convince an audience (through *ethos*) or a demonstration of his own character, or the creation of or appeal to emotion (through *pathos*), as well as through the word itself (*logos*). It is interesting to consider how often we are convinced by an argument on the basis of the supposed quality of the source, the arousal of our own emotion or the identification of the emotion with the source. Just so, we are easily persuaded through inventive argument or a witty turn of phrase.

Rhetorical strategies are as numerous as the choices available to us in every instance of communication. All of the categories of persuasion listed above ultimately derive from the communicative act itself. In other words, if the audience perceives emotion behind the argument of the speaker, it is because of some communicative act (that may or may not involve words). The artful display of images and text in an advertisement may have the cumulative effect of appealing to our moral and aesthetic sensibilities, building an argument, or showing and arousing emotion. While there are many ways of convincing us through language acts (including diction, tone, imagery, sentence length, repetition, volume, color, etc.), it is the skillful combination of these devices that ultimately persuades us. Rather than talking of some particular rhetorical devices (such as the degree of reinforcement through repetition, for example), we will outline some aspects of rhetoric that run through many media and genres.

Activity

Give me three

"Veni, Vedi, Vici" Julius Caesar

"Friends, Romans, Countrymen" Mark Antony in Shakespeare's *Julius Caesar*

"Life, liberty, and the pursuit of happiness" The United States Declaration of Independence

"Education, Education, Education" Tony Blair

You may recognize a few of these statements and you may recognize them because of the rhetorical principle, also put forward by Aristotle, that grouping in threes is an effective device for keeping attention and sticking to a number of ideas that can be recalled easily. Search for a political speech online and see how many times the speaker groups ideas, arguments, or points into threes.

In chapter 2 of this book, we talked about the importance of metaphor in literary language. The fact of the matter is that metaphor is a strong and common rhetorical device in both persuasive and informational writing. As in the example of a weather report, metaphor helps to make communication descriptive and to give it character, tone, and force. The metaphors we choose in persuasive speaking and writing create an impression on an audience and help to present our ideas in a favorable way. By comparing new ideas or information through metaphor to something we already know and value (or not), speakers can influence our opinions.

Another common rhetorical technique used in media communication is the art of clustering. While advertising and persuasion relies on the complex use of imagery, tone, and metaphor, these elements are often highlighted in some way. Repetition alone does not always lead to the desired effect of a communicative act on an audience, so producers may rely on building a group of signs that gather around a single idea or impression. The intention is to make sure that the viewer or listener both understands the point that is being made, and that extraneous ideas and information are not getting in the way of the intended message. Look at the image below and think in terms of clusters. What elements do you see in this picture? How are individual words, images, or colors linked together? How do individual elements work together to give a unified impression? What elements, that may have appeared naturally or realistically, have been left out of the advertisement?

Gatorade Fierce, "Boogie Board." DDB Mexico, December 2004.

Some of the elements you may have noticed in this picture include the dam releasing a controlled outpouring of water, braced and suspended by its armature of industrial scaffolding, the dark muscled back of the man holding his boogie board with a tense but determined posture, and the steely blue-grey lighting that is both atmospheric and hard at the same time. In particular, the color-coding is graphically emphasized in the overall monotone color of the composition, and it's one high-key point of a more lustrous acqua blue to denote the icy blue thirst-quenching drink, Gatorade. All of these elements work together to give the message that the Gatorade drinker is tough and adventurous. Everything in this ad reinforces that single idea. If this image was "real" the water may have been less rough, the lighting less atmospheric, flowers might have grown on the hillside, and a more natural waterway might have replaced the impossibly risky and probably illegal dive into the waters of an industrial site under construction. But then, we would have had a poorly clustered, less rhetorically effective advertisement!

When metaphors and **clusters** accumulate or work in a seemingly integrated way to influence ideas they can be said to "frame" our perceptions. In other words, by setting up powerful mental pictures of how the world *should* or *seems* to operate, metaphors simplify problems, issues, and choices for us and influence our actions. You have probably heard the term "framing the debate" which essentially means to put forward the terms that will be used in a debate or to characterize the issues at hand. Each side in a political debate would naturally try to frame the issue from its own perspective. In the United States, where there has been no government-controlled healthcare, the Democratic Party (the liberal party), have attempted to "reform" the system, looking to provide "universal coverage" to citizens. The Democrats attempt to create the frame, the overarching images and metaphors, to portray the issue as one of keeping healthcare from becoming something only available to the elite or provided only by private, profit-seeking companies. On the other side of the debate, the Republicans (the conservative party in US politics), have attempted to reframe the debate from their perspective. The healthcare bill becomes an attempt at "socialism" (a word that has negative implications to many people in the United States) and an attempt to impose "expensive" "government control" over the people that would "curb medical care" by restricting options for people who may otherwise have privately funded their care. The audience for these debates is often caught in the rhetorical war, when faced with actual bills and proposals that are long and complicated, making it difficult to judge the best options for their own health and wellbeing and the health and wellbeing of a large number of people. Sometimes, in a media war, the one who frames best wins.

A **cluster** is a grouping of distinct textual or graphic elements that together, convey an idea more strongly than when taken in isolation.

The power of narrative

Storytelling is a powerful force across media. While the power of narrative may be best explored by reading novels and short stories, as discussed in the literature section of this course, it is important to remember that we seem naturally to gravitate to storytelling to order and make sense of our experience. A good definition of narrative is

Activity

Ad analysis

While this advertisement may make some obvious use of narrative, examine the image and words together and see how many elements from your study of fiction you can recognize. What is the story behind this advertisement? Who is the main character? What is this main character like? What are the main ideas, issues, or themes being communicated? Who is the implied reader of this story and how is the reader supposed to relate to the ad?

simply the communication of a chain of events. A key word here, perhaps, is chain. When we enjoy a story we may be attracted to a plot, a sequence of events, that we can arrange in our minds in a temporal way (we know what happens first, next, and what may happen later) and which often suggests a causal relation between events. A good story, a story with what may be called "aboutness," is often not a collection of unrelated events, characters, or observations but an ordered sequence of events in which characters act, interact, and work toward some resolution. Surely you have heard someone on a Monday morning at school attempt to tell a story about something funny that happened over the weekend. After the storyteller makes a stumbling attempt at a bad story, someone remarks, "I guess you had to be there." Someone else, on the other hand, may be able to take the same events and put together an engaging tale that results in gasps of disbelief, laughter, or further curiosity. Creating a narrative around an idea can be a very effective rhetorical device and is often at the heart of a political campaign, an advertising campaign, or even an argument in a newspaper editorial. In this course, as you move from section to section with different focus points, you will find that the questions you consider in relation to a work of literature like a novel or a short passage will apply across media and allow you to discuss the effects of narrative in mass communication.

Critical study of mass communication

During your study of language and mass communication you will use some of the practices we outlined in the first three chapters of this book to take a close critical look at language and media. Paying attention to some of the details of the complex relationship between language and the purposes and means of communication to a large audience, you will study a few broad topics such as textual bias, stereotypes, and language and the role of the state. There are a variety of ways to organize the course but no matter what topic you choose to investigate you will be considering different genres within media, the way mass media uses language to inform, persuade, or entertain, and the potential for ideological influence of the media. In the second half of this chapter we will examine a series of texts under the three broad topics of news organizations, political speeches and campaigns, and popular culture. These topics are broad enough so that many of the issues you will address in your own school's particular focus will be touched upon here. Rather than giving you an in-depth analysis of language and mass communication through the lens of these topics we hope to give you a series of texts that will both raise important theoretical ideas and offer the chance for you to practice your skills of media analysis.

News organizations

The organizations that bring us news can be either public or private and can function across a wide variety of media. Until recently, news organizations or the institutions behind them (media conglomerates, the government) had to be relatively large, simply because these services are expensive. A newspaper, news gathering organizations such as Reuters or the Associated Press, television networks such as CNN, BBC, and ABC (Australia), are corporations that employ large numbers of people to create, distribute and determine the product that is printed or broadcast as news.

Quite early in school we are taught to be wary of media bias in news reporting. Using basic skills of critical reading we are able to discern the difference between a newspaper article that at least presents itself as informational and an article that is editorial- or opinion-based. Words and phrases like "perhaps," "it would seem," "in our opinion," or most likely" clue us in to the tentative or opinion-based nature of a piece. It is more difficult, however, to discern the political, social, or theoretical bias of a newspaper, magazine, journal, or television show. Understanding theoretical bias involves examining codes, assumptions, political affiliations and the social and professional context behind the argument and focus of the story. While some of the texts we will examine here involve a discussion of context and the underlying bias in particular organizations, it is important in the first instance to understand the institutional assumptions that are made when producing the news, regardless of any other political or theoretical leaning.

First and foremost, we should remember that the production of news is a profession like any other, with its own processes, rules, and routes to professionalization, all of which shape the communicative acts we finally call "news." From the very beginning of mass communication the dissemination of news has been one of its primary functions. Humans, it seems, have a basic need or desire for information in order to understand their world or make sense of their own culture, either in relation to their private lives or in relation to distant cultures. News, then, has always presented itself as truthful information and, as such, journalists have almost always taken a stance, as a matter of professionalism, of integrity and objectivity. In the early days of the United States, Thomas Jefferson, an early leader during the transition from colonies to the United States, famously added to the responsibilities of the press by suggesting it might play the role of a check on the honesty of government. "The way to prevent" citizens from being led astray by misguided leaders, suggested Jefferson, was "to give them full information of their affairs thro' the channel of the public papers, and to contrive that those papers should penetrate the mass of the people." Jefferson even went further, saying "were it left to me to decide whether we should have a government without newspapers, or newspapers without a government, I should not hesitate a moment to prefer the latter." This drive to inform, to remain unbiased, and to be a check on those in power, has remained a professional standard—if a sometimes lofty one—for news organizations and is a goal of both private and government-supported institutions.

But what other professional practices and conventions drive the production of news? While government-supported organizations such as the BBC may not have to rely on raising money in order to stay viable, they may have other obligations to consider when they produce a news program—they are influenced directly by the government agencies and committees that provide their funds and, less directly, by the impressions of the people who pay taxes that ultimately support their programs. Publicly funded news media must be aware of the desires and concerns of their audience. Private news media, of course, have to also be concerned with generating an audience for both sales of the news product itself or for the sale of advertising time or space. These financial and political forces are underscored by other, more immediate, restrictions and imperatives. First, the news has a deadline to reach a prime-time viewing audience or a print deadline (who knows, in the 24-hour news cycle, what developments the next day will bring?). News organizations, far from simply *finding* news, must *create* consumable and interesting news out of a mass of experience. News professionals go to school and apprentice, like lawyers and doctors, to learn the particular jobs involved in putting together the news, and this process leads to a predictable and automatically expedient or biased product. Consider the following process. Journalists and reporters, both freelance and those working for news organizations, get stories from various sources. Some reporters are assigned to "beats" that are considered frequently newsworthy or interesting, like police headquarters, government organizations, or financial centers. Reporters also rely on major organizations and corporations that issue press releases (promotional statements that are sent to news organizations), press briefings (short conferences or meetings with the press, often governmental, to explain issues or events), news conferences, or relations with public relations firms. News is sourced, in other words, through attention to the usual sources and to outlets that are designed to provide product to news organizations. The myriad stories collected this way are then reviewed by news editors who determine which stories deserve development and which stories will not be needed.

Activity

Broadcast media: public or private

Which broadcast media in your country are public and which are privately funded? Most countries today have a mix of private and public news organizations and some public broadcasters today are in reality partially funded by donors or advertisers. Public broadcasting has some obvious benefits: without the pressure of finding advertisers, broadcasters can cater to small interest groups, including minority language groups, or focus on stories of more community interest if not more entertainment value.

List as many news media institutions as you can that are based in the area where you live. Where do you find your news? Does your news come from private or public sources? Is there a difference between these sources? Using either the radio, television, or the Internet (searching on sites such as www.youtube.com), listen to or watch two news broadcasts from the same day, one from a privately funded station and one from a public station. Write a brief reflection on the differences you perceive, if any.

This naturally leads to a certain similarity, or familiarity in the approach, even when the stories have a different origin with news coming from such a variety of sources, Take the case of an individual reporter trying to get stories published in a newspaper for which she works. The reporter generally works on smaller stories, but knows that if she finds a lead that is interesting, or topical enough, she may be able to convince her editor to give her a bigger assignment, more space in the upcoming edition, or a position on a more important page. Faced with a variety of news events occurring on her usual "beat," how would the reporter prioritize her focus? How would she decide which story is going to have a higher chance of making the paper? What criteria would the editor be using when choosing stories? In what ways would the decisions to publish depend on the size, location, and advertising revenue of the newspaper? Stories often get to be news, and get to be news in a number of broadcast media, because they meet certain well-established criteria that guarantee a readership.

Activity

Media bias

Read the following extract from a book about the nature of the creation of the news by institutions. This extract considers biases not in terms of political agenda but in terms of a philosophy regarding what counts as news and what people need or want to consume as news.

Text 1

This extract outlines the attributes of what is frequently called the informational bias of the news, that is, the bias news has towards certain kinds of stories and the types of information they convey.

Personalization Most news stories focus on individuals rather than institutions, and emphasize human-interest angles and emotional impact over and often at the expense of broader social contexts and political perspectives. Simply put, news stories are people-centered; they rely heavily upon interviews, first-person accounts, eye-witness testimony and expert opinions. The focus on individual people is designed to make stories feel more personal, direct, and immediate. But by focusing on individual actors, such as the President, in a story about economic recession, for instance, audiences are encouraged to view political issues individually rather than socially. Consequently, they are more likely to blame specific political actors for social ills and less likely to understand the underlying factors and root causes of social problems.

Dramatization The news is overwhelmingly biased toward the narrative presentation of information. Regardless of the specific issues journalists are reporting on, those issues tend to be structured as stories... Moreover, to heighten audience interest, journalists frequently focus on the most sensational, scandalous, and shocking details of a story. The

insistence on narrativizing the news has at least two significant consequences. First, since some issues are difficult to pictorialize and require sustained analysis, their dramatization leads to inaccurate or misrepresentative reporting (if they get covered at all). Second, since narratives have beginnings, middles, and endings, dramatized news has the potential to impose a clean and tidy sense of closure on complex, enduring issues.

Fragmentation A third information bias in the news is the tendency to treat stories in isolation, ignoring their connection to other stories and the larger contexts in which they occur. Both newspapers and televised newscasts organize the news into brief, self-contained capsules. This can foster the misimpression that the world is just a series of random, unrelated events. The compartmentalization of news stories can obfuscate not only the interconnections among stories, but also their historical significance. Fragmented news makes the world appear chaotic and unpredictable. Indeed, the prevalence of fragmented news helps to explain why the 9/11 attacks were so utterly incomprehensible to most Americans, who had no context for understanding the connections between the economic and foreign policies of the USA, and the religious zealotry of... extremists. To most Americans, the attacks of September 11, 2001 on the World Trade Center and Pentagon are isolated events with no prior history or context.

Authority-disorder The fourth and final informational bias of the news is closely related to the first three, and in particular, the way that personalized news becomes dramatized. Since personalization leads to a focus on individuals and dramatization favors the sensational, it is common to depict the individuals and parties involved in a story as in conflict or tension. This tension is typically represented as one between authority (i.e. police, government leaders, public officials) and disorder (i.e. criminals, natural disasters, terrorism). Furthermore, since the news is comprised of individual capsules that require narrative closure, the authority-disorder tension is generally resolved either in the direction of authority through the restoration of normalcy or in the direction of disorder and the cynical view that public officials are incompetent.

Source: Ott, Brian L. & Mack. Robert L. 2010. *Critical Media Studies: An Introduction*. Oxford: Wiley-Blackwell. pp. 62–63.

Questions to the text

1 How do you react to the list presented in the passages above?

2 Do you think news organizations purposefully or subconsciously, as part of their professional practice, adhere to this list?

3 Can you think of other attributes that would either structure a news story or make an event newsworthy?

Activity

Front page news

Compare the front page news of several different newspapers from your city or region. Or, take a major international paper, like the *New York Times,* and review its North American, European and Asian editions (the *International Herald Tribune*).

What is noticeable about the priority given to major news stories of both a national and international relevance? How do you think the different editorial decisions reflect the priorities of the different regions and the target readership? How does the language reflect the readership? How do local or national news media groups differ in their approach to news coverage in comparison to an international consortium like the *New York Times*?

Activity

Television news

Watch at least two different news programs on television or through the Internet. Compare a "prime time" news program with a 24-hour news program on a cable or satellite station. What factors influence which stories count as news on television? How are videos used as sources of information? How are other visual factors such as set design, graphics, and newscaster appearance important?

What effect does music play in a news program? Why would one program use an anchor person who stands at the scene, while another is seated behind a desk? Expand your brief comparison of a daily news program, to compare it with the front page of the same day's newspaper. What is covered and what isn't? How does the medium and the intended audience change the news on offer?

The future of news

What changes will the Internet bring to news organizations or, more generally, to the type of news we encounter? As we write this book, the fate of many large newspapers remains in doubt. Over the past couple of decades private news organizations are increasingly being bought by multinational corporations that now control a large number of media outlets. Certainly, the centralization of news could be harmful to the variety and amount of bias in coverage. Now, small and large newspapers alike are under threat by the Internet, not only potentially affecting gathering itself. It would be difficult to outline here all of the possible effects the widening audience for Internet news and the shrinking audience for print newspapers will have on traditional news sources (including television). For one thing, we are in the middle of the changes now. Second, for every negative effect there is a possible positive effect. Here are a few issues to consider when thinking about the effect of the Internet on traditional journalism:

- **Local coverage** Smaller newspapers are often the first to feel the effects of shrinking readerships. The loss of local newspapers often means the loss of focus on smaller communities. At the same time, the growth of local websites, community bulletin boards, and local web magazines or newsletters could lead to greater coverage of community news through alternative sources. But what would happen to the regular features that we now consider to be the mainstay of the local press: the reporting of marriages, births, and obituaries for instance? If local newspapers move online, will they be able to generate enough revenue to hire staff and reporters?

- **In-depth reporting** As newspapers currently feel the pressure to provide more entertainment and light news in their pages, they justify the time spent on more frivolous content by stating that the money they make funds more serious, in-depth and often less flashy reporting. Some feel that the Internet will mean less funding for specialist reporters and expensive investigative journalism. On the other hand, some websites, because they do not have the obligation to be generalists, specialize in a given topic, politics for example, and provide continuous coverage. Other news sources on the Internet, and some print newspapers as well, are beginning to rely more on outside sources for most of their information, acting more as a collector of already produced news stories. Newspapers, and increasingly these aggregating websites, then grow and support their own smaller stable of expert reporters.

- **Financial resources** Ultimately, newspapers rely on money from sponsors, governments, or advertisers. All news sources are currently struggling to find where exactly revenue will come from as the digital age progresses. While the *New York Times* has a successful online presence, its print newspaper still generates the main share of its advertising revenue. In 2010, *The Times* in London began charging subscription rates for access to its online service, starting what may be a future trend. Professional journalists and editors can devote their time to the gathering of news because it is their job and they get paid. Some bloggers post "editorial" comments on their websites in their spare time or as an adjunct to their primary profession (an economics professor might blog in a less academic register about the economy online, for example), but is this likely to be a reliable source of information in the future?

- **Reporter access to information** Who gets to interview the prime minister? Who is given a press pass to watch and report on the finals of the French Open? Who gets to sit with a notepad in the front row of Armani's spring show? While news is often generated by those who have power and influence through events, announcements, and press conferences, access to this information is necessarily limited. While the Internet allows for easier public access to some events (YouTube has recently featured both live debates and live professional cricket matches), many organizations choose who they want to distribute a story and the choice usually falls on professional journalists. Will the producers of Internet news have the same access to information as other journalists? The answer is still up in the air. There are recent cases of online celebrity reporters who have "scooped" traditional media in key stories and some political news websites. Bloggers who have special access to information have been quoted as sources in the mainstream media.

- **Informational bias** Consider the "informational biases" in the front-page news stories you discussed. How many of these attributes would also apply to online news sites? Would the wide audience and wide number of sources on the Internet lead to a different set of news features becoming more prevalent?

- **Flexibility** How is a news-gathering organization able to respond to events as they happen, and to the changing needs of an audience? All news organizations have been influenced by increasingly more sophisticated digital technology. It is much easier for organizations to find, record, and send news through satellite, the Internet or cell phone connections. News services are able to draw on the insights of private individuals and local reporters who may have information that is easily communicated through contemporary technologies, rather than a regular foreign correspondent posted overseas. But are smaller organizations better able adapt to new technologies and pursue stories in the way they see fit? Or, are large organizations with substantial funding better able to consolidate and use new technologies to their advantage? Are small, user-generated organizations more flexible and quick to respond to news and audience demands, or do more well-resourced professional organizations play a greater role in keeping and creating new audiences?

- **Fragmented audience** There is something for everyone on the Internet. It is also relatively easy to avoid the things you *don't* want on the Internet. If your passion is road cycling, there are myriad sites that will fulfill your need for very specific and detailed information about cycling. And if you are not interested in hot air ballooning, just don't search for it. Or put a parent lock on ballooning sites. But is there a loss of a broader sense of community? One function of a strong local news presence may not only be the dissemination of news from an area but the building of a community of readers who share information and debate. Does the Internet create a broader, global news community or a more fractured whole? If large multinational newspapers like the *New York Times* do create a sense of community that crosses borders, is this beneficial or limiting?

Activity

The blog

Blogging is one of the online genres that has the potential to change the way news is produced and consumed. The power of the independent, informational blog is so strong that savvy traditional media outlets now produce their own blogs so that their staff writers and reporters have another outlet for their material—material that often sits outside traditional news boundaries. Look at the following extracts and consider the nature of the blog in relation to traditional news outlets like television news and newspapers. How do the "headlines" on a blog differ from the headlines in newspapers? Do the stories in a blog fit into the models of informational bias and newsworthiness as previously discussed? Does the language of the blog article indicate to you in any way that it is a different genre from a typical newspaper article? How is the article different in style, register, or content? Is the blog and its article more or less useful than a traditional newspaper? Do blogs add something to media culture that was not possible before the Internet? Does the language of the blog article indicate to you in any way that it is a different genre from a typical newspaper article?

Text 1

The "front page" of a private blog by the British journalist Toby Young.

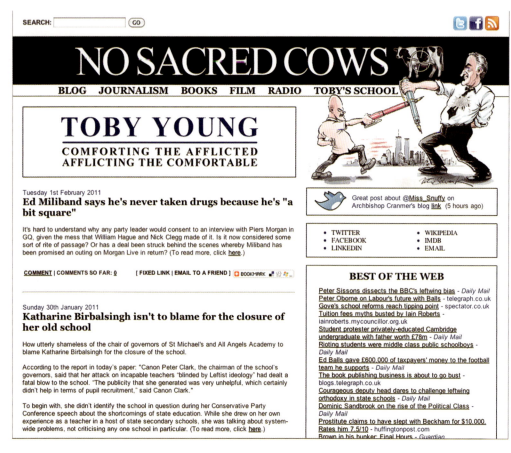

Source: http://www.nosacredcows.co.uk.

Text 2

The following is a complete article also taken from Toby Young's Blog:

Ed Balls's plans to privatise state education

BLOG	JOURNALISM	BOOKS	FILM	RADIO	TOBY'S SCHOOL

By **Toby Young** **Education** Last updated: March 31st, 2010 **5 Comments** **Comment on this article**

On March 12, *The Times Educational Supplement* ran an article entitled "Now Young turns to for-profit providers" in which it revealed that I'd been talking to various commercial education providers about the possibility of operating the West London Free School after it has been set up. That is to say, the school would be governed by a charitable trust which, in turn, would be sponsored by my parent group. But the trust would sub-contract the day-to-day operation of the school to a private company, such as IES or Kunskapsskolan, the two largest Swedish "free school" businesses.

> The TES journalist who wrote the piece (Richard Vaughan) had the wit to call up the leader of the NUT to see what she thought of this idea and—surprise, surprise—she denounced it in no uncertain terms:
>
> NUT general secretary Christine Blower said: "Those who run and manage schools should be education professionals with a public service ethos, not educational companies whose bottom line is serving the interests of their shareholders. Children and young people are not commodities; they are entitled within school to know that those who run and manage their school have purely their educational interests at heart."
>
> Ms Blower added: "Toby Young's suggestion of bringing in private companies on a service contract gives a lie to the Conservative's stated intention to introduce parent-led free schools. In practice, parents do not have the time or the expertise to run their own schools."
>
> "The Conservative's plans can lead in one direction only and that is the introduction of profit-making companies into the running of the English education system."

In fact, it's not a Tory policy at all—or, at least, not just a Tory policy. It's a Labour policy, too. On February 23, Ed Balls announced that he was putting in place a new system of accreditation whereby "outstanding school leaders" could apply to become Approved Providers and, if certified, go on "to run chains of secondary schools". In the Guidance on Becoming an Accredited School Provider published on the DCSF's website, there's a list of the type of groups who may be accredited as School Providers and it includes "private and third sector organisations".

In other words, Ed Balls was giving a green light to private companies to operate state schools—and they haven't been slow to respond. Since the new accreditation system was put in place, dozens of commercial education businesses have applied to become Approved Providers, including EdisonLearning, Serco and VT Group.

This radical new departure in Labour's education policy didn't receive any publicity at the time, but *The Times's* education correspondent has finally cottoned on to this and written it up in this morning's paper:

> Although both the Government and the Conservatives say that organisations driven by profit should not run schools, both have created a path for them to enter the sector. Governing bodies of new, or existing, schools can appoint a contractor to operate the school on their behalf—a model used widely in the US.

Now that the paper of record has made it clear that a plan the leader of the NUT denounced as "Toby Young's suggestion" is, in fact, official Labour Party policy, I look forward to a motion being passed at this weekend's NUT annual conference condemning Ed Balls in the same shrill tones that I've been condemned.

Tags: Christine Blower, DCSF, Ed Balls, EdisonLearning, IES,Kunskapsskolan, Mary Bousted, Serco, VT Group, West London Free School

Questions to the text

1 How is the article different in style, register, or content to a mainstream newspaper?

2 Is the blog and its article more or less useful than a traditional newspaper?

3 Do blogs add something to media culture that was not possible before the Internet?

Text 3

Following is a page from a website called "wikileaks.org" that is dedicated to providing public access to government and corporate documents and information that would otherwise not be readily available.

The webcapture is a page with a video taken from a US helicopter gunship that shows the killing of civilians and reporters in Iraq.

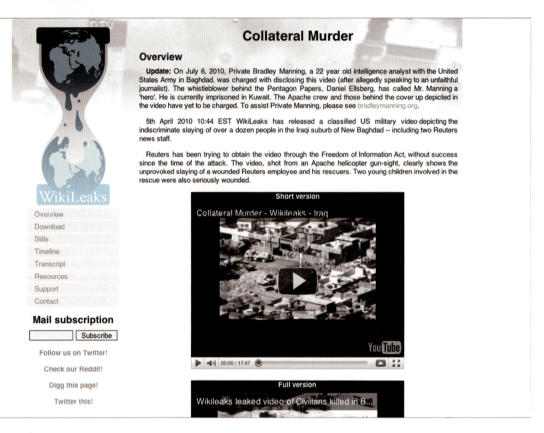

Questions to the text

1 What are the benefits of sites such as wikileaks.org that provide information to the public? What are the drawbacks?

2 What vital role do "whistleblowers" play in reporting on the wrong doings of large organizations?

3 What questions would you ask about any such website when considering relative truth or bias?

Political speeches and campaigns

The previous discussion focused on the institutions and outlets that actually function to harness various media formats in order to bring information to the public. When we think of the very purpose of mass communication—sending a message to an audience larger than one and potentially today numbering in the millions—it should be obvious that politics are intimately tied, if not dependent upon, mass communication. Almost every possible political message ranging from a speech to a small crowd to a mass emailing is an attempt at mass communication and these communicative acts are invariably communicated through a wide variety of media. Looking at mass communication through political speeches and campaigns provides a useful focus to see how language is crafted and consumed across a variety of media. In the political arena, language is power and an investigation of language allows us to see how power is gained and maintained through the combined effects of managing expectations, style, register, use of imagery, use of narrative and many other elements.

This brief outline of some of the issues to consider in an examination of the topic of politics and mass communication will help you to apply your analytic skills to a variety of texts that will spur thought around language. First, you should consider the broader elements of language and mass communication and the ways in which media formats and institutions shape language. Obviously, the concerns foregrounded in the discussion of media institutions and news organization are closely related to the ways in which political messages are both disseminated and reported. Even in the texts that follow, which are *about* speeches and campaigns rather than examples of primary political texts, you should be on the lookout for the way the *reporting of* political events—what is in a sense a remediation of a message—is itself intimately tied to the way messages get to us, the consumers. Political messages are important to examine for their potential manipulation of power through language and the implications this has for the way we organize our societies from how we learn in schools to how we decide to go to war.

It is sometimes difficult to analyze political texts that come from outside of our own culture because we are simply not aware enough of the particular context, concerns or debates in a given locality. We have attempted, then, to choose texts from a variety of cultures that represent a language and communication issue, rather than attempting to examine a particular campaign. You should read the examples almost as if they exist out of context, trying to get at the issue of communication and power and then you should apply these skills to political texts you find in your own community or that you might examine in your classroom.

Regardless of your own context, you will find that language and mass communication plays a role in how you are governed. Consider for now just these few examples of where and how language and mass communication figures in the political landscape by speeches, debates, sound bites, advertisements, and policy statements:

• **Political agenda** Mass communication influences what the general public considers to be the issues of the day, often determined by the focus of elected officials. Think about your own local community: what issues mattered in your most recent election? How do you know? What issues are government leaders currently addressing at the local or national level? How did these issues become important? The political agenda, the metaphoric list of items or issues that need to be or are being addressed by the government, is created through communication. Political leaders give speeches on issues related to polling data conducted by private organizations and media outlets; journalists write opinion pieces or editorials on issues they feel people are or should be concerned about (or that they think will sell magazines); private and public organizations attempt to alert the public to issues of health, safety, or economic wellbeing—these are all ways in which through language the political agenda is constructed.

- **Elections** Elections obviously affect the way we are governed and officials would not be elected if it were not for the successful marshalling of mass communication. Speeches may offer political candidates an opportunity to speak directly to a group of people but almost as soon as the carefully crafted words are spoken (from carefully crafted "sets" like schools, aircraft carriers, or drought-stricken regions) they are infinitely "spun" and remediated. While institutional media outlets play a large role in the election process in terms of communication and interpretation of ideas, mass communication by individuals, corporations, and institutions are almost infinitely variable and affect what the public thinks and how it votes.

- **Public policy** Much like the political agenda, public policy is affected by mass communication, the lobbying of pressure groups through the media. The public agenda is what we think of as important issues of the day while public policy is the set of decisions made by the government in relation to many of those issues. The question, then, is how do public officials make and modify policy decisions once they are elected? Once again, these decisions are made, influenced by, and communicated by a variety of people through a variety of media. Ultimately, a policy, like a law, is written so the rules we follow are closely tied to how meanings are communicated and consumed. Before policy is adopted, it is debated and discussed: almost every sentence, word, comma, or image, can lead to changes in how our lives are conducted within the governing social institutions.

Activity

Speeches

The two texts below are from speeches that have received acclaim for their rhetorical or persuasive power. The first speech, by then Deputy Prime Minister of South Africa, Thabo Mbeki, was given in 1996 to celebrate the first democratic elections in the post-apartheid era. The second speech was given by the British suffragette Emmeline Pankhurst as she campaigned for women's right to vote in the United States. As you read them, consider where the political power of a speech come from. Is it in the content of the speech? The stories told? The words, as they are spoken? In this case, it is worth considering that you have here the text of the speech and not the spoken version. You may consider as you read what elements may have been particularly effective or important as spoken words.

Text 1

The speech "I am an African" by Thabo Mbeki, Deputy President of South Africa, was given on 8 May 1996, on the occasion of the adoption by the Constitutional Assembly of the Republic Of South Africa Constitution Bill of 1996. Many commentators have suggested that

Thabo Mbeki's speech led to a resurgence of pan-African pride. Interestingly, some have compared Mbeki's speech to the popular "I have a dream" speech given by the US civil rights leader Martin Luther King Jr. Many critics have suggested that the original power of King's speech, delivered in 1963 came from his use of the rhythm and styles of African American Christian sermonizing which itself was indebted to the rhetorical styles inherited from Africa. Do you recognize these and other rhetorical devices in Mbeki's speech?

> Friends, on an occasion such as this, we should, perhaps, start from the beginning. So, let me begin.
>
> I am an African! I owe by being to the hills and the valleys, the mountains and the glades, the rivers, the deserts, the trees, the flowers, the seas and the ever-changing seasons that define the face of our native land. My body has frozen in our frosts and in our latter day snows. It has thawed in the warmth of our sunshine and melted in the heat of the midday sun. The crack and the rumble of the summer thunders, lashed by startling lightening, have been a cause both

of trembling and of hope … The dramatic shapes of the [landscape] have … been panels of the set on the natural stage on which we act out the foolish deeds of the theatre of our day.

At times, and in fear, I have wondered whether I should concede equal citizenship of our country to the leopard and the lion, the elephant and the springbok, the hyena, the black mamba and the pestilential mosquito. A human presence among all these, a feature on the face of our native land thus defined, I know that none dare challenge me when I say—I am an African! …

Today, as a country, we keep an audible silence about these ancestors of the generations that live, fearful to admit the horror of a former deed, seeking to obliterate from our memories a cruel occurrence which, in its remembering, should teach us not and never to be inhuman again. I am formed of the migrants who left Europe to find a new home on our native land. Whatever their own actions, they remain still, part of me. In my veins courses the blood of the Malay slaves who came from the East. Their proud dignity informs my bearing, their culture a part of my essence. The stripes they bore on their bodies from the lash of the slave master are a reminder embossed on my consciousness of what should not be done … My mind and my knowledge of myself is formed by the victories that are the jewels in our African crown, the victories we earned from Isandhlwana to Khartoum, as Ethiopians and as the Ashanti of Ghana, as the Berbers of the desert. …

I have seen our country torn asunder as … my people, engaged one another in a titanic battle, the one redress a wrong that had been caused by one to another and the other, to defend the indefensible. I have seen what happens when one person has superiority of force over another, when the stronger appropriate to themselves the prerogative even to annul the injunction that God created all men and women in His image.

I know what it signifies when race and colour are used to determine who is human and who, sub-human. I have seen the destruction of all sense of self-esteem, the consequent striving to be what one is not, simply to acquire some of the benefits which those who had improved themselves as masters had ensured that they enjoy. I have experience of the situation in which race and colour is used to enrich some and impoverish the rest.

I have seen the corruption of minds and souls [in] the pursuit of an ignoble effort to perpetrate a veritable crime against humanity. I have seen concrete expression of the denial of the dignity of a human being emanating from the conscious, systemic and systematic oppressive and repressive activities of other human beings. There the victims parade with no mask to hide the brutish reality—the beggars, the prostitutes, the street children, those who seek solace in substance abuse, those who have to steal to assuage hunger, those who have to lose their sanity because to be sane is to invite pain. Perhaps the worst among these, who are my people, are those who have learnt to kill for a wage. To these the extent of death is directly proportional to their personal welfare …

All this I know and know to be true because I am an African! Because of that, I am also able to state this fundamental truth that I am born of a people who are heroes and heroines. I am born of a people who would not tolerate oppression. I am of a nation that would not allow that fear of death, torture, imprisonment, exile or persecution should result in the perpetuation of injustice. The great masses who are our mother and father will not permit that the behaviour of the few results in the description of our country and people as barbaric. Patient because history is on their side, these masses do not despair because today the weather is bad. Nor do they turn triumphalist when, tomorrow, the sun shines.

Whatever the circumstances they have lived through and because of that experience, they are determined to define for themselves who they are and who they should be … As an African, this is an achievement of which I am proud, proud without reservation and proud without any feeling of conceit … But it seems to have happened that we looked at ourselves and said the time had come that we make a super-human effort to be other than human, to respond to the call to create for ourselves a glorious future, to remind ourselves of the Latin saying: *Gloria est consequenda*—Glory must be sought after! Today it feels good to be an African …

I am born of the peoples of the continent of Africa. The pain of the violent conflict that the peoples of Liberia, Somalia, the Sudan, Burundi and Algeria, is a pain I also bear. The dismal shame of poverty, suffering and human degradation of my continent is a blight that we share. The blight on our happiness that derives from this and from our drift to the periphery of the ordering of human affairs leaves us in a persistent shadow of despair. This is a savage road to which nobody should be condemned. This thing that we have done today, in this small corner of a great continent that has contributed so decisively to the evolution of humanity says that Africa reaffirms that she is continuing her rise from the ashes …

Whatever the difficulties, Africa shall be at peace!

However improbable it may sound to the sceptics, Africa will prosper! Whoever we may be, whatever our immediate interest, however much we carry baggage from our past, however much we have been caught by the fashion of cynicism and loss of faith in the capacity of the people, let us err today and say—nothing can stop us now!

Source: South Africa Government Information. http://www.info.gov.za/speeches/1996/960819_23196.htm.

Questions to the text

1 What is the effect of the repetition of structures like "I have" and "I know"?

2 What is the effect of referring to both negative and positive aspects of the history of South Africa? What is the effect of keeping these allusions general?

3 How does Mbeki employ the use of lists? What are the effects of these lists? What is the effect of a list with the repetitive use of "and," as opposed to a list using commas?

4 Where does Mbeki shift from use of the singular "I" to use of the first person plural "we" and what is its effect?

Text 2

The following speech, "Freedom or Death" by Emmeline Pankhurst, was delivered on November 13, 1913, in Hartford, Connecticut. She had been invited to the United States to defend female activists who were fighting for the right to vote and were beginning to use more physical, dangerous tactics. A few months before, in England, a member of the Women's Social and Political Union, Emily Davison, had, during an important horse race, thrown herself in protest in front of a horse owned by the King. Pankhurst and others viewed Davison as a martyr for the cause of women's suffrage. At the time of her speech, Pankhurst herself was on release from a series of jail sentences in England. In what was referred to as the "Cat and Mouse Act," female prisoners who protested their jail sentences with hunger strikes (as did Pankhurst) were briefly released from prison until they regained their health. In this speech Pankhurst attracted attention for the fame and extremity of her actions and called attention to the lengths to which women were willing to go to gain equality.

I do not come here as an advocate, because whatever position the suffrage movement may occupy in the United States of America, in England it has passed beyond the realm of advocacy and it has entered into the sphere of practical politics. It has become the subject of revolution and civil war, and so tonight I am not here to advocate woman suffrage. American suffragists can do that very well for themselves.

I am here as a soldier who has temporarily left the field of battle in order to explain—it seems strange it should have to be explained—what civil war is like when civil war is waged by women. I am not only here as a soldier temporarily absent from the field at battle; I am here—and that, I think, is the strangest part of my coming—I am here as a person who, according to the law courts of my country, it has been decided, is of no value to the community at all; and I am adjudged because of my life to be a dangerous person, under sentence of penal servitude in a convict prison.

It is not at all difficult if revolutionaries come to you from Russia, if they come to you from China, or from any other part of the world, if they are men. But since I am a woman it is necessary to explain why women have adopted revolutionary methods in order to win the rights of citizenship. We women, in trying to make our case clear, always have to make as part of our argument, and urge upon men in our audience the fact—a very simple fact—that women are human beings.

Suppose the men of Hartford had a grievance, and they laid that grievance before their legislature, and the legislature obstinately refused to listen to them, or to remove their grievance, what would be the proper and the constitutional and the practical way of getting their grievance removed? Well, it is perfectly obvious at the next general election the men of Hartford would turn out that legislature and elect a new one.

But let the men of Hartford imagine that they were not in the position of being voters at all, that they were governed without their consent being obtained, that the legislature turned an absolutely deaf ear to their demands, what would the men of Hartford do then? They couldn't vote the legislature out. They would have to choose; they would have to make a choice of two evils: they would either have to submit indefinitely to an unjust state of affairs, or they would have to rise up and adopt some of the antiquated means by which men in the past got their grievances remedied.

Your forefathers decided that they must have representation for taxation, many, many years ago. When they felt they couldn't wait any longer, when they laid all the arguments before an obstinate British government that they could think of, and when their arguments were absolutely disregarded, when every other means had failed, they began by the tea party at Boston, and they went on until they had won the

independence of the United States of America.

It is about eight years since the word militant was first used to describe what we were doing. It was not militant at all, except that it provoked militancy on the part of those who were opposed to it. When women asked questions in political meetings and failed to get answers, they were not doing anything militant. In Great Britain it is a custom, a time-honoured one, to ask questions of candidates for parliament and ask questions of members of the government. No man was ever put out of a public meeting for asking a question. The first people who were put out of a political meeting for asking questions, were women; they were brutally ill-used; they found themselves in jail before 24 hours had expired.

We were called militant, and we were quite willing to accept the name. We were determined to press this question of the enfranchisement of women to the point where we were no longer to be ignored by the politicians.

You have two babies very hungry and wanting to be fed. One baby is a patient baby, and waits indefinitely until its mother is ready to feed it. The other baby is an impatient baby and cries lustily, screams and kicks and makes everybody unpleasant until it is fed. Well, we know perfectly well which baby is attended to first. That is the whole history of politics. You have to make more noise than anybody else, you have to make yourself more obtrusive than anybody else, you have to fill all the papers more than anybody else, in fact you have to be there all the time and see that they do not snow you under.

When you have warfare things happen; people suffer; the noncombatants suffer as well as thcombatants. And so it happens in civil war. When your forefathers threw the tea into Boston Harbour, a good many women had to go without their tea. It has always seemed to me an extraordinary thing that you did not follow it up by throwing the whiskey overboard; you sacrificed the women; and there is a good deal of warfare for which men take a great deal of glorification which has involved more practical sacrifice on women than it has on any man. It always has been so. The grievances of those who have got power, the influence of those who have got power commands a great deal of attention; but the wrongs and the grievances of those people who have no power at all are apt to be absolutely ignored. That is the history of humanity right from the beginning.

Well, in our civil war people have suffered, but you cannot make omelettes without breaking eggs; you cannot have civil war without damage to something. The great thing is to see that no more damage is done than is absolutely necessary, that you do just as much as will arouse enough feeling to bring about peace, to bring about an honourable peace for the combatants; and that is what we have been doing.

We entirely prevented stockbrokers in London from telegraphing to stockbrokers in Glasgow and vice versa: for one whole day telegraphic communication was entirely stopped. I am not going to tell you how it was done. I am not going to tell you how the women got to the mains and cut the wires; but it was done. It was done, and it was proved to the authorities that weak women, suffrage women, as we are supposed to be, had enough ingenuity to create a situation of that kind. Now, I ask you, if women can do that, is there any limit to what we can do except the limit we put upon ourselves?

If you are dealing with an industrial revolution, if you get the men and women of one class rising up against the men and women of another class, you can locate the difficulty; if there is a great industrial strike, you know exactly where the violence is and how the warfare is going to be waged; but in our war against the government you can't locate it. We wear no mark; we belong to every class; we permeate every class of the community from the highest to the lowest; and so you see in the woman's civil war the dear men of my country are discovering it is absolutely impossible to deal with it: you cannot locate it, and you cannot stop it.

"Put them in prison," they said, "that will stop it." But it didn't stop it at all: instead of the women giving it up, more women did it, and more and more and more women did it until there were 300 women at a time, who had not broken a single law, only "made a nuisance of themselves" as the politicians say.

Then they began to legislate. The British government has passed more stringent laws to deal with this agitation than it ever found necessary during all the history of political agitation in my country. They were able to deal with the revolutionaries of the Chartists' time; they were able to deal with the trades union agitation; they were able to deal with the revolutionaries later on when the Reform Acts were passed: but the ordinary law has not sufficed to curb insurgent women. They had to dip back into the middle ages to find a means of repressing the women in revolt.

They have said to us, government rests upon force, the women haven't force, so they must submit. Well, we are showing them that government does not rest upon force at all: it rests upon consent. As long as women consent to be unjustly governed, they can be, but directly women say: "We withhold our consent, we will not be governed any longer so long as that government is unjust." Not by the forces of civil war can you govern the very weakest woman. You can kill that woman, but she escapes you then; you cannot govern her. No power on earth can govern a human being, however feeble, who withholds his or her consent.

When they put us in prison at first, simply for taking petitions, we submitted; we allowed them to dress us in prison clothes; we allowed them to put us in solitary confinement; we allowed them to put us amongst the most degraded of criminals; we learned of some of the appalling evils of our so-called civilisation that we could not have learned in any other way. It was valuable experience, and we were glad to get it.

I have seen men smile when they heard the words "hunger strike", and yet I think there are very few men today who would be prepared to adopt a "hunger strike" for any cause. It is only people who feel an intolerable sense of oppression who would adopt a means of that kind. It means you refuse food until you are at death's door, and then the authorities have to choose between letting you die, and letting you go; and then they let the women go.

Now, that went on so long that the government felt that they were unable to cope. It was [then] that, to the shame of the British government, they set the example to authorities all over the world of feeding sane, resisting human beings by force. There may be doctors in this meeting: if so, they know it is one thing to feed by force an insane person; but it is quite another thing to feed a sane, resisting human being who resists with every nerve and with every fibre of her body the indignity and the outrage of forcible feeding. Now, that was done in England, and the government thought they had crushed us. But they found that it did not quell the agitation, that more and more women came in and even passed that terrible ordeal, and they were obliged to let them go.

Source: MacArthur, Brian. *The Penguin Book of 20th Century Speeches*. New York: Penguin Books. 1999. pp. 33–37.

Questions to the text

1 How does Pankhurst use comparisons to elevate the status of the fight for voting rights for women?

2 How does Pankhurst call attention to the physical nature of the battle for equality?

3 What words indicate revolution? Suffering? Resistance?

4 What is the effect of Pankhurst's use of "we" and "they"?

5 How does the content of the speech itself draw attention to Pankhurst's issues?

Public debates

Public debates between candidates are often seen as an effective way to inform the public of the views of candidates. Many people also feel a debate gives them a chance to see how candidates handle themselves "on their feet" and in stressful situations. Political debates can take a variety of formats: they can include more than two candidates; they can be based on prepared questions; they can include impromptu questions from the audience; they may involve rebuttal or simply offer each candidate a chance to speak. An interesting question to ask is: "How do you win a debate?" The judges of a high school debating team may determine a winner based on a careful analysis of points made and lost. A debate is often won in the public's mind based on a combination of ideas presented, witty statements made, facial expressions or tone of voice. Success in a debate may also depend on the "spin" given to the debate by supporters or opponents who speak to the press after a debate.

Activity

Televised debates

Televised debates between political candidates have been popular since the 1960s in the United States, and have recently gained popularity in Australia and England. Debates are an interesting laboratory for investigating the use and power of language in a political context. Just as important as the answers to the particular questions are diction, modulation of voice, use of memorable phrasing and humor or wit. On your own, research political debates with a focus on the power of *how* something is said. Focus on one debate and make your own notes considering the following questions: what were the memorable words? Phrases? Which words were repeated? Did either candidate make a noticeable mistake? You could also research published analyses of the debates. What was your impression of the debate? What was the general reaction from the public? What was the verdict among political analysts?

Activity

Researching advertisements

Political advertisements are produced for large, national campaigns as well as for small, local elections. It is sometimes difficult to appreciate particular issues or concerns outside of the community in which you have political concerns as a citizen. On your own, look for as many political advertisements as you can find for a recent election that was relatively familiar to you. See if you can characterize or classify these advertisements broadly. Do they provide information about a politician's stance on major issues, or are they more intended to give a general impression? Are they celebratory? Sensationalist? Are they negative? After considering the possible type of advertisements you have found, begin to look at particular approaches. Are the advertisements thought-provoking? Funny? Disturbing? How are these emotions or ideas created by the words and images used in the advertisements? Finally, consider whether the advertisements serve a purpose beyond the possible election of the candidate.

Look up examples of advertisements on YouTube, or other new media sources.

Further questions

1 What is the advantage of being able to find advertisements on YouTube?

2 What is the effect of a viral ad—an advertisement that spreads through word of mouth or email forwarding—in comparison to more traditional advertising?

   Does the form of distribution have a greater influence on decisions you make in relation to a candidate? Are there different stylistic or rhetorical "rules" that govern viral advertisements in comparison to traditional client-generated advertisements that are paid for and placed during popular television viewing times?

Political advertising

Language in politics goes beyond political speeches and debates. Many citizens get their information and make voting decisions based on paid advertising from political campaigns and independent political groups with a variety of agendas. It seems to be easy to remember that advertisements on television or in print are trying to sell products. It may be difficult to remember, however, that political advertisements are not necessarily informative but meant to persuade or sell. With the proliferation of digital means of mass communication and the concurrent growth in the budget available to political aspirants, it is no wonder that political advertisements have become increasingly well-crafted. While debates and political speeches are venerable traditions in politics, the advertisement seems to have overtaken these longer formats because of their speed, wit, and catchiness.

Activity

Does font matter?

Sam Berlow and Cyrus Highsmith, two researchers and designers of typography, have suggested that the very shape of the letters that make up words act as a powerful form of image. A font, as you may know from playing with the various fonts in your word processor, can communicate a mood, or change the tone of a sentence. During the 2008 presidential election campaign in the United States, Berlow and Highsmith suggested that the fonts chosen to be used consistently by various campaigns in all of their signs and materials were carefully chosen to communicate a desirable attribute or attitude. Look at the collage of political logos below. Can you hypothesize what ideas are communicated by the combination of font and design?

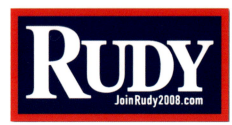

Popular culture

Mass communication is a significant form of entertainment. The popular songs, websites, films, and periodicals created through the mass media provide an outlet for thinking, feeling, and interaction and at the same time provides a means for community building and self-identification. While we saw in the chapter on language in cultural context the variety of contexts within which we use language, it is equally important to consider the mediation of language effects and how we by definition interact with popular culture in supposedly casual or off-hand way. Why do we enjoy certain songs? Why do we get hooked on a particular television program? The manipulation, broadcast, and reception of language makes up a large part of what we call popular culture.

Leisure, choice and commerce

As we pointed out in the very first chapter of this book, the line between what is considered high culture and what is considered popular culture is often blurred and even hotly contested. Viewing culture as a form of art and entertainment, and not in its more sociological and academic sense as the rules and actions of social groups, we see that cultural objects are created to entertain, communicate, and often build community. While cultural objects ranging from paintings and plays to posters, cards and newspapers; and from popular songs and productions to mass-disseminated recordings have been available in some form for centuries, the 20th and 21st centuries have seen an explosion in terms of what is available and how easily it is accessed. The increased availability and lower production costs have created greater demand, and the potential to generate income. We have constant access to a limitless supply of cultural products, ranging from must-read articles and news bites to the latest songs of a new band, and the circulation of jokes, art images and video clips. The sheer scale of production—amassed on a global level—requires us to be selective, critical consumers.

The media stream

River. Torrent. Flood. All of these words have been used by cultural critics to describe our current access to information through contemporary media. While some have suggested that we may be overwhelmed by the depth and breadth of sounds and sights available to us at all hours, others have suggested that all we get is more of the same, and it is important to control the river—the torrent— to discriminately dip into what we feel is entertaining, informative, useful, or important. To help us, corporations such as Apple, Sony or Amazon with products like the iPod and e-readers, allow us to listen to music and read books, with almost instant access to a vast online digital library, and help us to locate similar products. But, is there a downside to the control of such corporations, and their power to filter or mediate content? But how do we choose what we read, view, and listen to? How is our own cultural production influenced by the ever-present flood of words, tunes and images around us? Do we have power over all of the cultural choices we make, or are we simply swept along by the current of popular consumer choices?

In another sense, it is important to recognize that the forms of popular culture may have remained the same throughout the centuries. A comedic play may share attributes with a television situation comedy; word-of-mouth jokes may have been as popular in ancient Pompeii as they are today in the classroom. Perhaps the main difference today is that popular culture is more all-encompassing and global and offers, in its variety, at least the illusion of choice. This access to popular cultural products, however, can be as deadening or deafening as it is stimulating.

Deconstructing the playlist

What are your top ten favourite songs? Why are they your favourites? Where did you find these songs or first hear them? Do some informal research into your own favourite music and the favourites of fellow students. Digital players make it easy to find out what your real current favourites are by simply telling you what you listen to most frequently. Compile lists of the top ten favourites of as many people as you can and ask yourself some of these questions:

1 What are the similarities between the lists? What are the differences?

2 Where did the listeners first hear their favourite songs?

3 Where did the listeners get their music?

4 How much money was paid for the music?

5 Are their interesting or surprising choices on the lists?

Youth culture and commercialization

Read the following texts that are related to popular culture and commercialization. Popular youth culture is often considered "cutting edge" or as a form of expression that works in opposition to the culture at-large that is promoted by adults, schools and corporations. Corporations are always on the lookout for what the youth consider to be cool and interesting so that they can cultivate this growing market and its long-term brand loyalty. There is an interesting cycle in popular culture in terms of what is new, fresh, and original. In skateboarding culture, for example, young skaters may push away from what they think is corporate and develop a rebel style all their own. This new style, however, may be quickly copied by commercial producers wishing to profit from what is new and "cool." At other times, corporations put a lot of effort into predicting and determining what the next big thing will be.

What's new? What's cool?

Who, then, determines what is popular and original? How is language used to both rebel against established culture and to repackage corporate culture as something street-level or rebellious? Consider the following texts in relation to the ever-changing landscape of popular culture.

Text 1

Source: http://www.SBCskateboard.com

Text 2

Source: https://www.SLAMskateboarding.com.

Questions to the text

1 How do these two websites use graphics, images, and language to appeal to their readers?

2 How much advertising appears on the sites?

3 How do the advertisements use language and image, and to what effect?

4 How do the sites take advantage of the digital environment such as linking or social networking?

5 Who is sending the messages on these sites? Who is deciding what is cool?

Text 3

The following blog post from skateboardingmagazine.com offers an opinion on the problem of the commercialization of skateboarding in reference to one young skateboarder who has profited from his pastime. Do you agree with the point of view of the blogger?

Corporate contracts destroy skateboarding's basic principles

Posted on 16 March 2010

Skateboarding is not a sport. According to some of the biggest names in **skateboarding**, like Mark Appleyard and Frank Gerwer, skateboarding is not even an "extreme sport." Skateboarding is an art, a subculture and a world of its own. It possesses many of the same traits as any sport or pastime but the tie that holds skateboarders together is a tight one. Well, at least it used to be.

In August 2007, MTV single-handedly broke down the skate world's barriers by airing the reality TV show, "Life of Ryan," a show that displayed Ryan Sheckler's oh-so-awful life and times growing up in Orange County – with more money than my family, grandparents and uncle put together – while he skateboards and travels the world for a living.

Boohoo. As if the label of reality TV isn't misleading enough, the life of Ryan as depicted on the show is clearly far from reality. I'm not going to say I like Ryan Sheckler because that would be a lie. I will admit that he is a talented skateboarder, and deserves what he has (at least when it comes to sponsors). But do I respect the guy? No way. Ryan's oh-so-exciting life somehow gained the attention of hundreds of thousands of viewers throughout each season of his show's short career, leaving fans with one thought in their mind: "Skateboarding? Yeah, I could do that." Well, the joke's on you.

Meanwhile, the skateboarding world is blowing up online, in magazines, on blogs and elsewhere. Sheckler and MTV were the talk of the town. The real world adores skateboarders like Sheckler. He's been in everything from deodorant commercials to milk commercials. (Yep, he's one of the few to wear the milk mustache, skateboard in hand.) But who cares? Skateboarding isn't about being in milk commercials, or winning the X Games. Skateboarding isn't about having your own TV show or about being famous. Rather it is about the self-satisfaction of riding the board. It's about skating your surroundings – anything and everything.

I think it's sad that corporations such as MTV weasel their way into these kids' wallets. What is even more depressing, though, is when your favorite pros change companies they have been on for years just to boost up that paycheck. They gain money but lose respect. From a fan's perspective, it's just how you look at it. Skateboarding is branching into two major directions right now: you're either in it for the fame, money and sponsors who aren't even associated with skateboarding; or you're doing it for the thrill, passion and the feeling of bombing a hill at 6 a.m. to grab a cup of coffee.

I hate to admit it, but Sheckler does love skateboarding. He is a professional, and deserves his title. I just don't agree with advertisements in skateboarding magazines showing a kid posing for the camera like a model, without a skateboard in sight. Skateboarders used to make money by skateboarding – strictly and solely. They would take photos (yes, of them skateboarding), which would be published in skate magazines, and they would get paid for ads.

Most professional skateboarders in the 1990s and even into the 2000s lived in crammed apartments, with six or seven friends, skating to survive. They didn't drive around in Mercedes or BMWs, let alone shoot skateboarding ads flaunting them. A skateboarder's life was as raw and as exciting as you could imagine. Unfortunately, this was before industry-heads realized they could make a few bucks to be corny and ride for sellout companies. Many of them jumped on that wagon without thinking twice, although a fair share of professionals and skateboarders of all ages remained humble, and underground. MTV called Tim O' Connor, a pro for Habitat skateboards, more than three times to set up meetings and get a show started. He denied them every time. That is exactly how it should be.

Source: "Corporate contracts destroy skateboarding's basic principles." Posted March 16, 2010. http://skateboardingmagazine.com/blog.

Questions to the text

1 How would you describe the style and register of this blog post? Is it effective?

2 Who ultimately decides what is cool or not? Who decides what types of media messages the public will consume?

3 When corporate sponsorship is backing a popular pastime, how does it change people's attitudes? Who is the loser in the corporatization of leisure?

Text 4

The following excerpt is from *Pattern Recognition*, a novel by William Gibson. Gibson is most famous for coining the term "cyberspace" in his science fiction novel *Neuromancer*. *Pattern Recognition* investigates the intersections of identity, popular culture, and commercial interests. The protagonist of the novel, Cayce Pollard, is a "cool hunter" who helps companies find and market what is cutting edge.

The Website of Dreadful Night

Five hours' New York jet lag and Cayce Pollard wakes in Camden Town to the dire and ever-circling wolves of disrupted circadian rhythm.

It is that flat and spectral non-hour, awash in limbic tides, brainstem stirring fitfully, flashing inappropriate reptilian demands for sex, food, sedation, all of the above, and none really an option now.

Not even food, as Damien's new kitchen is as devoid of edible content as its designers' display windows in Camden High Street. Very handsome, the upper cabinets faced in canary-yellow laminate, the lower with lacquered, unstained apple-ply. Very clean and almost entirely empty, save for a carton containing two dry pucks of Weetabix and some loose packets of herbal tea. Nothing at all in the German fridge, so new that its interior smells only of cold and long-chain monomers.

She knows, now, absolutely, hearing the white noise that is London, that Damien's theory of jet lag is correct: that her mortal soul is leagues behind her, being reeled in on some ghostly umbilical down the vanished wake of the plane that brought her here, hundreds of thousands of feet above the Atlantic. Souls can't move that quickly, and are left behind, and must be awaited, upon arrival, like lost luggage.

She wonders if this gets gradually worse with age: the nameless hour deeper, more null, its affect at once stranger and less interesting?

Numb here in the semi-dark, in Damien's bedroom, beneath a silvery thing the color of oven mitts, probably never intended by its makers to actually be slept under. She'd been too tired to find a blanket. The sheets between her skin and the weight of this industrial coverlet are silky, some luxurious thread count, and they smell faintly of, she guesses, Damien. Not badly, though. Actually it's not unpleasant; any physical linkage to a fellow mammal seems a plus at this point.

Damien is a friend.

Their boy-girl Lego doesn't click, he would say.

Damien is thirty, Cayce two years older, but there is some carefully insulated module of immaturity in him, some shy and stubborn thing that frightened the money people. Both have been very good at what they've done, neither seeming to have the least idea of why.

Google Damien and you will find a director of music videos and commercials. Google Cayce and you will find "coolhunter," and if you look closely you may see it suggested that she is a "sensitive" of some kind, a dowser in the world of global marketing.

Though the truth, Damien would say, is closer to allergy, a morbid and sometimes violent reactivity to the semiotics of the marketplace.

Damien's in Russia now, avoiding renovation and claiming to be shooting a documentary. Whatever faintly lived-in feel the place now has, Cayce knows, is the work of a production assistant.

She rolls over, abandoning this pointless parody of sleep. Gropes for her clothes. A small boy's black Fruit Of The Loom T-shirt, thoroughly shrunken, a thin gray V-necked pullover purchased by the half-dozen from a supplier to New England prep schools, and a new and oversized pair of black 501's, every trademark carefully removed. Even the buttons on these have been ground flat, featureless, by a puzzled Korean locksmith, in the Village, a week ago.

The switch on Damien's Italian floor lamp feels alien: a different click, designed to hold back a different voltage, foreign British electricity.

Standing now, stepping into her jeans, she straightens, shivering.

Source: Gibson, William. 2003. *Pattern Recognition*. New York: Berkley, 2005. pp. 1–2.

Questions to the text

1 Why would Gibson title this chapter "The Website of Dreadful Night"? In what ways can an experience be described as a website?

2 How does Gibson show, through his use of language and imagery, that Cayce is both an analyst of popular culture and a consumer thoroughly immersed in it?

3 What is the relationship in this passage between commercialism and identity?

4 What is Cayce's attitude toward brands? How would this be useful in her job as a "cool hunter"?

Viral advertising

Viral marketing, or viral advertising, is a method of communication that uses social structures and web-based social networking to distribute its message. Like a virus that can find a host and then spread to others who come in contact with the host, a viral message is passed on through word of mouth, links, or other forms of user-generated sharing. Interesting or humorous commercials, for example, have been created specifically for YouTube and then have gained millions of "hits" because of their popularity without the corporation paying for any placement (as a television commercial, for example).

Viral marketing can be seen as an extreme form of demonstrating consumer choice, as a way of both influencing choice and creating the illusion of freedom and private action. If you forward a humorous advertisement to a friend, are you acting out of your own volition, in a genuinely participative way by selectively promoting a cultural product, or are you being manipulated into acting as a carrier, or agent, for an exploitative producer or corporation?

Conclusion

At the most basic level, the importance of mass communication lies in its very definition. Mass communication is the process of enabling a message to be sent from one to many. Developing broadcast and participative technologies means that mass communication has become more widespread, more effective, and more accessible both for the cultural producer and those on the receiving end. It requires our participation no less in stemming or questioning the flow or proliferation of media content, and potentially contributing to it in our own "viral" way. As such, the study of mass communication and the role of individual and group communicative acts, as a form of participation in global mass culture remains a critical dimension, worthy of close study and attention across its different forms.

7 Assessment in language and mass communication

As you will by now appreciate, the formal, summative assessments designed by IB are actually all assessments *for* learning. When you read or view, and respond to your reading and viewing by speaking and writing, you are actively engaged in learning and demonstrating to someone else what you know and are able to do. With this in mind, you should not approach the IB assessments with trepidation; but, rather, with a sense of personal and creative engagement in the concerns of the course. Of course, there is always some stress when a mark or grade gets thrown into the mix. This chapter is designed to give you more focused practice. We like to think that your teacher (and this course companion) should not have to "teach to the test" or worry about giving you certain information or basic formulas that you then have to repeat for an examiner; the test should be seen as a natural conclusion to your ongoing creative research.

Read the following student samples critically, considering the positive and negative aspects. You should also always think about what you would have done yourself and look at your own work with the same critical eye (an admittedly difficult task).

Written task 1

What is it?

The main features of written task 1 has already been discussed in chapter 5. The attributes of the task, the guidelines for production, the methods for organizing and writing your responses and meeting the assessment criteria remain the same for each section of the course. You are required to complete four written tasks at the higher level, or three at standard level for assessment; two of these are submitted for external assessment at the higher level and one at standard level. Since you must submit written tasks for both the language part of the course and the literature component, your teacher will most likely ask you to produce a task for each section. The example following will focus on a written task that has been produced to meet the objectives of the language and mass communication section of the course.

As discussed in chapter 6, the stylistic and formal qualities of the medium are very important to grasp when considering the use or effect of language in mass communication. The written task is a chance to mimic and show your understanding of a form, such as a newspaper article. For this written task, as in all of the written tasks for this course, you may include images as part of your assignment and call attention to formal elements such as layout, but you must also make sure not to exceed or go too far under the word count (a rationale of 200 to 300 words and a task of 800 to 1,000 words). It is important to consider, as in the case of a newspaper article, the most appropriate language (in terms of formality and accessibility), as well as the structure, propriety (in the naming of individuals, and quoting sources etc.), details (the event, location, age and number of people concerned), and any other relevant information as reference points. In regards to the content, remember that the rationale, and by implication the task itself, should make clear the audience, purpose and social, cultural or historical context for your written task.

How is it marked?

Before looking at the task below, it is worth remembering the criteria against which the task will be marked. Remember that through the production of a text type and by engaging in an analysis of the function of language in mass communication (by reproducing that language in your task) you are trying to demonstrate to an examiner your ability to write in a clear and organized way and, in a wider sense, demonstrate your competencies with a particular medium of textual practice. Refer back to the notes on the criteria for assessment on page 138.

Where do I start?

As teachers, we can say that this is the most commonly asked question in any classroom (besides "Can I go to the bathroom?") So, here are a few points about how to approach the production of this writing task:

- Keep the idea of this task and its requirements in the back of your mind as you proceed through the course.

- Make mental notes of the aspects of the course that you most enjoyed. Did you find an issue challenging or exciting? Did you enjoy reading a particular type of text? Is there a media form that you would like to write or create in the future?

- Pay attention to the daily work you do in class. What did you find most challenging? Was there an assignment that particularly appealed to you? What tasks were you most successful at, and when did you most actively participate in class discussions?

- Once you are assigned a task, start planning early. Even if you note only a few ideas for approaches as soon as you get the assignment, ideas can begin to germinate in the back of your mind based on this little seed of a start.

- Take notes and read or research the pieces that most relate to your own idea. Find examples of the same text type or relevant source material. Again, if you have the idea in the back of your mind, you never know what kind of reading (or viewing) might push you in an interesting direction.

- Last, but not least, get down to the final note-taking, organizing, and writing. This should always be the last stage and, if you have generated ideas from the start, this part shouldn't be too painful.

Student sample

Who is your favorite musician? Why do you like this person's (or group's) music? How is this musician portrayed in the popular press? In music videos? These are all questions that can lead to a legitimate and engaged response on a written task clearly related to the goals of the course in language and mass communication. Before reading the student sample below, brainstorm some ideas about how you could incorporate an interest in music into a written task that relates to media institutions, modes of communication, bias, power, class, or the production and spread of popular culture.

Rationale Rock stars are more than just musicians who write and perform popular songs. Rock stars seem to transcend the everyday world of making music and become idols that attract attention for their lives and lifestyles as much as for the crowds they draw at concerts. While it is obvious that the songs and exciting performances are what initiate the popularity for the most successful performers, media also plays a role in developing the myth of a particular star. The roles of the media and the roles of the individual star are quite interesting when considering the way a persona is developed and marketed to the consumer. A newspaper or magazine, for example, wants to sell issues by publishing articles about a musician and thus would like the musician to remain popular. The musician, while agreeing to be interviewed or profiled by a magazine, is also concerned with self-marketing. To add complexity, the musician and magazine are also in the business of selling other products or somehow manipulating an audience. For this written task I will create two magazine articles about a fictional Irish rock star named Bolo. The first article will be a "profile piece" from a popular music magazine such as *Rolling Stone*, and will focus on music and the band's success. The second article, an editorial from a news magazine such as *The Economist*, will focus on the humanitarian work that the artist has done as a celebrity. By juxtaposing the two articles I hope to highlight the idea of celebrity as a construction of language used to sell to a consumer both on the part of the magazines and the celebrity himself and the ways in which language changes for different audiences and for different purposes.

I like the immediate focus on a larger issue in relation to popular culture and mass communication.

Good point.

More than their success? I am wondering if RS is a good choice. Choose another magazine that is even more fawning?

This sounds very good but I hope you are not biting off more than you can chew. A lot to put into two short pieces.

Article 1

Pulling up to the front of the Regal Plaza in L.A. is disappointing. It's not because I'm driving a white Hyundai rental car. It's not because my jeans suddenly feel outdated when I look at the expensively dressed guests swishing through the revolving doors. I've grown up listening to the plaintive lyrics of Bolo and his legendary group UZ and when I was young these guys were rockers and rebels and now, I thought, as the valet sneered at my rental key chain, Bolo had finally sold out. UZ's newest album, the one we have all heard previewed on the Facebook page and piped through Gap stores, is supposed to be a return to their roots … but the Gap? A Starbucks promotion? Sitting around the pool at the Regal Plaza? I'm done with these guys.

So it is, with a mix of pleasure and ironic hesitancy, that I approach the pool and find Bolo, sure enough, splayed on a lounge, wearing his signature wrap-around shades and a mix of leather and denim, as the guests around him look at home in their impossibly small swimsuits. There he is: the rock star rebel. What can I say about this casually grungy get-up? Is it all for show? I am pleased because he looks different from the others, less polished but I am disappointed because he is fitting the mold of not fitting the mold. My confusion probably shows through in my awkward opening.

"This is about what I expected, I guess."

"Ah, you must be from the magazine. Then again, you could be anyone. I've been doing this for over thirty years and I've finally come to realize that no matter what you do it will go against and right bloody along with what people expect."

So, put in my place, I try to talk to Bolo, find out what he thinks, and more importantly, try to get a glimpse into what went in to the production of this new album. And I should say here that what we find in the album, what we get when we separate the music from the sales of jeans and t-shirts (yes, yes, I know, jeans sales that will eventually benefit malaria research and ethical development in Africa) is earthy, gut moving, and surprising. These are songs of nineteen-year-olds who don't want to work with their dads but have never eaten anything but food their mothers have made. These are songs of being young and out of work but put together with the slightly world-weary wisdom of a fifty-year old star. The first song on the album is the perfect example of a rock anthem that rebels but understands what it means to capture a feeling and entertain an audience. We know what we are getting in the song; we know that the guitar licks will make us progressively more excited. But just like meeting Bolo himself, listening to the song I find it fulfills my expectations and then laughs at me as it expands into something personal, self-conscious and a little bit pained.

"That's exactly what we wanted," says Bolo, "music that does what it is supposed to do but pushes some boundaries. It is tough always living up to expectations but isn't that what life is all about? Fulfilling a few expectations and using those ways of acting to push back a little bit too?"

The music on this album certainly does push back. As I listen to Bolo and the way he is both at ease with himself but also willing to keep experimenting, I realize that this is the mark of an artist. When UZ was an upstart band, what set them apart was that they took evident pleasure in their making of music. They played for

You have a clear tone here and a purpose. But does this read the same as Rolling Stone? This may be where you are in trouble and need a bit more length but I still think you have the right idea.

Good attention to celebrity/media.

A quick transition but I think the reader gets the point. Is there another way to start this paragraph?

Do you want to mention this tension (between the promotion in the article and the music criticism) in the statement of intent?

themselves and for the jumping audience crowding the local Dublin pub. For UZ now they still play for themselves and for what we might call a slightly larger pub.

This is the best aspect of the new album. As a listener I may approach the music with self-consciousness, expectations, and cynicism, but as soon as I listen, the joy and artistry takes over and I forget any of my worries or preconceived notions of what it means to rock.

A good article with a nice conclusion related to the music and some of the contradictory feelings of the journalist.

Article 2

The continued success and music industry domination of UZ is an intriguing story of the value of a strong, easily identified product combined with the ability to adapt to large but subtle demographic changes in audience and societal expectations. We have no issue with UZ as a producer of entertaining music and we certainly respect UZ for its talent as a marketing machine. We wonder, however, how genuine and effective the humanitarian efforts of Bolo, the band's lead singer and song writer, can be. The star power being brought to the humanitarian crisis reveals a level of vanity and a narrow perspective of the possibilities of the African continent.

Nice change in vocabulary here.

Bolo is an easily recognizable star capable of generating interest and money for humanitarian causes. The amount of money raised for malaria research in Africa, is quite significant in relation to the millions being spent by a number of publicly funded research agencies both in Africa and around the world. One wonders how more money being spent on research can be a bad thing. What is troubling is how this money ends up being directed, and by whom. "Research organizations are learning to play the game of tailoring their activities to match the desires of large private donor organizations in order to receive funding," says EU research biologist Stephen Harper. "When Redmond Tisch (Bolo's humanitarian coordinator) suggests that prophylactic drugs are a rich area for research," continues Harper "everyone abandons long range research to jump on board." Government funded research tends to allow for greater freedom for areas of research that may not be so glamorous but may offer longer term solutions.

A shift in focus but I like the comparison you are making.

On a more cultural level, the activities of Bolo suggest a mere marketing ploy that brings more exposure to his band, his future tours, and the products of companies allied with his activities. The sales of Bolo's awareness raising t-shirts, while raising money for research, has earned four times as much money for the clothing companies who have increased sales of other products because of Bolo's ability to attract business. Being an environmental and social reformer, for Bolo, is a more adult way of rebelling, fighting … and selling out tour dates.

A nice way of explicitly getting to some of the issues in your statement of intent.

Examiner comments

This is a clear, well-written approach to the task at hand. The rationale indicates an understanding of important concerns of this part of the course as well as some of the debates that may rise from the mass media's role in popular culture. The rationale also does a nice job of suggesting how popular culture goes beyond entertainment and may have social implications. The rationale nicely frames the various issues in relation to intentions, whether of the pieces themselves, the "rock star" profiled, or of the larger media institutions. This could also be one of the weaknesses of the written task. The rationale may be attempting to address too many issues in relation to mass communication in order to effectively demonstrate an in-depth understanding. Even the choice of writing two brief articles limits the candidate's ability to develop a voice, emphasize stylistic or generic techniques, and delve into the issues at hand.

The pieces themselves do a good job of imitating the styles of the text types being imitated and present an interesting contrasting focus. The candidate has also managed make links between the two pieces of writing beyond the persona of the celebrity. Both pieces mention social concerns, and both are concerned with marketing, promotion, and appeal though from different perspectives. The pieces show a good understanding of stylistic features of these text types as well. The second piece could, perhaps, be even more "factual," going beyond the quotes from the "source." Overall, presented in a clear, fresh voice, this written task shows a good understanding of the concerns of this section of the course and the types of texts studied.

Some other ideas for written tasks in relation to this section of the course include the following:

- The creation of a public information document explaining new legislation to the community.

- A newspaper report on a local news event from the perspective of a national newspaper (or vice versa).

- A screenplay for a documentary on the effects of global warming.

- The creation of a mass emailing campaign by a candidate running for public office.

Written task 2 (higher level)

What is it?

As we noted in chapter 5, written task 2 is an opportunity for students to demonstrate understanding and explore issues in language and literature in a slightly more detailed manner. Unlike written task 1, written task 2 is absolutely meant to be a more traditional persuasive academic essay. Although the topic will ultimately be decided by you, your written task 2 assessments are meant to respond to one of six set questions, with two questions coming from each of the following three areas of study. In this section we will give you an example of a student response to one of the prescribed questions. At this time, the prescribed questions, as listed in the guide for the course, are the following (the bullets under questions are examples of possible approaches or texts to study in relation to language and mass communication):

Reader, culture, and text

1 How could the text be read and interpreted differently by two different readers?

- the study and analysis of a public health brochure written for a rural area with limited healthcare access.

Activity

Be the examiner
Since you have had the chance to look at two examples of written tasks in chapter 5 and you have read the examiner comments, try writing comments of your own to the previous text. Re-read the rationale and the essay and write a paragraph or two about the paper's strengths and weaknesses. You should focus your comments on aspects brought up by the assessment criteria categories.

- the analysis of media material from a political campaign.
- the study of newspaper articles from different areas of the world related to the same information or incident.
- the study of advertisements for a particular type of product, such as kitchen supplies, from the 1940s to now.

2 If the text had been written in a different time or place or for a different audience, how and why would it change?

- a comic book originally produced in the 1950s rewritten for a contemporary audience.
- a newspaper article from one culture rewritten for another cultural audience, highlighting the different use of language directed at particular social groups.
- the study of two advertising campaigns for automobiles, each one focused on a different consumer profile related to age or gender.

Power and privilege

1 How and why is a social group represented in a particular way?

- The study of an article in which a native tribe is represented in a negative way.
- The study of a website that is designed to appeal to a particular powerful audience demographic.
- A study of the language used in a news editorial and the assumptions made about audience class.

2 Which social groups are marginalized, excluded, or silenced within the text?

- A study of the lack of the representation of minority groups in mainstream magazines.
- An analysis of the portrayal of women in a major sports magazine or on a major sports television network.

Text and genre

1 How does the text conform to, or deviate from, the conventions of a particular genre, and for what purpose?

- A study of a new situation comedy on television and the way it plays with the typical constraints of the genre.
- A comparative study of a Shakespearean comedy with a film version of a contemporary romantic comedy.
- An analysis of a novel in relation to its use of attributes from other media (showing the use of music video techniques in the structure of a novel or the use of letters, newspaper articles, or diaries).

2 How has the text borrowed from other texts? Which effects has it drawn on?

- An analysis of the ways in which print advertisements take advantage of more serious or informational journalistic genres.
- The study of religious imagery and its use in other media.
- A comparison of a short story and a feature-length magazine article in relation to narrative structure.

How to approach the task?

The questions that are set for this task are both intentionally broad and clearly linked to the main objectives of the course. If you look at the questions, you will probably see areas of investigation that are interesting to you or that you have already begun to explore in class or on your own. The best question to pursue would be one that links not just to what you have been taught but to the topics and particular texts that you have found the most interesting. It may be worth your while to look at these questions before you even begin studying a unit so that some of these major concerns are in your mind as you begin to reflect on examples of the various text types.

Once you have chosen a question to answer and a text to use in order to respond, you should spend some time re-reading, thinking and taking notes. We can't stress enough that all of the reading and thinking you do before writing is the most important part of completing an assessment. If you have an idea germinating in the back of your mind for a longer period of time before actually sitting down to write, you will give yourself the greater chance to refine and develop it, change your approaches, or even imagine a few great opening sentences. In terms of writing and development, there is nothing better than to have an idea for a paper, leave it for a day or two, and then find yourself waking up at night with the urge to get up and write it down before it slips away. Advanced thinking and planning gives your mind the opportunity to work.

How is it marked?

Very simply, there are four criteria used to assess written task 2: outline, response to the question, organization and language and style.

- **Outline** Does the outline adequately explain, define and highlight the focus of the essay?

- **Response to the question** Does the written task convey a developed and sophisticated understanding of the expectations of the question? Does the essay respond to the question or seek only to summarize information? Is the essay supported by well-chosen and thoroughly explained examples?

- **Organization** Are the structure and organization coherent and sustained? Has the word count been met (two marks will be deducted from tasks that fail to meet the word count)?

- **Language and style** Is the use of language and style effectively applied to the task chosen?

As with any assessment task, whether formative or summative, written task 1 or written task 2, examiners are looking for a strong sense of understanding of the works and topics studied as well as a thoughtful critical engagement.

Student sample

The following example of student writing for written task 2 focuses on an image from a print advertisement. Before reading the task itself, examine the advertisement. How could you use your knowledge of the language used in mass communication to analyze this advertisement? What prompts from the written task 2 prescribed questions would be appropriate to consider in relation to this advertisement? Finally, after reading the student response, and before reading the examiner's comments, be sure to think about approaches you may have taken that would differ from the approach of the student in this example.

"How and why is a social group represented in a particular way?"

"Bedouin: The desire to cut things up." Created for Stihl by the advertising agency Publicis Conseil Paris, France, in 2009.

We often do not think very deeply about the advertisements that we see on television, on the internet or in magazines. We see pretty pictures, get briefly excited about a story that is being told, or, more often, we laugh at a humorous idea or image. The advertisement above for a brand of chainsaws takes a moment of thought to understand why a chainsaw might be in the desert, but most viewers have a quick laugh and then do not think any more about the advertisement—except maybe to go on and remember or buy the product. All advertisements, however, in order to be attention getting, humorous, or memorable, have to work on many assumptions that the consumer will make. While this advertisement is visually striking and mildly humorous, it also shows the way advertizing can play to cultural and gender stereotypes, especially when marketing to an audience that is assumed to be Western and male.

The chainsaw advertisement is striking and funny, but why? The advertiser obviously wants to attract our attention and does so by using a beautiful but stark picture of a desert scene. The scene–including

This introduction comes to a strong conclusion but it lacks some specifics. The first two sentences generalize without getting to the image and in the last two sentences you could be more specific ... "striking," in what way? What particular "stereotypes"?

A good way to get at technique and meaning.

a broad expanse of desert, a man kneeling at work, a tent and camel—appeals to a romantic vision of what an exotic desert experience can be. The viewer's attention is drawn to the man and the product in the near center of the image and all of the objects in the image are pushed to the upper left hand corner, giving the viewer the sense of the emptiness in the surrounding environment. The humor comes from the juxtaposition of the image with the brief text. The French slogan loosely translates to "it gives you the desire to cut (or saw) (translation my own) and this idea, along with the smile on the face of the man, his posture near the box that suggests eagerness, juxtapose with the treeless surroundings. This is funny; this chainsaw induces strong desires even for someone living in the desert. It is important that this humor and the basic attraction even of the image relies heavily on the depiction of a culture (including a geographical area, a race, and a way of living) that may be foreign to many of the viewers, considering that they would live in an area with trees or in France where the advertisement would run.

Helpful description and beginnings of analysis.

Is it funny regardless of place?

Much of the force of the advertisement comes from playing on stereotypes of a North African or Arabian culture that is represented here with very typical, striking symbols that may be a form of racism. First of all, the image calls our attention to details that we assume are accurate in relation to the culture: the man is isolated, he wears a head scarf, his tent is made of carpet or old material, his mode of transportation is a camel, and the only visible piece of modern technology is the foreign, purposefully out of place chainsaw. The man lives in poverty but not in an impoverished situation that is realistic, but one that appeals partially to a romantic or typical view of what the desert is like in our imaginations. While we may laugh at the lack of trees in the barren desert, we may also be laughing at the possibility that such a person in such a place, would even have access to, let alone need, a chainsaw. The chainsaw creates desire even in this person who is obviously not the intended consumer or viewer of the advertisement. The viewer of the advertisement is above this person, the image implies, and may in fact need the chainsaw.

A good transition to some important cultural issues.

You may need more here. What do you mean by "above"? Are you saying the viewer looks down on the man in image? If so, why?

Some of the cultural assumptions on display in the advertisement are even more troubling even if they are not made on purpose by the advertising agency. While the image is "typical," what is typical may be reductive, racist, or gender biased. First, a male is portrayed in this advertisement. There *is* a connection between the consumer in the image and the possible consumer in real life. Pictured here is a happy man in a plaid shirt. This might correspond to the type of man this advertisement is marketing to. In this way, the advertisement makes assumptions about gender roles, about who does outdoor work with saws, and about the toughness of a consumer of chainsaws. This also may imply, however, something about the portrayal of culture again. With no woman in the picture we are shown an image of Arab society that is male. If there is a woman (if this were real life) she must be in the tent. Second, the

Interesting and nice detail.

A bit off-handed here. Are you reading too much into this or, conversely, do you need a bit more development of this idea?

image of the man uses another easily recognized sign or symbol and that is the prayer rug and the posture of the man. If we see the carpet in front of the tent as a small rug that a man would kneel on and the man in the position of prayer (even the shadow points to the fact that the man may be facing directly East in the direction toward which prayers are given) we have to wonder about what kind of statement the advertisement makes in relation to culture. This may be belittling of the religious practices of an individual or it may be insulting in that the man is now in a position of praising the chainsaw, or maybe the chainsaw takes his attention away from prayer. While this advertisement is obviously not trying to spread any kind of racism or hatred, in making a simple joke it calls upon many small assumptions a dominant Western male audience may make about a culture that is exotic, different, and less powerful.

Yes, good point.

Advertisements must market to a careful focused audience and must make references in their advertisements that that audience will understand. This advertisement attracts attention with something humorous and strange for the viewer but using signs that are quite familiar. You could say that the advertisement reflects the assumptions about race, gender, and culture that a particular consumer might have. At the same time, in the creation of a humorous image, the advertisement also perpetuates reductive notions of another culture and makes elements of the portrayed culture part of the humorous appeal of the piece. Even very simple advertisement can, through the communication system of words and images, perpetuate typical power relationships.

Examiner comments

This is a very thorough response that clearly responds to the demands of the question. Though the introduction does not make specific reference to any of the terms in the question, it is clear that the main point is relevant and thoughtful. It is important to keep in mind that in this task, as well as in paper 2 of the exam, you should come to a clear and succinct "answer" to the question.

The following analysis is interesting and insightful. The candidate manages to give a thorough and at times surprising view of a very "short" text. One clear strength of this piece is that the argument, while it may be unexpected at first, is convincing. At the same time, a drawback might be that upon consideration, the essay at times makes assumptions about audience and

intentions that aren't clearly supported or may be argued against. At times the writer of this piece just assumes that we, the readers, will take the analysis for granted. How do we know the assumed audience? How do we know that the viewer of the advertisement will feel "above" the person depicted in the image? Though these ideas could be supported, there needs to be more here.

It must be said, however, that overall, and considering the word limit on the assignment, the candidate has managed to show great skill at "deconstructing" the advertisement as well as the possible significance of an intended viewer's reaction to it.

Further oral activities

The further oral activity, as explained in more depth in chapter 5, is an internally assessed assignment that is completed for both part 1 (Language in cultural context) and part 2 (Language and mass communication) of the course. The marks for both of these assessments will be recorded by your teacher and one set of marks will be chosen as the final assessment as part of your overall grade for the course. The further oral activity also allows you the freedom to pursue your own interests and also gives you a chance to produce a complex mass media product in a group. As long as every member of your group contributes and that your portion of the contribution to the project can be judged by your teacher, completing a further oral activity with other members of your class can lead to projects that create a great springboard for class discussion.

In this section of the course, as you know from chapter 6, you will be paying attention to the medium and to issues related to the broadcast of information and entertainment to a large audience. The further oral activity in this section can be used to create newspapers, websites, multimedia or multimodal advertising campaigns, radio broadcasts, blogs, or vodcasts. The research and production put into this activity should pay off in that production will focus your attention on aspects that make medium and mass communication important and problematic. Since the assessment itself is actually an interactive oral presentation, you and your group, if you produce a newspaper for example, could present the product to the class, discuss the most important issues in relation to your production and the concerns of the course, and open up a discussion of concerns raised in relation to audience, bias, or intercultural relationships. Care should be taken in any project that the work somehow relates to texts or works studied in your course and that the discussion take a more formal, analytical approach (as academic criticism) rather than just raising issues around the group dynamics or the difficulties in production (although, these aspects could be briefly introduced).

Possible approaches to the oral

Here are some possible ideas, many of which can be done individually or conceived as a project for a group.

- Choose a product and design an entire advertising campaign that includes print and online advertisements and a television commercial. Present this campaign to the class or, better yet, survey class members' reactions to the campaign and use these results to start a discussion.

- Convert a traditional advertising campaign for an existing product into a viral form of advertising (you may create, for example, a YouTube video). In your presentation to the class, focus on reactions to the piece or to the challenges involved in this type of advertising.

- Collect public health information about the H1N1 virus or any communicable disease and consider the effectiveness of the methods of communication and education. Present your findings to the class, using case studies of communities affected. You could present some examples of effective and ineffective management of the spread of the disease, and policies that ensure access to treatment for those most at risk.

- Show videos of two different news presentations to the class and lead a structured discussion of the differing content, styles, and biases of the two programs, and the audience or target market for the two different reports. Write and deliver your own political speech. Open the floor for discussion and questions after your speech. Analyze both the formal presentation issues and the way you structured your ideas to persuade and convince your audience. Do an opinion poll of the class to see how they would rate your success at an election or legislative debate to pass a bill. Give an oral commentary or critique on a political debate. Analyze the general approach to issues, and opinions as they are presented through the media by the leading spokespeople and interest groups. Start out by researching the social and political context for the debate. Who serves most to benefit (or lose) if legislation is passed and acted upon, or further action is prevented? Discuss the difference between the presentation, purpose and effect of different types of popular music such as rap, hip hop, rock, or alternative. How diverse are the different practitioners within a chosen sub-group, based on region or nationality, ethnicity, race, gender etc. What sociopolitical agendas are reflected in the music? Who is the audience for this music, and how is it distributed?

- Create a blog site that serves as a response to the main student newspaper (print or online) at your school. Presentation to the class might include your "rationale," some of the challenges for production, and a discussion of the differences between the media and their intentions. Role-play a meeting between a cigarette manufacturer and an advertising agency. What are the sensitivities and the obligations of both the client and the agency. What provisional ideas or guidelines are discussed? What legal obligations are there for advertising or nicotine products in your country?

Always keep in mind that the presentation itself is judged not only for knowledge issues and critical relevance but also for logic of presentation, clarity and appropriate use of language. The oral presentation is meant "to engage with the process of intercultural understanding," so some consideration should be given to texts created outside of your own culture or texts that may themselves address wider cultural issues.

You will also be asked to produce a reflective statement on your oral activity. The statement will indicate your goals in the presentation, discuss your performance, and indicate the progress you have made in meeting the aims of the project or the relevant section of the course.

Exam paper 1

What is it?

You may remember from chapter 5 that paper 1 of the exam takes the form of textual analysis. At the higher level you will be expected to choose one of two pairs of texts and write a coherent commentary about the similarities and differences between the texts in relation to genre, text type, audience, content, theme or idea, formal and stylistic features. At standard level you will write a close analysis on only one passage, paying attention to the same details. In the activity below, if you are a standard level candidate, you may simply look at the passages individually rather than as pairs. Of course, comparing passages is good practice because looking at a second passage can often help to differentiate or call to attention the important aspects of the first passage. At the higher level the two passages may consist of one nonliterary text and one literary text or two nonliterary texts. At standard level, the two choices of individual passages will always be nonliterary (a newspaper article, an editorial, a blog, a passage from a historical text, etc.).

What kind of analysis is required?

Since exam paper 1 takes passages from nonliterary texts you will often find that the text type is one that has been considered during your study of language and mass communication. Remember that issues such as author/producer, intention, bias, attributes of the intended audience, and the effect of medium are all worth commenting on in your analysis. There is, of course, no sense in reading a book and waiting to hear what the teacher has to say about it or looking on the Internet in order to find the "right" meaning of a particular exchange or scene. Getting into the habit of textual analysis gives you the chance to demonstrate how you read, think, and respond on your own, and will in turn give you the confidence to be flexible in your approach once you become more familiar with the models and are able to refine your identification of the issues particular to each type of text.

Practicing on your own

It is very important to go through the process of writing a comparative textual analysis before actually doing one in an exam situation. You will be practicing this type of timed writing in school but you can certainly practice on your own at home or with the help of this book. Admittedly, writing in a timed exam situation is somewhat artificial but if you think about it, a timed exam, a situation where you must perform a skill under pressure, is not terribly unlike a sports contest, a test at a job interview, or even a pressure situation you might find in any life experience. The key to success is getting used to the expectations and getting used to your own areas of strength and weakness in relation to the task.

Students often wonder how much time to spend thinking and planning before writing. The best advice is to try to judge your own needs and to listen to the advice of your teacher who has become familiar with your work. In general, however, you should know that you can't simply read a couple of passages and start writing. Reading through four passages in order to make your choice about the pair you will discuss will take more than five minutes. You should always re-read the passages you will discuss before starting to write—another few minutes. You should then spend time jotting notes, thinking, marking, and prioritizing your observations and ideas—yet another few minutes. At this point, you can create a rough outline. You should set aside 15 to 20 minutes out of a two-hour exam to read, think, and plan.

Student sample

Text 1

Historic Goal gives South Africa the moment of national exultation it had craved. It would not be enough for an outright win, but Bafana Bafana can still feel triumph

Johannesburg, Saturday June 12, 2010

It was a glorious moment, for the team, for this country, and even if that's as good as it gets, the sound and the sense will live on in memory.

The perfect, angled pass from Teko Modise that set Siphiwe Tshabalala free, a half step clear of the lone Mexican defender. The shot, flawless, struck in full stride, cross goal from his left foot into the top right corner, unstoppable by any keeper. And then the roar: The *vuvuzelas* suddenly hitting a new amplitude, and high above that drone, in Soccer City and you knew everywhere in this country, a great collective exultation, the sound of joy.

Not enough, it turned out, for a historic victory, but at least enough for a historic 1–1 draw in the opening match of the first World Cup game ever played on the African continent.

South Africa will take it. They will absolutely take it. Bafana Bafana had seemed intimidated at the start on Friday afternoon, overwhelmed by the scene and their starring role in it, and who could blame them a bit? All of those years knowing as the host, they would be automatic participants, and standard-bearers, and symbols—and of knowing all of that would seem pretty much beside the point if they couldn't get a result. Home teams in World Cups are supposed to overachieve, but the consensus was there had never been one as weak as this.

Next the draw—a tough one—and the rigorous training under Carlos Alberto Parreira, and the surprisingly strong series of performances leading up to the tournament, which sent expectation meters here crazily into the red. Anyone who went on local television over the past few days and suggested South Africa would do anything less that win a quarter-final seemed like a piker—wild talk considering their real place in the football food chain.

The crowd in the stadium and on the streets, the speeches from FIFA boss Sepp Blatter and South Africa's president Jacob Zuma, the nod to the absent Nelson Mandela, the anthem, all heavy, heavy stuff. Not to mention that standing at the other end of the pitch was a very good side from Mexico, with its own pressures, its own expectations, but in this context mere supporting players.

For the first 40 minutes it was a mismatch. Mexico probed patiently, controlled the pace, seemed to be setting up an inevitable first goal, while the South Africans couldn't make the simplest of passes and mostly sat back in their own half of the field, as though they knew what was coming and were terrified of the consequences.

But then, in the final 10 minutes or so of the half, there was a subtle shift. The Mexico goal didn't come, and meanwhile, after conceding a couple of corners, they seemed a bit vulnerable when forced to defend. The 0–0 result at the half was flattering to South Africa, but also represented an opportunity found, and they took it, with Tshabalala's historic score in the 55th minute against a Mexican side whose initial confidence /overconfidence had turned to lethargy. …

Source: Brunt, Stephen. "Historic Goal gives South Africa the moment of national exultation it had craved. It would not be enough for an outright win, but Bafana Bafana can still feel triumph." *The Glove and Mail*. Toronto. June 12, 2010.

Text 2

The football World Cup may give South Africa's economy an astonishing extra 0.5% of growth, according to a recent report by Grant Thornton, a firm of accountants. That is quite a chunk of the country's forecast 3% rate for the year. Some 373,000 foreigners are now expected during the tournament, which kicks off on June 11th. On average they will stay for 18 days, go to five matches and spend 30,200 rand (nearly $4,000) each. Compelling figures for statistic-mad football fans. But South Africa's government is also taking them seriously because the same firm wrote a similar report on the cup's impact on South Africa just before the world financial crash two years ago.

There were fears that the recession might shrink the economic benefits of the tournament to South Africa. In fact, if Grant Thornton is right, the country has little to worry about. In 2007, the firm expected 483,000 foreign visitors, so that number is sharply down. Moreover, only about 11,300 ticket-holders are from African countries outside South Africa, surely a disappointment to the organisers. But each visitor is now expected to make more of his (or less often her) trip, staying a bit longer and shelling out a third more cash.

So the total effect on South Africa's economy should be roughly the same, with about 93 billion rand ($12.4 billion) injected, most of that having been generated before this year. Tourism should account for 16% of the final total. Much of the rest will come from the central government's spending on infrastructure.

Very nice for South Africa, perhaps. But South Africans themselves are grumbling about the eye-wateringly large amounts of money that FIFA, the world football body that is the monopoly organiser, is poised to make, even though South Africa is bearing most of the cost. FIFA is responsible only for the prize money paid to the teams along with the cost of their travel and preparation, which amounted to just $279m in Germany, where the tournament last took place, in 2006. This week FIFA said it would contribute an extra $100m to the South Africans to ensure that all the facilities are ready in time.

Yet the event's main direct benefits, from television and marketing rights, all go to FIFA. According to Citi, the research arm of Citibank, FIFA's profit in Germany came to $1.8 billion, equivalent to 0.7% of South Africa's GDP. FIFA will recycle much of that money into football development worldwide. Nonetheless, even a bit of it would help clear up some of the country's festering shanty towns.

Source: Editorial. "South Africa's World Cup: Who Profits most?" *The Economist.* May 13, 2010.

SECTION 2 • Language

Sample student notes

After reading the above passages twice and spending some time taking notes, consider the following notes taken by a student.

First text: a sports article (it says and it is obvious). focus on the game itself. vivid description of the goal ("perfect angled pass" "struck in full stride"). Seems to focus more on the goal itself from South Africa even though it goes on to discuss the game as a whole. An opinion piece as well as factual, an analysis of the game, what lead up to it and why it is important. The text is about glory and celebration (at the beginning and at the end). Though the text doesn't say it directly, it implies that the goal, and maybe the whole World Cup, is important for South Africa because of its history or the challenges in the country. I also noticed that the writer gives his opinion and suggests his hopes partly through the use of rhetorical devices that could come from a rousing speech. The last sentence sounds like a three part battle cry.

Second text This article is more of an economics article than a sports article though it also focuses on the World Cup. The article is a factual piece with many results from statistical predictions about the economic impact of hosting the tournament. The article also brings up important questions as an opinion piece or editorial would. While the first article hinted at benefits for South Africa and why the country might need some sort of boost, the second article directly states that South Africa could use some support or money for its "festering shanty towns." The piece brings up another important cultural issue wondering who really serves to benefit the most from the tournament, the South Africans or the FIFA organization. This piece makes you wonder about the first article, is it promoting South Africa? Football? The World Cup as a big money making enterprise? If South Africa were to perform well it would mean not only more pride but more money (maybe I can use this in my conclusion …)

More comparison Both articles seem to be written for a wide audience. You do not have to be an economist to read the second article even though that is the name of the magazine. Also I noticed that the first article starts on the front page of the newspaper. The game is big news and not just something that you would find on the sports page. The pieces do have different purposes though—the first one boosts and celebrates and the second one is more critical and removed from passion. The tone and register of the two pieces are different and match their purposes (I need to find words that support this. … in first piece the last sentence, the first sentence, "exultation," "joy," and informal register such as the use of "heavy, heavy stuff" to describe the ceremonial aspect of the game. The second piece is analytic and balanced in tone and formal in register especially through the use of references and statistics but even this piece shows some informality (and marks it as partly opinion or written not just as information) by saying for example "Very nice for South Africa, perhaps" or "grumbling about eye-wateringly large amounts of money."

215

I could maybe say something about culture as well. The first piece is from Canada and the second is from the U.K. but I know that it is sold all over the world (but is written in English). Both articles are writing about another culture and the possible harms and benefits the World Cup might have for a developing nation. Maybe the people in South Africa just want to enjoy the games and support their team (and make money?) but don't want to think for now about other problems. Maybe I'm reading too much into it but at least I can say that we don't get a South African perspective in either piece.

Compare your notes with the example quoted here. The notes above do show considerable reflection on the possible significance and intentions of the texts as well as some of the stylistic features and how they might indicate something about meaning or intention. Your notes may look a little different or be more scattered. Some of the conclusions you make may not be directly stated in sentence form but may be written quickly to remind yourself of the points you want to make. The notes above are very good, although the student probably needs to use even more specific examples from the texts (she has possibly underlining them in the texts). The next step would be to organize these notes, to think of a way to start the essay and a logical order for discussion.

This particular student organized her analysis this way:

Intro

What each piece is about. The main similarity and difference (the tournament, sports glory, economics)

The main focus to start is the way both pieces assume a consideration of the importance of the game or the whole tournament to South Africa as a whole.

Pragraph two

focus of each piece.

The implications of the focus of each.

Paragraph three

The register and style of each piece.

Bias, information, opinion.

Paragraph four

The social concerns and implications of the pieces including the lack of South African perspective.

The ways in which both articles show the larger concerns surrounding the tournament.

Paragraph five

Overall intention and effect on reader. (First one inspires, second one causes reader to question or criticize).

Final paragraph/conclusion—wrap things up, maybe make some extension.

Note: the student here created an outline but she did not follow a traditional outline style. She already had extensive notes and she felt that this basic outline would be sufficient to include all of the observations she had made. Also, notice that the student does not seem worried about a particular formula for the structure beyond the basic idea of having an introduction, a body, and a conclusion. She does not write (here at least) a three-part thesis statement, nor does she plan a "five paragraph" essay with each paragraph matching one of her points. The structure this student has chosen balances discussion between the two pieces in each paragraph while remaining true to the notes she has taken. The structure of your writing largely depends on the texts you are analyzing and the points that you want to make (you may have one important main point, three equally important points, or a couple of main ideas with sub-points).

At this point you should sit down and write a full comparative analysis of the texts. If you are a standard level candidate, write a detailed analysis of one text.

The marking criteria

Now that you have written a comparative textual analysis, try to see where you fall in a spectrum from weak to very strong performance. You will have access to assessment criteria when you study this course in your school, but for now, it is best to consider the range from poor to excellent (1 to 5). Looking at some of the criteria, even if you don't have a sense of the standards, will force you to think objectively about your own performance or at least to understand the goals of your practice.

Criterion A Understanding and comparison of the texts

1 Little understanding of the context and purpose of the texts and their similarities or differences. Summary predominates; and observations are rarely supported by references to the texts.

5 Excellent understanding of the texts, their context and purpose and the similarities and differences between them, comments are fully supported by well-chosen references to the texts.

Criterion B Understanding of the use and effects of stylistic features including the features of visual texts.

1 Little awareness of the use of stylistic features and little or no illustration of their effects on the reader.

5 Excellent awareness of the use of stylistic features, with very good understanding of their effects on the reader.

Criterion C Organization and development

1 Little organization is apparent with no sense of balance and very little development; considerable emphasis is placed on one text to the detriment of the other.

5 The comparative analysis is well balanced and effectively organized with a coherent and effective structure and development.

Criterion D Language

1 Rarely clear and appropriate language with many errors in grammar, vocabulary and sentence construction and little sense of register and style.

5 Very clear, effective, carefully chosen and precise language with a high degree of accuracy in grammar, vocabulary and sentence construction; register and style are effective and appropriate to the task.

After looking at the assessments in this chapter through a focus on the language in mass communication course component, remember not to forget the other aspects of language you have studied and to carry over your skills in media analysis to assessments in other sections of the course.

Activity

Practice with any texts

Practice the skills of paper 1 by considering closely short passages from almost anything you read. If you read, for example, an article in a popular magazine, try isolating the first page and considering issues such as the following: What is the genre or text type? Who is the intended audience? What literary, technical, or stylistic features do you notice and, most importantly, how do these affect meaning? You can then "compare" this passage to almost anything that you read next. Even if the piece is not similar in theme or content, it is a worthwhile exercise to consider the vast differences possible between texts.

Activity

Comparative analysis

Text 1

Hey mom,

I finished all the plums last night.
Sorry... I know you wanted to add
them to the fruit salad for the
picnic today but I was starving
and there was nothing else to eat!

Could you also pick me up some
face wash and Coke when you're
at the store?!

Love ya!

Text 2

This is Just to Say

I have eaten
the plums
that were in
the icebox

and which
you were probably
saving
for breakfast

Forgive me
they were delicious
so sweet
and so cold

William Carlos Williams, 1934

Questions to the text

1 What aspects are common between the two "notes?" What is the subject matter of the extract in each case?

2 What are the differences between the two texts?

3 Are the differences related to intention?

4 How do the two texts convey pragmatic intention? How do they convey purpose beyond this?

5 If the content of the "notes" can be said to be the same (or quite similar), what do you think distinguishes the poem by William Carlos Williams from the more prosaic version?

In this chapter, we will begin to look at literature as a particular form of intentional use of language. Literature is clearly not going to be an entirely new subject for you but the focus in this course may be different. The emphasis here is on defining the terms with which we address literature in relation to other communicative acts. Quite clearly, literature shares common concerns with other texts, while also maintaining the distinction of being a unique kind of discourse deserving specialized treatment. It is likely that your answers to the questions above in support of a comparative textual analysis went some way to shed light on this distinction.

In this section, you will be asked to treat literature as both a formal type of communicative act (a unique "literary" discourse) and as part of a larger social discourse and cultural context. The literature component of the language and literature course is not developed as a specific body of content to be mastered as a set of styles and techniques appropriate to the specific genres; rather, it is about developing a set of skills and sensitivities with which to approach any literary text you may encounter in this course and beyond.

Literature is generally understood to be writing that connects content with form: that is, literature is an expression of an idea, attitude or interest that draws attention to itself. The *way* of expressing this idea, attitude or interest can be as important as the idea, attitude or interest itself. Much of the literature we encounter is further defined as fiction. This term comes from the Latin *fictio*, meaning "counterfeiting," and although most literature we read is not entirely factual, we might expect to recognize some degree of verisimilitude in terms of setting, events or characters. Still, it is equally clear that most literature we read is at least partially imagined or artificial and that it is also intentionally so. Regardless of the degree of the use of fact or fiction, literature does not seek to chronicle real life; rather, it is asking us to pay attention to what is *worthy* of being remembered or conceived of in the act of constructing a mirror world. Ultimately, literature does not seek to communicate information as much as it seeks to communicate human experience as something we might willingly participate in.

One of the challenges for students of literature is how to treat these human experiences. A common mistake is to treat characters and texts as real life. Students often want to make statements about the merits of character or comment qualitatively about actions performed within literary works to the detriment of their literary understanding. Again, the key is to remember that literary works are generally symbolic, with a larger purpose or significance beyond the portrayal of reality.

Determining a larger purpose or significance is both the challenge and the pleasure of engaging literature. In the classroom, there are always funny moments where our students believe we are lying about accepted interpretations of literary works. They ask whether it is really possible that an author has had the wherewithal to actually have anticipated and controlled such possibilities and connections. Although this scenario is actually quite a complex consideration of intention and the role of reading and writing, at a basic level it does get at the core of what distinguishes critical readers: pattern recognition. For students, it is a matter of learning and becoming more familiar with these patterns rather than adopting any magic trick or technique. And, of course, students always bring with them unique perspectives and connections to the texts that can enhance appreciation or awareness of such patterns.

Activity

Pattern recognition

You are actually already very accomplished in recognizing patterns in language used for particular effect. Sometimes this works unconsciously. Look at the following text and pay attention to the patterns and expectations required to propel the narrative.

Person 1 Knock knock.

Person 2 Who's there?

Person 1 Banana.

Person 2 Banana who?

Person 1 Knock knock.

Person 2 Who's there?

Person 1 Banana.

Person 2 Banana who?

Person 1 Knock knock.

Person 2 Who's there?

Person 1 Orange.

Person 2 Orange who?

Person 1 Orange you glad I didn't say "banana?"

With a partner, think about and list the patterns you recognize, and how they are important to our comprehension of the text.

Questions to the text

1 How do you know that this will be funny?

2 How does the humor ultimately work?

3 What devices or strategies does this text employ to convey humor?

4 What expectations does the text meet or subvert to be effective?

Approaching texts

You may be thinking that the example in the preceding activity is all fine and good and that it is easy with a "knock knock" joke, but how does this apply to more complex texts? Clearly, practice and familiarity with a broad range of texts is necessary. Careful, close reading is also essential. Close reading is far more laborious than a passive recognition of words on a page. With close reading, the simple story—what happens—is taken for granted but the emphasis is instead placed on how such a story is conveyed, and for what purpose. Some people may refer to this as "reading between the lines," which is probably a perfectly apt description. But this might suggest, again, that magic trick of pulling something from nothing. We prefer to think about it as just plain hard work, and the cumulative experience of exposing yourself to as broad a range of texts as possible by subjecting them to close analysis.

Again, as the activity above suggests, you already have the basic skills—you know when you are expected to be scared during a horror film, or encouraged to connect having a brighter life with the right brand of toothpaste. The difference here is simply a conscious awareness of what you are doing and the level of difficulty or subtlety of texts. The best part of the challenge, and also the central caveat, is that this work with the text should not be formulaic. What patterns we see and appreciate or respond to may be different depending on our experiences and background (including our class background, race, gender, ethnicity etc.). As with anything that attempts to cover human experience, the possibilities and opportunities are as varied as they are significant.

A quick Internet search will reveal thousands of lists of suggestions, to say nothing of the number of books committed to the topic of approaching literature. This course companion does not seek to be exhaustive by covering all literary devices, but only to provide a general overview to be used in concert with your own work in the classroom. Having said that, many students do look for methodologies or processes for going about reading literary works. Although we would encourage you to be skeptical of such easy, formulaic approaches to literature, as with all texts, they can be quite useful. For less-experienced readers of literature, the following points may help with an initial approach to a text:

- What seems to be the literal topic of the work? What is its plot? Does the title affirm or problematize this? Who are the primary characters in the text? Are there, conceivably, nonhuman characters, like an animal or a house?

- What is the setting? Where and when does it take place and why might this be significant? Alternatively, why is the setting deliberately schematized, or made generic to be anywhere or everywhere (or even nowhere in particular)? How is the passage of time treated in the text?

- What is the point of view? Who speaks? Are they reliable? Does this change throughout the work? What makes us question the identity of the subject?

- What seems to be the apparent and obvious structure? If it is a poem, are stanzas of a consistent length? If prose, are paragraphs and/or sentences long? Are they short? How much consists of dialogue, either direct or in the form of reported speech? Are there long internal monologues, or lengthy descriptions? How do these relate to the reporting of actions or events?

- What impact or effect does the diction have? Are words highly formal or more colloquial? Is there diction that seems out of place or that attracts your attention? Are there particular effects as a result of the diction such as particular sound patterns, repetitions, or qualities?

- Are there strong images or key symbols that appear repeatedly in the work? Is the use of metaphor, such as associations with color, or weather, indicative of the mood? Do symbols play a pivotal role?

- What seems to be the overall attitude or feeling expressed? Is the tone light and happy or dark and depressed (or otherwise expressed)? Is the approach positive, critical, humorous or difficult to determine? Why might a feeling of unease or uncertainty be deliberate?

- Is there a theme or central purpose that makes itself known? What, beyond the essentials of plot, is the essential object of the account? How does this relate to the subject (the main character or point of view?)

With close reading and practice, your approach to the text will become increasingly more sophisticated and more natural. As you work toward this, it is worth considering some specific concerns based on the most common literary genres.

Fictional prose

Narrative

Narrative, or telling stories, is part of our universal human nature. Even before the advent of writing and other methods of recording, stories were passed from generation to generation for purposes of entertainment, education and art. But telling stories is even more central to our being than this: on a daily basis, we enjoy recounting and hearing about experiences and actions. Retelling what happened, how we felt and who said what make up the bulk of our interactions with people, and published accounts. Even more, we engage in the process of telling stories as a means of imagining or rehearsing possibilities. It is not surprising to know that theorists, like Frederic Jameson, consider narrative "the central function or instance of the human mind."

Although narrative is a universal function of humans, it should not be confused with every language act. It is possible, for instance, to simply describe a phenomenon such as "It is very hot today." This is not a narrative. Instead, at the very least narratives describe or represent a series of events or potential events. John le Carre, a British writer of espionage thrillers, once said that to write "the cat sat on the mat" is not a story. But to write "the cat sat on the dog's mat" presents an event, even if a small one, from which a true story may emerge. Following are further explanations of the main elements of a narrative.

Plot

All stories have plot; that is, something happens or becomes an "event," as described above. Beyond this simple understanding plot can be a very tricky term for many literary theorists and is often defined in relation to time and an arrangement of events within a larger story. This element of a narrative is meant to refer to the chronological time in which events in a story take place, and the order in which they occur.

This is not as simple as it may at first seem. In an essay, there is no passing of time. Even if the writer *refers* to an event that happened over time, an essay is meant to convey an idea in the moment and not a series of events unfolding over time. But a story asks readers to imagine events happening over time and this becomes plot. Even if it takes you the same amount of time to read the essay and the story, the intended "internal" time that is meant to have passed is "zero" with the essay and can be quite a long time—over many generations in some narratives—with a story. We understand that the time elapsing in a narrative can be either much shorter or much longer than the time it takes to hear or read a story.

Time is not always experienced as a linear chronology of events. Plots can begin in the middle of an event and move backwards and forwards across time. They can begin at the end and be filled in with flashbacks. Or they can operate as a more linear chronology starting with a clear beginning and moving through a middle on the way toward an end. Although plot may seem like a straightforward element, it is quite a remarkable achievement that we are able to hear or read narratives with widely varying plots and reconstruct them meaningfully. For this reason, some prefer to associate plot also with causality: it is not just that one event happens before or after another but that there is a recognizable causal link between events.

Freytag's pyramid

Gustav Freytag was a 19th-century German novelist who recognized patterns in the plots of stories and developed a diagram in the form of a pyramid to help analyze them. Although the patterns in many stories can occur in different orders, many find looking for the following points in a narrative helpful.

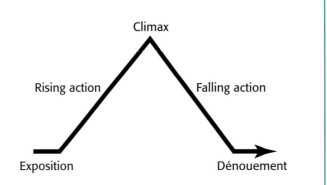

Exposition	Setting the scene. The writer introduces the characters and setting, providing description and background.
Rising action	Something happens (an event) to signal a conflict and the story builds and gets more exciting.
Climax	The moment of greatest tension in a story. This is often the most exciting event. It is the event that the rising action builds up to and that the falling action follows.
Falling action	Events happen as a result of the climax and leading to the resolution where the main problem or conflict is resolved.
Dénouement	The ending. All questions are solved or explained and we can contemplate futures for the characters. A theme may become apparent.

Point of view

All narratives have narrators; that is a person or persons who tells the story. When narrating the events of our day to one another, the narrator is easy to spot: they are the one telling the story. But literary narrative can be told from different points of view including combinations of points of view. Although there are several possibilities with point of view, for our purposes it is about determining who tells a story or the vantage point from which a story is told.

Usually, you will encounter literary narratives told from either a first-person or a third-person point of view. First-person point of view is when a story is told by a character within that story through the use of "I." In these cases, a writer chooses to adopt the persona of a character which can include limitations to understanding and **unreliable narration**. It would be wrong, however, to assume all stories told from first-person point of view are unreliable. Sometimes a writer includes multiple first-person points of view to give accounts of the same event from several perspectives.

Third-person point of view is also referred to as omniscient. In this case, although the literal meaning ("all-knowing") is an exaggeration, stories are told without the limitations of any one character and includes comment, thoughts, feelings and emotions that may exist outside of characters. Like other elements, point of view can be a complex consideration. Stories can also be comprised of a mix of first- and third-person narrative. Points of view can range from those of minor to major characters, and can seem to be all-knowing and objective to convey a summary viewpoint through more indirect or partial participation of a broad range of individual characters. Points of view can, of course, be more or less reliable and include a stream of consciousness. Being aware of such complexity can only aid in our understanding of a narrative.

> An **unreliable narrator** is a narrator who may be in error in their understanding or judgment of events and circumstance. An unreliable narrator can reveal more ambiguous authorial intentions than a straight account of the truth.

Character
The events that make up a narrative are not meaningful as narrative until a person, real or imagined, is involved. "Person" here can be taken to mean not just a flesh-and-blood individual but rather human characteristics or personalities that are familiar to us. "The cat sat on the dog's mat" conveys an emotional, and possibly physical, exchange that we can imagine occurring between people.

A character in a literary narrative may not be human at all: animals, the elements, unlikeable antiheros and other assorted creatures and creations may inhabit a story, but the character they convey tends to align itself with human attributes that provide motivation, growth and change from a decidedly human perspective. Characters can also be either static or flat (they do not change over the course of a narrative), dynamic or round (they do change over the course of a narrative). As with point of view, the thoughts and actions of even the most minor characters can make up important elements of a narrative.

Finally, a character can often be referred to as an archetype. An archetype is a model from which copies are made. In literature, this is often a character or an idea that represents the most essential characteristics or type in the form of a person or concept.

Theme
The theme of a narrative is the central or dominant idea that a work reveals. It can be helpful to think of this as the purpose of a narrative but it is generally understood that literary narratives contain themes (even if the theme is to avoid conveying a theme!). Locating the theme of a narrative may or may not be easy to do and can be represented through subtle relationships within narratives as much as straight-forward messages. Themes may also be determined to be constructed unintentionally within a narrative rather than as a purposeful construction of the author.

The novel

Henry James once referred to 19th-century Russian novels (particularly Dostoyevsky) as "loose baggy monsters." James' reference was intended to be disparaging and conveyed his feeling that these novels lacked a unity of purpose or meaning around which the many events floated by. Regardless of your position with regard to Dostoyevsky and the other major 19th century Russian novels, we think James' term is not a bad way of thinking about the novel more generally (and more positively).

The novel is defined in its most broad sense as any extended prose narrative. The key point here is that it is extended. Although a novel could be anywhere in length from a "mere" one hundred pages to several volumes of several hundreds of pages each, the novel offers the scope to see characters encounter multiple events and grow, change and adapt (even if they may be considered static by the novel's end). A lot can happen in a novel and the challenges presented to a reader are several:

- **Perseverance** You may be asked to read longer books that you've encountered previously. Fortunately, many novels make for entertaining narratives and after pushing through the first pages you will find you are "hooked" on the story.

- **Maintaining a map** It is unlikely you will be able to pick up a novel and read through in one sitting. More commonly, you will be searching for the opportunity to get through another chapter before sleeping or between classes. You will need to keep track of sometimes complex events and relationships in both time and space within the novel even as you pick up the novel to read in interrupted moments. Some novels include complicated family trees of histories or a timeline of events to aid in this endeavor.

- **Developing connections** You will need to be making connections across different events and developments to help understand what may be multiple themes arising in a novel, and their impact on the central characters that you might come to care about, and live through as a witness.

Fortunately, all this work with novels is worth it. Their very looseness, bagginess and monstrousness is part of their appeal. Novels are entertaining and stimulating; although the challenges can be great, the rewards are even greater.

Activity

The opening of a novel

Read the openings to the following novels and answer the questions below.

Text 1
Great Expectations by Charles Dickens.

> My father's family name being Pirrip, and my christian name Philip, my infant tongue could make of both names nothing longer or more explicit than Pip. So I called myself Pip, and came to be called Pip.

> I gave Pirrip as my father's family name, on the authority of his tombstone and my sister—Mrs. Joe Gargery, who married the blacksmith. As I never saw my father or my mother, and never saw any likeness of either of them (for their days were long before the days of photographs), my first fancies regarding what they were like, were unreasonably derived from their tombstones. The shape of the letters on

my father's, gave me an odd idea that he was a square, stout, dark man, with curly black hair. From the character and turn of the inscription, *"Also Georgiana Wife of the Above,"* I drew a childish conclusion that my mother was freckled and sickly. To five little stone lozenges, each about a foot and a half long, which were arranged in a neat row beside their grave, and were sacred to the memory of five little brothers of mine—who gave up trying to get a living exceedingly early in that universal struggle—I am indebted for a belief I religiously entertained that they had all been born on their backs with their hands in the trousers-pockets, and had never taken them out in this state of existence.

Ours was the marsh country, down by the river, within, as the river wound, twenty miles from the sea. My first most vivid and broad impression of the identity of things, seems to me to have been gained on a memorable raw afternoon towards evening. At such a time I found out for certain, that this bleak place overgrown with nettles was the churchyard; and that Philip Pirrip, late of this parish, and also Georgiana wife of the above, were dead and buried; and that Alexander, Bartholomew, Abraham, Tobias, and Roger, infant children of the aforesaid, were also dead and buried; and that the dark flat wilderness beyond the churchyard, intersected with dykes and mounds and gates, with scattered cattle feeding on it, was the marshes; and that the low leaden line beyond was the river; and that the distant savage lair from which the wind was rushing, was the sea; and that the small bundle of shivers growing afraid of it all and beginning to cry, was Pip.

"Hold your noise!" cried a terrible voice, as a man started up from among the graves at the side of the church porch. "Keep still, you little devil, or I'll cut your throat!"

Source: Dickens, Charles. 1861. *Great Expectations*. New York: Alfred E. Knopf, 1992. pp.1–2.

Text 2

The End of the Affair by Graham Greene.

A story has no beginning or end: arbitrarily one chooses that moment of experience from which to look back or from which to look ahead. I say "one chooses" with the inaccurate pride of a professional writer who—when he has been seriously noted at all—has been praised for his technical ability, but do I in fact of my own will choose that black wet January night on the Common, in 1946, the sight of Henry Miles slanting across the wide river of rain, or did these images choose me? It is convenient, it is correct according to the rules of my craft to begging just

there, but if I had believed then in a God, I could also have believed in a hand, plucking at my elbow, a suggestion, "Speak to him: he hasn't seen you yet."

For why should I have spoken to him? If hate is not too large a term to use in relation to any human being, I hated Henry—I hated his wife Sarah too. And he, I suppose, came soon after the events of that evening to hate me: as he surely at times must have hated his wife and that other, in whom in those days we were lucky enough not to believe. So this is a record of hate far more than of love, and if I come to say anything in favour of Henry and Sarah I can be trusted: I am writing against the bias because it is my professional pride to prefer the near-truth, even to the expression of my near-hate.

It was strange to see Henry out on such a night: he liked his comfort and after all—or so I thought—he had Sarah. To me comfort is like the wrong memory at the wrong place or time: if one is lonely one prefers discomfort. There was too much comfort even in the bed sitting-room I had at the wrong—the south—side of the Common, in the relics of other people's furniture. I thought I would go for a walk through the rain and have a drink at the local. The little crowded hall was full of strangers' hats and coats and I took somebody else's umbrella by accident—the man on the second floor had friends in. Then I closed the stained-glass door behind me and made my way carefully down the steps that had been blasted in 1944 and never repaired. I had reason to remember the occasion and how the stained glass, tough and ugly and Victorian, stood up to the shock as our grandfathers themselves would have done.

Directly I began to cross the Common I realized I had the wrong umbrella, for it sprang a leak and the rain ran down under my macintosh collar, and then it was I saw Henry. I could so easily have avoided him; he had no umbrella and in the light of the lamp I could see his eyes were blinded with the rain. The black leafless trees gave no protection: they stood around like broken waterpipes, and the rain dripped off his stiff dark hat and ran in streams down his black civil servant's overcoat. If I had walked straight by him, he wouldn't have seen me, and I could have made certain by stepping two feet off the pavement, but I said, "Henry, you are almost a stranger," and saw his eyes light up as though we were old friends.

"Bendrix," he said with affection, and yet the world would have said *he* had the reasons for hate, not me.

Source: Greene, Graham. 1951. *The End of the Affair*. New York: Penguin, 1999. pp. 7–8.

Text 3

The Last Report on the Miracles at Little No Horse by Louise Erdrich.

The grass was white with frost on the shadowed sides of the reservation hills and ditches, but the morning air was almost warm, sweetened by a southern wind. Father Damien's best hours were late at night and just after rising, when all he'd had to break his fast was a cup of hot water. He was old, very old, but alert until he had to eat. Dressed in his antique cassock, he sat in his favourite chair, contemplating the graveyard that spread just past the ragged yard behind his retirement house and up a low hill. His thoughts seemed to penetrate sheer air, the maze of tree branches waving above the stones, clouds, sky, even time itself, and they surged from his brain, tense, quickly, one on the next until he'd eaten his tiny meal of toast and coffee. Just after, Father Damien's mind relaxed. His habit was then to doze again, often straight into his afternoon nap.

A period of waking confusion plagued him, usually before the supper hour, sometimes and most embarrassingly while he said late afternoon Saturday Mass. When lucid again, Father Damien repaired for the evening to his desk, a place from which he refused to be disturbed. There, he wrote fierce political attacks, reproachful ecclesiastical letters, memoirs of reservation life for history journals, and poetry. He also composed lengthy documents, which he called reports, to send to the Pope—he had in fact addressed every pontiff since he had come to the reservation in 1912. During his writing, Father Damien drank a few drops of wine, and usually, by the time he was ready for bed, he was what he called "pacified." This night, however, the wine had the opposite effect—it sharpened instead of dulled his fervor, sped instead of slowed the point of his cracked plastic pen, focused his mind.

To His Holiness, the Pope
The Vatican, Rome, Italy
The Last Report on the Miracles at Little No Horse
From the pen of
Father Damien Modeste

Source: Erdrich, Louise. 2001. *The Last Report on the Miracles at Little No Horse*. New York: Harper Collins. pp. 1–2.

Questions to the text

1 Is the narrative written in first or third person? What effect does this seem to have?

2 What do we learn or assume about the narrator's character as a result? How does the narrative voice help convey this?

3 In addition to the narrator, are there other characters introduced? If so, what do we learn about them and how?

4 What is the setting? Is there a particular tone or atmosphere already introduced? How is setting conveyed—through straight-forward description or other means?

5 What is the style of the writing? Does the language seem to "fit" with the narrator or work against them? Is the language simple, complex or difficult?

6 Are there clues about potential themes or main ideas to come?

7 Where in the plot do we seem to begin? Does this appear to be the beginning, middle or end of the story and what clues convey this?

8 In a novel, where so much more is to come, what aspects might excite a reader's curiosity to read further?

The short story

If the novel is largely defined by its length and scope, then the short story is most known for its brevity. Like the novel, the short story has a simplistic broad definition: any brief prose narrative. But the short story has developed some particular attributes around the demands of brevity.

First, the short story must be distinguished from the tale, fable or parable. Although these early stories were also brief, these more ancient forms clearly stem from oral tradition and represent the continuation of "natural" human literary expressions. The short story is now recognized as a unique art form consciously formulated to convey unique structure and technique. This should not be taken to mean that the short story is a more progressive form of the tale, fable or parable or that it is superior in any way. Rather, it should be recognized that each is its own distinct form achieving its own effects.

The short story focuses more on the development of a detailed scene, or dramatic moment. The short story may make use of epiphany, or a sudden moment of insight on a character's behalf. In this way, the short story conveys insight into a character through reactions to a scene. A novel, on the other hand, can afford to show a character developing slowly over time through a variety of events.

The short story

Read the excerpts from the following short stories, and answer the questions that follow.

Text 1

"A Rose for Emily," by William Faulkner.

So she vanquished them, horse and foot, just as she had vanquished their fathers thirty years before about the smell. That was two years after her father's death and a short time after her sweetheart—the one we believed would marry her—had deserted her. After her father's death she went out very little; after her sweetheart went away, people hardly saw her at all. A few of the ladies had the temerity to call, but were not received, and the only sign of life about the place was the Negro man—a young man then—going in and out with a market basket.

"Just as if a man—any man—could keep a kitchen properly," the ladies said; so they were not surprised when the smell developed. It was another link between the gross, teeming world and the high and mighty Griersons.

A neighbour, a woman, complained to the mayor, Judge Stevens, eighty years old.

"But what will you have me do about it, madam?" he said.

"Why, send her word to stop it," the woman said. "Isn't there a law?"

"I'm sure that won't be necessary," Judge Stevens said. "It's probably just a snake or a rat that nigger of hers killed in the yard. I'll speak to him about it."

The next day he received two more complaints, one from a man who came in diffident deprecation. "We really must do something about it, Judge. I'd be the last one in the world to bother Miss Emily, but we've got to do something." That night the Board of Aldermen met—three graybeards and one younger man, a member of the rising generation.

"It's simple enough," he said. "Send her word to have her place cleaned up. Give her a certain time to do it in, and if she don't …"

"Dammit, sir," Judge Stevens said, "will you accuse a lady to her face of smelling bad?"

So the next night, after midnight, four men crossed Miss Emily's lawn and slunk about the house like burglars, sniffing along the base of the brickwork and at the cellar openings while one of them performed a regular sowing motion with his hand out of a sack slung from his shoulder. They broke open the cellar door and sprinkled lime there, and in all the outbuildings. As they recrossed the lawn, a window that had been dark was lighted and Miss Emily sat in it, the light behind her, and her upright torso motionless as that of an idol. They crept quietly across the law and into the shadow of the locusts that lined the street. After a week or two the smell went away.

That was when people had begun to feel really sorry for her. People in our town, remembering how old lady Wyatt, her great-aunt, had gone completely crazy at last, believed that the Griersons held themselves a little too high for what they really were. None of the young men were quite good enough to Miss Emily and such. We had long through of them as a tableau; Miss Emily a slender figure in white in the background, her father a spraddled silhouette in the foreground, his back to her and clutching a horsewhip, the two of them framed by the back-flung front door. So when she got to be thirty and was still single, we were not pleased exactly, but vindicated; even with insanity in the family she wouldn't have turned down all of her chances if they had really materialized.

When her father died, it got about that the house was all that was left to her; and in a way, people were glad. At last they could pity Miss Emily. Being left alone, and a pauper, she had become humanized. Now she too would know the old thrill and the old despair of a penny more or less.

The day after his death all the ladies prepared to call at the house and offer condolence and aid, as is our custom. Miss Emily met them at the door, dressed as usual and with no trace of grief on her face. She told them that her father was not dead. She did that for three days, with the ministers calling on her, and the doctors, trying to persuade her to let them dispose of the body. Just as they were about to resort to law and force, she broke down, and they buried her father quickly.

We did not say she was crazy then. We believed she had to do that. We remembered all the young men her father had driven away, and we know that with nothing left, she would have to cling to that which had robbed her, as people will.

Source: Faulkner, William. 1930. "A Rose for Emily." *The Portable Faulkner*. New York: Modern Library, Random House, 1970 pp. 52–54.

Text 2

"The Management of Grief," by Bharanti Mukherjee.

A woman I don't know is boiling tea the Indian way in my kitchen. There are a lot of women I don't know in my kitchen, whispering and moving tactfully. They open doors, rummage through the pantry, and try not to ask me where things are kept. They remind me of when my sons were small, on Mother's Day or when Vikram and I were tired, and they would make big, sloppy omelets. I would lie in bed pretending I didn't hear them.

Dr. Sharma, the treasurer of the Indo-Canada Society, pulls me into the hallway. He wants to know if I am worried about money. His wife, who had just come up from the basement with a tray of empty cups and glasses, scolds him. "Don't bother Mrs. Bhave with mundane details." She looks so monstrously pregnant her baby must be days overdue. I tell her she shouldn't be carrying heavy things. "Shaila," she says, smiling, "this is the fifth." Then she grabs a teenager by his shirttails. He slips his Walkman off his head. He has to be one of her four children; they have the same domed and dented foreheads. "What's the official word now?" she demands. The boy slips the headphone back on. "They're acting evasive, Ma. They're saying it could be an accident or a terrorist bomb."

All morning, the boys have been muttering, Sikh bomb, Sikh bomb. The men, not using the word, bow their heads in agreement. Mrs. Sharma touches her forehead at such a word. At least they've stopped talking about space debris and Russian lasers.

Two radios are going in the dining room. They are tuned to different stations. Someone must have brought the radios down from my boys' bedrooms. I haven't gone into their rooms since Kusum came running across the front lawn in her bathrobe. She looked so funny, I was laughing when I opened the door.

The big TV in the den is being whizzed through American networks and cable channels. "Damn!" some man swears bitterly. "How can these preachers carry on like nothing has happened?" I want to tell him we're not that important. You look at the audience and at the preachers in his blue robe with his beautiful white hair, the potted palm trees under a blue sky, and you know they care about nothing.

The phone rings and rings. Dr. Sharma's taken charge. "We're with her," he keeps saying. "Yes, yes, the doctor has given calming pills. Yes, yes, pills are having necessary effect." I wonder if pills alone explain this calm. Not peace, just a deadening quiet.

I was always controlled, but never repressed. Sound can reach me, but my body is tensed, ready to scream. I hear their voices all around me. I hear my boys and Vikram cry, "Mommy, Shaila!" and their screams insulate me, like headphones.

The woman boiling water tells her story again and again. "I got the news first. My cousin called from Halifax before six a.m., can you imagine? He'd gotten up for prayers and his son was studying for medical exams and heard on a rock channel that something had happened to a plane. They said first it had disappeared from the radar, like a giant eraser just reached out. His father called me, so I said to him, what do you mean, 'something bad'? You mean a hijacking? And he said, *Behn*, there is no confirmation of anything yet, but check with your neighbours because a lot of them must be on that plane. So I called poor Kusum straight-away. I knew Kusum's husband and daughter were booked to go yesterday."

Kusum lives across the street from me. She and Satish had moved in less than a month ago. They said they needed a bigger place. All these people, the Sharmas and friends from the Indo-Canada Society, had been there for the housewarming. Satish and Kusum made tandoori on their big gas grill and even the white neighbors piled their places high with the luridly red, charred, juicy chicken. Their younger daughter had danced, and even our boys had broken away from the Stanley Cup telecast to put in a reluctant appearance. Everyone took pictures for their albums and for the community newspapers—another of our families had made it big in Toronto—and now I wonder how many of those happy faces are gone. "Why does God give us so much if all along He intends to take it away?" Kusum asks me.

I nod. We sit on carpeted stairs, holding hands like children. "I never once told him that I loved him," I say. I was too much the well-brought up woman. I was so well brought up I never felt comfortable calling my husband by his first name.

"It's all right," Kusum says. "He knew. My husband knew. They felt it. Modern young girls have to say it because what they feel is fake."

Kusum's daughter Pam runs in with an overnight case. Pam's in her McDonald's uniform. "Mummy" You have to get dressed!" Panic makes her cranky. "A reporters' on his way here."

"Why?"

"You want to talk to him in your bathrobe?" She starts to brush her mother's long hair. She's the daughter who's always in trouble. She dates

Canadian boys and hangs out in the mall, shopping for tight sweaters. The younger one, the goody-goody one according to Pam, the one with a voice so sweet that when she sang bhajans for Ethiopian relief even a frugal man like my husband wrote out a hundred-dollar check., she was on that plane. She was going to spend July and August with grandparents because Pam wouldn't go. Pam said she's rather waitress at McDonald's. "If it's a choice between Bombay and Wonderland, I'm picking Wonderland," she said.

"Leave me alone," Kusum yells. "You know what I want to do? If I didn't have to look after you now, I'd hang myself."

Pam's young face goes blotchy with pain. "Thanks," she says, "don't let me stop you."

"Hush," pregnant Mrs. Sharma scolds Pam. "Leave your mother along. Mr. Sharma will tackle the reporters and fill out the forms. He'll say what has to be said."

Pam stands her ground. "You think I don't know what Mummy's thinking. Why her? That's what. That's sick!" Mummy wishes my little sister were alive and I were dead."

Kusum's hand in mine is trembly hot. We continue to sit on the stairs.

Source: Mukherjee, Bharati. 1988. *Middleman and Other Stories*. Toronto: Grove Press.

Questions to the text

1 How are dramatic moments created in each of the excerpts?

2 What tensions are present in each excerpt? How do the respective authors create such tensions in such short space?

3 What details are present in the excerpts that convey aspects of character, plot and conflict? How do these operate in each story respectively?

Nonfictional prose

Nonfiction, a broad definition of genre may include essays, biography, travel writing, autobiography, memoir, etc. The one common element, it could be construed from this list, is a focus on actual events and real people. Certainly, this is quite a distinction from the prose fiction option but you may be surprised how permeable the boundary is between the two. What we might find in any nonfictional prose will be examples of the recognizably fictional, including mood or atmosphere, setting and theme. In fact, it is likely that, should your school be selecting nonfictional prose as one of its genres, some of your study will be regarding the blending of fiction with nonfiction and vice versa. The good news for you is that your approach to nonfictional prose will be very similar to that of your approach to fictional prose. The only difference would be the requirement for supporting evidence as it relates to purpose, but even fictional texts demand a degree of authenticity to be effectively realized. Consider the following questions when you approach nonfiction texts:

● For what purpose has the writer chosen this topic? What is the writer trying to demonstrate or prove?

● What relationship is there between the subject and the form of writing?

Activity

Setting the scene

Text 1

The following opinion piece by the American writer Joan Didion is part of a larger work exploring changing norms and mores in the United States in the late 1960s. "Marrying Absurd," Set in Las Vegas, considers changing attitudes toward love and marriage.

To be married in Las Vegas, Clark County, Nevada, a bride must swear that she is eighteen or has parental permission and a bridegroom that he is twenty-one or has parental permission. Someone must put up five dollars for the license. (On Sundays and holidays, fifteen dollars. The Clark County Courthouse issues marriage licenses at any time of the day or night except between noon and one in the afternoon, between eight and nine in the evening, and between four and five in the morning.) Nothing else is required. The State of Nevada, alone among these United States, demands neither a pre-marital blood test nor a waiting period before or after the issuance of a marriage license. Driving in across the Mojave from Los Angeles, one sees the signs way out on the desert, looming up from that moonscape of rattlesnakes and mesquite, even before the Las Vegas lights appear like a mirage on the horizon: "GETTING MARRIED? Free License Information First Strip Exit." Perhaps the Las Vegas wedding industry achieved its peak operational efficiency between 9:00 p.m. and midnight of August 26, 1965, an otherwise unremarkable Thursday which happened to be, by Presidential order, the last day on which anyone could improve his draft status merely be getting married. One hundred and seventy-one couples were pronounced man and wife in the name of Clark County and the State of Nevada that night, sixty-seven of them by a single justice of the peace, Mr. James A. Brennan. Mr. Brennan did one wedding at the Dunes and the other sixty-six in his office, and charged each couple eight dollars. One bride lent her veil to six others. "I got it down from five to three minutes," Mr. Brennan said later of his feat. "I could've married them *en masse*, but they're people, not cattle. People expect more when they get married."

What people who get married in Las Vegas actually do expect—what, in the largest sense, their "expectations" are—strikes one as a curious and self-contradictory business. Las Vegas is the most extreme and allegorical of American settlements, bizarre and beautiful in its venality and in its devotion to immediate gratification, a place the tone of which is set by mobsters and call girls and ladies' room attendants with amyl nitrite poppers in their uniform pockets. Almost everyone notes that there is no "time" in Las Vegas, no night and no day and no past and no future (no Las Vegas casino, however, has taken the obliteration of the ordinary time sense quite so far as Harold's Club in Reno, which for a while issued, at odd intervals in the day and night, mimeographed "bulletins" carrying news from the world outside); neither is there any logical sense of where one is. One is standing on a highway in the middle of a vast hostile desert looking at an eighty-foot sign which blinks "STARDUST" or "CEASAR'S PALACE." Yes, but what does that explain? This geographical implausibility reinforces the sense that what happens there has no connection with "real" life; Nevada cities like Reno and Carson are ranch towns, Western towns, places behind which there is some historical imperative. But Las Vegas seems to exist only in the eye of the beholder. All of which makes it an extraordinarily stimulating and interesting place, but an odd one in which to want to wear a candlelight satin Priscilla of Boston wedding dress with Chantilly lace insets, tapered sleeves and a detachable modified train.

Source: Didion, Joan. 1968. "Marrying Absurd." *Slouching Towards Bethlehem*. New York: Farrar, Straus & Giroux. pp. 68–69.

Questions to the text

1 What techniques does Didion use to give readers a sense of setting? Are these techniques "factual" or "literary" in nature and what impact do they have?

2 How does Didion create a sense of emotion in the text?

3 What seems to be the writer's attitude toward the subject and how is this revealed?

Text 2

The following account by the English writer William Dalrymple relates a conversation with his landlady, Mrs Puri, in Delhi. It is from his travelogue *City of Djinns*.

Mrs. Puri had achieved all this through a combination of hard work and good old-fashioned thrift. In the heat of summer she rarely put on the air conditioning. In winter she allowed herself the electric fire for only an hour a day. She recycled the newspapers we threw out; and returning from parties late at nights we could see her still sitting up, silhouetted against the window, knitting sweaters for export. "Sleep is silver," she would say in explanation, "but money is gold."

This was all very admirable, but the hitch, we soon learned, was that she expected her tenants to emulate the disciplines she imposed upon herself. One morning, after only a week in the flat, I turned on the tap to discover that our water had been cut off, so went downstairs to sort out the problem. Mrs. Puri had already been up and about for several hours; she had been to the gurdwara, said her prayers and was now busy drinking her morning glass of rice water.

"There is no water in our flat this morning, Mrs. Puri."

"No, Mr. William, and I am telling you why."

"Why, Mrs. Puri?"

"You are having guests, Mr. William. And always they are going to the lavatory."

"But why should that affect the water supply?"

"Last night I counted seven flushes," said Mrs. Puri, rapping her stick on the floor. "So I have cut off the water as protest."

She paused to let the enormity of our crime sink in.

"Is there any wonder that there is water shortage in our India when you people are making seven flushes in one night?"

Old Mr. Puri, her husband, was a magnificent-looking Sikh gentleman with a long white beard and a tin zimmer frame with wheels on the bottom. He always seemed friendly enough—as we passed he would nod politely from his armchair. But when we first took the flat Mrs. Puri drew us aside and warned us that her husband had never been, well, quite the same since the riots that followed Mrs. Gandhi's death in 1984.

In was a rather heroic story. When some hooligans began to break down the front door, Mr. Puri got Ladoo (the name means Sweety), his bearer, to place him directly behind the splintering wood. Uttering a blood-curdling cry, he whipped out his old service revolver and fired the entire magazine through the door. The marauders ran off to attack the taxi rank around the corner and the Puris were saved …

Since the riots, Mr. Puri had also become intermittently senile. One day he could be perfectly lucid; the next he might suffer from the strangest hallucinations. On these occasions conversations with him took on a somewhat surreal quality:

Mr. Puri: (up the stairs to my flat) Mr. William! Get your bloody mules out of my room this minute!

WD: But Mr. Puri, I don't have any mules.

Mr. Puri: Nonsense! How else could you get your trunks up the stairs? During our first month in the flat, however, Mr. Puri was on his best behavior. Apart from twice proposing marriage to my wife, he behaved with perfect decorum.

Source: Dalrymple, William. 1993. *City of Djinns*. New York: Penguin Books. pp. 12–13.

Questions to the text

1 What methods does Dalrymple employ that would be commonly associated with novelists? What effect do these methods have?

2 What is the general impression Dalrymple gives regarding his surroundings (the setting)? How is this conveyed?

Defining poetry

Introducing poetic devices

Working with a partner, consider the following two poems to compare and contrast the way they are written. How does the poet use language and devices such as rhyme, meter and metaphor to achieve the particular qualities of tone and atmosphere?

Text 1

Mint

It looked like a clump of small dusty nettles
Growing wild at the gable of the house
Beyond where we dumped our refuse and old bottles:
Unverdant ever, almost beneath notice.

But, to be fair, it also spelled promise
And newness in the back yard of our life
As if something callow yet tenacious
Sauntered in green alleys and grew rife.

The snip of scissor blades, the light of Sunday
Mornings when the mint was cut and loved:
My last things will be things slipping from me.
Yet let all things go fee that have survived.

Let the smells of mint go heady and defenseless
Like inmates liberated in that yard.
Like the disregarded ones we turned against
Because we'd failed them by our disregard.

Source: Heaney, Seamus. 1996. "Mint." *The Spirit Level*. New York: Farrar Straus Giroux. p. 9.

Text 2

In Just-

in Just-
spring   when the world is mud-
luscious the little
lame balloonman

whistles   far   and wee

and eddieandbill come
running from marbles and
piracies and it's
spring

when the world is puddle-wonderful

the queer
old balloonman whistles
far   and   wee
and bettyandisbel come dancing

from hop-scotch and jump-rope and

it's
spring
and
        the

              goat-footed

balloonMan   whistles
far
and
wee

Source: Cummings, E. E. 1923. *Tulips and Chimneys*. New York: Thomas Seltzer.

Questions to the texts

1 How are grammatical conventions used in each of the poems?

2 Does one poem seem easier to paraphrase that the other? Why or why not?

3 How does the physical structure of each poem further consolidate their meanings or the atmosphere created?

4 How is punctuation significant in each of the poems?

Poetry is difficult to define simply although most students readily identify it as that which is "not narrative." What that "non-narrative" is, however, can vary greatly and range from song lyrics to simple aphorism to a sonnet. Despite the challenge and because of its range, poetry exists everywhere and for as long as we have had language; poetry, in fact, is the oldest literary art. Poetry is not defined by its length, subject matter, relationship to time or its dramatization; rather, it is defined, most particularly, by its use of language. While narrative, drama and nonfiction all make use of language, poetry seems to use language differently. Many describe this difference as one of *intensity*. More than description, persuasion or analysis, poetry attempts to offer an experience of ideas and things.

To be successful, poetry must be, as that noted authority *Perrine's Sound and Sense* calls it, "multi-dimensional"; that is, poetry invites a reader to participate through senses, emotions, imagination and intelligence. Multidimensional experience and participation may sound slightly "New Age" in tone, but it is useful for its focus on personal affect. A poet works very hard to stimulate multidimensional participation but the actual experience itself is intensely personal and unique to the reader. Someone once said that all poetry begins with poets but ends with readers. This is not meant to imply that "anything goes." Indeed, poetry incorporates a number of very particular elements to encourage participation and, even if we recognize that the most authentic responses are always those that are most personal, we can read poetry with an ear and an eye toward how participation is cultivated. Ultimately, the strongest personal experiences with poetry is developed through learning and being critically informed.

Poetry is also meant to be heard. Even when reading alone, so much of a poem is revealed through its sound (you will be surprised how much more you gain, even on an initial reading, if you read a poem aloud). Although this is not truly unique to poetry, it is worth remembering and practicing as you move forward with your study of poetry.

Elements of poetry

Diction/syntax

Obviously words are an important element of poetry. Much of a poem's intensity stems from a poet's diction, or word choice, and syntax (the way words are put together or arranged). Diction is a good place to start. Choosing the right word depends on multiple variables but with poetry, you can expect that the diction has been well thought-out and carefully selected. Looking closely at the words is always a requirement in understanding poetry and it can be useful to pay particular attention to the following:

- **Denotation and connotation** Denotations are literal dictionary definitions of words. But both poets and non-poets often express ideas in words where more than a dictionary definition is called for. Connotations are ideas, overtones and expressions of meaning over and above denotations. To call someone blind refers literally to a lack of the sense of sight but may be used in ways where the implications are more of ignorance, denial or inexperience than pure sight loss.

- **Imagery** Imagery is a representation of the physical senses in language. It is commonly thought of as the way the words in a poem paint a picture, but this is actually too limited as imagery may appeal to any and/or all of the senses. The term does, however, suggest an emphasis on the mental or representational aspect of imagery, not to be confused with psychological or emotional sensations that are not determined by forms.

- **Figurative speech** Figurative speech is language used to convey an idea in an unordinary or unfamiliar way rather than directly. This can come through many methods including metaphor, simile, allusion, symbol, allegory, personification, metonymy, hyperbole, irony and more. By using figurative speech, a poet can often convey even more than the words should allow. Figurative speech is a little like a closet whose interior exceeds its exterior dimensions, figuratively speaking.

Syntax is the arrangement of words. Poetry very often follows unique syntax and may not adhere to all rules of standard grammar. For effect, poets often rearrange words for emphasis or omit standard grammar, including punctuation. Making the verb appear first instead of having it appear last in a line of poetry, for instance, can change the particular attitude or tone. As with the choice of words, the arrangement is carefully planned. Poetry can achieve a fuller use of language that is more rich and intense than prose.

Activity

Poetry and language

Read through the following poems alone or with a partner, taking notes. Langston Hughes' "Harlem (A Dream Deferred)" from 1951 and William Blake's "The Chimney Sweeper" (1789) are quite different poems that make particular use of diction and syntax. Pay close attention to how each poem uses language.

Text 1

Harlem

What happened to a dream deferred?
    Does it dry up?
    like a raisin in the sun?
    or fester like a sore—
    And then run?
    Does it stink like rotten meat?
    Or crust and sugar over—
    like a syrupy sweet?
    Maybe it just sags
    like a heavy load.
    Or does it explode?

Langston Hughes

Questions

1 Hughes combines simile and metaphor in this poem. What effect does each have? How is the place of the metaphor effective?

2 What are the possible meanings around the term "dream" and how do they work in this poem?

Text 2

The Chimney Sweeper

When my mother died I was very young,
And my father sold me while yet my tongue
Could scarcely cry "'weep! 'weep! 'weep! 'weep!"
So your chimneys I sweep, and in soot I sleep.

There's little Tom Dacre, who cried when his head
That curled like a lamb's back, was shaved; so I said,
"Hush, Tom! never mind it, for, when your head's bare,
You know that the soot cannot spoil your white hair."

And so he was quiet, and that very night,
As Tom was asleeping, he had such a sight!
That thousands of sweepers, Dick, Joe, Ned, and Jack,
Were all of them locked up in coffins of black.

And by came an Angel who had a bright key,
And he opened the coffins and set them all free;
Then down a green plain leaping, laughing, they run,
And wash in a river, and shine in the sun.

Then naked and white, all their bags left behind,
They rise upon clouds and sport in the wind;
And the Angel told Tom, if he's be a good boy,
He'd have God for his father, and never want joy.

And so Tom awoke, and we rose in the dark,
And got with our bags and brushes to work.
Though the morning was cold, Tom was happy and warm;
So if all do their duty they need not fear harm.

William Blake

Questions to the text

1 What are the possible meanings around the term "dream" in this poem and how do they compare to the Hughes poem above?

2 Like Hughes, there seems to be a sense of irony here. How does this operate and what specific words help create this voice?

3 How are the boys characterized in the poem? What specific language creates these characterizations?

Tone in literature

In literature, tone is defined as a speaker's attitude toward a subject. This is often treated as a simple element but it can be challenging to identify. Without inflection, the determining voice and tone comes through careful attention to any and all aspects that might suggest attitudes. But all poems have a tone or even multiple tones and understanding a poem begins with understanding of its tone. Commonly, poems can have tones ranging from serious to playful and satirical, or from detached and clinical to highly personal and confessional.

It can be helpful, in determining tone, to also consider voice. Voice may be also understood as persona, or who or what is "speaking" in the poem. Determining whether the speaker of a poem is a young and innocent little boy or a wise even god-like figure with deep experience and understanding would likely lead to very different tones. Although it is possible that the former speaker adopts a deep, serious tone or that the latter takes on a playful, innocent tone, even an awareness of this reversal of expectations would enlarge a reading. Together, tone and voice create mood, or general atmosphere in a poem. While there are clear links between the elements, each has its own unique qualities.

Activity

Poetry and tone

Read the following poems by Eavan Boland (1982) and Gerard Manley Hopkins (1918). Pay particular attention to the tones created and the language that gives rise to these attitudes.

Text 1

Woman in Kitchen

Once I am sure there's nothing going on
Breakfast over, islanded by noise,
she watches the machines go fast and slow.
She stands among them as they shake the house.
They move. Their destination is specific.
She has nowhere definite to go:
she might be a pedestrian in traffic.

White surfaces retract. White
sideboards light the white walls.
Cups wink white in their saucers.
The light of day bleaches as it falls
on cups and sideboards. She could use
the room to tap with if she lost her sight.

Machines jigsaw everything she knows.
And she is everywhere among their furor:
the tropic of the dryer tumbling clothes.
The round lunar window of the washer.
The kettle in the toaster is a kingfisher
swooping for trout above the river's mirror.

The wash done, the kettle boiled, the sheets
spun and clean, the dryer stops dead.
The silence is a death. It starts to bury
the room in white spaces. She turns to spread
a cloth on the board and irons sheets
in a room white and quiet as a mortuary.

Eavan Boland

Questions to the text

1 What connotations and denotations does the title have?

2 Considering the language, does the tone seem formal, informal, affectionate, violent, pleased, unhappy or some combination of these?

3 What seems to be the attitude of the speaker toward housework or domesticity more generally?

4 Define as precisely as possible the tone of the poem as precisely as possible.

Text 2

Spring

Nothing is so beautiful as spring—
   When weeds, in wheels, shoot long and lovely and lunch;
   Thrush's eggs look little low heavens, and thrust
Through the echoing timber does so rinse and wring
The ear, it strikes like lightnings to hear him sing;
   The glassy peartree leaves and blooms, they brush
   The descending blue; that blue is all in a rush
With richness: the racing lambs too have fair their fling.

What is all this juice and all this joy?
   A strain of the earth's sweet being in the beginning
In Eden garden.—Have, get, before it cloy,
   Before it cloud, Christ, lord, and sour with sinning,
Innocent mind and Mayday in girl and boy,
   Most, O maid's child, thy choice and worthy the winning.

Gerard Manley Hopkins

Questions to the text

1 What is the attitude of the speaker to the subject of spring?

2 How do the formality and tone of the language affect this attitude?

3 What seems to be the attitude of the speaker toward housework or domesticity more generally?

4 How does the comparison of spring to Eden work in this poem? Is it effective? Does in confirm or confuse the tone for the reader?

Structure and form

One of the first elements of poetry a reader encounters it its structure or form; a reader is made immediately aware of a poem in its physical format just on first glance. At the simplest level, poetry is divided into long, unbroken poems that are called stichic or poems that are divided into smaller groups of lines or words called strophic. In strophic poetry, the smaller groups of lines or words are called stanzas and strophic poetry is sometimes popularly referred to as stanzaic. While recognizing this most basic form cannot tell you everything, even an awareness of this level of structure begins to set an experience in motion. Seeing lines that are composed of only one word versus lines that are composed of many tens of words creates a different impression directly from the page. **Concrete poetry**, in particular, makes strong use of this effect.

Form can be closed or open. Closed form attempts to adhere to a fixed format, whether with regard to the number of syllables per line, lines per stanza or overall structure. Open form avoids trying to adhere to fixed structures.

Structure in poetry is a little more complex to define. The use of aspects such as enjambment or caesura affect the reading of a poem that may or may not align with its physical layout and, as with all poetic syntax, is used intentionally. But these aspects speak to a larger field of structural issues: those to do with sound arrangements.

> **Concrete poetry** is written/structured in such a manner that it creates a visual or graphic representation of the writing

Rhythm

Rhythm is the patterning of stress and sound that helps create a mood or sense. Stress can be created by familiar pronunciations of a word (syllable stress), by particular word placements or by word use (emphatic stress). This patterning of stresses is known as meter, a patterning of stressed and unstressed syllables in the words used (it can be helpful to think of this as similar to the musical "beat" of a poem). Meter is an interesting poetic form as it is intentional and there can be particular moods, tones or attitudes associated with different metrical constructions. Of course, poets often subvert common metrical associations for very nontraditional affect as well.

Meter

Meter begins with a pattern of syllables within words and then within lines. Syllables are grouped as pairs or trios which are referred to as a foot and categorized according to the order of stress and unstress. Lines are then patterned and labeled according to the number of feet they contain. Sometimes, analyzing meter can best be served by reversing the order (looking at numbers of feet in a line before determining the kind of foot). The process of analysis is formally known as scansion.

Foot	Lines
iambic = unstressed-stressed	one foot = monometer
trochaic = stressed-unstressed	two feet = dimeter
dactylic = stressed-unstressed-unstressed	three feet = trimester
anapestic = unstressed-unstressed-stressed	four feet = tetrameter
spondaic = stressed-stressed	five feet = pentameter
	six feet = hexameter
	seven feet = heptameter
	eight feet = octameter

Rhyme

Rhyme is another familiar way of structuring poetry. Incorporating rhyme has a natural impact on meter and rhythm but can also be used to add emphasis, unity or other effect. Rhymes can occur as any of a variety of aural features (including whole rhymes, half or slant rhymes,) but can also be physical in the form of sight rhymes. Together, rhythm, meter and rhyme help create a structure that is both physical and metaphoric.

Rhyme scheme

One way of recognizing a structure through the use of rhyme is through a poem's rhyme scheme. The rhyme scheme is the patterning within a stanza and/or poem that occurs with end rhymes, or the final syllable(s) of lines. This is usually described using small letters, as in the following example:

Roses are red	*a*
Violets are blue	*b*
You love me	*c*
And I love you	*b*

The rhyme scheme of this short poem is *abcb*.

One last note regarding structure and form is, ironically, a form of anti-form. Free verse intentionally avoids adherence to strict patterns and patterning with all of the above aspects, reworking lines at will to best achieve a desired effect. As with all poetry, however, even free verse is exceptionally well-crafted.

Activity

Poetry: Form and structure

Read through the following poems looking at form, structure and rhyme. How do they use structure to help convey meaning?

Text 1

Death, be not proud

Death, be not proud, though some have called thee
Mighty and dreadful, for thou art not so;
For those whom thou think'st thou dost overthrow
Die not, poor death, nor yet canst thou kill me.
From rest and sleep, which but thy pictures be,
Much pleasure—then, from thee much more must flow;

And soonest our best men with thee do go,
Rest of their bones and soul's delivery.
Thou art slave to fate, chance, kings, and desperate men,

And dost with poison, war, and sickness dwell;
And poppy or charms can make us sleep as well,
And better than thy stroke. Why swell'st thou then?
One short sleep passed, we wake eternally,
And death shall be no more; death, thou shalt die.

John Donne

Questions to the text

1 Look closely at the rhyme scheme and meter of the poem. What effect does the sonnet form have in contributing to tone and meaning?

2 In what ways does the form of the poem aid in making the "arguments" persuasive or logical?

Text 2

Disillusionment of Ten O'Clock

> The houses are haunted
> By white night-gowns.
> None are green,
> Or purple with green rings,
> Or green with yellow rings,
> Or yellow with blue rings,
> None of them are strange,
> With socks of lace
> And beaded ceintures.
> People are not going
> To dream of baboons and periwinkles.

> Only, here and there, an old sailor,
> Drunk and asleep in his boots,
> Catches tigers
> In red weather.

Wallace Stevens

Questions to the text

1 Despite a lack of clear meter or rhyme, there seems to be a form of intentional structure in this poem. How do lines 4 to 6 operate and to what effect? How do references to color help provide form in a poem that is otherwise blank verse?

2 Does there seem to be a rhythm in the poem, even if inconsistent? What effect might this have?

Reading for effect and meaning

If poetry is meant to be an intense and personal experience, the question of meaning remains complex. As already mentioned, this is a challenging issue but there are literary effects that invite participation and that can be analyzed as well as larger, or more "complete" meanings to be addressed. There are no clear lines dividing the two, necessarily, but intellectual engagement with the former can enhance our experience of the latter.

The particular and intentional use of language in poetry gives rise to particular effects. The use of structure, diction and tone, for instance, will create an effect and this is important to consider. But the effects created through particular uses of language will ultimately only allow for a reader's participation. The completion of the ideas will necessarily be experiential, and include our willingness to engage a poem to determine how meaning is conveyed and emerges for you, the individual reader.

Although there are no rules for reading and understanding poetry, keep in mind the following habits of experienced poetry lovers:

- Read poems more than once. The first reading rarely, if ever, delivers its full potential experience.

- Pay careful attention to the use of language and make notes. Because words are treated intensely, it is important to weigh all of them. This includes using a dictionary when necessary.

- Read poems aloud. Even if you don't actually speak the words aloud, read a poem so that you can hear the sounds in your mind. This also requires practice and attention, figuring out rhythms and patterns and managing punctuation.

- Begin right away to consider what a poem is about. Be careful not to be frustrated if this proves elusive, especially on first reading.

- Read a lot. Reading many poems, and a variety, will greatly aid in your understanding of poetry in general.

Elizabeth Bishop's "Imaginary Iceberg" is a challenging poem exploring the nature of cold reality and fertile imagination. In the style of Wallace Stevens or the French Symbolist poets (who argued that truths could only be gleaned indirectly and through obfuscated means), Bishop is concerned with the role of metaphor and imagination in constructing reality.

What do you think the iceberg represents?

The Imaginary Iceberg

We'd rather have the iceberg than the ship,
Although it meant the end of travel.
Although it stood stock still like cloudy rock
And all the sea were moving marble.
We'd rather have the iceberg than the ship;
We'd rather own this breathing plain of snow
Though the ship's sails were laid upon the sea
As the snow lies undissolved upon the water.
O solemn, floating field,
Are you aware an iceberg takes repose
With you, and when it wakes may pasture on your snows?

This is a scene a sailor'd give his eyes for.
The ship's ignored. The iceberg rises
And sinks again; its glassy pinnacles
Correct elliptics in the sky.
This is a scene where he who treads the boards
Is artlessly rhetorical. The curtain
Is light enough to rise on finest ropes
That airy twists of snow provide.
The wits of these white peaks
Spar with the sun. Its weight the iceberg dares
Upon a shifting stage and stands and stares.

This iceberg cuts its facets from within.
Like jewelry from a grave
It saves itself perpetually and adorns
Only itself, perhaps the snows
Which so surprise us lying on the sea.
Goodbye, we say, goodbye, the ship steers off
Where waves give in to one another's waves
And clouds run in a warmer sky.
Icebergs behoove the soul
(Both being self-made from elements least visible)
To see them so: fleshed, fair, erected indivisible.

Elizabeth Bishop, 1946

Drama: setting the scene

Read the following extracts from the opening scenes of two plays. Pay close attention to the setting of the scene and the creation of atmosphere. What can you glean about each of the individual characters and about the relationships likely to exist between them? Consider the significance of any stage directions and the approach to language.

Text 1

The following extract is from a three-act play by Irish playwright John Millington Synge. It is set in a public house in County Mayo (on the west coast of Ireland) during the early 1900s.

> **SCENE** Country public-house or shebeen, very rough and untidy. There is a sort of counter on the right with shelves, holding many bottles and jus, just seen above it. Empty barrels stand near the counter. At back, a little to left of counter, there is a door into the open air, then, more to the left, there is a settle with shelves above it, with more jugs, and a table beneath a window. At the left there is a large open fire-place, with turf fire, and a small door into inner room. Pegeen, a wild-looking but fine girl, of about twenty, is writing at table. She is dressed in the usual peasant dress.

> ***

> **Pegeen** (*slowly as she writes*). Six yards of stuff for to make a yellow gown. A pair of lace boots with lengthy heels on them and brassy eyes. A hat is suited for a wedding-day. A fine tooth comb. To be sent with three barrels of porter in Jimmy Farrell's creel cart on the evening of the coming Fair to Mister Michael James Flaherty. With the best compliments of this season. Margaret Flaherty.

> **Shawn** (*a fat and fair young man comes in as she signs, looks round awkwardly, when he sees she is alone*). Where's himself?

> **Pegeen** (*without looking at him*). He's coming. (*She directs the letter.*) To Mister Sheamus Mulroy, Wine and Spirit Dealer, Castlebar.

> **Shawn** (*uneasily*). I didn't see him on the road.

> **Pegeen** How would you see him (*licks stamp and puts it on letter*) and it dark night this half hour gone by?

> **Shawn** (*turning towards the door again*). I stood a while outside wondering would I have a right to pass on or to walk in and see you, Pegeen Mike (*comes to fire*), and I could hear the cows breathing, and sighing in the stillness of the air, and not a step moving any place from this gate to the bridge.

> **Pegeen** (*putting letter in envelope*). It's above at the cross-roads he is, meeting Philly Cullen; and a couple more are going along with him to Kate Cassidy's wake.

> **Shawn** (*looking at her blankly*). And he's going that length in the dark night?

> **Pegeen** (*impatiently*). He is surely, and leaving me lonesome on the scruff of the hill. (*She gets up and puts envelope on dresser, then winds clock.*) Isn't it long the nights are now, Shawn Keogh, to be leaving a poor girl with her own self counting the hours to the dawn of day?

> **Shawn** (*with awkward humour*). If it is, when we're wedded in a short while you'll have no call to complain, for I've little will to be walking off to wakes or weddings in the darkness of the night.

> **Pegeen** (*with rather scornful good humour*). You're making mighty certain, Shaneen, that I'll wed you now.

> **Shawn** Aren't we after making a good bargain, the way we're only waiting these days on Father Reilly's dispensation from the bishops, or the Court of Rome.

> **Pegeen** (*looking at him teasingly, washing up at dresser*). It's a wonder, Shaneen, the Holy Father'd be taking notice of the likes of you; for if I was him I wouldn't bother with this place where you'll meet none but Red Linahan, has a squint in his eye, and Patcheen is lame in his heel, or the mad Mulrannies were driven from California and they lost in their wits. We're a queer lot these times to go troubling the Holy Father on his sacred seat.

> **Shawn** (*scandalized*). If we are, we're as good this place as another, maybe, and as good these times as we were for ever.

> **Pegeen** (*with scorn*). As good, is it? Where now will you meet the like of Daneen Sullivan knocked the eye from a peeler, or Marcus Quin, God rest him, got six months for maiming ewes, and he a great warrant to tell stories of holy Ireland till he'd have the old women shedding down tears about their feet. Where will you find the like of them, I'm saying?

> **Shawn** (*timidly*). If you don't, it's a good job, maybe; for (*with peculiar emphasis on the words*) Father Reilly has small conceit to have that kind walking around and talking to the girls.

> **Pegeen** (*impatiently, throwing water from basin out of the door*). Stop tormenting me with Father Reilly (*imitating his voice*) when I'm asking only what way I'll pass these twelve hours of dark, and not take my death with the fear.

> (*Looking out of door.*)

Source: Synge, J. M. 1907. *The Playboy of the Western World*. Dublin: Maunsel & Co. pp. 1–2.

Text 2

The Zoo Story is American playwright Edward Albee's first play, written in 1958. This one-act play concerns two characters, Peter and Jerry. Peter is a family man and a book publisher. Jerry lives in a boarding house. These men meet on a park bench in New York City's Central Park.

As the curtain rises, Peter is seated on the bench stage-right. He is reading a book. He stops reading, cleans his glasses, goes back to reading. Jerry enters.

Jerry I've been to the zoo. (*Peter doesn't notice*) I said, I've been to the zoo. MISTER, I'VE BEEN TO THE ZOO!

Peter Hm? … What? … I'm sorry, were you talking to me?

Jerry I went to the zoo, and then I walked until I came here. Have I been walking north?

Peter (*puzzled*). North? Why … I … I think so. Let me see.

Jerry (*pointing past the audience*). Is the Fifth Avenue?

Peter Why yes; yes, it is.

Jerry And what is that cross street there; that one, to the right?

Peter That? Oh, that's Seventy-fourth Street.

Jerry And the zoo is around Sixty-fifth Street; so, I've been walking north.

Peter (*anxious to get back to his reading*). Yes; it would seem so.

Jerry Good old north.

Peter (*Lightly, by reflex*). Ha, ha.

Jerry (*after a slight pause*). But not due north.

Peter I … well, no, not due north; but, we … call it north. It's northerly.

Jerry (*watches as Peter, anxious to dismiss him, prepares his pipe*). Well, boy; you're not going to get lung cancer, are you?

Peter (*looks up, a little annoyed, then smiles*). No, sir. Not from this.

Jerry No, sir. What you'll probably get is cancer of the mouth, and then you'll have to wear one of those things Freud wore after they took one whole side of his jaw away. What do they call those things?

Peter (*uncomfortable*). A prosthesis?

Jerry The very thing! A prosthesis. You're an educated man, aren't you? Are you a doctor?

Peter Oh, no; no. I read about it somewhere; *Time* magazine, I think. (*He turns to his book.*)

Jerry Well, *Time* magazine isn't for blockheads.

Jerry No, I suppose not.

Jerry (*after a pause*). Boy, I'm glad that's Fifth Avenue there.

Peter (*vaguely*). Yes.

Jerry I don't like the west side of the park much.

Peter Oh? (*Then, slightly wary, but interested*) Why?

Jerry (*offhand*). I don't know.

Peter Oh. (*He returns to his book.*)

Jerry (*he stands for a few seconds, looking at Peter, who finally looks up again, puzzled*). Do you mind if we talk?

Peter (*obviously minding*). Why … no, no.

Jerry Yes you do; you do.

Peter (*puts his book down, his pipe out and away, smiling*). No, really; I don't mind.

Jerry Yes you do.

Peter (*finally decided*). No; I don't mind at all, really.

Jerry It's … it's a nice day.

Source: Albee, Edward. 1959. *The Zoo Story*. New York: Coward-McCann. pp. 1–2.

Questions to the text

Although both of the above excerpts are largely exposition and the larger conflicts in both plays have not yet been established, what kinds of expectations might already be created for an audience? What aspects in particular suggest such expectations?

Drama

… the first thing to realise when we open a play is that the words in front of us are not designed to function in the same way as the words in a novel or poem. The words are designed to become a performance.

Wallis, Mick & Shepherd, Simon. 2002. *Studying Plays*. London: Arnold.

The quote above may seem obvious but the repercussions run deep. Narrative prose, a novel for instance, addresses a reader directly, offering everything needed to read the entire world of the work. Even as readers may "stage" the events of a novel in their heads, the fictional world is complete. Drama, however, is not. Drama is more like a recipe for a fictional world rather than the completed dish: it lists the ingredients—dialogue, stage directions, breaks and perhaps some stage props—but it asks to be put together through interpretation and, ultimately, performance. In this way, drama may be viewed as a kind of indirect literature that does not offer a reader a completed fictional world but asks readers to consider the relationship between a dramatic text and a dramatic production.

This can be easily forgotten as readers get caught up in the "story" of a play. Reading the one-act play *Trifles* by Susan Glaspell, for instance, it is easy to get caught up in the murder mystery and human conflict and not think about how the play might be performed. We can rush over stage directions and character names, changing typography and the very "scriptness" of a play to see only a story. This is not a bad thing; good playwrights create good stories and good plays are devoured by isolated readers as much as public audiences. But part of the pleasure and excitement of drama is that it offers readers the opportunity to extend their engagement not only in reading a great narrative but in bringing it to life with a fresh and unique interpretation. The main elements of a drama are as follows.

Performance

Viewing the script for a play immediately reveals the difference between drama and literary narrative. Quite simply, you notice a lot of "other" writing like information about the first performance, stage directions, lists of characters and setting that speak most obviously to drama as performance. Some readers may dismiss this as extraneous information but this information actually has a substantial impact on the larger story. It is, at the same time, necessarily distinguished from the dialogue of a play and is certainly different to what you would normally expect to find in literary narrative.

Stage directions

Stage directions can do more than just set the scene, although this is also important. Considering stage directions helps a reader know something of the conventions and conditions common to the time of writing and the play's relationship to those conventions. This, in turn, greatly informs both a literal reading and a larger interpretation. Stage directions can be telling for quite different reasons, including their presence or absence, the frequency with which they occur and the content. Props, costumes and set design can be a part of stage directions and together stage directions form a significant part of a drama that readings and performances can embrace challenge.

Activity

Drama: stage directions

Read through the opening stage directions and stage manager comments from American playwright Thornton Wilder's *Our Town*.

Act I

No curtain. No scenery. The audience, arriving, sees and empty stage in half-light.

Presently the **Stage Manager***, hat on and pipe in mouth, enters and begins placing a table and three chairs downstage left, and a table and three chairs downstage right. He also places a low bench at the corner of what will be the Webb house, left."Left" and "right" are from the point of view of the actor facing the audience."Up" is toward the back wall. As the house lights go down he has finished setting the stage and leaving against the right proscenium pillar watches the late arrivals in the audience.*

When the auditorium is in complete darkness he speaks:

Stage Manager This play is called "Our Town". It was written by Thornton Wilder; produced and directed by A. … (or: produce by A. …; directed by B. …). In it you will see Miss C…; Miss D…; Miss E…; and Mr. F…' Mr. G…' Mr. H …; and many others. The name of the town is Grover's Corners, New Hampshire—just across the Massachusetts line: latitude 42 degrees 40 minutes; longitude 70 degrees 37 minutes. The First Act shows a day in our town. The day is May 7, 1901. The time is just before dawn.

A rooster crows

The sky is beginning to show some streaks of light over in the East there, behind our mount'in. The morning star always gets wonderful bright the minute before it has to go,—doesn't it?

He stares at it for a moment, then goes upstage.

Well, I'd better show you how our town lies. Up here—

That is: parallel with the back wall. is Main Street. Way back there is the railway station; tracks go that way. Polish Town's across the tracks, and some Canuck families.

Toward the left.

Over there is the Congregational Church; across the street's the Presbyterian. Methodist and Unitarian are over there. Baptist is down in the holla' by the river. Catholic Church is over beyond the tracks. Here's the Town Hall and Post Office combined; jail's in the basement.

Bryan once made a speech from these very steps here.

Along here's a row of stores. Hitching posts and horse blocks in front of them. First automobile's going to come along in about five years—belonged to Banker Cartwright, our richest citizen … lives in the big white house up on the hill.

Here's the grocery store and here's Mr. Morgan's drugstore. Most everybody in town manages to look into those two stores once a day.

Public School's over yonder. High School's still farther over. Quarter of nine mornings, noontimes, and three o'clock afternoons, the hull town can hear the yelling and screaming from those schoolyards.

He approaches the table and chairs downstage right.

This is our doctor's house,—Doc Gibbs'. This is the back door.

Two arched trellises, covered with vines and flowers, are pushed out, one by each proscenium pillar.

There's some scenery for those who think they have to have scenery.

This is Mrs. Gibbs' garden. Corn … peas … beans … holly-hocks … heliotrope … and a lot of burdock.

Crosses the stage.

In those days our newspaper come out twice a week—the Grover's Corners *Sentinel*—and this is Editor Webb's house. And this is Mrs. Webb's garden. Just like Mrs. Gibbs', only it's got a lot of sunflowers, too.

He looks upward, centre stage.

Right here …'s a big butternut tree.

He returns to his place by the right proscenium pillar and looks at the audience for a minute.

Nice town, y'know what I mean? Nobody very remarkable ever come out of it, s'far as we know. The earliest tombstones in the cemetery up there on the mountain say 1670–1680—they're Grovers and Cartwrights and Gibbses and Herseys—same names as are around here now.

Well, as I said: it's about dawn. The only lights on in town are in a cottage over by the tracks where a Polish mother's just had twins. And in the Joe Crowell house, where Jo Junior's getting up so as to deliver the paper. And in the depot, where Shorty Hawkins is getting' ready to flat the 5:45 for Boston.

A train whistle is heard. The **Stage Manager** *takes out his watch and nods.*

Source: Wilder, Thornton. 1938. *Our Town*. New York: Perennial Classics, 1998. pp. 3–8.

Questions to the text

1   What effect do the stage directions and stage manager comments have in the way you might approach this play?

2   How do the stage manager comments either connect or challenge you as a reader and/or viewer of the play? Do these seem to be part of the play or "outside" of the play? For what effect might this be done?

Dialogue and character

In a novel, a writer can provide significant background and history that gives a reader a rich idea about characters. Drama faces many more restrictions. Although the stage directions can speak directly to the characters of a play, most of what we learn about characters comes from their speech and interactions with others. Both of these occur primarily through dialogue, sometimes in what a character says, sometimes in what is said about a character and sometimes through dialogue exchanges or comparisons between characters. Unlike dialogue in "real" life (a conversation between two or more people), whether it is an exchange between multiple characters or a lone speech, dialogue in drama is intended to be heard first and foremost by an audience. Even when one character appears to be speaking to another, there is another line of communication open with an audience that is intended to be just as direct.

Activity

Drama: establishing character

Read the following section from Arthur Miller's *Death of a Salesman*. In this scene, Willy Loman and his nephew Bernard—who Willy has always thought of as weaker and less capable than his own son Biff—share an exchange that establishes each character as well as further tensions in the "story."

Light rises, on the right side of the forestage, on a small table in the reception room of Charley's office. Traffic sounds are heard. Bernard, now mature, sits whistling to himself. A pair of tennis rackets and an overnight bag are on the floor beside him.

Willy *(offstage)* What are you walking away for? Don't walk away! If you're going to say something say it to my face! I know you laugh at me behind my back. You'll laugh out of the other side of your goddam face after this game. Touchdown! Touchdown! Eighty thousand people! Touchdown! Right between the goal posts.

Bernard is a quiet, earnest, but self-assured young man. Willy's voice is coming from right upstage now. Bernard lowers his feet off the table and listens. Jenny, his father's secretary, enters.

Jenny *(distressed)* Say, Bernard, will you go out in the hall?

Bernard What is that noise? Who is it?

Jenny Mr. Loman. He just got off the elevator.

Bernard *(getting up)* Who's he arguing with?

Jenny Nobody. There's nobody with him. I can't deal with him anymore, and your father gets all upset everytime he comes. I've got a lot of typing to do, and your father's waiting to sign it. Will you see him?

Willy *(entering)* Touchdown! Touch— *(He sees Jenny.)* Jenny, Jenny, good to see you. How're ya? Workin'? or still honest?

Jenny Fine. How've you been feeling?

Willy Not much any more, Jenny. Ha, ha! *(He is surprised to see the rackets.)*

Bernard Hello, Uncle Willy.

Willy *(almost shocked)* Bernard! Well, look who's here! *(He comes quickly, guiltily, to Bernard and warmly shakes his hand.)*

Bernard How are you? Good to see you.

Willy What are you doing here?

Bernard Oh, just stopped by to see Pop. Get off my feet till my train leaves. I'm going to Washington in a few minutes.

Willy Is he in?

Bernard Yes, he's in his office with the accountant. Sit down.

Willy *(sitting down)* What're you going to do in Washington?

Bernard Oh, just a case I've got there, Willy.

Willy That so? *(indicating the rackets.)* You going to play tennis there?

Bernard I'm staying with a friend who's got a court.

Willy Don't say. His own tennis court. Must be fine people, I bet.

Bernard They are, very nice. Dad tells me Biff's in town.

Willy *(with a big smile)*: Yeah, Biff's in. Working on a very big deal, Bernard.

Bernard What's Biff doing?

Willy Well, he's been doing very big things in the West. But he decided to establish himself here. Very big. We're having dinner. Did I hear your wife had a boy.

Bernard That's right. Our second.

Willy Two boys! What do you know?

Bernard What kind of deal has Biff got?

Willy Well, Bill Oliver—very big sporting-goods man—he wants Biff very badly. Called him in from the West. Long distance, carte blanche, special deliveries. Your friends have their own private tennis court?

Bernard You still with the old firm, Willy?

Willy (after a pause) I'm—I'm overjoyed to see how you made the grade, Bernard, overjoyed. It's an encouraging thing to see a young man really—really—Looks very good for Biff—very— (He breaks off, then.) Bernard— (He is so full of emotion, he breaks off again.)

Bernard What is it, Willy?

Willy (small and alone): What—what's the secret?

Bernard What secret?

Willy How—how did you? Why didn't he ever catch on?

Bernard I wouldn't know that, Willy.

Willy (confidentially, desperately) You were his friend, his boyhood friend. There's something I don't understand about it. His life ended after that Ebbets Field game. From the age of seventeen nothing good ever happened to him.

Bernard He never trained himself for anything.

Willy But he did, he did. After high school he took so many correspondence courses. Radio mechanics, television; God knows what, and never made the slightest mark.

Bernard (taking off his glasses) Willy, do you want to talk candidly?

Willy (rising, faces Bernard) I regard you as a very brilliant man, Bernard. I value your advice.

Bernard Oh, the hell with the advice, Willy, I couldn't advice you. There's just one thing I've always wanted to ask you. When he was supposed to graduate, and the math teacher flunked him—

Willy Oh, that son-of-a-bitch ruined his life.

Bernard Yeah, but, Willy, all he had to do was go to summer school and make up that subject.

Willy That's right, that's right.

Bernard Did you tell him not to go to summer school?

Willy Me? I begged him to go. I ordered him to go!

Bernard Then why wouldn't he go?

Willy Why? Why! Bernard, that question has been trailing me like a ghost for the last fifteen years. He flunked the subject, and laid down and died like a hammer hit him!

Bernard Take it easy, kid.

Willy Let me talk to you—I got nobody to talk to. Bernard, Bernard, was it my fault? Y'see? It keeps going around in my mind, maybe I did something to him. I got nothing to give him.

Bernard Don't take it so hard.

Willy Why did he lay down? What is the story there? You were his friend!

Bernard Willy, I remember, it was June, and our grades came out. And he'd flunked math.

Willy That son-of-a-bitch.

Bernard No, it wasn't right then. Biff just got very angry, I remember, and he was ready to enrol in summer school.

Willy (surprised) He was?

Bernard He wasn't beaten by it at all. But then, Willy, he disappeared from the block for almost a month. And I got the idea that he'd gone up to New England to see you. Did he have a talk with you then?

Willy stares in silence.

Bernard Willy?

Willy (with a strong edge of resentment in his voice) Yeah, he came to Boston. What about it?

Bernard Well, just that when he came back—I'll never forget this, it always mystifies me. Because I'd though so well of Biff, even though he'd always taken advantage of me. I loved him, Willy, y'know? And he came back after that month and took his sneakers—remember those sneakers with "University of Virginia" print on them? He was so proud of those, wore them every day. And he took them down in the cellar, and burned them up in the furnace. We had a first fight. It lasted at least half an hour. Just the two of us, punching each other down in the cellar, and crying right through it. I've often thought of how strange it was that I knew he'd given up his life. What happened in Boston, Willy?

Willy looks at him as at an intruder.

Bernard I just bring it up because you asked me.

Willy (angrily) Nothing. What do you mean, "What happened?" What's that got to do with anything?

Bernard Well, don't get sore.

Willy What are you trying to do, blame it on me? If a boy lays down is that my fault?

Bernard Now, Willy, don't get—

Willy Well don't—don't talk to me that way! What does that mean, What happened?"

Source: Miller, Arthur. 1949. *Death of a Salesman*. New York: Viking Compass, 1971. pp. 90–94.

Questions to the text

1 How does dialogue work to create the characters of Willy and Bernard in this exchange?

2 How does the exchange between Willy and Bernard reveal aspects of Biff's character?

3 What kinds of ideas or "communications" seem to be intended for an audience that arise out of the dialogue between Willy and Bernard? How is the audience intended to experience the characters?

Soliloquy and aside

Revealing a character's internal thoughts and feelings could be problematic to manage if it had to always be delivered as an exchange of dialogue on the stage. The unique dramatic convention of the soliloquy and the aside is an important characteristic of staged drama, as it allows a playwright to navigate the limits of the genre. Very simply, an aside is defined as a convention whereby an actor addresses the audience directly to reveal inner thoughts and feelings. The aside is intended to be a private exchange between actor and audience and understood to be secret or unshared with other characters in the play. An aside is spoken when other characters are on stage and is rather like a whisper or a comment made to oneself in order to be heard by the audience but not by others on stage.

A soliloquy is a kind of aside but is spoken when a character is on stage alone, or at least believes they are alone. A soliloquy usually intends to reveal even more honesty of feeling or thought on the part of a character by virtue of its staging as a character safely buffeted from the attitudes, influences and judgments of other actors.

Activity

Drama: the speech

Consider the following speeches from Shakespeare's *Othello* and Margaret Edson's contemporary play *Wit*. Although all three examples are a form of soliloquy, the styles vary greatly.

Text 1

In this speech, the villain Iago admits to the audience his intentions to deceive Othello (the Moor). How are poetic language, contrast and dramatic irony employed to create heightened tension in the speech?

Roderigo I'll sell all my land. (*He exits.*)

Iago

> Thus I do ever make my fool my purse.
> For I mine own gained knowledge such profane
> If I would time expend with such (a) snipe
> But for my sport and profit. I hat ethe Moor,
> And it is thought abroad that 'twixt my sheets
> Has done my office. I know not if't be true,
> But I, for mere suspicion in that kind,
>
> Will do as if for surety. He holds me well.
> The better shall my purpose work on him.
> Cassio's a proper man. Let me see now:

> To get his place and to plume up my will
> In double knavery—How? how?—Let's see.
> After some time, to abuse Othello's (ear)
> That he is too familiar with his wife.
> He hath a person and a smooth dispose
> To be suspected, framed to make women false.
> The Moor is of a free and open nature
> That thinks men honest that but seem to be so,
> And will as tenderly be led by th' nose
> As asses are.
> I have't. It is engendered. Hell and night
> Must bring this monstrous birth to the world's light.
> (*He exits.*)

Source: Shakespeare, William. 1603. *Othello*. New York: Washington Square Press. 1993. Act I. Scene iii. pp. 426–47.

Text 2

In this speech, Iago continues to enact his plans for bringing Othello to ruin, but this speech does so through legitimate "honest" counsel (he has persuaded Cassio, Othello's wrongly-accused friend, to appeal to Othello's wife, Desdemona, for character support). Once again, he makes clear his intentions (although only to the audience) and once again, does so through juxtaposing opposites. How are language, contrast and dramatic irony use here to create heightened tension and how is it different from the previous speech?

Cassio Good night, honest Iago. (*Cassio exits.*)

Iago

> And what's he, then, that says I play the villain,
> When this advice is free I give and honest,
> Probal to thinking, and indeed the course
> To win the Moore again? For 'tis most easy
> Th' inclining Desdemona to subdue
> In any honest suit. She's framed as fruitful
> As the free elements. And then for her
> To win the Moor—(were't) to renounce his baptism,
> All seals and symbols of redeemed sin—
> His soul is so enfettered to her love
> That she make make, unmake, do what she list,
> Even as her appetite shall play the god
> With his weak function. How am I then a villain
> To counsel Cassio to this parallel course
> Directly to his good? Divinity of hell
> When devils will the blackest sins put on
> The do suggest at first with heavenly show,
> As I do now. For whiles this honest food
> Plies Desdemona to repair his fortune,
> And she for him pleads strongly to the Moor,
> I'll pour this pestilence into his ear
> That she repeals him for her body's lust,
> And by how much she strives to do him good,
> She shall undo her credit with the Moor.
> So will I turn her virtue into pitch,
> And out of her own goodness make the net
> That shall enmesh them all.

> **Source:** Shakespeare, William. 1603. *Othello*. New York: Washington Square Press. 1993. Act II. Scene iii. pp. 356–82.

Text 3

Margaret Edson's play *Wit* concerns a renowned and demanding professor of English grappling with cancer. Through frequent use of soliloquy/monologue (there are occasionally nurses on stage but they are unhearing of Vivian's speech), we watch as Dr. Bearing struggles to analyze and understand her disease as she would the poetry of John Donne.

Vivian (*Hesitantly.*)

> I should have asked more questions, because I know there's going to be a test.

> I have cancer, insidious cancer, with pernicious side effects—No, the *treatment* has pernicious side effects. I have stage-four metastatic ovarian cancer. There is no stage five. Oh, and I have to be very tough. It appears to be a matter, as the saying goes, of life and death.

I know all about life and death. I am, after all, a scholar of Donne's Holy Sonnets, which explore mortality in greater depth than any other body of work in the English language.

And I know for a fact that I am tough. A demanding professor. Uncompromising. Never one to turn from a challenge. That is why I chose, while a students of the great E. M. Ashford, to study Donne. (*Professor E. M. Ashford, fifty-two, enters, seated at the same desk as Kelekian was. The scene is twenty-eight years ago. Vivian suddenly turns twenty-two, eager and intimidated.*)

Professor Ashford?

The scholarly study of poetic texts requires a capacity for scrupulously detailed examination, particularly the poetry of John Donne. The salient characteristic of the poems is wit: "Itchy outbreaks of far-fetched wit," as Donne himself said.

To the common reader—that is to say, the undergraduate with a B-plus or better average—wit provides an invaluable exercise for sharpening the mental faculties, for stimulating the flash of comprehension that can only follow hours of exacting and seemingly pointless scrutiny. (*Technician 3 puts Vivian back in the wheelchair and wheels her toward the unit. Partway, Technician 3 gives the chair a shove and Susie takes over. Susie rolls Vivian to the exam room.*)

To the scholar, to the mind comprehensively trained in the subtleties of seventeenth-century vocabulary, versification, and theological, historical, geographical, political, and mythological allusions, Donne's wit is … a way to see how good you really are.

After twenty years, I can say with confidence, no one is quite as good as I. (*By now, Susie has helped Vivian sit on the exam table. Dr. Jason, Posner, clinical fellow, stands in the doorway.*)

> **Source:** Edson, Margaret. 1993. *Wit*. New York: Dramatists Play Service, Inc. 1999. pp. 13, 18.

Questions to the text

1 How does this speech address different audiences at different times and to what effect?

2 How does this soliloquy function as the concluding lines of the play? What effect does it have to end with a soliloquy? Does this final speech seem to "close" the play neatly or leave some confusion and uncertainty? Does this fit with the style of the soliloquy in general?

Plot and action

Unlike plot in narrative, plot in drama is generally free from chronological considerations. Time is less important in drama than action. Action, however, needs to be more fully understood than simply a physical event. In some plays, for instance Samuel Beckett's *Waiting for Godot*, many argue that nothing happens but even in this play with its famous last lines ("let's go, let's go, they do not go") there is plenty of action.

Plot and action in drama are more about movement that occurs via conflict, opposition and difference. Characters either experience events or perform physical or verbal actions that create tension and crises that must be explored, resolved or overcome. Interestingly, these tensions and crises may be on stage between actors or beyond the stage between the actor and audience, and the play and society. But plot and action in drama, unlike in prose, is about movement from episode to episode via conflict of one sort or another. Drama uses debate to maintain its dynamism.

Activity

Drama: the shape of action

With drama, many people talk about the "shape" of the action, which is like the diagrams mentioned earlier that attempt to map plot and geography in a novel. The shape of action can be as simple as two characters colliding before finding resolution (probably a simple triangular shape) but will more often involve multiple conflicts and, perhaps, multiple resolutions during the course of a play. Because of this, fewer critics use fixed systems such as Freytag's pyramid , even though aspects such as exposition, initial conflict, rising conflict, climax and resolution are very often found in drama.

As an exercise, try sketching a diagram of the plot and action of a play, television show or film with which you are familiar or are currently studying. How does the diagram enhance your understanding of the work?

Tragedy and comedy

The familiar symbols of drama are the twin masks of tragedy and comedy that supposedly encompass all of the possible stories to come out of the theatre, and by extension, human experience. These are powerful modes and do indeed play a role in all narrative produced, but perhaps as much through their interconnectedness as their distinctions. For the sake of simplicity, tragedy and comedy are distinctly defined genres, but in reality these modes sit together in a common continuum that overlaps, intertwines and is generally more complex than is often recognized.

Along this spectrum, tragedy is where things end badly and comedy is where things end well. With the former, a character often falls against great odds as a result of some inherent flaw and we are sad or afraid to see it; while, with the latter, we simply laugh (although, a character, is not usually entirely brought down by ridicule). But from such simplistic distinctions a great deal of complexity can arise. Friedrich Nietzsche viewed tragedy as the most noble human aspiration: to be aware of our own mortal limitations and still strive to overcome them is both flaw (because impossible, and only the most arrogant would believe they could overcome mortality) and worthy of celebration (although, ultimately, always viewed as tragic). On the other hand, the film director Quentin Tarantino has made a career of getting viewers to laugh during the most horrific, violent and sorrowful events that might involve murder, abuse, drug overdose and petty crime.

251

What is clearer than a distinction between tragedy and comedy is that these modes continue to inform not just drama but all of life.

Space

A final element of drama is the significance and use of space in a play. Although space is obviously a component of stage direction, spacing can communicate unique ideas about a drama. It can occur in multiple ways in a drama including the following:

- **Setting on the stage** The space can be an interior room or an entire landscape. It can involve movement through set changes or a static quality without change. This might also occur through lighting.

- **Space between actors** The kinesthetic movements of actors obviously affect space which communicates ideas. Do actors cross barriers of space physically or verbally? What effect does this have?

- **Space between the stage and an audience** This is known as a "fourth wall" and is the partition that separates actors as characters in a play from actors and performers. What kinds of barrier this is or ways (even the lighting that is dimmed in a theatre but for that on stage may contribute to this) that the barrier is overcome will communicate different ideas.

As with the shape of the action described above, the use of space is frequently best understood when diagrammed. To consider its implications, you could try sketching a diagram of the uses of space in a play, television show or film with which you are familiar or are currently studying. How does the diagram enhance your understanding of the work?

Conclusion

In the beginning of this chapter, we noted that recognizing patterns can aid the study of literature. To read closely while paying attention to potential patterns, forms and techniques specific to the different genres and the craft of writing, as highlighted above, certainly will make you a better student of literature. But many students continue to wonder why this kind of formal study might be valuable at all or why it isn't all "just a waste of time."

"What about the overriding value of the aesthetic encounter," you might ask? "What about just reading for pleasure." Or, even for information, like the setting and period being discussed? All of these motivations, and many more, are appropriate too. But in the context of this book, the strongest value for studying literature is the heightened attention to the intentional use of language both as a producer and as a consumer. Learning to value your own responses through encounters with literary texts as well as striving for more authoritative readings that consider genre, intention and context will not only enhance the values of literature but provide useful communication skills in your encounters with all language. As this book suggests, language is everywhere. If nothing else, then, practice and expertise with the pleasurable, complex, challenging and rewarding uses of language that make up literature will certainly help you be prepared to explore language and its place in communicative acts of any sort and mode.

Assessment in literature: critical study

This chapter focuses on assessment in literature: critical study, but many of the activities could apply across other parts of the course. While it is hoped that these examples and ideas might provide some support for your own activities and assessments, you should aim to approach these examples critically: They are not perfect but represent interesting approaches, some strengths and some weaknesses. Look closely at the examples and work to recognize what you find to be positives on which to build and negatives to avoid. Ultimately, you will want to develop that critical perspective in your approach to the different texts in this course, as well as in your own work and future reading.

Written task 1

For this section of the course you will be writing another written task 1. Remember that in this task you have several options for choosing an appropriate topic and text type. Of course, for this particular task, you must attempt to demonstrate you understanding of a work of literature from part 4 of the course. For details about the rules of the assignment and the way in which it is marked, refer to the written task 1 section of chapter 5. Although the focus here is on the study of literature, the written task itself does not have to model a literary genre. While you may decide to produce something literary such as a short story in response to a poem you have read, you may just as well write a newspaper book review or an editorial about important issues raised in a novel.

Warm-up activities

There is never a time in school when you should undertake a major assessment without having practiced or attempted to master the many skills necessary for success. Sometimes these warm-up activities do not involve simply writing model assessments or complete works. Instead, focused exercises that help us master component parts of a large assessment can be just as valuable in the long run. You may want to try some of the following activities at any point during your study of this section of the course in order to prepare for the formal written task ahead:

- **Record your process** We never come to a final analysis of a text from only one reading. At the same time, after several readings of a text and discussions in class, we sometimes forget the mental process we have gone through to make meaning. One way to focus your attention on important aspects of a text is to try to record how you have become a more experienced reader of the text. For example, you may write a brief journal entry about your initial impressions of a text. What was confusing? What were your initial thoughts about the meaning of the text? What did you simply "get wrong?" Write a second entry that describes how you answered some of these questions or how you came to see the text in a different light. Finally, write a brief entry that discusses the meaning and significance of the text. This process is a way of focusing your attention on the complexity of a work and, perhaps, the elements that may be interesting to develop as part of a written task 1 and share with another reader.

- **Writing about ideas** Have you ever sat in class during a discussion and suddenly thought that you had something urgent to share? Maybe you had an interesting response to something a classmate suggested, a sudden idea or an additional point to add? But before you could share your thoughts, someone else spoke, the class ended or the conversation moved on. Don't let your ideas go to waste! When you have such an experience— and these are probably more common than believed—make sure you find an opportunity to record your thoughts for further development. During a free moment or at home later in the day, write down your ideas and spend some time free-writing thoughts. This will not only help you remember and solidify your thoughts about a text, but will give you practice with recording your thoughts about literature in writing and develop a repertoire of ideas for later use with the written task.

- **Thinking about text types** Practice text types by imitating text types and genres you study or by taking an idea from one text type and rewriting as another text type. This will help you with your writing but will also help you consider the importance of genre and the particular aspects of different genres that you may want to highlight in a written task. Are you in a band? Write a song based on parts of a novel that you have found interesting. Go ahead and produce an entire album based on the poems of an author you have studied. Do you enjoy drawing? Create a graphic novel, using image and text, detailing the episodes of a set of short stories you are reading.

Marking criteria

Before reading the sample of the written task below, it is worth revisiting how you will be assessed. Again, for more detailed information refer to the written task section in chapter 5 but for now, keep in mind that you will be assessed in relation to how well your rationale explains your intentions, your understanding of the primary work and the appropriateness of the task chosen, the organization of your task, and the effectiveness of your language.

Student sample

For literature: critical study, there are many written task 1 possibilities with which to explore literary works. The following student sample is based on a reading and interpretation of several Edgar Allan Poe short stories. This particular example chooses to explore the style of Poe and, in particular, the significance of the narrative perspective in creating both the psychological tension and the focus of the plot.

Rationale In many Edgar Allan Poe Stories, such as "The Black Cat," "The Cask of the Amontillado," and "The Tell Tale Heart" a dark and very isolated narrator is featured as the main character. But more importantly these narrators possess warped minds and certain abnormalities that propel the story forward. But it is important to take note of the fact that Poe doesn't portray an inanely abnormal and confused narrator but rather a narrator who at one point was a normal person but *has become* irrational and obsessive under circumstances that he has amplified or overreacted to. Furthermore once this overreaction has taken place the narrator often has second thoughts as to why he may have overreacted or why he should continue with his evil deed. Or he sometimes tries to place the blame on someone else for his own abnormalities and quirks.

A succinct opening discussion.

This is best displayed in the story of "The Tell Tale Heart" where the narrator becomes scared of his master's "vulture eye" and uses this as an excuse to kill him even though his master does nothing whatsoever to incite this motive. He then regrets his decision when he "hears" his master's beating heart from underneath the floor board when the police arrive and this causes him to crack. This same chain events occurs in the "The Cask of Amontillado" where Montressor [narrator] is bent on seeking revenge on Fortunato for some reason, which is strange because it could not have been such a huge reason that Fortunato would not know of it in the first place. And when Montressor finally does chain Fortunato in his cellar he begins to have pangs of guilt as he laying the brick wall foundation, when Fortunato stops responding to his taunts.

Although, this pastiche will try to recreate this story format it will not adhere strictly to it, because the objective of this pastiche is to recreate the archetypal narrator that Poe has shown in many of his stories. This is because often in many Poe stories it is not the narrator who is in the story but actually the story which is in the narrator.

Good literary focus to your task.

Written task 1

"Sire!" "Sire!" the cry came. My ears and eyes were not working in coordination as my head spun in circles. I needn't looked further as a body collapsed at my feet. The man staring back at me was one I didn't recognize. His mangled body, glassy eyes and the bloody gash beneath his right eye looked like a man robbed of life. The truth was I had robbed Brooks. But it wasn't my fault. It was that silvery creature that drove me to this state. Oh how I craved for the blood of that vicious creature. The very fluid that fueled that creature was the very same that I thirsted for. In a single day that beast reduced me from what took me a lifetime to capture. For twelve hours luck alone had saved its wretched life.

You have a recognizable style and tone here but you still have to be careful about grammar/syntax.

I am a hunter you see. Not just any hunter, but the very best. Even before I could scribe, my begetter guided the young fledgling I was into the matured assassin that had snared every unreasonable creature from the rainforests of the Amazon to the jungles of Rhodesia. I was

We are getting into the story here but again you should be careful of language use.

relishing the thought of disappearing into comfort only enjoyed by the satisfied folk when I was nauseated by thought of inadequacy in my unfulfilled supremacy. The tale of the white tiger penetrated my mind and failed to exit, for it was an undiscriminating man-eater. But I am no man, so I resolved to hang its hide above my fireplace. Hurriedly I phoned Brooks, who too was onto greater things. His exuberance towards the matter was not on par with mine, but he nevertheless agreed simply out of favor for his trap-shooting teacher.

You may need to give us more details from the start or offer a bit more of a hint of the narrator's particular "problem."

Here I lay staring at the hazy sky and blistering sun penetrating through the tree tops, emasculated and alone. But the battle was not over yet, Brooks was no more but his sacrifice had not gone in vain. I had taken what was more valuable to it than my flesh. I glanced inside his partially torn rucksack. And there it was sound asleep, the cub of the beast. A horrible idea crossed my vulnerable mind. Sliding my palm into the sheath hanging beside my waist, I retrieved my jackknife. The power that lay in my palm was realized when the light from the sun accented the blade's fine grooves which was clean of the viscous blood I so desired. I angled the blade and accelerated its descent towards the awaiting target, when I suddenly stopped. The offspring wasn't my fight; its death would not satisfy the hunger of my revenge of the humiliation the beast caused upon me. I sat up, slung the rucksack over my shoulder and sprinted through the dense jungle towards the tiger's cave. Brooks wouldn't have wanted it this way, but it was I and I alone who now made the decisions. Brooks, what a clever rogue, I thought to myself as I ran.

A bit too much of a confusing leap in this paragraph. I think you are getting some of the tone correct but is this all a Poe narrator would do? To whom is this narrator speaking, for example?

"Sire, are you sure we shouldn't take rest," Brooks said as we trekked through the vast jungle.

"Nonsense, Brooks I didn't spend six months on the tug to rest," I had said walking ahead.

"Nevertheless sire there is no point in beginning our hunt today," he replied. "The tiger could be anywhere in this vast jungle."

"That's where you are mistaken my boy," I said curtly. "Every creature needs water." From the look on Brooks' face, he knew I would forever be his teacher. He understood we were to find the tiger today itself.

Good use of dialogue.

"Sire, there is a river bank about 2 kilometers north where the Yamuna drains," he suggested. "We could intercept him there." I slyly smiled at him and nodded my head. This was the answer I was looking for and so we set off. Upon arriving at the bank, it appeared quite peaceful and devoid of animal life. I unhooked my rifle and held it ready. An hour passed. Two hours passed. Three hours passed. Brooks' expression exhibited frustration, while I remained calm. Eventually the feline emerged from the thick shrubbery on the opposite bank. Alas the moment I had been waiting for had arrived. I lifted his rifle motioned for Brooks to lift his rifle and to begin the count. One, I encircled the tiger. Two, I clicked the hammer and placed my hand on the trigger. Just as Brooks had said three the jungle cat lifted its head and glared directly at me. Its eyes pierced my very inner being that the chill it sent down my spine sent my shot off-balanced. Fortunately Brooks' bullet had grazed the tree above the tiger's head and missing his target by mere inches. Watching the tiger flee I grew enraged at my sudden inability. The protégé had surpassed the teacher. How could I have let this happen? I thought to myself. I snatched Brooks' opportunity as his hands no longer deserved it. "Leave, I shouted, and don't come back until you can prove your worth." I snarled at him. Brooks gave me a look of disbelief and left, I soon regretted those words as it was the last moment I saw him … alive.

Do you want to do more with this earlier? If the actions of Brooks damage the narrator's ego, perhaps you want to let us in on this or show us how clever or infuriating Brooks can be.

I ran to the river bank, the mud still imprinted with the tiger's tracks. Diligently I retraced the savage's footprints to his lair. Oh with such diligence! The entrance to the tiger's cave said enough as there were footprints leading into the cave, but not a single one coming out. I withdrew my torch and proceeded into what could seal my fate. Hearing the progressive volume of the growls, I walked deeper and deeper into the cave. And lo and behold there was no beast at the end of the cave. Puzzled I spun around and saw the beast perched on an elevated ledge of the cave. Instinctively, I placed the rucksack on the floor, and the cub that had by now awoken climbed out and scurried to his mother. I inched towards my pistol, but the cunning feline was anticipating this move, and leaped on its enemy. The impact sent me sprawling ten meters and the pistol even further. The beast then walked around me in circles, while I helplessly watched on all fours. Seeing my vulnerability the tiger leapt towards me, at which I pulled the jackknife and plunged it in its neck. The savage's face turned from anger to pain to motionless and keeled over. I sighed as the dark red blood spewed from its neck and formed a puddle. Impulsively, I scooped a handful and drank it. It tasted of jealousy and betrayal.

You are going to need to clarify a bit here. Not exactly sure why this would be Brooks. Again I think you need to build some tension between the two.

Examiner comments

There are several strengths with this pastiche even if not a perfect paper overall. The rationale is quite good recognizing several aspects of Poe's writing and taking an interesting approach to the task. The focus on a narrator is a strong point and the candidate conveys understanding of the works studied.

The pastiche itself starts off equally strong. The candidate does quite a nice job capturing the style of Poe. The narrative perspective is certainly in the style of Poe and this mimics his larger style while being something far more unique than the more typical gothic environment in which most Poe stories mentioned take place. The candidate does a nice job building tension subtly and shifting tension from outside or environmental factors toward internal perspectives. The language can sometimes read as overdone or overstylized but does capture a style and mood common with Poe.

Probably the area for improvement is with the resolution of the story. Admittedly, this can read like Poe and his somewhat abrupt conclusions but there is some confusion in the end. I am not quite sure of the tension between the narrator and Brooks and the ultimate jealousy remains a little elusive (as does the foreboding line of not seeing Brooks again alive). Still, the candidate does a very good job building tension that is psychological as much as anything else and this does convey an interesting approach to these works while also demonstrating understanding and interpretation.

Suggestions for topics

Topics to explore in written task 1 for this part of the course will be largely determined by the particular literary works studied in your school. Certain tasks will be better suited to particular genres. Beyond this, you are free to explore a wide array of elements related to the literary works in your study. You may choose to explore a cultural aspect of the text, or use the writer as a particular reference point. Alternatively, you could focus on different critical receptions, a thematic issue or stylistic aspects. Much of your exploration will be tied to what you study in your class and topics will be made in consultation with your teachers. For this part of the course, you are not asked to write a critical, persuasive essay but to engage more creatively (also as a means of demonstrating your knowledge) in a competent manipulation of different text types.

Deciding on a particular text type, then, may be a challenge. You will want to select a text type that is of interest to you but also that makes sense in relation to the topic selected. You will need to articulate why you have selected a particular text type and then demonstrate mastery of the type in performance.

A brief list of potential written task 1 text types useful for this part of the course includes the following:

- An exchange of letters between characters in a literary work articulating their beliefs about and approach to a central problem in the work.
- A multimodal digital project that traces and highlights complex narrative trajectories.
- An imaginary interview with the author of a literary work regarding its adaptation as a movie.
- A critical review of a performance of a text.
- An editorial letter objecting to critiques of a work and arguing for its artistic or aesthetic merits.
- An additional scene, chapter or stanza drawing more particular attention to an important aspect of the larger literary work.

Written task 2 (higher level)

As we have noted in earlier assessment chapters, at higher level you will be asked to produce a written task 2. This task is a critical essay based on questions that we will repeat below. Keep in mind that the assignment is meant to be a formal essay in which you consider the questions, analyze the text you have studied in relation to the questions, and support your idea with evidence from the text. As always, you should attempt to write a clear, well-organized discussion based on your consideration of the question. For specific details about the rules and the marking criteria for this task, refer to chapter 7 of this course companion. Remember that written task 2 must address a particular question that is reproduced in the course guide. You will find those questions as well in chapter 7.

Warm-up activities

While any practice with writing will help you to produce a well-organized and clearly written piece, you should also be attentive to the analysis and pointed response called for in written task 2. Much of your time in class is taken up with the practice of analysis. Any time you engage in a class discussion or listen to a teacher's or classmate's ideas about a text, you are working your way toward analysis. At the same time, the progression from fleeting thoughts about a text or confused ideas to a well formulated response does not necessarily come naturally. A little pointed practice in writing a literary response will help you to clarify your own thinking about a text and help you in making written arguments. Try any of the following activities:

- **Answer questions** As an exercise you can consider any of the questions posed for written task 2. It is important, though, to take another step: write at least a paragraph in response to the question and try to include at least one quotation from the text in your discussion. Forcing yourself to answer a question in writing helps you to clarify your thinking while giving you writing practice at the same time. Another idea is to make up questions about the text on your own. Again, push yourself further and write an answer to these questions. As you begin thinking about the formal completion of written task 2 you may find that your short writing exercises lead to further brainstorming, planning, and a well-argued draft.

- **Write a short commentary** A commentary, much like the comparative analysis you will do on paper 1 of the exam, is a piece of writing that describes and discusses the significance of a short text selection. In order to focus your attention to the important details of a literary work you can choose a short section of text (the opening page, the end of a chapter, a key moment), take notes on the selection, and then write a brief piece discussing why the extract is interesting. Your writing should take into account what the text means, what it suggests, and how it is written. This kind of close attention will help you to keep a literary focus in your written task and will give you needed practice in writing about literature.

- **Make a chart** When reading a novel, play, or even a collection of poems, you may find it useful to keep a record of the ideas, issues, characters, events and literary features that you encounter while reading. It is not unusual to study a work for four to five works and keeping a record of interesting points you have noticed can come in handy when preparing for your written task. First, you could look at the questions for the task. One chart might keep track of short extracts from your text that may relate to one of the questions. In a second column you could jot down your ideas about what the extract suggests or why it is interesting. Another type of chart could track interesting aspects of a character. In another column you could suggest how the thoughts and actions of the character are relevant to a particular question. In the end, simply noting and recording elements that you find interesting can help you to deepen and then organize your thinking so that your final assessment piece gives evidence of a developed, personal response.

Student sample

In this sample approach, a student has decided to explore question 2 under **Power and privilege** ("Which social groups are marginalized, excluded or silenced within the text?") in reference to William Faulkner's *Absalom, Absalom!* This is not a complete sample, but it shows the students initial planning processes that will eventually give rise to a written task—it is this kind of pre-writing and thinking process that can be valuable for not just written task 2 but all of your asessment tasks.

Complete samples of student work with written task 2 can be found in chapter 7 (Assessment in language and mass communication) and chapter 9 (Assessment in text and context).

Student notes: free writing

This has been a very hard book to read but in class we have discuss many issues that make it interesting and make it a good fit for w.t.2. I could actually write on any of the six questions and there is a lot to discuss with the different voices and mix of fact and fiction as well as appeal to other texts like the Old Testament.

I think some of these ideas would be interesting but I also think they could be difficult to discuss in only a short essay. What is really interesting is the emotional feelings that change around Charles. Thomas Sutpen is not very likeable so his reactions to Charles are sort of understandable. When Henry leaves his father and joins Charles in the war, I felt like I could understand his fighting against his father's wishes. There is always the threat of race with Charles and his mother being from Haiti but it remains below the surface. When Henry comes back after the war and his father tells him that Charles is part black, it is interesting and sad that Henry reacts as his father would wish. Even though Thomas is guilty of miscegenation, this is such a powerful "crime" that the white people will do almost anything to prevent it.

It can be kind of obvious that the miscegenation shows the exclusion and silencing of the blacks in the American South of this time period. But the more interesting aspect is the result. "Purity" is totally absent just like truth even though everyone is so keen to chase after it. But the exclusion of blacks and miscegenation in particular in the Sutpen family is not just the story of marginalizing others but ultimately of destroying themselves. I think in this written task, I will show the miscegenation but focus on how this ultimately leads to the destruction of the Sutpens themselves.

Student outline

1 Introduction

   a The question

   b The approach

2 Miscegenation of Thomas excludes population

   a Initially leads to split between father and son(s)

      i Thomas and Henry (and Charles)

      ii Henry and Charles are in Civil War in more ways than one—excludes black but also own sons

3 Miscegenation is larger emotional issue

   a Henry turns against Charles when he knows about his mother

   b Race is greater than family or truth—a focus on race destroys everyone

4 Destruction of Charles is Henry's ruin (and Thomas')

5 Conclusion

   a Miscegenation excludes the (Bons) black but also destroys the Sutpens (whites)

   b This is all one family

Individual oral commentary

What is it?

The individual oral commentary is an opportunity for students to demonstrate detailed and sophisticated understanding and interpretation of a literary work. The individual oral commentary is a highly formal assessment task where you will receive a short excerpt—approximately 40 lines—from one of the literary works in this part of the course and with a limited amount of preparation, offer a detailed commentary of that excerpt lasting approximately 15 minutes. The primary focus of the individual oral commentary is on close analysis of language, literary features and any other formal elements, arguing precisely how the language used gives rise to significant effects and/or ideas. Individual oral commentaries are recorded for external moderation and the excerpts selected may come from any of the works you study in this part of the course.

What are the rules?

- Excerpts for you individual oral commentary are approximately 40 lines in length and may be selected from any of the works studied. If the work is poetry, excerpts will be one complete poem whenever possible. Excerpts will not be known to students before the individual oral commentary begins.

- Students receive their excerpts and have 20 minutes of supervised preparation time. You may annotate or make notes on your excerpts or even note key points. But you are not to prepare a complete body or work to be read during the commentary.

- Excerpts will include guiding questions. The questions are to assist students as needed but should not form the totality of the commentary. A student who only responds to the guiding questions will not offer a complete commentary.

- After completing the 20 minutes of preparation, students deliver approximately 10 minutes of commentary which is recorded. Commentaries are delivered in front of the teacher only. Teachers will follow up with further questions to help complete or "round-out" the commentary lasting approximately 5 minutes.

- Individual oral commentaries are formal and should be both organized and delivered with as much care as possible. Although there is an element of the impromptu, all works should be familiar to students and it is expected that part of the 20 minute preparation time is dedicated to organizing thoughts and responses.

- Individual oral commentaries are submitted for external moderation.

When is it done?

As a highly formal activity, the individual oral commentary will come at the conclusion of your study in this part of the course. However, you will probably get to perform several "practice" individual oral commentaries under far less formal conditions. Unlike previous oral activities, the individual oral commentary is unique to this part of the course. Literature: critical study, will not necessarily be studied last in the language and literature course nor will it necessarily be studied uninterruptedly; these details will be specific to your school and your classroom.

How is it marked?

Very simply, there are four criteria used to assess the individual oral commentary: knowledge and understanding of the text(s) and subject matter, understanding of how language is used, organization and language and style.

- **Knowledge and understanding of the text or extract**
  Does the commentary adequately convey knowledge and understanding of the work referred to and its larger meaning or significance?

- **Understanding of the use and effects of literary features**
  Does the commentary demonstrate awareness of significant contributions of different literary features? Does the commentary convey such awareness through detailed examples of the way language and style are used to create meaning and/or effect?

- **Organization and argument** Is the structure and organization coherent and sustained?

- **Language and style** Is the use of language effective and appropriate to formal literary commentary?

As with any assessment task, whether formative or summative, examiners are looking for a strong sense of understanding of the work or topic and a thoughtful critical engagement. While meeting the course objectives, this should also reinforce with confidence, your own unique personal style of presentation and analysis.

How should I approach this task?

One of the biggest errors students make with the individual oral commentary is to treat it as a purely impromptu exercise. Although you are asked to prepare a formal commentary under a time constraint and exam conditions, you will have studied all of the texts from which your extract is chosen and should, therefore, be substantially prepared to discuss any of the works. While it is highly unlikely, you will have covered every text in exacting detail, the individual oral commentary is the moment where you are able to demonstrate your familiarity with general themes, styles and effects encountered throughout the larger works. Part of this preparation involves a knowledge of the works studied but, as with all of the work in the course, your best preparation will not be reviewing a set of data to have at hand for an exam but through constant honing of the skills of close reading and analysis.

With all of the works studied, whether those primarily literary or those featuring other language aspects, it can be helpful to do the following:

- Read carefully and critically. Take notes on your reading, noting aspects which are interesting, confusing, or noteworthy for any reason.

- Participate actively in class while discussing texts. Consider notes and ideas from your own reading in light of class discussion in altering, strengthening or supplementing ideas.

- Consider literary features but only those that contribute significantly. It is better to focus on fewer literary devices with more analysis of effect than simply listing as many as you can identify.

- Review the text selection noting themes, aspects and literary techniques commonly used or approached in the different works. Expect that the extract will be significant and representative (IB examiners are not trying to play a trick on you!) Do organize your thoughts and prepare both an introduction and a conclusion, as the individual oral commentary demands some formality.

- Relax. If you "know" the texts, this should be an easily-enough accomplished assessment task. The individual oral commentary is an opportunity to showcase your by-now well-honed skills in presentation and analysis.

Sample of individual oral commentary

The individual oral commentary will be unique to your school and the literary works you study. Following is a transcript of one student's presentation in response to an extract from Michael Ondaatje's non-fictional text, *Running in the Family*. The example work has several strengths but is far from perfect; pay attention to aspects you would like to emulate as well as aspects you would like to enhance. As an oral commentary, the language is formal but you will see that there are some awkward constructions which occur in speaking tasks that would likely be polished in written works. This is not a mark of a weak commentary but rather does demonstrate some of the differences between assessment tasks. What is common, however, is an approach to literary works that aims to demonstrate understanding and an intellectual interpretation of the work through attention to how language is manipulated in a highly stylized fashion to achieve a particular effect.

Extract

Two weeks after he arrived in Ceylon, my father came home one evening to announce that he was engaged to a Doris Gratiaen. The postponed argument at Cambridge now erupted on my grandfather's lawn in Kegalle. My father was calm and unconcerned with the various complications he seemed to have created and did not even plan to write to the Roseleaps. It was Stephy who wrote, setting off a chain reaction in the mails, one letter going to Phyllis whose holiday plans were terminated. My father continued with his technique of trying to solve one problem by creating another. The next day he returned home saying he had joined the Ceylon Light Infantry.

I am not sure how long he had known my mother before the engagement. He must have met her socially now and then before his Cambridge years, for one of his closest friends was Noel Gratiaen, my mother's brother. About this time, Noel returned to Ceylon, sent down from Oxford at the end of his first year for setting fire to his room. This in fact was common behavior, but he had gone one step further, trying to put out the fire by throwing flaming sofas and armchairs out of the window onto the street and then dragging and hurling them into the river—where they sank three boats belonging to the Oxford rowing team. It was probably while visiting Noel in Colombo that my father first met Doris Gratiaen. At that time Doris Gratiaen and Dorothy Clementi-Smith would perform radical dances in private, practicing daily. Both women were about twenty-two and were greatly influenced by rumours of the dancing of Isadora Duncan. In a year or so they would perform in public. There is a reference to them in Rex Daniels' journals:

A garden party at the Residency Grounds … Bertha and I sat next to the Governor and Lady Thompson. A show had been organized for them made up of various acts. First on was a ventriloquist from Trincomalee whose act was not vetted as he had arrived late. He was drunk and began to tell insulting jokes about the Governor. The act was stopped and was followed by Doris Gratiaen and Dorothy Clementi-Smith who did an item called "'Dancing Brass Figures'". They wore swimsuits and had covered themselves in gold metallic paint. It was a very beautiful dance but the gold paint had an allergic effect on the girls and the next day they were covered in a terrible red rash.

Source: Ondaatje, Michael. 1982. *Running in the Family.* New York: Norton. pp. 33–34.

Questions

1 Discuss the mix of narratives and narrative styles including their larger effect(s).

2 What aspects of culture might be suggested in this passage?

Student response

For my formal oral commentary, I have received a passage from Michael Ondaatje's *Running In the Family*. This passage comes toward the beginning of the book where Ondaatje is kind of, where his stories are not as detailed as they are toward the end of the book. He is, basically, on this trip to find out more about his roots and his family but there is a really specific focus on his father who he is very curious about, has a lot of questions about because his mother and his father divorced while he was still a child and he is attempting to piece together much of his own life and own history by asking and investigating questions about both of his parents and, specifically, questions about their early lives together. This passage incorporates a lot of aspects that we see throughout the book such as the mix of comedy and tragedy, truth and supposition and cultural mixes that include the elite and privileged, the local and colonial and the serious and irresponsible. Through these layered juxtapositions, we get a picture that emerges of a family far from a simple homogenous identity but more a mosaic of influences and experiences that can also only be told and understood through a similar collage of perspectives and voices.

This passage begins with a focus on his father and talks about a story about how he broke off his engagement to another woman to marry Ondaatje's mother. The way this talks about … the way this passage shows how Ondaatje's father breaks off an engagement to marry his mother shows his kind of sudden quick changes of mind which later become more pronounced with his drunken episodes where he makes rash and careless decisions without thinking about them. This passage also highlights other antics by the father such as lying to his parents about admittance and attending Cambridge University and how he just lives off of his parents' money and foreshadows how when he comes back and after breaking off the engagement, he changes his life completely by rashly joins the Ceylon Light Infantry which, again, just highlights how his father is as a person. In this book, these sorts of anecdotes are important for Ondaatje as they make a more complete picture of his family than a book, say, that just talks about geneology would. There are many characters beside the father thrown in and the combination of voices, even when confused, can make a complete portrait of the family and how they function despite some difficult, funny or horrible issues.

The first lines, the whole first paragraph, has a very factual tone and reads like it is retelling established facts. The specific use of "two weeks" and even the description of the father as "calm and unconcerned with the various complications" seems very matter-of-fact as though it will simply retell factual notes of the father's life. This is in contrast to the subject matter, though, that should be far more emotional. His announcement of his engagement seems taken lightly by its abruptness. And of course this is unexpected because he is already engaged to another woman so that makes the tone even more jarring—you expect some more emotion there. The only emotion that is described is the use of "erupted" in line three but that doesn't seem to carry to much weight and even this is immediately followed by the description of the father as "calm and unconcerned." It might be interesting that the ex-fiancé is British and the Doris is not and that this has happened since Mervin arrive back to Ceylon—there is a hint of some division between the cultures. Even Mervin's lack of planning to write the Roseleaps and even inform them about the broken engagement is a kind of distance between England and Sri Lanka, between the proper or expected behavior and the more irascible actions of the father that just reaffirms contradictions in this passage.

The first paragraph also includes foreshadowing of Mervin's tendency to disregard the concerns or needs of others. It falls to his sister to relay the broken engagement and even ruining his cousin's—Phyllis'—summer plans, but the father doesn't seem to care. The last two lines of this paragraph really emphasize this. Ondaatje says that this continues his technique of solving one problem by creating another and this factual tone doesn't really convey maybe some of the sadness of emotion or irresponsibility of the event. But then it factually shows Mervin do this again; he doesn't just solve the problem of his engagement to Kaye with a new engagement to Dorris but solves the problem of solving this problem by joining the Ceylon Light Infantry. So this is told very unemotionally as just a statement of fact but this seems really a very emotional response, even crazy. This beginning represent a very messy situation for the father and it's not too good that this is the beginning of the relationship between Ondaatje's father and mother but none of the real fighting or sadness or madness or confusion gets established. All of these things are there for the reader, I think, and we know this must all be here but we don't expect that you could convey all this with so little narration. A lot of time and emotion is very abruptly shown in a very abbreviated manner. So much of the book is Ondaatje discovering himself to being a mix of very different forces and we see this through the beginning of the passage with a mix of narrative style and effects.

The next paragraph is really different with an initial tone of uncertain and very personal involvement. This paragraph begins with a first-person supposition rather than a more fact-like account of dates and events. The first words "I am not sure" really capture the personal exploration of the book that can seem unexpected in a non-fiction piece. The whole paragraph continues with a mix of some apparent fact but far more supposition and when viewed closely, is actually a work of more imagination or fiction than fact. Ondaatje says "he *must* have met her socially. The "must" is interesting because is suggests certainty though it is clear that this is all an imaginative act on the part of Ondaatje. Some of the humor is that the meeting of Ondaatje's parents remains a mystery but that might also be some of the reality of all families and family narratives that are always mixes of stories, of facts and fictions and productions or constructions of a viewer rather than easy-to-connect causalities. This is reaffirmed in the last line of the paragraph where Ondaatje says "it was probably while visiting Noel in Colombo that my father first met Doris Gratiaen." Though this tries to be certain and would make logical sense, there is enough in this book that the reader learns there is often much more than just logical sense.

It is the lack of this sense that makes up most of the body of this paragraph with the story of Noel that is very similar in both humor and tragedy to that of Mervin. The story of Noel's expulsion from Oxford is funny but also suggests the privilege enjoyed but all of these wealthy students and especially those Sri Lankans able to afford and manage it and their abuse of this privilege. But even the abuse seems because they aren't really familiar with the British customs. Noel's behavior is described as "common" and the mistake he makes is trying to put the fire out which causes more trouble for the rowing team. Marvin doesn't seem to even have had this much understanding and lied about going to Cambridge because he seems to think that was what one did. This paragraph reminds us of so much of the cultural confusion that exists and that exemplifies both Ondaatje as a Sri Lankan-Canadian and his family that consists of such a mix of social and ethnic cultures. Maybe this is also why he would choose to break his engagement with Kaye and choose someone in Sri Lanka but this is as much speculation as anything Ondaatje writes. The style of the passage is what we encounter throughout the book. It is very informal and personal and sounds like how a family member might tell a story to you without polishing as a written work. Any reader can identify with how these stories are told even when there are omissions or things are slightly confused. In the end, the personalities come across and this is also a mix of these effects: amidst a cacophony of overlapping voices, a clearer picture actually emerges.

The passage now switches to a focus on his mother but this is kind of strange. First, the focus is on her at a time that is imagined as the time when his father first met Doris. Again, there is a mix of fact and speculation. There is a tone of factual information about Doris and Dorothy and their dancing in the style of Isadora Duncan, how much they practiced, their influence and performances. But the inclusion of this information as meaningful to the larger picture is less obvious. Its place in Ondaatje lore is hinted at by being included but because it is so loosely connected to a time that may or may not have been a time when the parents really met makes this a far more uncertain "history."

We do learn more about the social cultural of the family members though. Doris and Dorothy are influenced by the dances of Isadora Duncan and clearly have the opportunity to dance rather than toil in labor so they are of some of the privileged class. And the dances are called "radical" which also hints at a kind of privilege where they can play and experiment. This fits in with the family that is described as upper class and privileged and elite but also more native that the British even though there is a connection to Dutch colonialism. But the names are anglicized and do suggest foreign and privileged influence and the mix of social and ethnic cultures found throughout the book. So specifically in this section there is a mention of how these people who live in Sri Lanka have this interesting blend of eastern and western cultures and influences. They are not indigenous natives of Sri Lanka, but at the same time they are not British or other colonizing people. They are somewhere in between or a mix or the two. They are of a privileged culture but they live in a way that is different from the native culture and the expatriate foreign population. They have this sort of life that focuses a lot on parties and entertainment because they are well-off and continue to live in an old-world elite style. But family, tradition and lineage are still important which we can see in the big event of Mervin Ondaatje's changing his engagement and the impact on the family.

There is a lot of mention throughout the book of drinking and parties, both their good and bad points, which shows both their importance but also a very authentic and human element to this story. It seems very real and funny and sad at different times. At first this seems more a clash of cultures but then it becomes more of a blend which gives a true picture of the character. They aren't all one way or another but they are a mix. These behaviors and things are not just with the Ondaatjes but many families in this group. The story of Noel and his dismissal from Oxford for throwing burning furniture out of the window is just a reminder that the atmosphere of this place and all this family and these friends are almost trying to one-up each other with wildness and that the Ondaatje's were not unique but part of a larger culture. We see this in the next section which is a section from Rex Daniels' journals that basically describes a party. The party is clearly the upper class being held at the Residency Grounds and guests like the Governor and Lady Thompson and different acts. But there is still the drunken ventriloquist and the allergic reaction to the paint that show the slightly inappropriate or less-polished or … um, not the sophisticated party that is expected. But this also puts a more local stamp on the party and this reads like a more local version of the foreign garden party and this shows that mix of cultures and social influences that ultimately makes up Ondaatje's family and life. The description of Dorris and her dancing are a little bit elegant but also a little bit comical with the rash and that also foreshadows some of the tragedy that we see throughout even when it is mixed with comedy. And also that this is all with a mix of sophisticated garden party but also a drunk ventriloquist that insults the governor.

All of these anecdotes are all told with a light tone using simple language. The stories are told without judgment. Maybe the tone is funny and light but not judgmental. However the anecdotes have a lot of deeper undertones. As we see later in the book when Mervin Ondaatje gets into all these scrapes in his fits of dipsomania he … the stories are told as if they are funny but you also get that sense that Michael Ondaatje is distressed and upset by the fact that his father behaved like that. Somehow the plainness of the tone almost highlights the confusion and the sadness that Ondaatje must feel when he hears these things. This happens in this passage. These stories of expulsion from college and breaking off engagements are told off-handedly or lightly and are funny to read but they are actually serious things and the hurt does come across as Ondaatje mentions the letters needing to be written and the big fights occurred to mollify the fiancé's family. You can also detect Mervin's own remorse and maybe understanding of the seriousness when he decides to join the Ceylon Light Infantry. In this way, this passage and much of the book highlights the darker side to the light-hearted partying and atmosphere and the very real repercussions to everything. Like with the woman drowning in the sea during a beach picnic, there can be frightening results to this play.

Because this passage comes at the beginning of the book you don't get the full sense of the morbid that occurs later but you still get a sense of that semi-tragic feeling. But this passage is a kind of foreshadowing of other anecdotes about his father where his actions and behaviors add up to a tragic and sad story rather than the funny story they may seem on the surface. Even when it isn't a bad event, like with the story of Dorris and Dorothy working so hard to practice for their radical dance event in the style of Isadore Duncan only to get allergic reactions to the makeup they use, there is always a kind of tragic-comedy irony that always has a sad tone. So this passage introduces a lot of this mix of tone and narrative style that is plain but speaks and is funny but also tragic.

This is probably the reason for the inclusion of Daniel's journal in this passage. It is to highlight that matter of factness of both the happy things and the darker tones that can be just underneath many of the events that take place. This use of a light tone that highlights some of the darkness of the content is an example of how everything has to be endured and should be endured or that it is normal that we have to endure difficulties. This could be seen later when we see Ondaatje's mother stay with his father despite the extreme alcoholism and problems it causes.

TEACHER QUESTION—okay a couple things; one of the things you talk about is the use of the journal as suggesting the complexity of the humor and the sadness. Look at the way the subject matter changes in the course of the passage. You start off with what we think is talking about the father but after the first paragraph, with no explanation, we jump to "I don't know how he met my mom," then on the Noel, then on to another story about his mother though focalized through another teller. What do you think Ondaatje is doing with this mix of voices and mix of stories here? Maybe you can also comment on the lack of connection between these different stories included here and what effect this might have.

Well, on the first things that does come across is the way that Ondaatje tells the story it sounds like a story that is jumbled up and told by many different people at the same time is connected to his afterward when he writes that he couldn't have written this book without the help of all his relatives and I think that that is what he is trying to achieve by writing the story like this and how there is no obvious connection between all the stories and paragraphs—the first is about him, the second is about his friend and the third is about his mother—there is that subtle connection with maintaining the actual way people talk and make connections and make sense of the world around them. A conversation might start off about the father, then someone will remember another thread of another event and a third person might add that this actually can shed light on an interesting story about the mother. And by doing this and making this mix of anecdotes and mix of voices, it makes the story richer because it is a tapestry of different peoples' opinions. None of this is strictly factual. None of this can be a scientific understanding of the history of the Ondaatjes because that kind of understanding of self and family is impossible. But what it is is actually more valid than that kind of knowledge because it gives a more genuine and human sense of both the comedy and the tragedy of real life. It

is interesting that this is non-fiction but not a non-fiction that presents purely factual accounts. It is non-fiction because it is genuine, in the words and stories and anecdotes of real people, flaws and all, trying to make the most of their lives. Ondaatje lets them all speak know that this is the only way he can "write" his own mixed history.

TEACHER QUESTION—Okay. You also mention the combination of humor and sadness or comedy and tragedy. What do you think the larger or ultimate tone is when he mixes the two so much?

Again, it seems to be about how there is no story that isn't a mix of these voices and styles and emotions and responses. Just like when later someone comments on how wonderful their childhood must have been after having heard some of the stories, his sister says that it wasn't; that it was terrible. But he also isn't agreeing that is was only terrible. We see these glimpses of exotic and exciting his life was. So by giving us all sides of a story and allowing them to contrast and mix together, he shows us what his life really was. And how life really is; how it is a mix of tragedy and comedy and people have to opportunity and privilege but also challenges and ordeals to face.

TEACHER QUESTION—Okay. One final point though it's probably connected to the previous two questions. It

does note overtly that it is a journal entry. What is really different or distinct with using the journal entry from Ondaatje writing about his father or mother or Noel?

Although I did suggest that his tone is objective, he can't help but convey some emotion when talking about his family members and especially his parents. Daniel's journal is simply relating events as though from an unbiased eyewitness. The paragraph that Ondaatje writes is not laden with emotion but there is some personal information. His story is a mix of all of these elements—stories passed down, or factual information and dates or personal interpretation. This use of the journal is to highlight this style of learning about oneself and one's family. It's a collage of voices and stories, truth and exaggerations, humor and terror, comedy and tragedy, information from others and from yourself that makes life so the most truthful way to convey that—the most non-fictive way—is to add all of this in his own writing and story.

Examiner comments

This candidate does attempt to locate the passage in the context of the larger work though this work does remain somewhat vague. This is partially due to the nature of this work that consists of short vignettes rather than a progressive narrative but slightly more specific work might still have been realized here. The can does, though, try to recognize and highlight elements common to both this passage and the larger work. There is a sophisticated notion of juxtapositions that the candidate notes.

The ideas are generally strong in the beginning even when the language used lacks some fluency. As an oral piece and one that is close to impromptu, it is expected that the language will be imperfect with some repetition but interesting ideas are still able to come across in the presentation.

After trying to offer some context, the candidate does a good job focusing on some specific elements of the passage. They try to touch on the use of specific words and lines and even offer some extensions of their thoughts to

consider possible alternatives and ideas related to culture. Paying attention to specific words and lines is always a strength and this candidate is able to do that quite well. Attention to tone is significant and convincing.

The candidate does lose some ground as it moves into the third paragraph as there is far less attention to specific language. There is still a sense of understanding and engagement but the work would be strengthened with more attention to the lines and words in the passage. This continues through to the end where there is more attention to the larger action on plot (again, understanding is evident) than on more specific effects. The candidate probably misses an opportunity to focus on the journal entry and the effect and purpose of its sudden inclusion though they are able to respond to it in subsequent questions.

This work would be strengthened with a little more focused conclusion but the candidate is able to respond to the teacher questions. Overall, there is a sense of good understanding, an attempt to organize the response around some specific and cohesive features and some attention to detail. The work could still be strengthened with more attention to specific usages of language and looking more attentively at the specific lines, but there is a strong attempt to organize a larger interpretation of the passage as a whole and its relationship to the larger work.

Conclusion

It is important to remember that the assessment for literature: critical study is not intending to measure your mastery of any particular body of content. Instead, throughout the course you are asked to demonstrate understanding and critical exploration of issues around language and literature and the assessments, as a result, are attempting to gauge your skills and abilities in *approaching* works of literature. This part of the course focuses on more formal language aspects that make a work a piece of literature but, in truth, the same attention to reading, thinking about and presenting ideas that you bring to all parts or the course will best serve you here as well. As already mentioned in chapter 3, formal assessments represent only those "live performances" where you present the same material you have been rehearsing but in full-costume and make-up. The assessments, then, are not unique or distinct tasks but rather the natural culmination of your ongoing hard work and practice throughout the course.

Opening questions

Read the following two passages carefully. Rather than approaching them as texts that you would analyze for an unseen commentary of some sort, think of them for what they are: short sections from long, complicated novels. Both passages are from the opening sections of the novels. If you were sitting down to read these novels, what would you think about these opening sections? What would you want to know more about in order to help with your reading? After reading the passages, look at the questions that were asked by a group of students in relation to these passages.

Text 1

The following extract is from the opening to the *The Leopard (Il Gattopardo)*, written by Giuseppe Tomasi di Lampedusa in 1958.

Introduction to the Prince

May, 1860

"Nunc et in hora mortis nostrae. Amen."

The daily recital of the Rosary was over. For half an hour the steady voice of the Prince had recalled the Sorrowful and the Glorious Mysteries; for half an hour other voices had interwoven a lilting hum from which, now and again, would chime some unlikely word; love, virginity, death; and during that hum the whole aspect of the rococo drawing-room seemed to change; even the parrots spreading iridescent wings over the silken walls appeared abashed; even the Magdalen between the two windows looked a penitent and not just a handsome blonde lost in some dubious daydream as she usually was.

Now, as the voices fell silent, everything dropped back into its usual order or disorder. Benedico, the Great Dane, grieved at exclusion, came wagging its tail through the door by which the servants had left. The women rose slowly to their feet, their oscillating skirts as they withdrew baring bit by bit the naked figures from mythology painted all over the milky depths of the tiles. Only an Andromeda remained covered by the soutane of Father Pirrone, still deep in extra prayer, and it was some time before she could sight the silvery Perseus swooping down to her aid and her kiss.

The divinities frescoed on the ceiling awoke. The troops of Tritons and dryads, hurtling across from hill and sea amid clouds of cyclamen pink towards a transfigured Conca d'Oro and bent on glorifying the House of Salina, seemed suddenly so overwhelmed with exaltation as to discard the most elementary rules of perspective; meanwhile the major Gods and Goddesses, the Princes among Gods, thunderous Jove and frowning Mars and languid Venus, had already preceeded the mob of minor deities and were amiably supporting the blue armorial shield of the Leopard. They knew that for the next twenty-three and a half hours they would be lords of the villa once again. On the walls the monkeys went back to pulling faces at the cockatoos.

Beneath this Palermitan Olympus the mortals of the Salina family were also dropping speedily from mystic spheres. The girls resettled the folds in their dresses, exchanged blue-eyed glances and snatches of school-girl slang; for over a month, ever since the outbreaks of the Fourth of April, they had been home for safety's sake from their convent, and regretting the canopied dormitories and collective cosiness of the Holy Redeemer. The boys were already scuffling with each other for possession of a medal of San Francesco id Paola; the eldest, the heir, the young Duke Paolo, longing to smoke and afraid of doing so in his parents' presence, was squeezing through his pocket the braided straw of his cigar-case. His gaunt face was veiled in brooding melancholy; it had been a bad day; Guiscard, his Irish sorrel, had seemed off form, and Fanny had apparently been unable (or unwilling) to send him her usual lilac-tinted billet-doux. Of what avail then, to him, was the Incarnation of his Saviour?

Source: Tomasi di Lampedusa, Giuseppe (trans. Colquhoun, Archibald). 1958. *The Leopard*. London: Everyman's Library. 1998. pp. 5–6.

Student's questions

- "Where exactly is this taking place? Is it Italy?"
- "What kind of royalty are these people?"
- "Is there something important going on politically or historically in 1860?"
- "A lot of the references are difficult. Are they mythical and religious allusions important?"
- "Who is the author and why would he write a book taking place in 1860 in 1958?"
- "Is this a good translation?"

Text 2

The following extract is from *Notable American Women*, a novel by Ben Marcus, first published in 2002.

Bury Your Head

I offer this message under duress, hungry, winded, and dizzy, braving a sound storm of words meant to prevent me, I'm sure, from being a Father of Distinction. For the sake of those persons in the world who expect leadership, clarity, and a levelheaded account of the matterful times that my "family"—to hell with all of them—has witnessed, I will not succumb to the easy distractions of language poison, even if it kills the body that I'm wearing, even if I become just another dead man who once felt things keenly and wished only for the world to see inside his heart and mind. There is light enough for one hour of transcription each day, and it is within this time that I have assembled these remarks, having carefully considered the true nature of what I think and feel during my other twenty-three daily hours, allotted to me as darkness by my captors, a group also known as Everyone I Used to Love, Who Would Never Have Survived Without Me.

I am aware that Ben Marcus, the improbable author of this book, but better known as my former son, can pass off or structure my introduction in any way that he chooses: annotate, abridge, or excise my every comment. He will have the final cut of this so-called introduction to his family history, and I'll not know the outcome unless he decides to share with me how he has savaged and defathered me for his own glory. He can obviously revise my identity to his own designs, change my words altogether, or simply discard them in place of statements he wishes I would make. I would put none of these distortions past him and will only caution the careful and fair-minded reader to be ever vigilant against his manipulations, to remember that he is a creature, *if* that, of inordinate bias and resentment, for reasons soon to be disclosed, undoubtedly intimidated by the truth only a father can offer. Considering that I fathered him with the utmost precision, I am sorry that it should be this way. I fully expect even this statement to be omitted, given how it might contradict the heroic role he will no doubt claim for himself, in which case it is only you, Ben, my jailer, who will read this. Please let a father say his part. You have done enough harm already.

Source: Marcus, Ben. 2002. *Notable American Women.* New York: Vintage Contemporaries. pp. 3–4.

Student's questions

- "What is the meaning of the title of this section?"
- "The book is called *Notable American Women* and it says it is a novel. Is this fiction or nonfiction? What about the author's name being used in the passage?"
- "What is going on with the father? Is he in prison? Are we supposed to take this book seriously?"
- "What kind of writer is Ben Marcus? I am wondering if this is science fiction or mystery."

After you have read the text extracts that begin this chapter, we will answer some of the questions you may have about these passages without getting in to a commentary or discussion. *The Leopard* was published just after the death of its author, Giuseppe Tomasi di Lampedusa, the last in a line of Sicilian aristocrats and landowners. The Tomasi di Lampedusa family had at one time been quite wealthy but over the course of a few hundred years, their family shrank due to a lack of male heirs and their property holdings dwindled out of a combination of lack of interest (one member of the family donated his entire share of the family fortune to the Catholic Church and went on to become a priest and was eventually named a Saint), mismanagement, and general economic hardships. Young Giuseppe di Lampedusa was one of the last members of the family and had witnessed the decline not only of the family, but of the noble class of Sicily. Because of his relative wealth, Tomasi di Lampedusa spent most of his life traveling in Europe and studying his interests. *The Leopard* was his only novel and its portrait of declining Italian aristocracy was seen as a poignant picture of dissolution and social decline. Although it was rejected by two publishers during his own lifetime, essentially because it was not considered new or experimental enough, the novel went on to become a bestselling classic in Italy. The novel drew attention for its criticism of Sicily, feudal customs, the Catholic Church and for its considerations of honor and personal fortitude. The beginning of this chapter introduces the family but also makes important, and at times playful or irreverent, allusions to both the Catholic faith and Roman mythology, both of which were important to Sicilian society.

Ben Marcus, author of *Notable American Women*, is a contemporary author who is noted for his experimentation with language and narrative form. While many authors turn to realism as a way to tell a heartfelt or meaningful story, Marcus attempts to alter the meaning of familiar words, tell stories in a nonlinear, sometimes confusing order, and set his works in a world that may be similar to our own but is clearly not meant to be either "real," or "fantastic" in the way science fiction or fantasy would be. While ambiguity often rules in the fiction of Ben Marcus, his own nonfiction essays have clearly addressed the role he feels authors should play in the future of fiction in general and the novel in particular. *Notable American Women* tells a story with echoes of a dystopian world and, in sometimes oblique ways, addresses issues of family, religion, the rules of society, and writing itself.

Now you might ask yourself other questions. Do these brief summaries help with your reading? Is it possible to approach a text without this information? How much more information, and of what type, would help you further with your understanding?

What are contexts?

What exactly do you need to know about a work of literature in order to be able to understand or respond to it? On the one hand, we might answer that question by saying that you have to know very little other than how to read. Yet, can this supposedly pure attention to the text ever be a reality? First of all, what does it mean to be able to read? Reading is not simply a decoding of letters and words but a process through which we understand what a text or author is suggesting and what the words mean. We all bring knowledge and experience to our reading of the text—knowledge about history, geography, societies, and writing itself. While many teachers today may not focus on teaching the biography of an author in order to help with your understanding of a text, or may not make you memorize historical facts from the time period in which it is set, we still find ourselves looking outside of the texts themselves for a little help. When I read I necessarily use the information I learned as I studied literature. I use what I know about the world and sometimes I am helped along by the information found in an introduction … or even on the Internet. To be an informed reader is to be a reader who may know it is impossible to know and understand everything about a work of literature, but who understands the forces on an author, on the meaning and interpretation of a work, and on our own personal reactions. To be an informed reader is to consider not only a text but its contexts.

Context can be defined simply as the circumstances that surround a given text and help to specify its meaning. In approaching a short passage from a longer work we may first think of the context as the rest of the work. Looking at the context of a passage in this case means considering how the short passage is significant to the whole or how the whole affects meaning in the short passage. More frequently, however, we think of context as all of the possible circumstances that surround a work and somehow contribute to its meaning. You may have experienced literature classes where poems, novels and plays are approached in a predictable and somewhat orderly way that takes context into consideration. Perhaps a work is introduced with a short biography of the writer followed by a discussion of where the work fits in the history of literature. You may also have looked at a timeline that places the writer and the work itself in a broader political or historical context. This approach, however, may be misleadingly comforting and may imply that there is a basic, agreed upon set of facts and circumstances that need to be known in order to reach an accepted understanding. Context is far from simple, however. First, as you are probably starting to notice, and as you may have noticed from thinking about the passages above, context is best expressed as contexts (plural) because of the wide variety of external forces that affect the general reception or understanding of a work. You also may have noticed that the importance and usefulness of contextual information is somewhat problematic. It is difficult to decide what information is necessary to better understand a text and it is difficult to decide, once you start investigating a given critical position, historical fact, or biographical aspect of an author's life, where to stop and turn back to the text itself and your experience of it. To complicate matters even further, you yourself are part of a work's context. Once you approach a work as a reader, the meaning that is communicated, that is sent from the text to you, is influenced by everything that you bring to it, from your reading to your personal experiences and biases.

Contexts, then, are best approached as always plural, always problematic, and always a matter of possibilities. Every text, while best approached, starting from the text itself and moving out, can be understood in different ways and to different degrees depending on contextual knowledge. The contextual information itself, of course, is open to debate and can vary depending on the source or the depth of investigation. Most importantly, the study of texts and contexts can open reading to a myriad of possible readings and to a wide variety of types of study and enjoyment.

The life and times of the author

The life and times of the author are probably the first ideas that come to mind when we think about the context of a work. Learning about the life of the author and the broad political, cultural, and aesthetic concerns of the day are often a logical and seemingly straightforward first step to helping with our understanding of a text. It is common sense to think about when an author was writing in order to theorize the broader or underlying meaning of a text. A novel written in 1943 may be responding to events of the Second World War and certainly wouldn't be dealing with issues of the Cold War. Knowing that an author had survived the Holocaust may influence our reading of a novel about concentration camp experiences. But even these apparently logical pieces of information may complicate our understanding of a work as much as they bring clarity. Our work with context must always be a back and forth negotiation with the text.

Consider some of the assumptions we could make about the passages we have already looked at above and how these conceptions might clarify or complicate our understanding. In reference to the opening reading: Learning that Giuseppe Tomasi di Lampedusa was himself the last heir of a disintegrating noble family allows us to understand the privileged position of knowledge and insight the author had into his subject matter. But, do we need to know, when approaching a work of fiction, that an author has some personal experience similar to what he writes about? And in terms of knowledge and veracity, how much experience would Tomasi di Lampedusa have of events from 100 years before in his family history? And what of the historical period when the novel was written? A publication date of 1958 in Italy might not help us very much; it would be a mistake to see the novel as a response to Italy's experience during the Second World War. But what of Italy's experience as a new republic as it struggled to recover in the postwar years? Could Tomasi di Lampedusa's novel about the disintegration of a noble family in the late 1800s be read as commentary upon the tension between the old and new in Italian political and cultural life in the postwar period? Could the story of a disintegrating class of nobles, on the other hand, be a story of a culture's longing to return to that very period, a period that existed before the country was pushed and pulled between the new superpowers of the United States and the Soviet Union? These are all difficult questions that are raised by even a cursory glance at cultural and biographical contexts. Ultimately, the answers to questions raised by information that is external to the text lie in the text itself. Any reading of a text modifies itself as it goes along. As we read even the short passage from *The Leopard* we begin to see particular traits in the characters (boredom or devotion for example) particular attitudes (towards religion for example) that may change or develop as we read. In the same way, what we think of as contextual insights may increase or decrease in importance depending on our response to the text. A reading of *The Leopard* may convince us that the novel is an insightful character study more than a work with broader cultural concerns and we may discount information about Italy's political environment. Does this swing us towards a reading based on the personal story of Tomasi di Lampedusa? Perhaps, but what if we were to discover that the author had no noble lineage, that his life history was fabricated and the novel was based solely on his imagination (this isn't true … at least as far as we know)? Would we then understand the novel any differently? *Should* we read it any differently? Once again, understanding is a matter of degree and is always open to revision.

The story context

In discussing historical and cultural contexts we are usually considering the time and place of the text's production. Some critics, in fact, would pointedly leave out of a discussion of context an investigation of the subject matter within the text. But the background knowledge about the story being told, or about events recounted in a poem for example, are worth examining in relationship to a wider appreciation of context. Once again, the passage from *The Leopard* serves as a good example. While many works of fiction, through the course of a story or presentation of an event, provide the context necessary for understanding, at times a general knowledge of the historical background will support a better understanding. Although *The Leopard* was published in 1958, its story recounts events during the previous century. Just as an understanding of Italian politics and culture in the 1950s may offer certain insights, so might an understanding of the political and cultural situation in the 1860s.

General questions about context

Here are some questions or routes of investigation you might pursue when considering the biographical, historical, and cultural contexts of a work:

- What is the cultural and educational background of the author?
- What views on writing or culture has the author expressed?
- What are the values and aesthetic concerns of the culture of the author?
- What historical events may have influenced the ideas in the work?
- What are the political or economic issues of the times?
- What cultural issues may have influenced, challenged, or inspired the author?

The receptive reader

In order for a text to have meaning it has to be read by someone. Each individual brings a different background and set of experiences to a text and therefore experiences the text in a particular, individual way. It is worth considering our own backgrounds and biases as a way of examining another way that a text's meaning lies partly beyond the words on the page. In a classroom situation it is interesting in discussions or when looking at the writing of fellow students or the comments made by a teacher to reflect on the different works we have in front of us, the different meanings we experience, because of the way we receive the text. When we read texts, we are the actual or flesh and blood readers, who experience a work with all of our knowledge, biases, and very individual flaws. At the same time, we all have the ability to read a text and consider the implied reader, that reader with a particular type of knowledge and bias that we *assume* is addressed by the author. When we investigate the historical background of a text like *The Leopard* we may assume that the implied reader, the reader theoretically addressed by Tomasi de Lampedusa, would have an understanding of the historical and cultural milieu of Italy after the Second World War. Our personal reading often becomes a negotiation between our very personal understanding, and our assumptions about who the text is addressing.

Your values and assumptions are part of the context of a work. Even more importantly, your values and assumptions function in a relationship with the assumptions that other readers make about a text. Have you ever read and enjoyed part of a book for a homework assignment, thought of some interesting ideas, developed a response, and then been surprised the next day in school when your teacher or peers had very different ideas about the reading? Did you question whether or not your own response was correct. Or, did you simply modify your views, and add those experiences to your own to come up with a more complex understanding? We tend to develop an understanding of the meaning of a work not only through our own reading but through conversations with others about their reading. In a very similar way, we can be said to have a relationship with the history of the way a work has been read over time. When we study Shakespeare, we often consider the views of critics over the centuries. Critics over time have personal views that are influenced by the critics who have come before. When we read and consider these critical views ourselves our understanding of a text is obviously not coming solely from the text itself but from a complex context of readings and re-readings.

The passage from *Notable American Women* can serve as a good example of the ways in which reader experience and an understanding of the reception of a text—the way a text has been read over time or by critics and other readers—adds to the context that creates meaning. Your own reading of the passage would certainly be influenced by your previous reading experience. If you had come across experimental or postmodern texts you would read the passage differently from someone who may approach the work as a realistic first person confession. Most importantly, your understanding would be negotiated in a classroom where you would work with others to get at meaning. This is also where the broader critical reception of a work plays an important role in informative context. Many critics have written about Marcus and the way he experiments with form and language. If we read about Marcus's experimental style and consider the ways others have approached *Notable American Women* we may then read the text in a different light. Reading with an understanding of this critical context may be an important key to understanding the passage in a way that is not purely personal.

These are some questions and ideas that you may think about when investigating the context of the reception and reading of a work:

- Your own knowledge, values, educational background, and experiences.
- The current political and cultural factors that may influence you and your reading.
- How was the work initially received by critics? The reading public?
- What are some of the critical perspectives on the work?
- How would critics from different theoretical schools read the work?

How the text is built and functions

Another contextual issue to consider is the way the text itself has traveled from being an idea in the writer's mind to being the work in front of us. Considering how and why a text uses specific structures and types of language goes along with how a text relates to all of the works that have preceded it and how a publishing company or editor might decide to alter a text or shape its reception through marketing. People always say "don't judge a book by its cover" but maybe, when it comes to works of literature, we do and in some respects can.

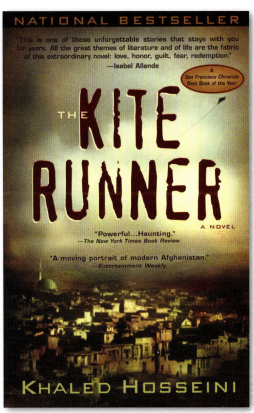

Take this example of *The Kite Runner* by Khaled Hosseini, first published in 2003. There are a number of elements that you may have noticed on this cover that may influence your reading of the text (or help you to consider whether you would buy the novel in the first place). First, the picture of a non-western city may look exotic or may convince you that this book is from or about another culture. As you read, because of the way the book is marketed, you may purposefully look for issues of difference. The deep red letters of the title may seem dramatic and along with words like "powerful", "haunting", "love", "honor", "guilt" will push you to reading for grand themes or for the similarities across cultures despite that difference you have noticed. You may also notice that the novel has been successful. While this fact may initially convince you to buy, it may also convince you to enjoy the work—certainly if it has been so wildly successful, it must be good, even despite any misgivings you may have. The cover of the book has also attempted to put the work in a literary framework. First of all, you are told that the work is a novel, which raises a variety of expectations for you as someone who has read a wide variety of novels—you expect fiction, you may be looking for realism, you may certainly expect a number of characters, a wide canvass. Second, you see that one of the "blurbs" is written by Isabel Allende. If you have read her before, you may think that this book shares some similarities with her works. You may wonder if this book is a generational saga, if it holds the power of magic and mystery, if it somehow fits into a tradition of Latin American "magic realism". All in all, the cover is part of, and represents, the literary and publishing context of the work and influences the meaning you derive from the work.

The above activity points to just some of the issues to consider when looking at the context of a work and its production. Decisions made in the creation of a work are influenced by a variety of factors including literary tradition and the desire to make money. These factors then influence the way we approach a work. When an author decides to write, the seemingly basic decision of what genre to work in—whether to write a novel, a poem, a work of nonfiction, etc.—the decision is based on the author's understanding of literary tradition. When we read a poem we may expect certain things—rhythm or imagery?—and so our path to understanding begins as a text either fulfills or subverts our expectations. When reading the Ben Marcus passage we may think that the text starts as any novel could, but when the narrator mentions the author's name, we wonder what is going on, we wonder whether this is a different kind of novel. These expectations hold true with structure and use of language. We are always ready to judge a text based on our expectations.

While it may be hard to separate the meaning of a work from a broader context, it is also hard to separate the work itself from a broader literary context. Any novel could be said to be an allusion to

Activity

Judging a book ...

Look at the cover of a popular novel. Based on the cover, would you want to read this book? Why or why not? What information do you learn about this book? Would this information shape your reading of the text?

Write a short account of your interest in a book that was inspired by seeing the cover.

novels that have come before. Writers also make more pointed and purposeful allusions that can be recognized to better understand how a text operates. Just as a novel may push and pull against the expected form of a novel, a writer pushes and pulls with literary forbears. Shakespeare makes references to Greek myths in his plays or rewrites older poems as plays, and these allusions add richness to his plays and help us to understand the ideas he is trying to express. James Cameron's film *Avatar* is said to strongly allude to the early American story of Captain John Smith and Pocahontas. By alluding to, or even "rewriting" an older story, Cameron is not copying or plagiarizing but calling attention to, and highlighting what he wants us to see as the truth of important themes like conservation or the nature of shared humanity. At the same time, allusion to an older tale calls attention to what he is doing that is new, the way he uses technology, for example, or the ways in which humanity is facing a similar, yet perhaps more chilling, crisis in the present and a revised look at what it means to be "human." A text seldom works alone; rather, it is part of a rich, intertextual network, in which it can be said that a work of literature enters into a conversation with all of the works that have come before.

The somewhat theoretical nature of the writing of a text and its relation with the larger literary history is linked to more mundane issues of production such as publication. From an author (or an agent) a work travels to a publishing house where it is turned into a commodity that is sold to the public. The cover of *The Kite Runner* suggests a number of ways texts are marketed and how that marketing might affect our reading. Texts go through a number of changes before they appear in a bookstore or library. An editor may make quite significant changes to a text. We may not be aware of these changes (although in some cases, with older works, we do have records of revisions and drafts), but it is at times worth considering the nature of authorship or the way a text has already been read and modified. The nature of a text's distribution also affects our reading. How would you approach a book from a small publisher, given to you by a friend who tells you that the little known work is a special find. Will you trust your own judgment with the book? Will you trust your friend? How much do you trust or distrust the judgment of book reviewers in large newspapers? What about the judgment of critics from your local newspaper or a blog you frequent? If an author on a "book tour" appears on your favorite television talk show, are you more or less likely to take the work seriously. Interestingly enough, when adults are polled about what books were the *most important* works they have read, they invariably point to the books they were given to read in high school. Is this because of the books themselves, or because these books have been "marketed" to them in the context of an important secondary school class (the *most* important secondary school class)?

Here again are some further ideas and questions you can explore in relation to the form and production of a work of literature:

● What is the genre of the work and how does the work either fulfill or go against your expectations of the genre?

● How is the narrative structure of the work either familiar or surprising?

- How are techniques ranging from diction to characterization either familiar or surprising?

- How does the work relate to a broader literary tradition?

- What are the possible sources of the work?

- What allusions does the work make?

- What is the publishing and marketing history of the work?

Case studies

The texts you study in school may be from a variety of genres and may just as likely be from a variety of cultures or time periods. It is also important to note that the value of different types of contextual information varies from text to text. While the biography of Giuseppe Tomasi di Lampedusa may shed light on *The Leopard* a more rhetorical approach that considers critical and linguistic contexts may be appropriate when approaching a work like *Notable American Women*. In this section of the chapter we have attempted to select, in just six short sections, a variety of texts that offer different ways to study the interaction of reader, text, and context. In each short section we will give you some suggested ways of approaching the work, a passage from the text for closer analysis, and a variety of critical and contextual perspectives. Our intention here, however, is *not* to give you a critical and contextual overview of the works. Our hope is, rather, that you will see here, even if you are unfamiliar with the works, that context can be approached from a variety of sometimes surprising angles. While you may never study these works in school we hope that you will both think of new ways of looking at the texts you encounter on your own and that you may be inspired to pick up these works for further reading and investigation.

Purple Hibiscus by Chimamanda Ngozi Adichie

Chimamanda Adichie's *Purple Hibiscus* is an interesting work to study because it invites a variety of approaches to addressing its various literary and cultural contexts. The novel, written in the United States, by a woman who was educated both in Nigeria and at graduate programs in creative writing in the United States, tells the story of a young girl coming of age in Nigeria during a time of political strife. The main character and narrator, Kambili, finds herself pulled in many directions as she deals with her brutal, conservative father, her liberal and exciting aunt, and not least of all, her own thoughts and desires. Besides the many cultural contexts these issues may encourage us to investigate, the novel also follows the literary tradition of a *bildungsroman*—a story of growth and development taking the young protagonist to the threshold of adulthood—and stands against some traditions as what has been called by critics a "third generation" Nigerian novel.

While this section of the chapter is not meant to be a comprehensive study of Adichie's novel, it attempts to show some of the complexities of looking at a novel that, although written in English, may deal with an unfamiliar culture. While we could argue that the novel is actually written from within the 21st-century US culture and seems to be addressed to an audience somewhat unfamiliar with Nigerian culture, the text itself is to a degree *about* context, or about trying to make sense of a landscape of conflicting cultures or allegiances. Kambili, the narrator, asks us to examine from the outside cultural constructs such as religion (Catholicism and traditional Igbo religion), education, rural life and city life, class, politics, the media (her father owns a newspaper), customs around food (traditional versus Western), puberty, adulthood, and marriage. Before looking at a selection from the novel, consider what the author herself says about the contextual issues. The following passage is from an essay entitled "Authenticity" by Chimamanda Ngozi Adichie:

I grew up in Nsukka, a small university town in southeastern Nigeria, and started reading when I was perhaps four years old. I read a lot of British children's literature, and I was particularly enamored of Enid Blyton. I thought that all books had to have white people in them, by their very nature, and so when I started to write, as soon as I was old enough to spell, I wrote the kinds of stories that I was reading. All my characters were white and had blue eyes and played in the snow and ate apples and had dogs called *Socks*. This, by the way, at a time when I had not been to England and had never seen snow and was more familiar with mangoes than apples. My characters drank ginger beer, a staple of Enid Blyton's characters. Never mind that I had no idea what ginger beer was. For many years afterward, I would have a desperate fascination for ginger beer, but that is another story.

Then, when I was perhaps eight or nine, I read Chinua Achebe's *Things Fall Apart* (1958). It was a glorious shock of discovery. Here were characters who had Igbo names and ate yams and inhabited a world similar to mine. Oknonkwo and Ezinma and Ikemefuna taught me that *my* world was worthy of literature, that books could also have people like me in them. It was about the same time that I read Camara Laye's novel *The Dark Child* (1953), a beautiful, elegiac, and in some ways wonderfully defensive book that also played a role in making me see my African world as a worthy subject of literature.

I like to think of Achebe as the writer whose work gave me permission to write my own stories. But, although Achebe's characters were familiar to me in many ways, their world was also incredibly exotic because they lived without the things that I saw as the norm in my life: they did not have cars and electricity and telephones. They did not eat fried rice. They lived a life that my great-grandfather might have lived, which brings me to a second *Things Fall Apart* story.

I came to the United States about ten years ago to go to college because I was fleeing the study of medicine in Nigeria. As is the case in many places, when you do well in school in Nigeria, you are expected to become a doctor or to pursue some other exalted science. I had been in the science track in secondary school and matriculated at the University of Nigeria to study medicine, but after a year I realized I would be a very unhappy doctor. To prevent the future inadvertent deaths of patients, I fled. Before I arrived in Philadelphia, my friend Ada, who had been in the United States for some years, found a four-bedroom apartment which I would share with three American students. Because Ada had made all of the arrangements, my future roommates did not see me until I arrived at the door. I remember them opening the door and looking at me in shock. There was also some disappointment on their faces: I was not what they had expected. "You are wearing American clothes," they said (about the jeans I had bought in the Nsukka market). "Where did you learn to speak English so well?" They were surprised that I knew who Mariah Carey was; they had assumed that I listened to what they called "tribal music." I remember looking at them and being surprised that twenty-year-olds knew so little about the world. And then →

I realized that perhaps *Things Fall Apart* had played a role in this. These students, like many Americans, had read Achebe's novel in high school, but I suspect that their teacher forgot to explain to them that it was a book set in the Nigeria of a hundred years ago. Later, one of my new roommates told me that I just didn't seem *African*. Clearly, they had expected that I would step out of the pages of *Things Fall Apart*.

Source: Ngozi Adichie, Chimamanda. 2008. "African 'Authenticity' and the Biafran Experience." *Transition*, no. 99. pp. 42–43.

The opening of *Purple Hibiscus* allows the reader to quickly engage with the reflections of the first person narrator. While the reader may be aware of the genre, may be prepared to read the story of a young girl and troubles brewing at home, the reader is also aware of the complex cultural contexts of the story itself. Read the beginning of the novel here and consider the way Adichie chooses to introduce us to the fictional world of Kambili, the narrator:

Discussion Point

1 How are our personal experiences important to what we write or how we respond to literature?

2 In what ways are we affected by the cultural context of a work?

3 What are the benefits and limitations of a cultural gap between reader and text?

4 Based on Adichie's experience with *Things Fall Apart*, how might *Purple Hibiscus* best be approached?

Things started to fall apart at home when my brother, Jaja, did not go to communion and Papa flung his heavy missal across the room and broke the figurines on the étagère. We had just returned from church. Mama placed the fresh palm fronds, which were wet with holy water, on the dining table and then went upstairs to change. Later, she would knot the palm fronds into sagging cross shapes and hang them on the wall beside our gold-framed family photo. They would stay there until next Ash Wednesday, when we would take the fronds to church, to have them burned for ash. Papa, wearing a long, gray robe like the rest of the oblates, helped distribute ash every year. His line moved the slowest because he pressed hard on each forehead to make a perfect cross with his ash-covered thumb and slowly, meaningfully enunciated every word of "dust and unto dust you shall return."

Papa always sat in the front pew for Mass, at the end beside the middle aisle, with Mama, Jaja, and me sitting next to him. He was first to receive communion. Most people did not kneel to receive communion at the marble altar, with the blond life-size Virgin Mary mounted nearby, but Papa did. He would hold his eyes shut so hard that his face tightened into a grimace, and then he would stick his tongue out as far as it could go. Afterward, he sat back on his seat and watched the rest of the congregation troop to the altar, palms pressed together and extended, like a saucer held sideways, just as Father Benedict had taught them to do. Even though Father Benedict had been at St. Agnes for seven years, people still referred to him as "our new priest." Perhaps they would not have if he had not been white. He still looked new. The colors of his face, the colors of condensed milk and a cut-open soursop, had not tanned at all in the fierce heat of seven Nigerian harmattans. And his British nose was still as pinched and as narrow as it always was, the same nose that had had me worried that he did not get enough air when he first came to Enugu.

Source: Ngozi Adichie, Chimamanda. 2007. *Purple Hibiscus.* London: Harper Perennial. pp. 3–4.

The opening line of the novel makes a very pointed reference to the title of Chinua Achebe's *Things Fall Apart*. Adichie herself has suggested the importance of this novel to her own writing and here she alerts the reader to the novel's self-conscious place in the Nigerian literary tradition and perhaps also to the way the novel may, after the opening line, move away from the earlier work. In fact, we find in the story that follows that not only have things been falling apart in this family for quite some time, but that the strong male character of this novel, Kambili's father, is strongly attached to his Catholicism, in contrast to Okonkwo of *Things Fall Apart*, who with equal passion opposed early missionaries.

In addition to introducing us to a new step in a literary tradition, the novel suggests its own special context and its own preoccupation with cultural difference. The opening paragraph takes place in a Catholic Church and references, ranging from holidays to objects and practices, help to draw the borders of the cultural landscape. References to Catholicism, however, are also embedded within a larger Nigerian setting. This is a place of blazing sun, "harmattans," and "soursop" that is obviously familiar to the narrator, if not necessarily the reader. And difference, from the start of the novel, matters. The narrator is careful to point out her own recognition of difference in the priest who leads the service and has "taught" the people.

Culture and the child narrator

In a critical essay about the role of child narrators in contemporary African fiction, the literary critic Madelaine Hron discusses the ways in which a young person's perspective in a novel, far from making the novel "juvenile," allows readers to experience culture and cultural conflicts from a naive perspective. A reader who is not familiar with Nigerian culture, for example, may discover the tensions in a society along with the narrator who is maturing and coming to her own understanding.

In the article, Hron brings up some interesting points that relate both to *Purple Hibiscus* and the larger role of literature in relation to both "teaching" culture and representing our own complex relationship with the cultures that surround us. The suggestion that Western readers, less familiar with Nigerian culture, may be more apt to relate to or learn from the child's perspective in the novel may be true but it also suggests that entering a novel that is rooted from deep within a culture, that makes dense and complicated reference to its own culture, may be may be difficult for any but a special few to access. How is narrative perspective, then, related to the way a reader approaches the culture represented in a work?

Also worth noting, is the way Hron suggests that novels told from a child's perspective deal with "negotiation" and "navigation" of cultural contexts. In an interesting way, the narrator of Adichie's novel is trying to get a handle on her own world at the same time the reader is trying to develop a relationship with the fictional yet Nigerian world of the novel. While Kambili, the young narrator, is clearly familiar with her Catholic faith, the politics of Nigeria, and the traditional religion still followed by her estranged grandfather, she is also only just coming to an awareness of the complexities of identification with these cultural conventions. Kambili thinks she understands Catholicism as taught to her by her father, or the danger of traditional religion, also taught by her father but she learns, when she travels to live with her aunt, that there are other sides, more inviting to her, of both Catholicism and Igbo traditions. When her father is eventually caught up in the growing political unrest in Nigeria, she also learns that political forces, once seen as distant, can be quite personal. For many readers of the novel, starting from outside of the novel's cultural network, the experience of the novel itself moves from being one of an outsider looking in to one who is caught in a difficult back and forth relationship with familiarity and unfamiliarity—a situation not unlike the narrator's.

Here is another short passage from *Purple Hibiscus*. Consider the way the narrator describes this simple event, packing a car before going on a holiday during the Christmas season, while the author may be asking the reader to think about both the narrator's and our position in relation to culture.

> Papa stood by the hibiscuses, giving directions, one hand sunk in the pocket of his white tunic while the other pointed from item to car. "The suitcases go in the Mercedes, and those vegetables also. The yams will go in the Peugeot 505, with the cases of Remy Martin and cartons of juice. See if the stacks of *okporoko* will fit in, too. The bags of rice and *garri* and beans and the plantains go in the Volvo."

While there are times when certain contextual information must be understood in order to understand a situation, this easily understood situation, packing the car, seems to suggest that, far from needing to know what *okporoko* and *garri* are, this passage is *about* the way the known and unknown are often thrown together, that any situation may be the mix of the familiar and unfamiliar. Rather than "teaching" the reader about Nigerian culture, this passage reminds the reader that cultural understanding is a back and forth movement.

We have noted that *Purple Hibiscus* self-consciously steps forward from Achebe's *Things Fall Apart* which itself, according to Achebe, was a way of moving forward from the representation of African culture by outsiders in works like Joseph Conrad's *Heart of Darkness*. At the same time, *Purple Hibiscus*, as a literary work, looks backward to the long tradition of coming-of-age novels and, more historically, to the political history of Nigeria. While a reader unfamiliar with Nigerian culture is clearly made aware of the cultural negotiations taking place within the novel, readers unfamiliar with a broader literary context may not be aware of the literary negotiations taking place. In the short autobiographical excerpt above, Adichie makes mention of her own early exposure to British children's literature. *Purple Hibiscus* may both draw from and push against earlier traditions in British literature, even beyond the more obvious response to Conrad and Achebe. The literary critic Lily G. N. Mabura has pointed out that the novel's exploration of the growth of a young girl along with the explicit imagery of isolation, trauma, and growth places it clearly in the tradition of the Gothic novel of the late 1700s. In echoing the Gothic tradition, the novel may be finding another way to interrogate culture and the narrator's place within cultural traditions. In other words, just as the narrator finds herself examining the traditions of her family, her religion, her country, and her own growing identity, Adichie both feels comfortable within, and grows away from, literary tradition. While the context of the novel can be examined from the perspective of Nigerian cultural traditions and issues, the context may just as easily be studied from literary contextual perspectives and, ultimately, it may be discovered that the tensions found in both examinations mirror each other.

Pride and Prejudice by Jane Austen

Jane Austen's *Pride and Prejudice* is another interesting work to study because its context is something very often taken for granted in English literature classrooms. As a commonly read and discussed classic English work, the novel is often taught and read with closer attention to its theme and style than to context.

Interestingly, such a treatment is itself extremely contextual. The context described above is a specifically literary context involving a canon of great works of literature that many people believe ought to be read and studied as part of a larger acculturation process. To read the great works of a culture is to become fluent with the cultural values and norms commonly shared across that culture, including attitudes about what makes a book great. What may be slightly ironic is that this very contextual approach regarding cultural values is often overlooked as context at all: to be affirming (or reaffirming) the prevailing norms of a "great work" *might* lead to questions of what really distinguishes a "great" work but very often this meta-cognitive approach is omitted and such works are read instead because they are "great" in the first place.

In fairness to *Pride and Prejudice*, this is an intentionally exaggerated claim. In fact, this novel continues to draw intense scrutiny and consideration both popularly and critically and this is a work that has been approached from multiple contextual perspectives. We add it here as an example of how context can be considered in even the most familiar of literary works.

Pride and Prejudice, quite simply, follows Elizabeth Bennet as she deals with a life of manners, propriety, good upbringing and marriage in 19th-century England. The Bennet family, particularly the mother, is keen to marry off her five daughters in order to procure more long-term financial stability. As various suitors for the daughters come and go, both for good and ill, we begin to focus on Elizabeth and her relationship with Mr. Darcy. As the most interesting and aware of the characters (with a very well developed sense of irony), we follow Elizabeth through the trials and tribulations of their romance (including a very inauspicious introduction, and an initial rejection) against the backdrop of several other couplings in the novel.

"She is tolerable," Darcy said of Elizabeth.

Jane Austen and women's emancipation

The following extract comes from Vivien Jones's introduction to the Penguin edition of *Pride and Prejudice*. Here Jones refers to Mary Wollstonecraft, a famous 18th-century British feminist, who was instrumental in feminist and emancipation movements in both Europe and the United States:

> For Wollstonecraft, it is culture, not nature, which dictates that women behave like merely passive creatures of feeling, just as it is culture, not nature, which has allowed a self-perpetuating ruling class to reach a similar state of decadent self-indulgence. The ideal which she offers as an alternative to both—and to Burke's defence of tradition—is that of the professional middle class, where education is a process of self- as well as public improvement:
>
>> In the middle rank of life … men, in their youth, are prepared for professions, and marriage is not considered as the grand feature of their lives; whilst women, on the contrary, have no other scheme to sharpen their faculties. It is not business, extensive plans, or any of the excursive flights of ambition, that engross their attention; no, their thoughts are not employed in rearing noble structures.
>
> Women have only one route to self-improvement: 'To rise in the world, and have the liberty of running from pleasure to pleasure, they must marry advantageously, and to this object their time is sacrificed, and their persons often legally prostituted.' Instead, Wollstonecraft envisages the possibility of women becoming more publicly active participants in a middle-class meritocracy.
>
> The characterization of women as 'rational creatures,' the question of whether marriage is the only legitimate goal for a woman, the promotion of an active feminine identity and a professional ideal: these issues, raised by Wollstonecraft and others in the cause of revolutionary change, reverberate in political writing—and in fiction—throughout the 1790s and beyond. And they are clearly still very much current in *Pride and Prejudice*. In the 1790s radical women such as Mary Hays, Charlotte Smith and Wollstonecraft herself wrote experimental novels with active—even unchaste—heroines, novels which exposed the stifling limitations of the conventional happy-ever-after marriage; in response, anti-revolutionary novels by, for example, Jane West or Elizabeth Hamilton reasserted a virtuous, domestic feminine ideal, often
>
> through plots which demonstrate the catastrophic personal consequences of taking up radical ideas—or of giving to in 'first impressions'. Drafts of Austen's *First Impressions* (the initial title of *Pride and Prejudice*) have not survived, so we can't know precisely how her original novel might have fitted into this fictional 'war of ideas'. What is evident, however, is the broad resemblance between Austen's plot and the plots of some of the more conservative novels of the 1790s. In Austen's novel, Elizabeth has to learn to revise her first impressions, not just of Darcy but also of the unscrupulous Wickham; in conservative fiction, heroines similarly over-confident of the capacity to make independent decisions, and to act on them, learn the error of their self-assertive ways—often (unlike Elizabeth) by suffering near or utter ruin.
>
> More than ten years intervened between the writing of *First Impressions* and the publication of *Pride and Prejudice* in January 1813. Austen 'lopt and cropt' *First Impressions* to produce the novel as we now know it, in a rather different political climate. In the 1790s, with the failure of revolutionary ideals in France and repressive domestic policies at home, English radicals lost confidence and their voice became more muted; during the next decade, as the Napoleonic Wars went on, the sometimes hysterical reactionary atmosphere at the turn of the century also gradually gave way to a precarious conservative consensus, at least among the increasingly confident middle classes. Again, ideas about the role of women played a crucial part in these shifts of opinion. Conservatives and traditionalists could not ignore the new Wollstonecraftian femininity. It was violently discredited in some anti-revolutionary propaganda, usually by depicting Wollstonecraft and other radical women as prostitutes … But the idea that women might be active participants in culture also had a more complicated and pervasive effect: in a much modified form, active femininity was appropriated for the conservative cause of national family values…

Source: Introduction by Vivien Jones in Austen, Jane. 1812. *Pride and Prejudice*. London: Penguin. pp. ixx–xxi.

Questions to the text

1 What degrees of emancipation and/or conservative reinforcement of 18th-century family values does Elizabeth Bennett's marriage to Mr. Darcy support?

2 What attitudes to marriage does *Pride and Prejudice* convey? What other options did Elizabeth Bennet have?

3 How does this introduction affect your reading and approach to the novel?

4 How could the social circumstances and contexts of *Pride and Prejudice* apply to different cultures and contexts today?

On the surface, *Pride and Prejudice* does not offer the kind of revolutionary narrative of female emancipation of which Mary Wollstonecraft would approve, with its focus on marriage as a legitimate and rational goal, and as form of natural adaptation to the cultural and social circumstances of life in the Regency period in England (roughly approximate with Jane Austen's own life span of 1775–1817). But in this period, making the right marriage was the only way to maintain a position within this social structure, as women were prevented by law from the right to inherit property.

The essential question we have to ask ourselves about Elizabeth, however, is how much her character is conditioned by the limitations of the age and social context. And, how is the more self-conscious desire for a life of her own choosing, as someone in control of her own destiny, possible in these circumstances? How does the character of Elizabeth support or reinforce the values of the right to self-fulfilment and personal independence, as discussed by Wollstonecroft? How, in essence, the far-less-revolutionary drive of finding "degrees of personal happiness" (as she believes, by the end of the novel, only Mr. Darcy can offer her) can be achieved through being true to herself, and not just the expectations of society. In your own reading, imagine a country very much torn about the future role of women in society, how useful a role model is the character of Elizabeth? Why do you think she continues to be one of the most popular female role models in fiction (witnessed by the plethora of adaptations of the novel)?

Chatsworth House, in Derbyshire, was a possible model for Mr. Darcy's country house and grounds, Pemberley.

Matrimonial prospects in *Pride and Prejudice*

Relatively early in the novel, Elizabeth receives a proposal for marriage from her cousin Mr. Collins. Mrs. Bennet is excited by the prospect of marrying off a daughter to the man who will control the Bennet estate after Mr Bennet's death (and therefore potentially secure the long-term future of the family) but Elizabeth, who does not like him, refuses Mr. Collins in no uncertain terms. In this episode from the novel, that follows, Elizabeth's good friend Charlotte Lucas surprises everyone by positioning herself as the next Mrs. Collins.

Text 1

The Bennets were engaged to dine with the Lucases, and again during the chief of the day, was Miss Lucas so kind as to listen to Mr. Collins. Elizabeth took an opportunity of thanking her. "It keeps him in good humour," said she, "and I am more obliged to you than I can express." Charlotte assured her friend of her satisfaction in being useful, and that it amply repaid her for the little sacrifice of her time. This was very amiable, but Charlotte's kindness extended farther than Elizabeth had any conception of;—its object was nothing less, than to secure her from any return of Mr. Collins's addresses, by engaging them towards herself. Such was Miss Lucas's scheme; and appearances were so favourable that when they parted at night, she would have felt almost sure of success if he had not been to leave Hertforshire so very soon. But here, she did injustice to the fire and independence of his character, for it led him escape out of Longbourn House the next morning with admirable slyness, and hasten to Lucas Lodge to throw himself at her feet. He was anxious to avoid the notice of his cousins, from a conviction that if they saw him depart, they could not fail to conjecture his design, and he was not willing to have the attempt known till its success could be known likewise; for though feeling almost secure, and with reason, for Charlotte had been tolerably encouraging, he was comparatively diffident since the adventure of Wednesday. His reception however was of the most flattering kind. Miss Lucas perceived him from an upper window as he walked towards the house, and instantly set out to meet him accidentally in the lane. But little had she dared to hope that so much love and eloquence awaited her there.

In as short a time as Mr. Collins's long speeches would allow, everthing was settled between them to the satisfaction of both; and as they entered the house, he earnestly entreated her to name the day that was to make him the happiest of men; and though such a solicitation must be waived for the present, the lady felt no inclination to trifle with his happiness. The stupidity with which he was favoured by nature, must guard his courtship from any charm that could make a woman wish for its continuance; and Miss Lucas, who accepted him solely from the pure and disinterested desire of an establishment, cared now how soon that establishment were gained.

Sir William and Lady Lucas were speedily applied to for their consent; and it was bestowed with a most joyful alacrity. Mr. Collins's present circumstances made it a most eligible match for their daughter, to whom they could give little fortune; and his prospects of future wealth were exceedingly fair. Lady Lucas began directly to calculate with more interest than the matter had ever excited before, how many years longer Mr. Bennet was likely to live; and Sir William gave it as his decided opinion, that whenever Mr. Collins should be in possession of the Longbourn estate, it would be highly expedient that both he and his wife should make their appearance at St. James's. The whole family in short were properly overjoyed on the occasion. The younger girls formed hopes of

coming out a year or two sooner than they might otherwise have done; and the boys were relieved from their apprehension of Charlotte's dying an old maid. Charlotte herself was tolerably composed. She had gained her point, and had time to consider it. Her reflections were in general satisfactory. Mr. Collins to be sure was neither sensible nor agreeable; his society was irksome, and his attachment to her must be imaginary. But still he would be her husband.—Without thinking highly either of men or of matrimony, marriage had always been her object; it was the only honourable provision for well-educated young women of small fortune, and however uncertain of giving happiness, must be their pleasantest preservative from want. This preservative she had now obtained; and at the age of twenty-seven, without having ever been handsome, she felt all the good luck of it.

Source: Austen, Jane. 1812. *Pride and Prejudice.* London: Penguin. 2003. pp 119–20.

Text 2

Jane received an astonishing (to her) proposal of marriage from Mr. Darcy when she visits her now married friend Charlotte in Kent. Read carefully his proposal and her response. What is the significance of their reactions in reflection upon the title of the novel?

"In vain I have struggled. It will not do. My feelings will not be repressed. You must allow me to tell you how ardently I admire and love you."

Elizabeth's astonishment was beyond expression. She stared, coloured, doubted, and was silent. This he considered sufficient encouragement; and the avowal of all that he felt, and had long felt for her, immediately followed. He spoke well; but there were feelings besides those of the heart to be detailed; and he was not more eloquent on the subject of tenderness than of pride. His sense of her inferiority—of its being a degradation—of the family obstacles which had always opposed to inclination, were dwelt on with a warmth which seemed due to the consequence he was wounding, but was very unlikely to recommend his suit.

In spite of her deeply-rooted dislike, she could not be insensible to the compliment of such a man's affection, and though her intentions did not vary for an instant, she was at first sorry for the pain he was to receive; till, roused to resentment by his subsequent language, she lost all compassion in anger. She tried, however, to compose herself to answer him with patience, when he should have done. He concluded with representing to her the strength of that attachment which, in spite of all his endeavours, he had found impossible to conquer; and with expressing his hope that it would now be rewarded by her acceptance of his hand. As he said this, she could easily see that he had no doubt of a favourable answer. He spoke of apprehension and anxiety, but his countenance expressed real security. Such a circumstance could only exasperate farther, and, when he ceased, the colour rose into her cheeks, and she said:

"In such cases as this, it is, I believe, the established mode to express a sense of obligation for the sentiments avowed, however unequally they may be returned. It is natural that obligation should be felt, and if I could feel gratitude, I would now thank you. But I cannot—I have never desired your good opinion, and you have certainly bestowed it most unwillingly. I am sorry to have occasioned pain to anyone. It has been most unconsciously done, however, and I hope will be of short duration. The feelings which, you tell me, have long prevented the acknowledgment of your regard, can have little difficulty in overcoming it after this explanation."

Text 3

The following extract describes Elizabeth's visit to the elegant house and grounds of Pemberley, where Mr. Darcy lives. How does this episode anticipate the rewards of marrying into a rich and noble family?

Elizabeth's mind was too full for conversation, but she saw and admired every remarkable spot and point of view. They gradually ascended for half a mile, and then found themselves at the top of a considerable eminence, where the wood ceased, and the eye was instantly caught by Pemberley House, situated on the opposite side of a valley, into which the road with some abruptness wound. It was a large, handsome, stone building, standing well on rising ground, and backed by a ridge of high woody hills;—and in front, a stream of some natural importance was swelled into greater, but without any artificial appearance. Its banks were neither formal, nor falsely adorned. Elizabeth was delighted. She had never seen a place for which nature had done more, or where natural beauty had been so little counteracted by an awkward taste. They were all of them warm in their admiration; and at that moment she felt, that to be mistress of Pemberley might be something!

Source: Austen, Jane. 1812. *Pride and Prejudice*. London: Penguin, 2003. p. 235.

Questions to the text

1 Summarize Charlotte's approach to Mr. Collins. What does she hope to get out of a marriage with Mr. Collins? Would you describe Charlotte as a strong or a weak character? Explain.

2 How does Austen present Elizabeth and Mr. Darcy as acting upon their natural emotions and instincts? Do you think Elizabeth's response is extreme? What is conflicted in Mr. Darcy's representation of his feelings for her, that she so strongly objects to?

3 How do Elizabeth's perceptions of Pemberley suggest her changed feelings for the owner of the house and grounds? How does nature here reflect a view of cultural attitudes and human attributes?

Atonement by Ian McEwan

The novel *Atonement* by Ian McEwan offers an interesting perspective on the idea of context and a novel's relationship to time, place, and even authorial intention. Written in 2002, the story takes place mostly during the 1930s in England, and the early days of the Second World War in London and Dunkirk. For the most part, the story is told by an adult Briony Tallis who sees through the eyes of her younger self. At the beginning of the novel, Briony is a bright, observant, and somewhat fanciful girl who writes plays and invents intrigue. Why would McEwan write from the point of view of a woman recalling her childhood in the 1930s? What is the effect of creating this distance in his novel? These are questions we may have from the start but they are further complicated when, in the last section of the novel, we meet the adult Briony, who is the "author" of the novel we have just read. We learn that she herself has altered events of the past for her own purposes, skewing this semi-autobiographical account, to grant herself the privilege of atonement. McEwan, then, is writing as an older woman looking back to two different stages of her own life, and who writes as a younger fictional version of herself, writing from or about the perspective of an even younger self. Confusing? Perhaps, but what is clearly important is that the story within *Atonement*, the main plot line of the romance between Briony's sister Cecelia and Robbie Turner, and the false accusation that splits them apart forever, is a mistake that Briony has to live with for the rest of her life. Read the following extract from the novel about Robbie's experience during the evacuation from Dunkirk, and the critical article that follows. Consider, as you read the following, the importance of context. Later in the chapter, you will read a critical article that may shed some light on additional contextual issues.

A still from the 2007 film adaptation of *Atonement*.

Read

Read the following passage and try to think about it as you would an unseen commentary. In other words, analyze the passage in terms of what is happening, what ideas or feelings are being suggested and issues of literary technique such as who the narrator is. Who is speaking or seeing in the passage? Who is seeing the events taking place? What is the setting? What do we know about what is going on?

There was more confusion ahead, more shouting. Incredibly, an armored column was forcing its way against the forward press of traffic, soldiers, refugees. The crowd parted reluctantly. People squeezed into the gaps between abandoned vehicles or against shattered walls and doorways. It was a French column, hardly more than a detachment—three armored cars, two half-tracks and two troop carriers. There was no show of common cause. Among the British troops the view was that the French had let them down. No will to fight for their own country. Irritated at being pushed aside, the Tommies swore, and taunted their allies with shouts of "Maginot!" For their part, the *poilus* must have heard rumors of an evacuation. And here they were, being sent to cover the rear. "Cowards! To the boats! Go shit in your pants!" Then they were gone, and the crowd closed in again under a cloud of diesel smoke and walked on.

They were approaching the last houses in the village. In a field ahead, he saw a man and his collie dog walking behind a horse-drawn plow. Like the ladies in the shoe shop, the farmer did not seem aware of the convoy. These lives were lived in parallel—war was a hobby for the enthusiasts and no less serious for that. Like the deadly pursuit of a hunt to hounds, while over the next hedge a woman in the backseat of a passing motorcar was absorbed in her knitting, and in the bare garden of a new house a man was teaching his son to kick a ball. Yes, the plowing would still go on and there'd be a crop, someone to reap it and mill it, others to eat it, and not everyone would be dead …

Turner was thinking this when Nettle gripped his arm and pointed. The commotion of the passing French column had covered the sound, but they were easy enough to see. There were at least fifteen of them, at ten thousand feet, little dots in the blue circling above the road. Turner and the corporals stopped to watch and everyone nearby saw them too.

An exhausted voice murmured close to his hear, "F…Where's the RAF?"

Another said knowingly, "They'll go for the Frogs."

As if goaded into disproof, one of the specks peeled away and began its near-vertical dive, directly above their heads. For seconds the sound did not reach them. The silence was building like pressure in their ears. Even the wild shouts that went up and down the road did not relieve it. Take cover! Disperse! At the double!

Source: McEwan, Ian. 2002. *Atonement*. New York: Doubleday. pp. 220–21.

Dunkirk, France, in 1940, after the evacuation of British and French troops.

Reading this passage without any information about the text at hand, other than perhaps a date, many readers would remark on the portrayal of war and the strange sense of imminent danger alongside a world or a life that keeps going in a relatively ordinary fashion. Most readers would remark on the almost stream-of-consciousness perspective of the first part of the passage from the perspective of the soldier in the battle, followed by the change in voice to the narrator who has been present from the start. There is a separation between the thoughts of Robbie Turner in the first half and the voice of the narrator who comes in to describe more broadly the scene at hand. Who is the narrator? What perspective does the narrator have that Robbie Turner does not?

Many readers of this passage might guess that it describes the evacuation of French and British soldiers from Dunkirk near the beginning of the Second World War. But is this identification necessary? Does it matter that this is a pivotal moment in history? We are beginning to consider the broader context. Besides wanting to know what else is going on in the novel, what other information do you feel would help in your understanding? Does the political or historical context of this passage matter? How naive would it be to consider this passage just as it appears in front of us on the page? Does the meaning of the passage change when we know that the author of the passage is Ian McEwan writing in 2001? Does the meaning of the passage change when we know the author is Ian McEwan pretending to be the 77-year-old author Briony Tallis, 59 years after the initial events, writing a fictional account out of a sense of guilt for Robbie Turner's experience in Dunkirk?

Authorial intentions

Read the following extract that comes from the beginning of a critical article about *Atonement*. How important is an understanding of context to the writer's interpretation of McEwan's novel?

In his review of *Atonement* for *The Times Literary Supplement,* Robert Macfarlane observes that "the question of how the past is represented in language has become the central obsession of British fiction over the past three decades". I would argue that the tendency has been far more marked in the 1990s and early 2000s, when British novelists have engaged with the past in ways that have little to do with the traditional forms of historical fiction or with the self-conscious parody of the historiographic metafictions of the previous decades…

The attraction of the past has proved so strong that it has reached writers long known for their immersion in the present and the creation of self-enclosed fictional worlds. Ian McEwan's novels of the 1990s marked a departure from the suffocating atmosphere of his ealy fiction, which is best symbolized perhaps by the body of the mother encased in cement in *The Cement Garden* (1978) or the surreal quality of the unnamed city of Venice in *The Comfort of Strangers* (1981). Perhaps it was inevitable that, as he grew older, McEwan would leave behind the cool analysis of incest, sadism, and abjection that had gained him notoriety and would explore the power of evil in twentieth-century European history.

In the introduction to the edition of his television plays, McEwan spoke of his intention to write about World War II:

> *Three years later I read* The People's War, *a social history of World War II, and resolved to write something one day about the war. I come from an Army background and although I was born three years after the war ended, it was a living presence throughout my childhood. Sometimes I found it hard to believe I had not been alive in the summer of 1940.*

An event in the summer of 1940, the retreat of the British Expeditionary Army to Dunkirk, features in *Atonement*, but the story the novel tells is far more complex and nuanced than a mere fictional account of one of the great military disasters in British history. The epigraph, the well-known moment in the conversation between Henry Tilney and Catherine Morland in *Northanger Abbey* in which the young man tells Catherine how unfounded her surmises about General Tilney have been, relates to *Atonement* in two ways. In an interview with Jeff Giles in *Newsweek*, McEwan says that in his notebooks he called *Atonement* "my Jane Austen novel"; and in a long conversation focusing on *The Child in Time, Enduring Love,* and *Atonement,* he makes explicit the connection embedded in the epigraph:

> *What are the distances between what is real and what is imagined? Catherine Morland, the heroine of Jane Austen's* Northanger Abbey, *was a girl so full of the delights of Gothic fiction that she causes havoc around her when she imagines a perfectly innocent man to be capable of the most terrible things. For many, many years, I've been thinking how I might devise a hero or heroine who could echo that process in Catherine Morland, but then go a step further and look at, not the crime, but the process of atonement, and do it through writing—do it through storytelling, I would say.*

The Jane Austen connection is thus twofold. On the one hand, Briony Tallis, like Catherine Morland, is a heroine whose perception is distorted by literature and an imperfect knowledge of the world. On the other, in the first part of *Atonement,* set in 1935, the country house as a literary motif makes ironic intertextual allusions to *Mansfield Park* (the rehearsal of a play that finally is not performed, Robbie Turner's fleeting interest in landscape gardening, the sexual predator from London) and to twentieth-century works of fiction such as E.M. Forster's *Howards End* and Evelyn Waugh's *Brideshead Revisited.* Thus, in his exploration of the gap between what is real and what is imagined, McEwan deploys a variety of stylistic devices and narrative techniques that give the novel its multilayered texture. Hermione Lee put it this way in her review of *Atonement* for *The Observer:*

Atonement asks what the English novel of the twenty-first century has inherited, and what it can do now. One of the things it can do, very subtly in McEwan's case, is to be androgynous. This is a novel written by a man acting the part of a woman writing a "male" *subject, and there's nothing to distinguish between them.*

Source: Hidalgo, Pilar. "Memory and Storytelling in Ian McEwan's Atonement." *Critique* vol. 46, no. 2. Winter 2005. pp. 82–83.

Discussion Point

Role models

Think of works of recent fiction to support discussions around the following questions.

1 Think of characters in fiction that are modelled on other fictional characters, like the many attempts to insert the characters and plot of Jane Austen novel into a fictional work of contemporary life. What is the challenge in doing this?

2 How do we use our knowledge of the past and of historical literature, to recreate historical periods in contemporary literature? What skills does the author use to make these scenes and interior monologues of fictional characters believable?

3 Find examples of men writing as women, and women writing as men. Many critics have pointed out that Jane Austen rarely presented a male character with a private internal monologue, or in a scene that wasn't told from the point of view of a female observer, due to her extremely limited social circumstances, and her desire to retain a sense of authenticity in her writing. What are the benefits and limitations of this approach? Why do other authors, like McEwen, take the opposite approach? What is in it for them?

4 Do you think that the passage about the evacuation of Dunkirk would fulfil McEwan's desire to write about the war? Whose vision of the war is depicted: Robbie's, Briony's, McEwan's, or those of his sources?

The narrator of *Atonement*, Briony Tallis as a young adult woman, looks back on her past and tries to make amends for ruining the lives of her sister Celia and Celia's boyfriend Robbie Turner. Her story ends with a kind of reconciliation with her sister. As we meet Briony Tallis as an older woman, however, we learn that what we have just read is a fictional attempt at atonement, and that the reconciliation with her sister never actually happened. We realize that the past has been filtered through a fictional recollection. At the same time, as readers we are aware that none of these moves are happening in "real life," that the author Ian McEwan wants us to consider the purposes and uses of storytelling to recreate the past, to make amends, and to tell a kind of truth. The very title of the novel, *Atonement*, like Jane Austen's *Pride and Prejudice*, signals the development of some form of emotional maturity and a lesson that is learned. Not only has McEwan completed a complex task of finding a way to recreate a past England, past English forms of the novel, and important historical moments, but he wants his reader to understand that this task itself is at the center of the novel.

Activity

Historical truth

Consider the following brief passage. On the way to a tribute to her career as a writer, Briony Tallis considers her recent work. She has recently been told by her doctor that she has been diagnosed with Alzheimer's and will soon be losing her memory completely. Before arriving at the tribute, she decides to visit the Imperial War Museum library in London where she had done much of the research for her last novel:

> I spent a while chatting with the Keeper of Documents. I handed over the bundle of letters Mr. Nettle wrote me about Dunkirk—most gratefully received. They'll be stored with all the others I've given. The Keeper had found me an obliging old colonel of the Buffs, something of an amateur historian himself, who had read the relevant pages of my typescript and faxed through his suggestions. His notes were handed to me now—irascible, helpful. I was completely absorbed by them, thank God.
>
> "Absolutely no (underlined twice) soldier serving with the British army would say 'On the double.' Only an American would give such an order. The correct term is 'At the double.'"
>
> I love these little things, this pointillist approach to verisimilitude, the correction of detail that cumulatively gives such satisfaction.
>
> "No one would ever think of saying 'twenty-five-pound guns.' The term was either 'twenty-five pounders' or 'twenty-five-pounder guns.' Your usage would sound distinctly bizarre, even to a man who was not with the Royal Artillery."
>
> Like policemen in a search team, we go on hands and knees and crawl our way toward the truth.
>
> "You have your RAF chappie wearing a beret. I really don't think so. Outside the Tank Corps, even the army didn't have them in 1940. I think you'd better give the man a forage cap."
>
> Finally, the colonel, who began his letter by addressing me as "Miss Tallis," allowed some impatience with my sex to show through. What was our kind doing anyway, meddling in these affairs?
>
> "Madame (underlined three times)—a Stuka does not carry 'a single thousand-ton bomb.' Are you aware that a navy frigate hardly weighs that much? I suggest you look into the matter further."
>
> Merely a typo. I meant to type "pound." I made a note of these corrections, and wrote a letter of thanks to the colonel. I paid for some photocopies of documents which I arranged into orderly piles for my own archives. I returned the books I had been using to the front desk, and threw away various scraps of paper. The work space was cleared of all traces of me. As I said my goodbyes to the Keeper, I learned that the Marshall Foundation was about to make a grant to the museum. After a round of handshaking with the other librarians, and my promise to acknowledge the department's help, a porter was called to see me down. Very kindly, the girl in the cloak-room called a taxi, and one of the younger members of the door staff carried my bag all the way out to the pavement.
>
> During the ride back north, I thought about the colonel's letter, or rather, about my own pleasure in these trivial alterations. If I really cared so much about facts, I should have written a different kind of book. But my work was done. There would be no further drafts.

Source: McEwan, Ian. 2002. *Atonement*. New York: Doubleday. 2002. pp. 339–40.

Questions to the text

1 How can Briony's position in this passage in relation to historical fact be related to the position of McEwan"

2 What is suggested here about the nature of truth in relation to history? What is suggested about the difficulty of conveying historical context within a novel?

3 Does an immersion in, or fascination with, facts contradict the desire to tell a fictional story?

Poetry by Wislawa Szymborska and Carol Ann Duffy

Wislawa Szymborska is a Polish poet born in 1923. She has experienced firsthand the turbulent history of contemporary Poland from the Nazi invasion to socialist military rule to the contemporary free market economy of post-1989 Central and Eastern Europe. Szymborska won the Noble Prize for Literature in 1996 and is known for poems that explore existential themes in a deceptively simple manner. Many of Szymborska's poems seem to address hardship, chance, and the fleeting beauty of life but end up embracing these difficulties as that which, in fact, give life its special meaning.

The poet Carol Ann Duffy was born in Glasgow in 1955. After a long career in writing that has included work in drama and television but most famously poetry, Duffy was appointed Poet Laureate of Britain in 2009. Duffy's poetry is notable for its variety and its exploration of a wide range of registers and it is also particularly interesting for its treatment, at times seemingly autobiographical, of the roles of women in contemporary society. In her collection *The World's Wife* Duffy attempts, sometimes playfully and sometimes poignantly, to give voice to historical and fictional "wives" of famous male figures. These poems capture Duffy's clear and interesting diction and also show her ability to touch matters of universal significance.

Szymborska's poetry was originally written in Polish and Duffy writes in English. In the poems that follow, both Szymborska and Duffy create fictional voices and discuss issues of both broad philosophical and more everyday routine concern. In terms of cultural context, these poems call for specific literary or cultural knowledge in order to understand the general implications, conveyed through the complex fusion of voices and literary allusions.

An allusion, or an implied or stated reference to another work of art or literature, functions as a way of pulling context into the text itself. In other words, by making an allusion, a writer is able to broaden the implications of the text at hand. At one level, an allusion functions as a way of establishing context. By containing a reference to another work or historical period a text identifies its historical, philosophical, or artistic concerns. By consciously linking to another work, allusion also functions to broaden the thematic concerns of the text. An allusion allows a writer to examine issues in the original work or to put those issues into a new light. Allusion can often self-consciously create tension between new and old works. In a sense, allusion allows writers to both build on the past and push against it. While in many works authors make allusions in subtle ways to literary traditions (by appropriating a rhyme scheme or a particular metaphor, for example), in the examples that follow Szymborska and Duffy make more concrete allusions to the past signaled through the titles of their poems. In the process, they reconsider accepted stories and traditions to reflect on more contemporary concerns.

Cassandra In Greek mythology Cassandra was the daughter of King Priam and Queen Hecuba of Troy. As a young woman the god Apollo was consumed by her beauty and granted her the gift of prophecy. When she didn't return his love, however, she did not have her gift taken away but was cursed with the fate that no one would ever believe her telling of the future. Cassandra foretold the fall of Troy but no one believed that they would eventually see their great city in ashes. No one believed Cassandra, in fact, until she foretold and walked to her own death at the hands of Clytemnestra.

Activity

Poetic allusion

Read each of the poems that follow and take some brief notes about their meaning or significance. Then read the brief explanation of the main allusion following each poem. How has your understanding changed? How necessary is such an explanation?

Soliloquy for Cassandra

Here I am, Cassandra.
And this is my city under ashes.
And these are my prophet's staff and ribbons.
And this is my head full of doubts.

It's true, I am triumphant.
My prophetic words burn like fire in the sky.
Only unacknowledged prophets
are privy to such prospects.
Only those who got off on the wrong foot,
whose predictions turned to fact so quickly—
it's as if they'd never lived.
I remember it so clearly—
how people, seeing me, would break off in mid-word.
Laughter died.
Lovers' hands unclasped.
Children ran to their mothers.
I didn't even know their short-lived names.
And that song about a little green leaf—
no one every finished it near me.
I loved them.
But I loved them haughtily.
From heights beyond life.
From the future. Where it's always empty
and nothing is easier than seeing death.
I'm sorry that my voice was hard.
Look down on yourselves from the stars, I cried,
look down on yourselves from the stars.
They heard me and lowered their eyes.
They lived within life.
Pierced by that great wind.
Condemned.
Trapped from birth in departing bodies.
But in them they bore a moist hope,
a flame fueled by its own flickering.
They really knew what a moment means,
oh any moment, any one at all
before—
It turns out I was right.
But nothing has come of it.
And this is my robe, slightly singed.
And this is my prophet's junk.
And this is my twisted face.
A face that didn't know it could be beautiful.

Source: Szymborska, Wislawa. 1967. "Soliloquy for Cassandra." *View With a Grain of Sand*. New York: Harcourt, 1995 pp. 45–46.

Lot's Wife

They say I looked back out of curiosity,
but I could have had other reasons.
I looked back mourning my silver bowl.
Carelessly, while tying my sandal strap.
So I wouldn't have to keep staring at the righteous nape
of my husband Lot's neck.
From the sudden conviction that if I dropped dead
he wouldn't so much as hesitate.
From the disobedience of the meek.
Checking for pursuers.

Raphael (school), a fresco of scenes from the Story of Abraham and Lot in the Vatican, Rome.

Lot's wife In the Old Testament of the Bible, Lot and his family settled near the cities of Sodom and Gomorrah. When God decided to punish the cities for their sinful ways, Lot and his family were saved because of the kindness they had shown to Angels who had come to visit the cities before their destruction in search of good people. The Angels rush Lot and his family out of the city with one warning: not to look back on the destruction of Sodom. As the family flees, however, Lot's wife looks back and is turned into a pillar of salt. In the New Testament of the Bible, Jesus reminds his followers of the story of Lot's wife as a way of telling them not to look back with longing to their previous sinful ways.

Struck by the silence, hoping God had changed his mind.
Our two daughters were already vanishing over the hilltop.
I felt age within me. Distance.
The futility of wandering. Torpor.
I looked back setting my bundle down.
I looked back not knowing where to set my foot.
Serpents appeared on my path,
spiders, field mice, baby vultures.
They were neither good nor evil now—every living thing
was simply creeping or hopping along in the mass panic.
I looked back in desolation.
In shame because we had stolen away.
Wanting to cry out, to go home.
Or only when a sudden gust of wind
Unbound my hair and lifted up my robe.
It seemed to me that they were watching from the walls of Sodom
and bursting into thunderous laughter again and again.
I looked back in anger.
To savor their terrible fate.
I looked back for all the reasons given above.
I looked back involuntarily.
It was only a rock that turned underfoot, growling at me.
It was a sudden crack that stopped my in my tracks.
A hamster on its hind paws tottered on the edge.
It was then we both glanced back.
No, no. I ran on,
I crept, I flew upward
until darkness fell from the heavens
and with it scorching gravel and dead birds.
I couldn't breathe and spun around and around.
Anyone who saw me must have thought I was dancing.
It's not inconceivable that my eyes were open.
It's possible I fell facing the city.

Source: Szymborska, Wislawa. 1976. "Lot's Wife." *View With a Grain of Sand*. New York: Harcourt, 1995 pp. 101–102.

Mrs Lazarus

I had grieved. I had wept for a night and a day
over my loss, ripped the cloth I was married in
from my breasts, howled, shrieked, clawed
at the burial stones till my hands bled, retched
his name over and over again, dead, dead.
Gone home. Gutted the place. Slept in a single cot,
widow, one empty glove, white femur
in the dust, half. Stuffed dark suits
into black bags, shuffled in a dead man's shoes,
noosed the double knot of a tie round my bare neck,
gaunt nun in the mirror, touching herself. I learnt
the Stations of Bereavement, the icon of my face
in each bleak frame; but all those months
he was going away from me, dwindling
to the shrunk size of a snapshot, going,
going. Till his hame was not longer a certain spell
for his face. The last hair on his head

The wife of Lazarus Another story from the Bible, this one from the New Testament, tells the story of Lazarus, a friend of Jesus' who takes ill and dies. While the sisters of Lazarus (a wife is not mentioned in the Bible story) had pleaded with Jesus to come to visit Lazarus while he was sick, Jesus intentionally waited two days before arriving. While the sisters were upset with Jesus, he assured them that Lazarus would be fine. Jesus had the stone moved away from the entrance to Lazarus' grave and Lazarus walked out in his death shroud.

floated out from a book. His scent went from the house.
The will was read. See, he was vanishing
to the small zero held by the gold of my ring.
Then he was gone. Then he was legend, language;
my arm on the arm of the schoolteacher—the shock
of a man's strength under the sleeve of his coat—
along the hedgerows. But I was faithful
for as long as it took. Until he was a memory.
So I could stand that evening in the field
in a shawl of fine air, healed, able
to watch the edge of the moon occur to the sky
and a hare thump from a hedge; then notice
the village men running towards me, shouting,
behind them the women and children, barking dogs,
and I knew by the shrill light
on the blacksmith's face, the sly eyes
of the barmaid, the sudden hands bearing me
into the hot tang of the crowd parting before me.
He lived. I saw the horror on his face.
I heard his mother's crazy song. I breathed
his stench; my bridegroom in his rotting shroud,
moist and disheveled from the grave's slack chew,
croaking his cuckold name, disinherited, out of his time.

Source: Duffy, Carol Ann. "Mrs Lazarus." 1994. *Selected Poems*. Penguin Books, New York. pp 135–36.

Mrs Aesop

By Christ, he could bore for Purgatory. He was small,
didn't prepossess. So he tried to impress. *Dead men,
Mrs Aesop,* he'd say, *tell no tales.* Well, let me tell you now
that the bird in his hand shat on his sleeve,
never mind the two worth less in the bush. Tedious.
Going out was worst. He'd stand at our gate, look, then leap;
scour the hedgerows for a shy mouse, the fields for a sly fox, the sky for
one particular swallow that couldn't make a summer. The jackdaw,
according to him, envied the eagle. Donkeys would, on the whole,
prefer to be lions.
On one appalling evening stroll, we passed an old hare
snoozing in a ditch—he stopped and made a note—
and then, about a mile further on, a tortoise, somebody's pet,
creeping, slow as marriage, up the road. *Slow but certain, Mrs Aesop,
wins the race.* Asshole.
What race? What sour grapes? What silk purse,
sow's ear, dog in a manger, what big fish? Some days,
I could barely keep awake as the story droned on
towards the moral of itself. *Action, Mrs A., speaks louder
than words.* And that's another thing, the sex was diabolical. I gave him
a fable one night
about a little cock that wouldn't crow, a razor-sharp axe
I'll cut off your tail, all right, I said, *to save my face.*
That shut him up. I laughed last, longest.

Source: Duffy, Carol Ann. "Mrs Aesop." 1994. *Selected Poems*. New York: Penguin Books. pp 141–42.

Aesop Aesop (*circa.* 620–564 BCE) was the ancient Greek writer of fables. Although he may not have written or composed them all, a large number of fables are attributed to Aesop. As an interesting side note the ancient Greek philosopher Himerius said that Aesop "was laughed at and made fun of not because of his tales, but on account of his looks and the sound of his voice." Some of the famous fables attributed to Aesop include "The Tortoise and the Hare," "The Ant and the Grasshopper," "The Lion and the Mouse," "The Boy Who Cried Wolf," "The Fox and the Grapes," and "The Wolf in Sheep's Clothing."

Questions to the text

1 How many of the above allusions do you recognize?

2 When looking at the poems for a second time, how do the poets comment on and take advantage of their basic allusions?

3 In what ways do the poems comment on or ammend the allusions?

4 How do the poets manipulate or move away from their original material?

5 How are the poems important beyond the allusions they are making?

6 In what way is giving voice to these "wives" a feminist project or an attempt to give forgotten women their place in history? In what ways do the poems represent a larger consideration of human existence and concerns?

The Echo Maker by Richard Powers

The Echo Maker tells the story of a young man who, because of a car accident, is afflicted with Capgras syndrome, a condition that causes him to have all of his memories and mental powers except for the ability to recognize the people closest to him—to in fact recognize loved ones but to think they are impostors. While the novel is a realistic and contemporary engagement with the lives of people who are struggling with physical and emotional pain, it is also an exercise in contemplating the nature of the human mind versus the spirit—knowledge versus belief—and the underlying mental and spiritual aspects that make us human. The writer, Richard Powers, is known for his intricate and detailed storytelling and novel approaches to the intersections of art and science. Powers has written novels that consider the ability of computers with artificial intelligence to understand literature, the difference between virtual reality and the wandering thoughts of a person in solitary confinement, and the fictional discovery of a gene for happiness. *The Echo Maker* takes place in the US state of Nebraska near the Platte River. Every year in this location thousands of cranes stop and rest for a few days on their migration towards the warmer south. Powers uses this conceit to wonder about the capabilities of the mind. How are birds able to find the same place year after year on their migration? Do the birds have a memory, in the way we would describe memory, of place? Is it a special kind of memory that makes us human? What happens when a person loses the most personal and comforting part of memory.

Activity

Instinct

Read the passage below from *The Echo Maker* by Richard Powers and answer the questions below.

Cranes keep landing as night falls. Ribbons of them roll down, slack against the sky. They float in from all compass points, in kettles of a dozen, dropping with the dusk. Scores of *Grus Canadensis* settle on the thawing river. They gather on the island flats, grazing, beating their wings, trumpeting: the advance wave of a mass evacuation. More birds land by the minute, the air red with calls.

A neck stretches long; legs drape behind. Wings curl forward, the length of a man. Spread like fingers, primaries tip the bird into the wind's plane. The blood-red head bows and the wings sweep together, a cloaked benediction. Tail cups and belly buckles, surprised by the upsurge of ground. Legs kick out, their backward knees flapping like broken landing gear. Another bird plummets and stumbles forward, fighting for a spot in the packed staging ground along those few miles of water still clear and wide enough to pass as safe.

Twilight comes early, as it will for a few more weeks. The sky, ice blue through the encroaching willows and cottonwoods, flares up, a brief rose, before collapsing to indigo. Late February on the Platte, and the night's chill haze hangs over this river, frosting the stubble from last fall that still fills the bordering fields. The nervous birds, tall as children, crowd together wing by wind on this stretch of river, one that they've learned to find by memory.

They converge on the river at winter's end as they have for eons, carpeting the wetlands. In this light, something saurian still clings to them: the oldest flying things on earth, one stutter-step away from pterodactyls. As darkness falls for real, it's a beginner's world again, the same evening as that day sixty million years ago when this migration began.

Half a million birds—four fifths of all the sandhill cranes on earth—home in on this river. They trace the Central Flyway, an hourglass laid over the continent. They push up from New Mexico, Texas, and Mexico, hundreds of miles each day, with thousands more ahead before they reach their remembered nests. For a few weeks, this stretch of river shelters the miles-long flock. Then, by the start of spring, they'll rise and head away, feeling their way up to Saskatchewan, Alaska, or beyond.

This year's flight has always been. Something in the birds retraces a route laid down centuries before their parents showed it to them. And each crane recalls the route still to come.

Tonight's cranes mill again on the braided water. For another hour, their massed calls carry on the emptying air. The birds flap and fidget, edgy with migration. Some tear up frosty twigs and toss them in the air. Their jitters spill over into combat. At last the sandhills settle down into wary, stilt-legged sleep, most standing in the water, a few farther up in the stubbled fields.

A squeal of brakes, the crunch of metal on asphalt, one broken scream and then another rouse the flock. The truck arcs through the air, corkscrewing into the field. A plume shoots through the birds. They lurch off the ground, wings beating. The panicked carpet lifts, circles, and falls again. Calls that seem to come from creatures twice their size carry miles before fading.

By morning, that sound never happened. Again there is only here, now, the river's braid, a feast of waste grain that will carry these flocks north, beyong the Arctic Circle. As first light breaks, the fossils return to life, testing their legs, tasting the frozen air, leaping free, bills skyward and throats open. And then, as if the night took nothing, forgetting everything but this moment, the dawn sandhills start to dance. Dance as they have since before this river started.

Source: Powers, Richard. 2006. *The Echo Maker*. New York: Farrar, Straus and Giroux. pp. 3–4.

Questions to the text

1 What is the central activity in this passage?
2 How are the cranes described?
3 How are the cranes compared to humans? How are they differentiated from humans?
4 Beyond migration itself, what ideas does the narrator seem to consider in relation to the cranes?
5 What is the effect of the brief description of the car accident? In what ways is it both significant and insignificant?

Activity

Technology as context

When Powers considers scientific phenomenon he often wonders about the relationship between contemporary advances and the nature of the human mind. After winning the National Book Award for *The Echo Maker*, Powers shocked many people by revealing the fact that he had "written" his novel by dictating directly into a word processing document using speech recognition software. Many people wondered if this dictation could even be considered writing. The following excerpts from an essay by Powers address the nature of the use of dictation software. Powers considers it as both a new technological advancement that allows him to write laying in bed and also as a nod to the past, to an oral age when words in storytelling may have been, so to speak, closer to our lips. Does the following article push you to reread the passage from *The Echo Maker* to look for its oral qualities?

How to Speak a Book

Except for brief moments of duress, I haven't touched a keyboard for years. No fingers were tortured in producing these words—or the last half a million words of my published fiction. By rough count, I've sent 10,000 e-mail messages without typing. My primary digital prosthetic doesn't even have keys.

I write these words from bed, under the covers with my knees up, my head propped and my three-pound tablet PC—just a shade heavier than a hardcover—resting in my lap, almost forgettable. I speak untethered, without a headset, into the slate's microphone array. The words appear as fast as I can speak, or they wait out my long pauses. I touch them up with a stylus, scribbling or re-speaking as needed. Whole phrases die and revive, as quickly as I could have hit the backspace. I hear every sentence as it's made, testing what it will sound like, inside the mind's ear.

Like all good Jetson futures, speech recognition is really a memory. Speak the thing into being: as dreams go, that's as old as they get. Once, all stories existed only in speech, and no technology caused more upheaval than the written word. In the "Phaedrus," Socrates—who talked a whole lot but never, apparently, wrote a word—uncorks at length about how writing damages memory, obscures authority and even alters meaning. But we have his warning only through Plato's suspect transcript.

For most of history, most reading was done out loud. Augustine remarks with surprise that Bishop Ambrose could read without moving his tongue. Our passage into silent text came late and slow, and poets have resisted it all the way. From Homer to hip-hop, the hum is what counts. Blind Milton chanted "Paradise Lost" to his daughters. Of his 159-line "Tintern Abbey," Wordsworth said, "I began it upon leaving Tintern ... and concluded ... after a ramble of four or five days. ... Not a line of it was altered, and not any part of it written down till I reached Bristol." Wallace Stevens used to compose while walking to work, then dictate the results to his secretary, before proceeding to his official correspondence as vice president of the Hartford insurance company. (I've tried dictating to my tablet while rambling; traffic and birdsong make it babble.)

Even novelists, working in a form so very written, have needed to write by voice. Stendhal dictated "The Charterhouse of Parma" in seven weeks. An impoverished Dostoyevsky had just six weeks to deliver the manuscript of "The Gambler" or face complete ruin. He hired a stenographer, knocked the book out in four weeks, then married the girl. ...

Why all this need for speech? Long after we've fully retooled for printed silence, we still feel residual meaning in the wake of how things sound. Speech and writing share some major neural circuitry, much

of it auditory. All readers, even the fast ones, subvocalize. That's why so many writers—like Flaubert, shouting his sentences in his gueuloir—test the rightness of their words out loud.

What could be less conducive to thought's cadences than stopping every time your short-term memory fills to pass those large-scale musical phrases through your fingers, one tedious letter at a time? You'd be hard-pressed to invent a greater barrier to cognitive flow. The 130-year-old qwerty keyboard may even have been designed to slow fingers and prevent key jamming. We compose on keys the way dogs walk on two legs. However good we get, the act will always be a little freakish ....

For one, I can write lying down. I can forget the machine is even there. I can live above the level of the phrase, thinking in full paragraphs and capturing the rhythmic arcs before they fade. I don't have to queue, stop, batch dispatch and queue up again. I spend less mental overhead on orthography and finger mechanics and more on hearing my characters speak themselves into existence. Mostly, I'm just a little closer to what my cadences might mean, when replayed in the subvocal voices of some other auditioner.

Writing is the act of accepting the huge shortfall between the story in the mind and what hits the page. "From your lips to God's ears," goes the old Yiddish wish. The writer, by contrast, tries to read God's lips and pass along the words, via some crazed game of Telephone, to a further listener. And for that, no interface will ever be clean or invisible enough for us to get the passage right. As Bede says of Caedmon, scrambling to transcribe the angelic hymn dictated to him in a dream: "This is the sense, but not the words themselves as he sang them in his sleep; for however well composed, verses cannot be translated out of one language into another without much loss of beauty and loftiness."

Everything we write—through any medium—is lost in translation. But something new is always found again, in their eager years. In Derrida's fears. Make that: in the reader's ears.

Source: Powers, Richard. "How to Speak a Book." *New York Times*. January 7, 2007.

Your turn

Here are a few ideas that could help you explore the context of *The Echo Maker* in terms of its subject matter and its production.

- Reasearch Capgras syndrome or read the popular work of neurologist Oliver Sacks (a character in the novel is modeled closely on Sacks) to learn more about brain disorders and what makes us human.

- Research the cranes of the river Platte and their annual migration.
- Consider the ways in which technology affects the way we create and disseminate works of fiction. How does the computer change reading and writing? What are the effects of e-readers on the way we find and read books? How would the invention of the printing press have changed not only access to books, but the kinds of books that were being written?

Questions to the text

1 In what way is Powers again interested in the intersection of art and science?

2 Do you think it would be freeing to "speak a book"? Does it count as writing?

3 Does knowing the work's mode of production influence your reading of it? Go back and reread the passage from *The Echo Maker*. Can you sense the rhythm of the human voice in the passage? If you can, do you think it is only because you now know it was dictated?

The Moor's Last Sigh by Salman Rushdie

Chowpatty Beach scene with Ganesha, India.

Activity

Cultural context

Before receiving any information about Rushdie's novel, read the following passage considering style, content and possible contextual issues.

> Once a year, my mother Aurora Zogoiby liked to dance higher than the gods. Once a year, the gods came to Chowpatty Beach to bathe in the filthy sea: fat bellied idols by the thousand, papier-mâché effigies of the elephant-headed deity Ganesha or Ganpati Bappa, swarming towards the water astride papier-mâché rats—for Indian rats, as we know, carry gods as well as plagues. Some of these tusk'n'tail duos were small enough to be borne on human shoulders, or cradled in human arms; others were the size of small mansions, and were pulled along on great-wheeled wooden carts by hundreds of disciples. There were, in addition, many Dancing Ganeshas, and it was these wiggle-hipped Ganpatis, love-handled and plump of gut, against whom Aurora competed, setting her profane gyrations against the jolly jiving of the much-replicated god. Once a year, the skies were full of Color-by-DeLuxe clouds: pink and purple, magenta and vermilion, saffron and

green, these powder-clouds, squirted from re-used insecticide guns, or floating down from some bursting balloon-cluster wafting across the sky, hung in the air above the deities "like aurora-not-borealis-but-bombayalis," as the painter Vasco Miranda used to say. Also sky-high above crowds and gods, year after year—for forty-one years in all—fearless upon the precipitous ramparts of our Malabar Hill bungalow, which in a spirit of ironic mischief or perversity she had insisted on naming *Elephanta*, there twirled the almost-divine figure of our very own Aurora Bombayalis, plumed in a series of dazzle-hued mirrorwork outfits, outdoing in finery even the festival sky with its hanging gardens of powdered colour. Her white hair flying out around her in long loose exclamations (O prophetically premature white hair of my ancestors!), her exposed belly not old-bat-fat but fit-cat-flat, her bare feet stamping, her ankles a-jingle with silver jhunjunna bell-bracelets, snapping her neck from side to side, speaking incomprehensible volumes with her hands, the great painter danced her defiance, she danced her contempt for the perversity of humankind, which led these huge crowds to risk death-by-trampling "just to dumpofy their dollies in the drink," as she liked incredulously, and with much raising of the eyes to skies and wry twisting of the mouth, to jeer.

Source: Rushdie, Salman. 1997. *The Moor's Last Sigh.* New York: Vintage Books. pp. 123–24.

Questions to the text

1. How would you describe the language in this passage?
2. Is the use of language familiar? Playful? Formal?
3. In what way does this passage address the sacred and the profane, or the religious and the secular?
4. How can this passage be seen as being both about celebration and a celebration in itself?
5. How would you describe the general cultural context of this passage? Is this context familiar to you?

The mixture of high and low register, of literary and local popular references, and of the traditional and modern in the passage above is only a small example of the narrative, linguistic, and contextual complexity of Rushdie's novel. *The Moor's Last Sigh*, narrated by Moraes, "Moor" Zogoiby, chronicles the Zogoiby family saga from its beginnings in Cochin in the south of India where two families, one Christian and one Jewish, come together, to Bombay (now called Mumbai) and even on to Spain. The novel is a mosaic of the many religions and cultures pieced together in a story that spans from the 1800s and the descendents of Vasco De Gama (at least in theory) on to the 1990s.

In response to the text

How do we, as individuals, relate to a text? How much context do we need to know or understand before we can say that we understand a given work? What does an individual bring to a text that can either help or hinder understanding? Explore your own personal reactions to Rushdie's novel and the ways in which your understanding is based on a knowledge and appreciation of literature and a broader cultural education. In the following paragraphs we have written a brief history of our reading (we both taught this book when it was first published) that may help to illuminate, in a different way from the other case studies, the complex relationship between text, reader, and context.

Going back to 1995, we first decided to read *The Moor's Last Sigh* simply because we had both read Rushdie before (his Booker Award winning *Midnight's Children* and the controversial *Satanic Verses*) and we wanted to read his latest work. We both enjoyed Rushdie because of his verve in storytelling and invention. He reminded us of Gabriel Garcia Marquez: Rushdie has a knack for telling involved, generational stories with a touch of magic realism—a literary movement that incorporates fantastic elements into a seemingly realistic world in a matter-of-fact way. We also enjoyed, because we like postmodern metafiction, the way his works are as much about the act of writing and storytelling itself as about the events at hand.

With these kinds of expectations and experiences in reading, *The Moor's Last Sigh* can be approached as a novel about a dying son and his relationship with his eccentric, artist mother. It is a story about how Moor, the narrator, grows up under the influence of a mother, a painter, who is consumed by her art and the family as a whole that cannot get out from under the intricate stories of its past. Just through reading the novel, the reader finds that the title comes from the name of a painting that depicts the last North African King of Spain as he is driven from the country by the new Christian rulers. Moor Zogoiby and his family obliquely trace their lineage back to this king but more importantly, the scene is re-figured in a modern painting by Moor's mother Aurora. The reader soon realizes as well that Moor himself is dying, breathing his last sigh, or telling his last story, in the form of the novel in our hands. *The Moor's Last Sigh* is a novel about the way families stay alive or keep hold of their past through inventive storytelling, or through constant re-writing (or re-painting) of old tales. As readers in 1995, we were absorbed into this as well as other themes, and we also enjoyed reading about Cochin, Bombay, the spice trade, Bollywood movies, and the underworld. On a stylistic level, the language of Salman Rushdie is always engaging. As in the passage above, Rushdie is well known for playing with language: he uses puns, Hindi, English, hyperbole, repetition, alliteration, and uses diction both high and low. We taught the book to our classes feeling sound in our knowledge and understanding of the novel.

In 2008 we came back to it with fresh eyes, with the added value of a recent relocation to Mumbai. This second experience of the novel while living in India brought new insight to some of the basic elements of setting in the novel as well as to some of the history or cultural baggage behind some of the events. You can't live in Mumbai without witnessing firsthand the everyday passion for cricket, the incredible visible mix of religions and languages, the pervasive influence of the Bollywood film industry, and the daily riot of colors, smells and sounds. All of these factor into the novel. The novel as well deals with the changes in India as it pushed for independence and built itself into a dynamic nation where the super-rich and the poor live side by side. The story of the nation is very much alive in India today and it is easy to see how a family story and its connection to a larger history is more than just a fictional conceit.

Perhaps the most striking discovery about Rushdie's writing was in relation to language. India, we both found, at different times on different journeys to the country, is a place where many languages coexist and where English, far from being a minor variation of "standard" English, is a thriving, dynamic, and changing language. Listening to accents, mixes of Hindi and English, and words that seem uncommon or outdated compared to typical North American, or even British, vernacular not only gives insight into the ways languages change over time but perhaps takes away from some of Rushdie's inventiveness. Rushdie wasn't creating a new language, he was meticulously documenting the English of Mumbai! Just the new verb "dumpofy" in the passage above seemed like a transcription of a word that might be heard on the streets from a vendor of chat (snacks).

Read

In response
Here is a brief excerpt from an informal essay by a student about the difficulty or reading texts that are either close to or very different from your own culture.

A student's response

One of the most pleasurable aspects of reading *The Moor's Last Sigh* is that it takes place in my home and my own life parallel's Rushdie's in some ways. Though I have only traveled to Cochin where the novel begins, I am very familiar with the area from vacations and my father has always talked about the proud independent state of Kerala. I have always known Cochin as a place where people read (the literacy rate is one of the highest in the world) and where every person seems to trace their roots to a different ancient culture. Mumbai, or Bombay still in the book, is a place I call home. Most of the novel takes place on Malabar Hill where I currently live. My own house overlooks Chowpatty Beach. I laugh at every twist and turn in the roads of the story because they are the same overcrowded twists and turns I use to come to school every day. I also understand how Rushdie can be an insider and outsider. I have lived for a long time outside of the country and

I feel like I am similar to so many Indians who have gone overseas to work. We always like to come back. This is a place that can get in your bones. At the end of the novel, as we realize that Moor is writing his last words and writing a testament about his life, if you are from India you also realize that he is writing a story about his home that he can't get out of his head.

The difficulty of reading this novel, though, is that my teacher doesn't understand it. First of all he thinks the language is authentic Indian English. I think that Rushdie is over playful and that he is almost making fun of Indian English. Some of the words, like "dumpofy" and all of the "fy" words Aurora uses I have never heard in my life. I think that if a Westerner reads this book he would think that Rushdie is being inventive or using Indian English. When I read this book I think that Rushdie is trying hard to sound authentic but he is really falling short. Unfortunately I can't appreciate some of the inventive language because it just doesn't sound right to me. Second, my teacher misses all of the good jokes in the book. In the first section, when we meet the brothers working at the spice business, my teacher didn't realize that their names were the Hindi words for popular spices. When Rushdie talks about the colors by "DeLuxe" my teacher didn't understand that this is the most popular paint in India and that everybody loves the fake, bright colors to use in their homes. The Bollywood references in the book are not just interesting or exotic, they are funny and relate to real stories about actors and actresses who are popular but who also have very famous private lives. The last thing, of course, is how little my teacher knew about the political parties in the state of Maharashtra where Mumbai is the capital. He doesn't know that many people didn't like the change in name from Bombay to Mumbai or that the Shiv Sena, one of the political parties here, is the model for the political group in the book run by the character "Mainduck." The whole political battle is about power for the people of Maharashtra and about giving jobs to these people before people from the outside. This is very important in a book that is about memories, ancestors, moving around, and coming to terms with your past. How can you even begin to correct your teacher about some misunderstanding on every page?

A teacher's response

Who is meant to read any novel? Maybe that is one of the questions we can always ask about a text. Who is Salman Rushdie's ideal reader? One student suggested that many of the stories Rushdie tells are almost too uninteresting, too common for an Indian audience. Perhaps Rushdie's ideal, or at least implied, reader is one who will be somewhat mystified by some of the allusions. At the same time, even if this is not true, allusions are tricky business. While I may not understand references to Hindi or popular Mumbai culture, many students miss allusions to Catholicism or jokes about popular American artists like Johnny Cash, or even scenes in the novel that relate to Rushdie's experience with the controversy surrounding his earlier work. I would still argue that the broader purposes of the book, the issues of art, the limits of representation, and the relationships between parents and children are both universal and perhaps best understood by an experienced reader, not necessarily by someone familiar with cultural context. But then again … a literary tradition and family dynamics are just another part of culture, aren't they?

To conclude this section, read this last short passage that is the very last section of the novel. Moor is about to lay down his pen for the last time. How many cultural and literary allusions do you recognize? How many of these allusions may be relevant no matter what cultural perspective you have?

> At the head of this tombstone are three eroded letters; my fingertip reads them for me. RIP. Very well: I will rest, and hope for peace. The world is full of sleepers waiting for their moment of return: Arthur sleeps in Avalon, Barbarossa in his cave. Finn MacCool lies in the Irish hillsides and the Worm Ouroboros on the bed of the Sundering Sea. Australia's ancestors, the Wandjina, take their ease underground, and somewhere, in a tangle of thorns, a beauty in a glass coffin awaits a prince's kiss. See: here is my flask. I'll drink some wine/ and then, like a latter-day Van Winkle, I'll lay me down upon this graven stone, lay my head beneath these letters RIP, and close my eyes, according to our family's old practice of falling asleep in times of trouble, and hope to awaken, renewed and joyful, into a better time.

Discussion Point

1 What do you think about the debate concerning cultural understanding and a reader's understanding of a text?

2 How has your own understanding of a text changed as either your reading experiences or life experiences have changed?

Assessment in literature: texts and contexts

As we have said repeatedly, reading and thinking about the works you encounter in the course will help you to develop your skills and prepare you for assessment. All of the work you do in the course whether summative or formative—through discussion, oral presentation, written essays or journals—is aimed toward the development of these skills, which are highly transferable to a broad range of content. The focus of this chapter is preparation for assessment in literature: texts and contexts. You should approach the examples supplied here critically, and learn from their strengths and weaknesses.

Written task 1

One of your written tasks will be completed during your study of literature: texts and contexts. For specific details about the nature of the task itself and how it is marked, refer to chapter 5. There may be some differences, of course, in the ways your approach your written task for this section of the course. This section of the course offers you an interesting opportunity to engage with a literary work and also to consider the importance of a wide variety of contexts. Your written task 1 should take into consideration both the texts you have studied and your particular views about the importance of context. You should consider some of the following ideas before determining the nature and content of your writing:

- Does your chosen format or text type relate to the work you have studied or to issues of context? You should keep in mind that you do not choose a text type for a written task haphazardly. An epistolary novel from the 1700s, for example, might be the perfect text to respond to with a letter. At the same time, if your intention is to comment on the ways modes of production influence meaning in a text, you may choose to rewrite the novel as a series of e-mails. Always think about how your choice of text type sheds light on an issue from the text itself or a broader issue of cultural context. You should also consider how the text type will allow you to demonstrate your own understanding throughout the piece itself.

- While your focus primarily will be on the text itself, you should consider how your task addresses contextual concerns. Keep in mind that "contexts" can include issues such as the background of the writer, the historical background of the time of production, the historical background of the text itself, issues of textual production, or issues relating to a reader's reception of the text.

The following student sample engages with issues of historical context and is written in the form of a letter in order to engage with contextual issues in two ways. Do you think the following example is successful in demonstrating an understanding of both the text and contexts?

Student sample

Rationale

Lazarillo de Tormes by an anonymous author and originally published in Spain in 1554 is a text that is considered one of the earliest examples of the novel. The novel, written in the first person, purports to be a letter written by Lazaro to his protector or "master" explaining his current situation in life and his upbringing. By broadly taking the form of a letter, the novel is able to use a form of personal address and raises issues about the motivations of the narrator (and the author) and his view on society. Since the entire novel is meant to be a letter in response to a request from an unidentified "your honor," for this written task I would like to create a context for the novel by writing the initial letter to Lazaro that has elicited the response we have in the text.

In this assignment I want to address the issues of religion, both as a commodity and a necessity, as well as the relation between Lazaro's rise in society and the statuses of his masters. I also wanted to note that this book was published shortly before the Spanish inquisition. To do this, I made the character of "Your Honor" be Gonzalo de Blas y Pradillo, a priest and also a wine merchant of dubious honesty and reputation. He has been somehow disadvantaged by the archpriest, and seeks to incriminate him with Lazaro's wife for some sort of personal gain—he does not tell Lazaro what he stands to gain, as he is trying to manipulate Lazaro into believing that it is for Lazaro's own interest that he writes the letter. This manipulative manner is similar to how men of the church act throughout "Lazarillo de Tormes." They take advantage of the status society awards them to take advantage of those they are responsible for. In "Lazarillo de Tormes," religion is a way of being upwardly mobile. By giving the priest a more extremist tone than that of the other priests in Lazaro's life, I wanted to make note that shortly after the book was published, the relatively liberal attitude of the time was dissolved and the Spanish inquisition was instituted.

Too much? Is religion related to this issue of status? A bit confusing here.

Nice job of tying the work to culture, context. You have good intentions in this rationale but you may need to tighten your focus. First, will you be able to show all this in the task itself? Next, this rationale is a bit long … it could do with editing and a tighter focus.

To Lazaro de Tormes, from the Honorable Gonzalo de Blas y Pradillo:

I am Gonzalo de Blas y Pradillo, a priest. You might remember me as having sold wine through you some months ago. You might also remember that I moved my enterprises to Tarragona with the Archpriest of San Salvador, our confrere's blessings and recommendation, fine man that he is. I have risen from the status of a mere presbyter to that of a priest, and I was far more successful in selling my wines in Tarragona. Unfortunately, the master, when sending me a letter of introduction to give to an acquaintance of his in the clergy there, must have forgotten that this man was recently revealed as being involved in a number of scandals. These scandals are of a Mercedarian nature that would sicken any devout Christian. He was often seen cavorting in taverns with disreputable women and local stable-hands and other such knaves. The master might be quite shocked at hearing this of his colleague! I toiled under this Man's blessings for a lengthy period of time and remained innocent of his wrongdoings; I was certainly appalled to hear of his reputation. I could clearly not remain in Tarragona with a clear conscience, and chose to return to Toledo and seek the kindness of our archpriest.

I have heard of your advancement in the world through my remaining acquaintances in Toledo—the ever-increasing patronage of our archpriest and your recent marriage are reasons to rejoice. However, I have also heard some beastly and despicable rumors about the purity of your patron's intentions, the poor man. These rumors even dare to call into question your own wife's chastity! I was horrified, and refused to believe this. You have always struck me as a man of good judgment, honesty, and lacking the greedy instinct for your own advancement. However, I must advise you that the slander-mongers will ruin your reputation as a man and a business-man. The soul is merely as virtuous as the mind of a man allows it to be, and one cannot think unjustified thoughts about those who care for us. However, a man haunted by the devil's horns must free himself of the devil using prayer and his own cunning. If he fails to do so, he is not worthy of the respect of his fellow men. A man, in his fear of Satan might forget to fear God himself. Of this, Lazaro, you must beware.

If you will forgive me for this intrusion, could you illuminate me on how such a terrible rumor sprang up, for I cannot imagine how righteous men such as the archpriest and of course yourself could be slandered in such a way. I cannot believe that it is merely the malicious jealousy of other men and the cruel tongues of fallen women that conceived of this terrible tale. There were many wicked tales told about yourself in the town when you first began to be noticed—that you were not of legitimate birth and that you were the a shrewd blind man's boy being those most commonly bandied about. The commonest people seek merely to entertain themselves with such tales, and luckily you were not damaged by them. However, Lazaro, I fear that you might one day feel the ramifications of such former misdemeanor, whether it is true or not. The clergy keep careful record of vagrants and vagabonds, and often seek to incriminate citizens who are innocent by using papers from their pasts to attest their degeneracy.

Upon my return to Toledo, I have noticed the holiness of the clergy in this city is being called into question by many. Even clergymen themselves misuse the powers that have been vested in them to manipulate the masses and advance their own status and wealth. It greatly distresses me to hear this. There are many who even claim that this problem has spread throughout the realm and even all throughout Christendom. We must cleanse our clergy of the debauched and greedy members. You, a god-fearing man with a wife and perhaps a family to care for, must be able to appreciate this sentiment. As a priest and also as a merchant, I observe the lowliest of men, and I cannot believe that they can be absolved of their sins by the current

An interesting way to get at some of the concerns of the book without simply rehashing the plot of Lazarillo. This reflects issues in the book without paraphrasing the text.

Not exactly chastity ... do you mean fidelity?

Is the horns reference meant also to refer to cuckoldry? You are using some of the language and ideas of the original text but you need to clarify your language? Whose intentions or "unjustified thoughts" are you talking about? The people who slander Lazaro or Lazaro's in the text?

OK. The end of this paragraph gives a nice overall context for Lazaro's response, the novel itself. There is also clearly an indication of the coming Inquisition—this might be a bit subtle but since you mentioned it in the rationale, the reader can recognize the suggestion here.

I like this paragraph but I wonder if you want to push to increase some of the irony here. You have indicated that this writer has had success as a merchant and you have indicated in your rationale that this man is as corrupt and manipulative as others in the novel. Can you show this more clearly? In other words, how can you make us (the readers) more clearly aware that this priest is corrupt (just as the reader of Lazarillo is clear that clergy, whose sins are far worse! You are rising above the public, and must take the god-given task of exposing such fraudulent "men of god" in all seriousness. The soul will rejoice as shepherds rejoiced at the birth of Christ, and you will not regret your deeds.

I await your speedy response,

Gonzalo de Blas y Pradillo

he is naïve) while managing to seem virtuous to the intended reader within the work, Lazaro. You are a little short in the word count of the task itself so you may want to see what you can do with the 30–200 words you have left for development.

Activity

Brainstorming ideas

Think about the texts you are studying in this section of the course and brainstorm as many ideas as possible of possible written tasks. One idea is to make a list of possible issues or concerns in the texts, make a separate list of important literary features, and make a third list of text types that may seem to have particular relevance to your texts (such as the letter above in relation to an epistolary novel (a novel that takes the form of a letter or series of letters). After creating these lists, start mixing and matching and see what you come up with.

Written task 2

If you are taking the language and literature course at higher level, you may write a written task 2 based on one of the texts studied in this part of the course. For detailed information about the nature of written task 2, the specific questions you should address, and the way it will be marked refer to the discussion of the task in chapter 7.

Obviously, the task you produce in relation to this section of the course should engage with the literature you have studied and with broader issues of cultural context and their effect on meaning. To a large extent, the questions for the task will naturally push you in the right direction for your analysis. In the end, your written task 2 will reflect your own interests, the avenues of investigation you took in class, and your personal engagement with one of the texts. The student sample below writes well about a work of literature, addresses a particular question, and is overtly engaged with issues of context.

Student sample

How and why is a social group represented?

"The Terrible Gift of Language in *The Tempest*"

The Tempest, one of Shakespeare's last plays, is the story of Prospero, the former Duke of Milan, who has been banished from Milan by his own brother and now lives alone on an island with his young daughter Miranda. The play centers on Prospero and his magic as he begins to get revenge on his brother and form new alliances with the King of Naples and finds a husband for his daughter in the King's son Ferdinand. To say that Prospero is alone on the island is an exaggeration, though. When he arrived on the island he found

Caliban, the son of the witch Sycorax and Ariel, a spirit who had been imprisoned by Sycorax. Caliban has the role of the villain in this play and is treated, especially as a villain by Prospero. *The Tempest*, however suggests that Caliban may only be a villain in Prospero's eyes and that Prospero was simply unwilling to treat Caliban as a human and instead forces his rule, and his language, on someone he sees as a "poisonous slave (I.ii. 319).

Okay. Nice clear introduction with an appropriate focus.

In the first act of the play Prospero recounts the story of his exile to his daughter and, in the process, tells the audience about his experience coming to the island and finding Ariel and Caliban. From the start, Prospero sees the island as empty or "not honored with a human shape (I.ii. 283–84). Prospero does not count Caliban as human. He goes on to admit, however, that he needs Caliban. "We cannot miss him," he tells Miranda, because "he does make our fire/Fetch in our wood, and serves in offices/That profit us" (I. ii. 311–313). In fact, Caliban, in his later anger at Prospero and Miranda outlines a plausible start to their relationship:

> This island's mine by Sycorax my mother,
> Which thou tak'st from me. When thou cam'st first,
> Thou strok'st me and made much of me; wouldst give me
> Water with berries in't; and teach me how
> To name the bigger light, and how the less,
> That burn by day and night. And then I loved thee
> And showed thee all the qualities o' th' isle,
> The fresh springs, brine pits, barren place and fertile.
> Cursed be I that did so! (I.ii. 54–55)

Caliban, seen by Prospero as nonhuman, plays a role similar to that of the native Americans who greeted the first explorers (this play is based on accounts of the first explorations of the New World and a shipwreck in the Caribbean): Caliban saves the "explorer" and then becomes his slave.

Very nice; a sophisticated approach with clear development and succinct / precise treatment.

In the play, Prospero is shown to have his reasons for making Caliban a slave. Caliban attempts to attack Miranda and, as he even says "people(ed) else/This isle with Calibans" (I. ii. 350–351). However, it seems that Prospero's disdain for Caliban comes first. The island, as he saw it, was not inhabited by a human being. Why did he think this? Miranda's story of her experience with Caliban gives us a clue. She, presumably unlike her father, felt sorry for Caliban:

> Abhorred slave,
> Which any print of goodness wilt not take,
> Being capable of all ill! I pitied thee,
> Took pains to make thee speak, taught thee each hour
> One thing or other. When thou didst not, savage,
> Know thine own meaning, but wouldst gabble like
> A think most brutish, I endowed thy purposes
> With words that made them known. (I. ii. 352–58)

Caliban is inhuman because of his looks and because of his language. Miranda's assumption is that Caliban speaks without meaning because she cannot understand his meaning, even suggesting that Caliban cannot understand himself. Her view is that though she taught him her language, she cannot teacher him how to act properly because the real learning "wilt not take."

Who is Caliban, though, and does he just gabble meaninglessly? Prospero tells Ariel that Sycorax, the mother of Caliban, was a witch "from Argier (Algeria)" (I.ii. 265). Could the babbling of Caliban be Arabic? Caliban, an unfamiliar name in English or in Italian (where the play supposedly takes place, or on an island between Italy and North Africa) but it does sound similar to a word such as *kelbayn* (two dogs) which would go along with Shakespeare's portrayal of him. Caliban's attitude toward the language of his oppressor's is perhaps understandable: "You taught me language, and my profit on't /Is I know how to curse. The red plague rid you/For learning me your language" (I.ii. 363–65). Now his life is taking orders from Prospero and cursing him for the pain he suffers.

Shakespeare does more than just give Caliban the ability to curse, however. In fact, Shakespeare cleverly allows for Caliban to be an expressive and interesting human in his own right. As Caliban is attempting to enlist the help of the fools Trinculo and Stephano, he attempts to soothe their worries at the unfamiliar sounds they encounter on the island. He says:

> Be not afeard; the isle is full of noises,
> Sounds and sweet airs, that give delight and hurt not.
> Sometimes a thousand twangling instruments
> Will hum about mine ears, and sometime voices
> That, if I then had waked after long sleep,
> Will make me sleep again: and then, in dreaming,
> The clouds methought would open and show riches
> Ready to drop upon me that, when I waked,
> I cried to dream again. (III. ii. 140–48)

This is an interesting short speech. As a reader familiar with the whole play, this can certainly refer to Ariel's magic or the larger magic of Prospero but it is not a stretch to see that this might also refer to unfamiliar language that, though strange, is beautiful and valuable in its own right. Like Caliban's own language, these noises can give delight and hurt not and may also even provide a kind of riches that are unique. Unlike Prospero's claims, then, Caliban's speech is beautiful and describes a potential of goodness and beauty that exists but simply may not always be understood by those unfamiliar with it. It is not a great stretch to apply the same thinking to Caliban's own language, whether Arabic or other.

Cleverly, Shakespeare hints at a more complex character for Caliban. Though the play ends "happily" with Caliban accepting his place and "recognizing" the righteousness of Prospero, we are equally aware that everything is a kind of mirage or performance or magical fantasy. Things are as we make and imagine them or, rather, maybe even only as we understand them. A man may be a drunkard or wise, a prince or slave, a brute or expressive individual depending on how

Yes, this is true. Good set-up thus far in the written task.

Very interesting approach with the Arabic reference. A nice segue into the thrust of your argument.

I really like this approach. This is a sophisticated and interesting reading that highlights cultural difference. There could be a little more direct attention to cultural context, i.e. as European or northern cultural expectation that defines both civilized and barbarian in curious ways. I like the idea of your reading Shakespeare as challenging these common notions though.

Overall, a succinct and sophisticated approach. Quite good work with a clear approach to cultural context and an engaged

we view them and what we understand. Though recognizing Caliban as an expressive individual may problematize somewhat the "neat" conclusion to the play, it is precisely this kind of ear for the unfamiliar and the real that we have come to expect in Shakespeare and can find celebrated in this play.

and unique consideration. You do still have a little more leeway with which to write about the topic—maybe just one more point or a little more explication would further enhance.

Further oral activity

As you have learned in earlier assessment chapters, the further oral activity is an assessment that gives you the chance to further explore some of the topics and issues raised by your study in particular sections of the course. It is part of your internal assessment and will be evaluated by your teacher. As we have stressed before, the further oral activity is a chance to be creative and personal in your approach to learning—and proving your learning—in the course.

Your job is to explore an aspect of a particular text in relation to issues discussed in class or based on your own interests. The approach should be related to the main aims of the course and you should certainly discuss your topic with your teacher. It would not be enough, for example, to give a "book report" or to summarize some of the main points of a text that you have already discussed in class. The further oral is meant to go into greater depth or to handle subjects only touched upon briefly. You may also find that a subject raised earlier in the course, language and minority communities for example, relates to the text you are studying now, and would serve as an interesting topic.

An important thing to remember with the oral in this section is to use clear supporting detail from the texts being studied. Here are some possible ways of approaching the further oral activity in this section:

- Discussion arising from the presentation of cultural or contextual background materials related to the texts being studied.

- A discussion of some particulars of the biography of the author in relation to details from the texts studied.

- A comparison of stylistic features and their varying purposes in two of the texts being studied.

- A commentary prepared for the class based on a key passage in the texts.

- The preparation of a multimedia presentation that is shown to the class and then discussed as a group.

- The creation of a short film based on an aspect of the texts studied. This film would be shown and the discussion could revolve around its production, its intent, and its relative success.

- The role play of a dialogue between the author and an interviewer.

- The presentation of a prepared monologue based on the thoughts or concerns of a minor character in the work.

- The writing and performance of a dramatic scene based on one part of the work studied.

How do I give a better presentation?

One aspect we have not discussed in earlier chapters is how to give a better oral presentation. Partly, this answer depends on what type of activity you intend to complete: a guided class discussion is different from a formal presentation which, in turn, is different from a dramatic scene. In all of these, however, preparation, organization, and clarity are keys to success. First, remember the criteria for judgment in the oral activity:

- Knowledge and understanding of the text(s) and the subject matter.

- Understanding of how language is used (this could be related to rhetorical language use in the text, style, literary features, etc.)

- Organization. In a presentation it may be even more important to plan your argument and make your structure clear to your audience.

- Language. While there may be some natural informality in a spoken presentation, you should still be concerned with register, clarity, and precision.

Your preparation and delivery of the further oral activity may take the following steps:

- Develop an appropriate topic and determine an appropriate size for your group (or if you will do the oral individually). Make these decisions with the help of your teacher.

- Plan and delegate the work for your activity. Will you write a play? Perhaps you should plan with your partner, outline together, then each write one half of the play, and finally revise together. Research a multi-aspect topic? Everybody finds information on one part.

- Create your product for presentation or plan your speech. If you are leading a class discussion, be sure to prepare questions and a basic progression beforehand. You can let a discussion take its own path but remember that you are trying to show your own knowledge and understanding of the work or subject matter.

- In any oral presentation or commentary, organization is especially important because it is harder for an audience to follow a speech than it is for a reader to follow an argument in a written text. Have a clear introduction. Tell the audience where you are going to go, or what your main points will be. Signpost your topics for your audience: "Now I will talk in more detail about the way women are represented in chapter 6."

- Do not let your presentation or discussion die out at the end. You should both know when to end and give an appropriate conclusion to either your discussion or your other activity.

- In relation to dramatic works, avoid the silly skit. A skit is entertaining but it can be informal and sloppy and can easily stray from the issues in the text at hand. At the same time a "skit" gives the impression of lack of preparation. If you write or perform for the class, plan, memorize, decide your props, plan your movements, and practice before the day of your presentation.

Building oral skills

In school, you may do more formal preparation for written assessments than you do for oral activities. Speaking up in class and gaining confidence offering your opinions in front of your peers is a good way of practicing your oral skills too. If you are used to speaking in a class discussion, leading a class discussion should come quite naturally. On the day of your presentation it is natural to be nervous but you will be less anxious if you have found some way to practice. First, remember to always rehearse your performance. Although it may be embarrassing, running through your presentation out loud beforehand (at home or with a friend) always helps.

There are a few other ways, however, to practice oral work in general. If you have a blog try podcasting or vodcasting. Speaking your opinions into a microphone or into the camera on a computer can mimic many of the skills and much of the anxiety involved in oral presentation. If you have a website that is meant for close friends in family—a place where you post pictures of your vacations or your school activities—try posting audio and video here as well. Even better, try getting your whole class involved in some of this practice in a more formal, academic manner. Posting and sharing regular podcasts with other class members based on the material studied throughout this course can lead to great further oral activities, strong oral commentaries, and better analysis and presentation in general.

Exam paper 2: essay

What is it?

Paper 2 of the exam is an essay written in response to a question in an exam situation (1 hour 30 minutes for standard level and 2 hours for higher level) at the end of your final year of the Diploma Programme. Paper 2 consists of six questions based on the literary texts studied. For this paper, your well-organized essay should show not only your ability to craft an organized response but should show your knowledge and understanding of the works you have studied, your ability to respond to the demands of a specific question, and your understanding of the use of stylistic or literary features in the works you have studied. In this paper of the exam you are trying to show that you have met the broad objectives of this literature section and the course as a whole. In other words, you should be demonstrating your understanding of the content and form of the works you have studied, the significance and meaning of these texts, the importance of contexts in relation to these texts, and your own aesthetic appreciation of the works.

While you may feel some pressure going into the exam session, you should know that students often feel very successful with this type of essay because hard work and preparation can clearly pay off in results. The questions asked are flexible enough to be able to be applied to a wide range of texts and they are directly related to the main ideas that you will discuss in class throughout the entire two years of the Diploma Programme and especially during the texts and contexts section. You are also required to demonstrate your knowledge of texts you have studied extensively in class. If you read, think, practice, and pay attention, you should find that you are going into the exam with the appropriate level of knowledge and understanding.

What are the rules?

Very broadly, you will be given six questions of which you must choose one to answer. You must then write a response to the questions that uses both of the works you have studied. Be sure to stay focused on the question and analyze your works in light of the way the contexts of production and reception affect meaning. The course guide lists the following areas of discussion that you need to consider in order to prepare for the assessment:

● How can we explain the continued interest in a particular work in different contexts and at different times?

● What do you think of the assertion that the meaning of a text is fixed and does not change over time?

● If beauty is a relative term, how do one or more of the works you have studied explore this idea?

● How valid is the assertion that literature is a voice for the oppressed?

● To what extent do male and female literary characters accurately reflect the role of men and women in society?

● To what purpose do authors sometimes choose not to follow a chronological sequence of events in their literary works?

● Do works of literary merit both reflect the spirit of the time and challenge it?

Students studying at the higher level may, in addition to the above, consider questions or suggestions for discussion such as these:

● What groups are omitted in a text and what might this reflect about its production?

● Test the validity of the assertion that the meaning of a text is fixed and does not change over time.

● How does a particular term or concept, such as childhood, change in the way it is represented in the texts you have studied?

● Why do authors sometimes choose not to follow a chronological sequence of events in their literary works?

● How is the critical approach taken to the analysis of a text influenced by specific cultural perspectives.

How is it marked?

Following is a broad outline of the marking criteria:

● **Criterion A** Knowledge and understanding: How much knowledge and understanding of the part 3 works and their context has the candidate demonstrated in relation to the question answered?

● **Criterion B** Response to the question: To what extent is an understanding of the expectations of the course shown? How relevant is the response to these expectations and how far does it show critical analysis?

● **Criterion C** Understanding the use and effects of stylistic features: To what extent does the essay show awareness of how the writer's choices of the stylistic features in the texts, such as characterization, setting, theme, narrative point of view, structure, style and technique are used to construct meaning? To what extent does the essay show understanding of the effects of stylistic features?

- **Criterion D** Organization and development: How logical and developed is the argument of the essay? How coherent and effective is the formal structure of the essay?

- **Criterion E** Language: How clear, varied and accurate is the language? How appropriate is the choice of register and style? (Register refers, in this context, to elements such as vocabulary, tone, sentence structure and terminology appropriate to the task).

Over the years examiners have found that the best essays written by students in response to questions show personal engagement, flexibility with the texts, and a strong focus on the question. While you can prepare for this exam by working in class and reading with care, memorizing rote responses to texts or rehearsing answers to sample questions seldom pays off for students because the responses do not use interesting or surprising details from texts that demonstrate a more *personal* engagement, or the response betrays a lack of flexible understanding because you are not shaping your knowledge to a fresh, original question. For example, you might study the concept of the unreliable narrator in class. Perhaps you read a text in which we as readers doubt the knowledge or intentions of the narrator or in which the author clearly wants us to see the narrator's naiveté (think of works you may have studied such as *Huckleberry Finn*, *Heart of Darkness*, *Lolita*, *Catcher in the Rye*, *One Flew Over the Cuckoo's Nest*, *Death in Venice* or many others). If a question were to ask you about the relationship between the narrator and his or her community, a response that spends too much time dwelling on the unreliable narrator without getting to other issues might indicate some knowledge and understanding, but not much personal engagement, understanding of subtleties, or an ability to respond to a question.

Here are some of the top weaknesses that examiners notice in papers:

- Repetition of memorized information without clear evidence of understanding.

- Lack of textual detail used as support for an argument or answer.

- Lack of a focus on the question at hand.

- An inability to discuss literary or stylistic features and their effect on meaning in the works.

In relation to the crafting of the essay itself, examiners notice the following weaknesses:

- Lack of a clear structure or basic introduction, body, and conclusion.

- A lack of transition between paragraphs or between discussion of one text and the other.

- An inability to effectively compare (and contrast) texts in relation to the question rather than writing an individual "mini essay" on each text.

How do I prepare?

Our first piece of advice for preparation is "don't panic." All of the reading, thinking and discussing you have been doing for two years, in fact for all of the years that you have been in school, has lead up to this assessment. In this exam you are asked to demonstrate your thinking about particular works and works of literature in general. So, what you need to do to prepare for this exam is build your knowledge of the prescribed texts in this section. You also need to build two kinds of knowledge about these texts. First, you should try to understand everything that you are told or that is brought up in discussion in your class at school. Second, you should be thinking about your own personal reaction to the texts. What is most interesting to you? What particular quotations, scenes, or issues do you find interesting and why? Here are some initial tips for building knowledge:

- Read all of the texts. Don't just skim. Don't read one well and the other quickly.

- Re-read the texts. Think about watching a favorite movie. The second time you saw the film you probably noticed things you didn't the first time. Or perhaps you thought "Oh … now I understand why the character said this at the beginning of the movie…" A second reading helps you to understand the construction of a work. Take notes. I often do not take notes while reading a text for the first time; it takes away from some of the pleasure of getting caught up in the reading. Picking apart a text and referring to specific details, will follow when you re-read and mark up the texts.

- Listen attentively in class. Actively participate in class discussion. Don't think of the teacher as someone who can give you all the right answers. Think of talking and developing your own ideas, and listening to and reacting to the ideas of classmates, as a chance to practice the skills of literary criticism. The exam paper is asking you to think out loud so practice putting your thoughts out in class.

- Do some traditional studying. Make charts of characters, events, themes and issues, and stylistic features of works. Try to see the relationships between elements on the chart (how does "setting" reflect the position of "women in the text, for example). Compare the results of charts you have made for different books.

Here are just a couple of *don'ts*:

- Don't rely only on memorizing notes from class.

- Don't rely on websites and study guides to give you all of the answers you need.

- Don't think that memorizing a list of literary terms is all you need to understand the importance of literary features in your works. Appreciating literary features is not simply identifying and defining.

What to do in the exam
Here are some basic tips to follow when you get into the exam room. It is important to get used to the idea of having two hours to respond to a question so, even if you don't have this kind of time in school, practice for two hour periods on your own at home.

During the exam itself:

- Read all of the questions. Choose the question you understand and that clearly relates to the texts you have studied.

- Go with what you think and feel during the exam and don't "overthink" your choice. It is a myth that "harder" questions allow for higher scores than "easy" ones. Pick apart the question. Make sure you understand the terms of the question and make sure that you will answer all parts of the question (it may, for example, ask you to discuss *how* an author uses an element such as setting and *to what extent* this feature is related to criticism of an aspect of society).

- Take notes on the works you will use. Think of examples and support for your argument by noting specific details and features of the text.

- When you begin to write, try to get to a reasonable, clear, and succinct answer to the question as quickly as possible in your introduction. The rest of the essay will be your chance to develop ideas and provide support.

- In the answer itself *do not* simply paraphrase the texts or retell the "story." A good idea is to come straight out with an idea or make an observation, supporting this observation with specific detail from the text and explaining the connection you have made, with reference to extended arguments or knowledge (to demonstrate why this observation is important).

Student sample

While so-called "high literary art" is said to deal with the noblest aims of humanity, popular culture takes obvious pleasure in more pedestrian entertainment. Referring to at least two of the works you have studied, consider the ways in which these texts either embrace or reject popular culture and to what effect?

If on a Winter's Night a Traveler by Italo Calvino and *The Snapper* by Roddy Doyle are two very different novels when it comes to their relationship with popular culture. Popular culture can be described as the events, fads, and activities that are found entertaining to a majority of people. The idiom of popular culture, by definition, has mass appeal. While Doyle embraces popular culture, Calvino overtly rejects it.

Good clear start but could you give us an idea of how or why right from your introduction? This may also be the place to give us a sentence or two about the works.

Calvino is an intellectual whose interest in the vocabulary of popular culture seems purely academic. He is a writer's writer. It is as if his intended audience is other authors who struggle with the art of writing. The structure of his book is unorthodox and clever. The concepts that Calvino presents in his novel such as the nature of reading and writing, do not necessarily appeal to the mainstream. They are more in the nature of a philosophical rumination. Doyle on the other hand, explores difficult social and moral dilemmas that have universal appeal. The story of a young, Irish working class woman having to deal with the stigma of rape and an unwanted pregnancy has resonance with a large audience and is written in a simple, direct style.

OK. But how do we know this? Is it evidenced in his writing? You will have to show us.

All of this is correct but you need specific examples (Also, what of the "chapters"? Aren't they in some way modeled after popular novels?)

Perhaps a concluding sentence here that summarizes the view of the two authors' purposes and forms would help.

Calvino's is a work of metafiction. Metafiction is a branch of fiction that playfully and self-referentially deals with the writing of fiction and its conventions. Calvino explores the fundamental dilemmas of all writers: should a writer be writing to please the maximum number of readers, or should he be writing to express a distinctive voice and style? Should an author rely on inspiration (like the "tormented writer") or should he rely on diligence, craftsmanship and formulae (like the "productive writer")? He notes that each type of writer envies the other. In Chapter 8, Calvino uses the voice of Silas Flannery, a successful novelist suffering from a creative block, to explore a number of these questions. Silas notes down his reflections in a diary and observes that an author who thinks too much about pleasing all types of audiences risks losing his or her style. The "readers are [his] vampires," and in his struggle to please the ideal reader, what he is writing is no longer "[his] anymore." Calvino uses the reflections of Silas to explain the intellectual basis for his book and its structure. Calvino sets for himself an ambitious goal: to "[to write] the books of all possible authors,"—to write a book that never loses its novelty therefore constantly keeping the reader on his or her toes.

OK. One more statement to clearly link to question? Perhaps need an explanation above of his structure as well. This is good use of quotations in an exam situation but remember to focus on the question (don't just imply a link to the question! (Is the effect or intention simply to keep the reader on his or her toes? Go beyond this basic, and questionable, emotional effect.

Calvino uses the technique of an embedded narrative harking back to a story telling technique that goes to the "Arabian Nights". The story follows "the Reader" (the main character) who has come across a book of incomplete manuscripts. While every odd numbered chapter follows the actions of the Reader, each even numbered chapter is a piece of the book which he (the Reader) is reading. It is through this structure that Calvino explores different genres of creative writing, including popular writing like Japanese eroticism.

You are not really addressing the question. So, in this paragraph, could you say that Calvino is embracing popular culture? Or is he creating high art by commenting on popular culture? Get back to the question.

With these elements, Calvino has produced a complex novel that addresses the nature of reading and writing provides an entirely different reading experience through its style of writing and structure. This different writing style is a form of high art because in its complexity it asks the reader to examine popular forms of storytelling. While this is entertaining, it is more of a comment on popular entertainment than a popular form itself.

Finally, back to the question! Some of this discussion could have been integrated above.

In contrast, Roddy Doyle's novel is embedded in popular culture. It focuses on issues that have universal appeal. The story is about the impact of an unwanted pregnancy on the Rabbitte family, especially on Jimmy Sr., father of the expectant mother. The novel addresses issues like alcohol and sexual abuse, issues that loom large in contemporary Irish society. It traces the challenges faced by a very brave and determined Sharon who, having been raped by a drunken friend of her father's, decides to have the baby in the face of rejection from her father and her own friends. In the end her very proud father becomes her strongest ally as the whole family rallies around her. The tale is an artful retelling of a timeless story about the ultimate strength of the love that binds parent and child, of love overcoming prejudice. Doyle has made a powerful use of a subject matter firmly rooted in popular culture to tell a story that would appeal to a large contemporary audience—so much so that the book has been adapted into a movie.

OK. But so far this broad summary hasn't gotten to a discussion of how the novel itself is high art or popular...

In addition, Doyle uses language specific to Irish English – the idiom of the novel allows Doyle to connect with a wider readership. Doyle uses Irish English vocabulary and expressions to keep the novel very real and also to inject humor into the story. This colorful use of language helps make Jimmy Sr. what one critic has called "one of the most engaging and loveable arseholes to ever grace the written page." Compared to Calvino's work, *The Snapper* uses language that is easy to understand and a structure that is easy to navigate. Without underlying complexities, *The Snapper* makes for an easy read.

All of this is reasonable, but do you want to hedge your bets a bit? In other words … isn't there something beyond the popular here … Or at least a comment on the way the general population lives? Is there any literary leaning in Doyle? And regardless of these questions, you must make a more specific link to the question here.

Doyle also embraces popular culture in the structure of his novel. Each chapter of the novel is an entertaining episode with a very traditional story arc. We start a chapter in the middle of an argument or a conversation or "in medias res." It is action from the start. Then as the chapter goes on, complications develop until the problem is partially resolved with a funny punch-line. In one early chapter the reader feels sorry for Mrs. Rabitte who seems to have no power in the novel. She slaves in the kitchen as everyone else is off to school, work, or the pub. But one morning she makes "easy slices" sandwiches for her husband for lunch, even though he hates them. As he walks out the door he asks if he has easy slices and she says no. She laughs, we laugh with her, and the chapter ends. It is as if we are watching a sitcom on television. Roddy Doyle uses very familiar structures to tell a story that is supposed to be very familiar or at least ordinary.

This is a good idea. The first part of this paragraph is correct but lacks support. You bring in the support at the end but it is a little bit vague, relies a bit too heavily on simply retelling the story. How could this idea be expressed more clearly, succinctly?

Whereas the subject matter and idiom of Doyle's novel is firmly and deliberately embedded in popular culture, Calvino's book is a cerebral work intended for the intellectual reader. Calvino's novel (if it can be called that), is an exploration of the dilemmas and challenges facing a writer and the nature of the relationship between reader and writer. In it Calvino references popular culture only as an example of a style of writing that a writer may chose in order to reach a wider readership. Both are very different authors, with completely opposite implicit attitudes towards popular culture.

Activity

Sample exam questions

Use the following example questions for practice essay questions. If you do not happen to be studying this section of the course, use whatever works you are studying now to answer the question.

- Artists often choose to focus their attention on issues that are either distinctly local, universal or arise out of tensions between the two. Referring to at least two of the works you have studied, consider the ways in which these works treat the local or the universal and to what effect.

- Referring to at least two of the works you have studied, how has place or location been created and to what significant effect.

- Even when the subject matter is of a serious nature, artists often use humor to convey meaning and create effect. Referring to at least two of the works in your study, consider the ways in which these works employ humor and to what effect.

- Developing technologies can inspire both celebration and concern. Referring to at least two of the works in your study, how have the works treated technology and to what larger effect?

- Though much art is concerned only with the aesthetic, there are works that pursue obvious political ends. Referring to at least two of the works you have studied, how have the works pursued overt political aims and to what larger effect?

Conclusion

It is important to remember that the assessment for part 3 (literature: texts and contexts) of the course—and for all parts of the course for that matter—is not intending to measure your mastery of any particular body of content. Instead, throughout the course you are asked to demonstrate understanding and critical exploration of issues around language and literature and the assessments, as a result, are attempting to gauge your skills and abilities with *approaching* works and issues. Part 3 of the course does focus on a slightly unique usage of language in that this part of the course focuses on both formal language aspects that make a work a piece of literature and cultural contexts that affect reading and reception of the work but, in truth, the same attention to reading, thinking about and presenting ideas that you bring to all parts or the course will best serve you here as well. Formal assessments represent only those "live performances" where you present the same material you have been rehearsing but in full-costume and make-up. The assessments, then, are not unique or distinct tasks but rather the natural culmination of your ongoing hard work and practice throughout the course.

A

abbreviations 68
Achebe, Chinua
  Things Fall Apart 282–4, 285
Addison, Joseph 68
Adichie, Chimamanda Ngozi
  Purple Hibiscus 281–6
advertising
  analysis 157, 168
  commercialization of youth culture
    194–7
  comparative study 158
  gender stereotyping 127
  infomercials 159
  narrative in 174
  political 191–2
  rhetorical devices 171, 172–3
  viral 198
  written task 1 145
Aeschylus
  Agamemnon 11
  Oresteia 10–11
aesthetic response 46–50
African American Vernacular English
  (AAVE) 101
Albee, Edward
  The Zoo Story 244
alliteration 75
ambiguity 19, 73
analysis 72
analyst commentator 93
anapestic foot 239
Anzaldua, Gloria
  "How to Tame a Wild Tongue" 131–2,
    133
archetypes 225
argot 87–95
Aristotle 10
  Rhetoric 171
Arnold, Matthew 38, 40
articulation 36
asemic writing 28
aside (in drama) 249–50
assessment
  exam paper 1 149–55,
    211–18
  exam paper 2 316–23
  formative 134–6
  further oral activities 147–8, 210–11,
    314–16
  general considerations 134–6
  language and mass communication
    199–218
  literature: critical study
    253–71
  literature: texts and contexts 308–23
  practising for 136–7
  summative 134–6
  written task 1 137–46,
    199–204, 308–11
  written task 2 (higher level) 146–7,
    204–9, 311–14
assonance 75
atmosphere 74
Atwood, Margaret
  You fit into me 14–15
audience and text, interaction between 85
Austen, Jane
  Pride and Prejudice 286–90, 294
author, life and times of 275–6, 277
authority-disorder 178–9

B

back-channeling 66
Barthes, Roland
  "The Death of the Author" 69–70
beauty, appreciating 46–50
Beckett, Samuel
  Waiting for Godot 251
bias 45
bildungsroman 281
bilingualism 37
binary operation 19
Bishop, Elizabeth
  "Imaginary Iceberg" 242
Blair, Tony 171
Blake, William
  "The Chimney Sweeper" 236–7
Blau, Sheridan 81, 82
blog
  keeping 80, 136
  as mass communication 159
  news coverage in 180, 182–3
  reliability 180
  written task 1 145
body language 31
Boland, Eavan
  "Woman in Kitchen" 238
Bolter, Jay David 164
books
  cover designs 279, 280
  ebooks 62, 64, 67–8, 162
  marketing 279, 280
  printed 160, 161–2
bricolage 40

C

Caesar, Julius 171
Cameron, James
  Avatar 280
canonical works 20
Casey, Susan 93
censorship 11–12
Chandler, Raymond
  The Big Sleep 75
characters 74
  archetypes 225
  drama 247–9
  fictional prose 225
  literary texts 220, 222
  nonhuman 222, 225
checklists
  critical reading 70–1, 73–5
  responding to texts 45
Chomsky, Noam 33–4, 36, 86
Cixous, Hélène
  "The Laugh of the Medusa" 128–9
class discussion 135
class, language and 86, 101, 105
climax 224
close reading 72, 221–2
  New Criticism 13–14, 46–7, 69
clustering 172–3
code-switching 111–12, 117–20
cognition, language and 86
cognitive science 34–5
  narrative in 26–7
colour commentator 93
comedy 251–2
commercialization of youth culture 194–7
communication
  language as 31–4, 157–8
  mass *see* mass communication
  models 160–1
Communication Accommodation Theory
  112
communicative act 8
community, language and
  96–110
  dialect 101–7
  regional and social variation 101
comparative analysis 158
comparative textual analysis (higher
  level) 149–55, 204–9
  language and mass communication
    204–9
  literature 219
concrete poetry 239
connotation 52–3, 236
  connotative translation 58
Conrad, Joseph
  Heart of Darkness 285
context 43, 53, 274–307
  case studies 281–307
  definition 274–5
  how text is built and functions 278–81
  reader's values and assumptions 277–8
  see also cultural context, language in
Corpus Linguistics 98
creativity 66, 70
critical awareness, developing 80
critical literacy 44–5, 49–50
critical reading 69–80
  of literary works 219–23
  pattern recognition 221
  showing in writing and speaking 80–2
criticism, literary
  ancient Greek culture 10–11
  basic assumptions 44–5
  bias 45
  cognitive science, narrative in 26–7
  Cultural Materialism 21–2
  cultural poetics 21–2
  cultural studies 20–2
  deconstruction 19
  feminist 21
  gender studies 21
  historical background 10–22
  horizon of expectations 16
  identity politics 20
  interpretive community 16
  legal narrative 23, 25
  Marxist 20–1
  medical narrative 23–5
  modern applications 23–7
  New Criticism 13–16, 46–7, 69
  New Historicism 21–2
  postcolonial 22–3
  postmodernism 18–20
  poststructuralism 18–20
  psychology, narrative in 23, 25–6
  reader-response criticism 15–16
  Romanticism 12–13
  science, narrative in 26–7
  scientific determination 13
  structuralism 16–18
  transcendentalism 13
Crystal, David 67–8, 87, 88
cultural context 275–7
cultural context, language in 83–6
  accent 101, 111
  cognition and language 86
  community and language 96–110
  dialect 101–7
  ethnicity and language 85
  gender and language 85, 121–33
  graphic representation 106
  identity and language 111–20
  jargon and argot 87–95
  key questions 86
  knowledge and language 86–95
  legal language 88–9
  meaning, construction 85
  political correctness 96
  regional and social variation 101–7
  scientific language 89–92
  social identity, and 87
  social interaction 85

sport, language in 92–5
time and place, effect 85
Cultural Materialism 21–2
cultural poetics 21–2
cultural values and belief systems 48–9
culture 29
cultural boundaries 40
cultural relativism 41
cultural studies 20–2
definition 37–9
describing 42
high and low 10, 40–3, 193
and identity 42–3
and language 37, 42–3
popular 27, 193–8
symbols and 39
theories of 38, 40–1
Cummings, E.E.
"In Just-" 234

D
dactylic foot 239
Dalrymple, William
City of Djinns 233
Darwin, Charles
Descent of Man 33
Origin of Species 13
deconstruction 19
denotation 52–3, 236
denotative translation 58
dénouement 224
descriptive grammar 30, 113
dialect 84, 101–7, 165
in mass communication 167
online language use 106–7
dialogue in drama 245, 247–9
diary, written task 1 146
Dickens, Charles
Great Expectations 71–2, 226–7
Dickinson, Emily 57–8
Emily Dickinson archive 64–5
diction 13, 74, 222
identity, and 111
in your own writing 81
Didion, Joan
"Marrying Absurd" 232–3
digital technology
ebooks 62, 64, 67–8, 162
film industry 162
mass communication media 159, 163, 179–84
news media 179–84
viral advertising 198
see also technology, using
dimeter 239
DiMicco, Joan Morris 114–15
discourse 21–2
discourse analysis 44
disfluencies 112–13
distance reading 62–3
Donne, John
"Death, be not proud" 240
Dostoyevsky, Fyodor 226
Crime and Punishment 59
drama 243–5
ancient Greek 10–11
aside 249–50
dialogue and character 245, 247–9
fourth wall 252
plot and action 251
soliloquy 249–50
space, use of 252
stage directions 245–6
tragedy and comedy 251–2
duality of patterning 30
Duffy, Carol Ann 296

The World's Wife 296, 298–9

E
ebooks 62, 64, 67–8, 162
Eco, Umberto 70
Edison, Thomas 162
editing 120, 278–9
editorial 145
Edrich, Louise
The Last Report on the Miracles at Little No Horse 228
Edson, Margaret
Wit 250
Eigner, Larry 56–7
email 95
phishing 159
emergentist perspective 35–6
emotional response 46–50
emotive language 555
emphatic stress 239
epistemology 10
Erard, Michael 113
essay-writing skills 136
ethnicity, language and 85, 122
Euripedes
Medea 127
exam paper 1
assessment criteria 149–50, 217–18
comparative textual analysis (higher level) 149–55, 211–12
language 150, 218
language and mass communication 211–18
organization and development 150, 218
percentage of marks 149
rules 149
student samples 213–17
text types 149, 212
textual analysis (standard level) 149–50, 211–12
exam paper 2 316–23
assessment criteria 317–18
duration 316
higher level 316
knowledge and understanding 317
language 318
organization and development 318
response to question 317
standard level 316
student sample 320–2
understanding stylistic features 317
exposition 224

F
fable 228
Faulkner, William
"A Rose for Emily" 229
feminism 21, 127–31
fictional prose 220
characters 222, 225
Freytag's pyramid 224
hypertext fiction 62
narrative 223
narrator 224–5
novels 226–8
plot 223–4
short stories 228–31
theme 225, 226
figurative speech 236
filler words 112–13
film 9
censorship 11–12
genres 169
as mass communication 157, 160, 162
popular culture 193

font, choice of 75, 192
foot 239
formative assessment 134–6
free verse 240
Freytag's pyramid 224, 251
further oral activity 147–8, 210–11
assessment 210
knowledge and understanding of text(s) and subject matter 148, 315
language 148, 315
language and mass communication 210–11
literature: texts and contexts 314–16
organization 148, 315
potential forms 147, 148, 210–11
reflective statement 147, 211
understanding of language use 148, 315

G
Geertz, Clifford 38
gender issues
advertising stereotypes 127
feminism 127–31
language and gender 85, 121–33
political correctness 96
gender studies 21
genre 75, 169–70
classification by 169
determination 167
mass communication, discourse genres 169–70
gesture 31
Gibson, William
Pattern Recognition 197
Giridharadas, Anand 95
Glaspell, Susan
Trifles 245
Glück, Louise
"The Drowned Children" 71–2
Gombrowicz, Witold
Ferdydurke 77–9
Google Books 64, 67
Google jockey 66
grammar 112–13
descriptive 30, 113
prescriptive 30, 113
Universal 34
graphic representation 64
Greek civilization
drama 10–11
philosophy 10
poetry 10
rhetoric 171
Greene, Graham
The End of the Affair 227
Grusin, Robert 164
Gugala, Jon 94
Gutenberg, Johannes 161

H
Hagege, Claude
Life and Death in Language 37
Heaney, Seamus
"Mint" 234
hegemony 20
heptameter 239
hexameter 239
high and low culture 10, 40–3, 193
historical context 275–7
history, cultural poetics 21–2
Homer
The Iliad 165
The Odyssey 127
Hopkins, Gerard Manley
"Spring" 238
horizon of expectations 16

Hosseini, Khaled
  The Kite Runner 42–3, 279, 280
Hron, Madelaine 284
Hughes, Langston
  "Harlem (A Dream Deferred)" 236–7
human rights, universal 41
hyperbole 74
hypertext fiction 62
hypothetical intentionality 70

I
iambic foot 239
identity
  accent 101, 111
  code-switching 111–12, 117–20
  and culture 42–3
  diction 111
  and language 111–20
  social networking sites
    106–10, 114–20
identity politics 20
idiolect 112–14
image 13
  aesthetic response to 46–50
  analysis 46, 75, 104–5
  comparison and contrast 104–5
  elements to consider 73–5
  visual language 51
imagery 74, 222, 236
imitation, learning through 136, 137, 254
infomercial 159
intentional fallacy 13
interactivity and creativity 66
Internet 60, 64–5, 162
  broadcasting 163
  mass communication 157, 159, 160, 163
  net speak 107
  online communities 106–10
  online language use 106–10
  social networking sites
    106–10, 114–20
  Web 2.0 114
interpretation of text 45
interpretive community 16
interventionist forms 62
irony 13, 167

J
James, Henry 226
Jameson, Frederic 223
jargon 54–6, 87–95
  in mass communication 167
Jefferson, Thomas 176
Jones, Vivien 287
journal, keeping 80
Joyce, James
  Ulysses 10

K
Kahar, Priti
  Untitled 57–8
Kamel, Deena 99
Kelso, Megan 131, 132–3
knowledge, language and 86–95
  jargon and argot 87–95
  knowledge engendered by language 95
  legal language 88–9
  medium of transmission 95
  scientific language 89–92
  sport, language in 92–5
Kruger, Barbara 129–31
  We don't need another hero 131

L
Lakoff, George and Johnson, Mark
  Metaphors We Live By 86–7

Lakoff, Robin
  Language and Women's Place 122
language
  animal language 33
  as area of knowledge 56–8
  articulation 36
  as communication 31–4
  competence and performance 36
  and culture 37, 42–3
  definition 29–30
  development 32–7
  diverse usage 44–5
  emergentist perspective 35–6
  emotive 555
  graphic representation of development
    106
  inherent nature 31, 33–4
  intentionality 31–3
  language instinct 34, 35
  langue and *parole* 36
  social functions 35
  specialist 54–6
  spoken and written 51
  stylized manipulation 9
  theory of knowledge 50–2
  and thought 36
  usage, changes in 113
Language Poets 56–7
language policy, IB 101
language-use survey 101
langue 36
Lasswell model 160–1
Laye, Camara
  The Dark Child 282
le Carre, John 223
Lee, Harper
  To Kill a Mocking Bird 42–3
legal language 88–9
legal narrative 23, 25
Levi-Strauss, Claude 38
Lewin, Tamar 109
literacy 8
  critical 44–5
literature
  comparative analysis 219
  content and form, connection 220
  contexts *see* context
  critical study 219–71
  criticism *see* criticism, literary
  cultural context 42–3
  definition 8–9, 220
  drama 243–52
  fictional prose 220, 223–31
  historical literary study 10–13
  individual oral commentary 261–71
  language manipulation 9
  nonfictional prose 231–3
  novels 221–8
  poetry 234–42
  short stories 221–5, 228–31
  symbolic nature 220
  texts and contexts 272–323
  tone 237–8

M
Mabura, Lily G.N. 285–6
McEwan, Ian
  Atonement 290–5
machinima 62
Macintyre, Been 100
magic realism 305
Marcus, Ben
  Notable American Women 273, 274, 278,
    279, 281
Marquez, Gabriel Garcia 305
Marxist literary criticism 20–1

mass communication
  advertising *see* advertising
  analyzing 168
  assessment in language and mass
    communication
    199–218
  audience fragmentation 163
  broadcast media 162–3
  and commercialization 194–7
  critical study 175–9
  definition 158–9
  dialect 167
  digital technology 159, 163, 179–84,
    193
  film 157, 162
  genres 169–70
  Internet 157
  jargon 167
  language and 157–8
  media 157–65
  media convergence 163
  media mobility 164
  multimedia 164
  multimodality 164
  narrative, use of 173–5
  news media *see* news media
  political speeches and campaigns
    184–92
  popular culture 193–8
  print media 159, 161–2, 179
  pronunciation 167
  register and style 165–7
  remediation 164–5, 185
  rhetorical strategies 170–3
  signs and sign systems 158
  speech and writing 167
  television 157
  vernacular language 167
  wikileaks 184
Mbeki, Thabo 186–8
meaning
  audience and text 85
  creation in language 30
  language in cultural context 85
media 158–61
  broadcast media 162–3
  convergence 163
  digital 159, 162–3, 193
  film 159, 162
  gender stereotyping 127
  media stream 193–4
  media studies 27
  mobility 164
  multimedia 164
  news organizations 175–9
  print media 159, 161–2
  remediation 164–5, 185
  rhetoric 170–3
  television 159
medical narrative 23–5
medium of transmission 95
metacognition 9
metaphor 53–4, 74, 172, 183, 222
meter 239, 240
Millen, David R. 114–15
Miller, Arthur
  Death of a Salesman 247–9
mimesis 17
mixed media 145
monometer 239
Moretti, Franco 62–3
morpheme 30
Morrison, Toni
  Beloved 102–3
Mukherjee, Bharanti
  "The Management of Grief" 230–1

multimodality 164

N

narrative
  in cognitive science 26–7
  definition 173
  fictional prose 223
  image analysis 46
  legal 23, 25
  in mass communication 173–5
  medical 23–5
  overlapping 75
  in psychology 23, 25–6
  theme 225
  voice 73
narrator or speaker 73
  fictional prose 224–5
  first-person 224–5
  omniscient 225
  third-person 224, 225
  unreliable 225
net speak 107
New Criticism 13–16, 46–7, 69
New Historicism 21–2
news media 175–9
  authority-disorder 178–9
  bias 17, 178–9, 181
  digital media 179–84
  dramatization by 178
  financing 176–8, 180
  fragmentation in 178, 181
  future of 179–84
  news creation 177
  news organizations 175–9
  ownership 176–8, 180
  personalization by 178
  political events, reporting 185
  print media 159, 161–2, 179
  reliability 180
  wikileaks 184
Nietzsche, Friedrich 251
nonfictional prose 231–3
note-taking 72, 73, 76, 80
novel
  critical study 221–8
  definition 226
  see also fictional prose

O

objective correlative 13–14
octameter 239
Ondaatje, Michael
  Running in the Family 263–71
Ong, Walter 67–8
online communities 106–10
ontological certainty 18–19
ontology 10
oral commentary
  assessment criteria 262–3
  literature: critical study
    261–71
  practising for 137, 316
  sample 263–71
oral traditions 8–9
outline plan 81

P

pamphlet 145
Pankhurst, Emmeline 186, 188–90
parable 228
parole 36
pattern recognition 221
pentameter 239
performing arts 9
  see also drama
personal vocabulary 113

philosophy, Greek 10
phishing 159
phoneme 30
Pinker, Steven 34, 35
planning 81
Plato 10, 67–8
plot 222–3
  drama 251
  fictional prose 223–4
  time, passing of 223–4
podcast, creating 137, 316
Poe, Edgar Allan 254–7
poetry
  concrete 239
  critical reading 241
  definition 235
  denotation and connotation 236
  figurative speech 236
  foot 239
  free verse 240
  Greek 10
  imagery 236
  intensity 235, 241
  Language Poets 56–7
  meter 239, 240
  multidimensional participation 235
  poetic devices 234
  rhyme 240
  rhythm 239, 240
  scansion 239
  SMS 62
  stanzaic 239
  stichic 239
  strophic 239
  structure and form 74, 239, 240–1
  syntax 236
  tone 237–8
  voice 237–8
politeness 96
political mass communication
  advertising 191–2
  public debates 190–1
  speeches and campaigns 184–92
politically correct language 96
popular culture 27, 193–8
  commercialization 194–7
  media stream 193–4
postcolonial literary criticism 22–3
postmodernism 18–20
poststructuralism 18–20, 52
  critical literacy 44
power relationships, establishing 85, 87, 102–4
Powers, Harriet 104–5
Powers, Richard
  The Echo Maker 300–3
Preminger, Otto
  Fallen Angel 75
prescriptive grammar 30, 113
print media 159, 161–2
  news media 159, 161–2, 179
  popular culture 193
  textbooks 165–6
printing press 160, 161
pronunciation 167
prose
  fictional 223–31
  nonfictional 231–3
  structure 74
Proulx, Annie
  "Brokeback Mountain" 50
psychology, narrative in 23, 25–6

Q

Queer Theory 21

R

Rabinowitz, Peter 159
racist language 96
radio 158–9, 162–3, 168
  see also news media
reader-response criticism 15–16
reading 134
  active reading 69–70
  basics of 70–2
  close reading 13–14, 46–7, 69, 72, 221–2
  contexts see context
  critical literacy 44–5
  critical reading 69–80
  elements to consider 73–5
  log, keeping 136
  marking a text 72, 76–9
  note-taking 72, 73, 76, 80
referent 17
register 165–7
remediation 164–5, 185
repetition 172, 222
reviews, book 136
rhetoric 170–3
rhyme 75, 240
rhythm 75, 239, 240
Richards, I.A. 14, 15–16
Rivera, Diego
  mural 48
Romanticism 12–13
Rosaldo, Renato 38
rules of notice 73
Rushdie, Salman
  The Moor's Last Sigh 303–7

S

Sandburg, Carl 107
sarcasm 96, 167
Saussure, Ferdinand de 17–18, 36
scansion 239
science, narrative in 26–7
scientific determination 13
scientific language 89–92
semiotics 27
setting 73, 74
Shakespeare, William 278, 280
  Hamlet 10
  Julius Caesar 171
  Othello 249–50
  Titus Andronicus 40
Shannon–Weaver model 160
short story
  critical study 221–5, 228–31
  definition 228
  see also fictional prose
signifier and signified 17–18, 45
  transcendental signified 18
signs 45
  definition 17
  duality of patterning 30
  mass communication 158
  semiotics 27
  structuralism 16–18
  thinking through 52
  words and language 28–30
simili 74
Skinner, B.F. 33
slang 87, 107
SMS poetry 62
social identity, language and 87
social interaction, language as tool for 85
social networking sites 106–10, 114–20, 198
sociolinguistics 98
soliloquy 249–50
Sophocles
  Oedipus Rex 11

Soulja Boy
  Turn My Swag On 103–4
speaker *see* narrator or speaker
speech 51
  improving speaking skills 135, 136
  register and style 167
spondaic foot 239
sport, language in 92–5
stage directions 245–6
stereotyping 555
Stevens, Wallace
  "Disillusionment of Ten O'Clock" 241
story within a story 75
Stowe, Harriet Beecher
  Uncle Tom's Cabin 104–5
stress 239
structuralism 16–18
structure 74, 222, 239, 240–1
style 75, 165–7
subjectivity 51
summative assessment 134–6
Swift, Jonathan 68
syllable stress 239
symbols 39, 222
Synge, John Millington
  The Playboy of the Western World 243
syntax 236
synthesizing 72
Szymborska, Wislawa 295, 296
  "Lot's Wife" 297–8
  "Soliloquy for Cassandra" 296–7

T
tale 228
Talking Tom app 111
Tannen, Deborah
  "The Talk of the Sandbox" 122–6
Tarantino, Quentin 251
technology, using 60–8
  changing technology 60–1
  and communication 61
  digital software 65
  evaluating resources 60
  graphic representation 64
  interactivity and creativity 66
  interventionist forms 62
  online resources 64–5
telephone communication 159, 160
television 162, 167, 168
  as mass communication 157, 160, 162–3
  political debates 190–1
  see also news media

tension or conflict 75
tetrameter 239
text 9
textbook 165–6
text type 9, 75
texting 68
theory of knowledge 50–6
thought and language 85, 134, 135
Tomasi di Lampedusa, Giuseppe
  The Leopard 272, 273–4, 276, 277, 281
tone 74, 222, 237–8
Tower of Babel 35
tragedy 251–2
transcendental signified 18
transcendentalism 13
translation, works in 58–9
trimester 239
trochaic foot 239
truth, social aspect 95
Tyler, Edward 38, 40
typography 75, 192

U
Universal Grammar 34
US Declaration of Independence 171

V
Van Gogh, Vincent
  The Sower 47–8
Vermeer, Johannes 74
vernacular language 107, 167
visual arts 7–8, 9, 39
visual language 51
vocabulary
  personal 113
  text 74
vodcast, creating 137, 316
voice 73, 88, 237–8

W
Whitman, Walt 86
wikileaks 184
Wilder, Thornton
  Our Town 246
Williams, Raymond 38
Williams, William Carlos
  "This is Just to Say" 219
Wilson, Chris 115–16
words 28–9
  denotation and connotation 52–3
  dictionary definitions 53
  spectrum, creating 53

Wordsworth, William
  "The Solitary Reaper" 12–13
World Wide Web *see* Internet
writing 28–9, 67–8
  developing writing skills 80–1
  first person, use of 82
  for purpose and clarity 81
  register and style 167
written task 1 137–46, 199–200
  assessment criteria 138, 200, 254
  language and mass communication 199–204
  language and style 138, 200
  length 137, 199
  literature: critical study 253–8
  literature: texts and contexts 308–11
  organization and argument 138
  part 1 language and cultural content 138
  potential text types 137, 138, 145–6, 199, 258
  propriety 200
  rationale 137–8, 200
  structure 200
  student samples 139–44, 201–4, 254–7, 309–11
  suggestions for topics 145
  task and content 138
written task 2 146–7, 204
  assessment criteria 146–7, 206
  essay 146
  language and mass communication 204–9
  language and style 147, 206
  length 146
  literature: critical study 258–61
  literature: texts and contexts 311–14
  organization 147, 206
  outline 146, 206
  power and privilege 205
  questions to be answered 146
  reader, culture, and text 204–5
  response to the question 146, 206
  student samples 207–9, 260–1, 311–14
  text and genre 205

Y
Young, Toby 182–3

Acknowledgments

Cover Page: Henriette v. Muenchhausen/Getty Images; **p7:** An Acrylic on Canvas painting by the artist Kiran Chandra, titled *"Displace"*, 2006; **p28:** Patricia Dunn; **p32:** Leo Cullum/The Cartoon Bank; **p35:** Photo Scala, Florence/British Library/c. 1025-1050; **p39l:** Photo Scala, Florence; **p39r:** Photo Scala, Florence/20th cent.; **p39b:** Photo Scala, Florence/Digital image, The Museum of Modern Art, New York; **p41:** Bjørn Hovdal/Dreamstime; **p46:** Peter Dazeley/Photographer's Choice/Getty Images; **p47:** The Granger Collection, New York; **p48:** The Granger Collection, New York; **p49:** Blank Archives/Hulton Archive/Getty Images; **p57:** Priti Kahar; **p62:** AFP; **p63:** Verso; **p64:** Randall Munro; **p65:** Houghton Library, Harvard University; **p69:** Chris Madden; **p75:** SNAP/Rex Features; **p92:** Bilderschorsch/Dreamstime; **p105t:** The Granger Collection, New York; **p105b:** Powers, Harriet (1837-1911)/Museum of Fine Arts, Boston, Massachusetts, USA/Bequest of Maxim Karolik/The Bridgeman Art Library; **p106:** Peter Steiner/The Cartoon Bank; **p111:** Andrey Kravchenko/Outfit7; **p117:** CJG - Technology/Alamy; **p127:** Wieden+Kennedy Advertising Agency; **p131:** Mary Boone Gallery; **p151:** The Granger Collection, New York; **p157:** Axe/Lowe Bull; **p165:** E. Caldwell/The Granger Collection; **p168:** Copyright 2011, DDB Worldwide Communications Group Inc.; **p172:** Stephanie Roldan/Rainter Strauss/Antonio Ramirez/Ricardo Trabulssi/Yosu Aranguena/Sebastian Arrechedera/Ricardo Cie,Sergio Ramirez,Miguel Fragoso/David Alvarez DDB Mexico advertising agency; **p174:** Geoff Wilson, Grant Booker/Christine Blackburn/Red Spide; **p182:** No Sacred Cows; **p184:** Collateral Murder; **p192tl:** http://www.mikehuckabee.com/; **p192tr:** BarackObama.com; **p192ml:** JoinRudy2008.com; **p192mr:** HillaryClinton.com; **p192b:** John Edwards Presidential Campaign, 2008; **p195t:** SBC Skateboard; **p195b:** 2009 SLAM Skateboarding Magazine; **p207:** Stihl/Charles Guillemant/Marie-France Capri/Jean-Yves Lemoigne/Publicis Conseil Paris; **p223:** Neiromobile/Dreamstime; **p232l:** Rick Rhay/Istockphoto; **p232r:** travelstock.ca/Alamy; **p234:** Hafiz; **p279:** Riverhead Books; **p283:** Ulf Andersen/Getty Images Entertainment/Getty Images; **p286:** The Granger Collection, New York; **p288:** Holmes Garden Photos/Alamy; **p291:** c.Focus/Everett/Rex Features; **p292:** The Granger Collection, New York; **p297:** Ullstein Bild - SV-Bilderdie/The Granger Collection, New York; **p303:** AFP.

Illustrations by Q2A Media, Lisa Hunt.

We have tried to trace and contact all copyright holders before publication. If notified the publishers will be pleased to rectify any errors or omissions at the earliest opportunity.